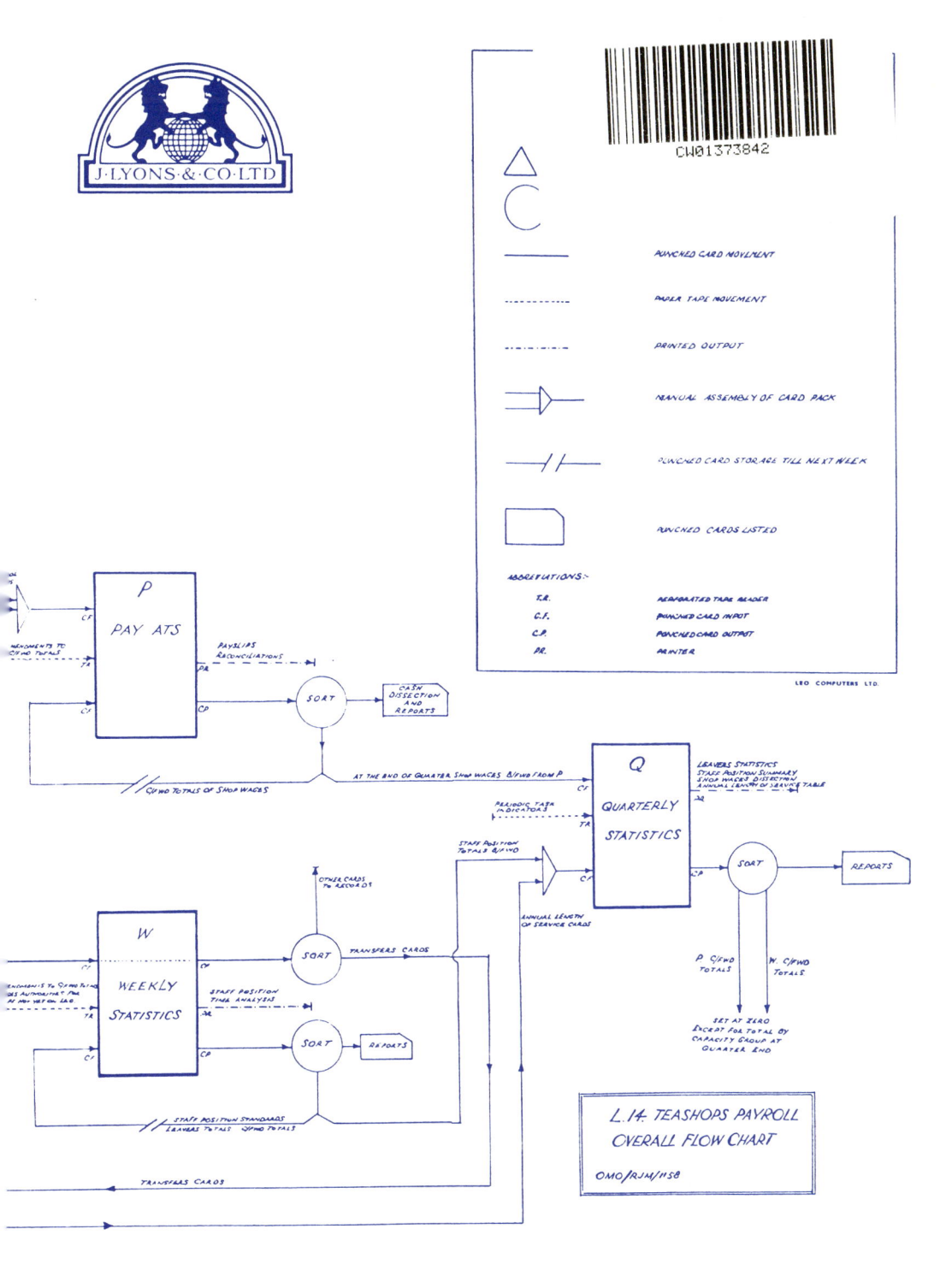

The overall flowchart for teashop payroll prepared in December 1958. Because if its complexity the teashops payroll was one of the last to be computerised. Two calculations were made for each person: one using Catering Wage Act rates and one for J. Lyons rates. The greater was paid. The running costs were calculated at 7.2 pence per person. *Reproduced by kind permission of J. Lyons & Co Ltd.*

LEO: The First Business Computer

By
Peter J. Bird

Hasler Publishing Limited
1994

Hasler Publishing Limited
4 Luckley Wood
Wokingham
Berkshire
RG11 3EW

© *Peter J. Bird 1994*

All rights reserved. No part of this publication may be reproduced, stored in a retrieval system, or transmitted, in any form or by any means, electronic, mechanical, photocopying, recording, or otherwise, without the prior permission of Hasler Publishing Limited.

British Library Cataloguing in Publication Data
Bird, Peter John
LEO: First business computer
I. Title
004.1

ISBN 0-9521651-0-4

Printed in Great Britain by
Biddles Limited
Guildford & King's Lynn

For Sylvia

CONTENTS

Foreword 8
Acknowledgements 9
Introduction 10
    The origins of computing 11

Chapter 1. Company origins 16
    Laying the business foundations 18

Chapter 2. Clerical efficiency endeavours 27
    Reorganising for efficiency 28
    Technological innovations 33
    The trip to America 35
    The radical proposal 37
    The Cambridge connection 40
    Building the team 42
    The programming team 47
    From calculator to computer 52
    Diagnosing program faults 58

Chapter 3. Computer construction begins 63
    EDSAC succeeds 66
    LEO is born 67
    A change of plan 68
    Manchester's Mark I computor 70
    LEO: design features 71
    Thompson's inspirational leadership 76
    Boat builders help 77
    In search of reliability 78
    The first job is run 86
    Bureau operations start 87
    The first computerised payroll 91
    A quiet revolution 93

Chapter 4. Full computer manufacture — 96
    The Samastronic printer — 97
    Magnetic drum storage — 98
    The computer manufacturing subsidiary — 100
    The wider context — 102
    LEO II: development and marketing — 105
    External work — 110
    The first order — 113
    Experimenting in automation — 116
    The first multiprogramming computer — 123
    Going further afield — 128
    The Master Plan — 130

Chapter 5. Further automation improvements — 140
    Broido's tabulator 7 — 140
    The development of the document reader — 143
    From Lector to Autolector — 148
    Rank's xerographic printer — 153

Chapter 6. End of an era—a new beginning — 169
    Disposal of computer interests — 174
    The death of LEO I — 179
    Centralised computer policy is challenged — 182

Sources and chapter notes — 189

Biographies — 200

Appendix 1 Program actions on the LEO I computer — 213
Appendix 2 LEO II features at February 1958 — 217
Appendix 3 LEO I and II summary of machine test programs — 220
Appendix 4 LEO II prices quoted to NRDC in January 1959 — 227
Appendix 5 The first clerical jobs: LEO I and II — 228
Appendix 6 Sales of LEO II computers — 234

Appendix 7	Program actions on the LEO III computer	235
Appendix 8	Components required to manufacture a LEO III	239
Appendix 9	Sales of LEO III computers	240
Appendix 10	Standard utility software supplied with LEO III	244
Appendix 11	Sales of Autolector (document reader)	245
Appendix 12	Sales of Xeronic printers	246
Appendix 13	How LEO I worked—a semi-technical description	248
Appendix 14	Summary of LEO characteristics	257

Index   260

FOREWORD

This book gives an interesting survey of the pioneering effort of J. Lyons & Co. in the field of business computing. Although I did little to contribute to this project, I was seconded to Lyons from the Mathematical Laboratory in 1948 and spent a few weeks at Cadby Hall doing some of the earliest business programming. It made a welcome contrast to the scientific programming being developed at Cambridge University, where a student's appreciation of Lyons was limited to discussing problems in the economical surroundings of Joe's!

The book is unique in the way it relates the computing to the historical background. It gives a brief history of the firm before computers existed, when it was justly famed for its catering, especially for major events, and its meticulous and efficient office methods. Thus, the ground-work was laid before computers were envisaged. It makes clear how the seed of innovation needs a prepared and fertile environment to survive.

The efforts made by the Lyons' team to give sufficiently reliable consistent results are exhibited quite well. I feel that the younger generation who are accustomed to present-day hardware reliability (measured in faults per year) will find the battle against errors very revealing. The pioneers were happy with only a few faults per day. The effort required to obtain fast reliable input and output will be a revelation to those of us who are now supplied with reliable peripherals and the simplest of which can out-perform the early ones.

Perhaps the most significant and underrated innovation introduced by Lyons was the quasi on-line service for attending to customers' needs by the next day, using the telephone for controlling the operator, who punched the orders into cards. LEO then calculated the loading schedules for the delivery vans. This was not done elsewhere until much later, as most early applications tended to be payroll calculations.

Another striking feature of this story is the small number of people who guided this project—quite different from today's large teams.

The later chapters tell of the death of the LEO company but we can see that many of the attitudes, techniques and facilities pioneered by LEO are still thriving.

To conclude, this is a fascinating book which will appeal to old timers like myself and give to others a true and detailed picture of the birth of the business computer.

Professor David Wheeler FBCS, FRS. Cambridge University. 1993

ACKNOWLEDGEMENTS

In writing this history I have tried to tell a story which spanned some 15 years when J. Lyons & Company were at the forefront of office automation. Many sources of information and much expert knowledge has been drawn on for its compilation and I consider this history a tribute to the people who made it possible. Many have been pestered by me during the course of my research and it now gives me great pleasure to put on record my appreciation of the help they unselfishly gave.

I am particularly grateful to J. Lyons & Company Ltd, and their archivist Yvonne Walker, for allowing me to have access to historical papers. I am equally grateful to International Computers Limited, and their archivist Gordon Collinson, for allowing the reproduction of photographs. Of the individuals, I would like to single out Derek Hemy; he has provided an abundance of information and has contributed to this work in many other ways, not least of which has been the meticulous reading of my manuscripts. Tony Morgan has provided most of the LEO III installation dates in the appendices. Alan King has supplied much of the information on the clerical tasks of LEO and has advised on Autolector programming.

Many former Lyons employees and the overseas companies for whom they work (worked) have contributed dates, costs, photographs and other information which has enabled me to accurately record the export events. These include the former LEO installations in Australia, Czechoslovakia and South Africa.

I acknowledge also, in alphabetical order, the valuable help given by the following: Leonard Badham (1923-1992), Norman Beasley, Dan Broido (1903-1990), Ian Brotherton, David Caminer OBE, Arthur Christian (1898-1993), Mary Coombs, Harry Dagnall, William Dunlop, Leo Fantl, John Gosden, John Grover, Mavis Hinds, Ernest Kaye, Frank Land, Ernest Lenaerts, Dr. John Pinkerton, Anthony Salmon, Raymond Shaw, George Stevens, Stanley H.A. Thompson and Professor David Wheeler.

Many more people, whose contributions have not been less valuable, helped with written enquiries to my advertisements. I offer them all my thanks and hope I have not caused offence by failing to mention them by name.

Every effort has been made to identify photograph and other illustration copyright. If any have been wrongly attributed I apologise.

INTRODUCTION

I joined J. Lyons & Company Ltd at a time when the pioneering years of computing had become no more than folk history, the subject of a wide variety of anecdotes in which it was difficult to distinguish fact from fiction. I worked with and talked to some of the old timers who remembered those days, but many of those who had been most closely involved had since moved on to other companies or countries. It appeared that no attempt had been made before their exodus to set down a full and accurate account of what had happened. No one can be blamed for this historical oversight; at the time, the full significance of the events which unfolded during the 1950s was not fully appreciated.

What little I was able to piece together during my first twenty years with the company convinced me that this was a unique story which deserved to be told, and I began in earnest to seek fuller information. But, as I made progress, it seemed to me even more interesting to discover how such an imaginative project came to be conceived and carried forward in such an unlikely milieu. This led me to consider the nature of Lyons in the immediate post-war years, but it soon became clear that the answers lay further back in time: it was only by studying the history of the Company—how it started and how it developed—that it would be possible to understand the path that led to the LEO project and to the part it played in the Information Technology (IT) industry. Thus, I found that there were two stories that needed to be told, each with its own interest, and neither previously recorded. Both were necessary for an understanding of how the ground was prepared for LEO, how the seed was sown, and how the project grew into what it ultimately became.

Unfortunately the information available was fragmentary. Little documentary evidence has been systematically preserved, but I started to piece together an account of the early years of LEO. As I contacted more sources, including some 150 people, the picture began to take shape, but identifying the sequence of events in the interrelated development of hardware and software was made more difficult by conflicting evidence from different sources. In the end I managed to contact most—though unfortunately not all—of the early pioneers and was able, by collating and cross-checking the evidence, to arrive at what I consider to be a true picture of the project.

Clearly there may be some who feel that too little—or indeed too much—credit is given to individuals or events; in the absence of detailed contemporary records this is perhaps unavoidable. In any event, it is perhaps much less important than it might seem, for I discovered from many sources that the project was particularly remarkable for the lack of regard given to individual success. Indeed, there was a well-developed corporate pride in the achievement of the team as a whole, which percolated throughout the company and was, no doubt, one of the factors that contributed to the progress that was made.

Scholars may find my treatment of the events insular and lacking in analytical style, in that I have, with one or two exceptions, neglected to take account of other office and business developments occurring elsewhere at the time. Let me say here that my research has deliberately been confined to the events taking place within Lyons since this is essentially a Lyons story. With this in mind I have interpreted the limited research documentation and my discussions with former employees accordingly. Having said that, however, I must admit that I have included some detail of the Xeronic printer, which was developed independently of the events taking place at Lyons: the two are unconnected except that this peripheral device was imaginatively used by Lyons on their LEO computer. In any event, little has been written about early peripheral technology and it did not seem out of place to record this matter here.

The Origins of Computing

Before starting on the story of Lyons and LEO, it is first appropriate to consider briefly the origins of computing. These date back to man's earliest times, and the oldest and most important piece of apparatus was probably the abacus. It is known to have been in use in 3000 BC in Mesopotamia (now part of modern Iraq). So successful was its design that it is still in use today in Asia and many western cities, mainly in its original form. Some have suggested that this was the first calculating machine; however, this is untrue since the abacus is merely a device for storing numbers, the calculation being performed by the operator.

The Scottish mathematician John Napier (1550–1617), best known for his invention of logarithms, devised a simple calculating system made of rods (Napier's bones) in 1617. However, it is Blaise Pascal (1623–1662), French scientist, philosopher and writer, but by profession a tax collector, who is generally credited with having invented the first calculating machine in 1642, at the age of 19. Pascal was to produce more than fifty calculators before he was 30. He obtained letters patent preventing competitors from selling similar devices, but although his inventions brought him fame, they were a financial failure because the aristocracy of the day believed that his devices would put men out of work.

It was not until the nineteenth century that any further significant advances were made in calculator design, brought about perhaps by improved engineering techniques. While working with the astronomer Sir John Herschel (1792–1871), Charles Babbage (1792–1871) had his original idea of a calculating machine. It is alleged that the repetitive, mundane calculations he was doing with Herschel for the Royal Astronomical Society prompted his idea, and that he hoped to produce mathematical and navigation tables to an accuracy of twenty decimal places. His machine would become an obsession, and would occupy his time, on and off, for the rest of his life. He called his device the Difference Engine.

After a great deal of lobbying, Charles Babbage secured a small grant from the Government towards the cost of the development of his Engine. The project took much longer than expected, and, indeed, his machine was never built. Many historians put this down to the limited engineering techniques available at the time. However, to mark Babbage's bicentenary year a project was undertaken, under the direction of Doran Swade of the Science Museum, London, during 1990–1991 to test his ideas. Using original drawings, and materials and engineering techniques similar to those which would have been available to Babbage, the Science Museum researchers successfully built his second Difference Engine, thus confounding the idea that the parts could not be made to the required engineering tolerances of the period. Although a complete set of drawings survived, no attempt had previously been made to build the Engine, which after completion weighed three tons and consisted of some 4,000 parts—without the printing mechanism—engineered from cast iron, bronze and steel.

Although many historians have described Babbage as well ahead of his time, some recent scholarship has emphasised how traditional his designs were, suggesting that he was designing a machine for which there was no market. It is interesting that some European inventors succeeded where Babbage failed. He was to work further on calculating machines and went on to design an even more ambitious project, which he described as an Analytical Engine.

In 1884, Dorr Eugene Felt (1862–1930), a 22-year-old American inventor, built a prototype machine that was operated by striking a keyboard and which incorporated a numerical carrying system, from units to tens, to hundreds, and so on. In 1887 he patented his device, which he called a Comptometer, and it was soon in use at the United States Treasury and the New York State Weather Bureau. The principle of his machine would be utilised by others over the next fifty years. The Comptometer was subsequently refined, notably by William Seaward Burroughs (1855–1898), who added a printing mechanism that recorded both separate items and final results. The Comptometer became the most widely used electromechanical accounting machine of the early twentieth century.

A few years later, another American inventor, Herman Hollerith (1860–1929), introduced his punched card system, which would have profound implications for large volume data sorting. His system gained wide acceptance, and gave birth to the tabulator in all its guises. In December 1896, after many setbacks, Hollerith, with the help of friends, formed the Tabulating Machine Company to develop and market his equipment. In 1911, because of ill health, he sold out to Charles Ranlett Flint (1850–1934), a colourful character who was said to be a gunrunner, a pioneer of the rubber industry and a confidential agent of the United States in the negotiation for war vessels. Flint had put together a consortium of companies which became known as the Computer Tabulating-Recording Company, more familiar, perhaps, as C-T-R. The term "Computing" in the title was derived from the Computing Scale Company, "Tabulating" from Hollerith's Tabulating Machine Company, and "Recording" from International Time Recording Company. There was a fourth component, sometimes forgotten, the Bundy Manufacturing Company of Endicott, New York. It has been suggested by some wags that Bundy merely contributed the word "Company" to the new title. In 1914 Thomas John Watson (1874–1956) was recruited from National Cash Register (NCR), where he had been dismissed as Sales Manager, to head C-T-R as General Manager. Although Hollerith became a millionaire overnight, by the sale of his substantial stock, he stayed on as General Manager and later as Consulting Engineer. In 1924 the C-T-R company changed its name to International Business Machines (IBM). It is now one of the largest computer manufacturers in the world with annual sales in 1989 in excess of $63bn. (In 1992 IBM reported a loss of nearly $5bn, the world's worst corporate loss to date.)

In 1914, James Powers (1871–1915), whom the US Government had earlier employed together with Hollerith's foreman Charles Spicer to break Hollerith's stranglehold on tabulating machinery, formed the Accounting and Tabulating Company of Great Britain. The Prudential Assurance Company was his largest customer. In 1919 the company separated from the American parent and became Powers Accounting Machines Limited. It formed a link with the French Powers distributor in 1929 and became known as Powers-Samas Accounting Machines Ltd, Samas being the acronym for the French company Société Anonyme des Machines a Statistiques. Several other mergers and distribution agreements followed, and Powers-Samas became a wholly owned subsidiary of Vickers in 1955. Four years later, the wheel had turned full circle when Powers-Samas and the British Tabulating Machine Company merged to form the nucleus of International Calculators and Tabulators (ICT).

By the 1930s universities and other research institutions had started experimenting with a whole range of mechanical, electromechanical and electronic calculating devices. One of the more famous was the Colossus experiment, designed by Dr Thomas Flowers while working at the General Post Office (GPO) Research Establishment at Dollis Hill, London. It was by this means that the Enigma machine codes of the *Oberkommando der Wehrmacht* during World War II, thought to be impregnable, were deciphered. (The Poles had captured an early Enigma machine which helped in this process.) The GPO's Colossus Mark 1 was the world's first working electronic computer—capable only of working on the Enigma problem—when it began work at Bletchley Park, Buckinghamshire, in 1943. Experience of this machine led to further improvements and the introduction of Colossus Mark II, which had 2,400 thermionic valves. It was considered a feat of engineering, and was capable of reading Baudot coded perforated paper tape—after Jean Maurice Emile Baudot (1845–1903), a pioneer of telegraphic communication—at a rate of 5,000 characters per second. While Colossus is now generally accepted as the first electronic computer, it was not thought of as such by its designers; indeed the term "computer" had not been coined at the time. It was described as a digital data processor, conceived by telephone engineers familiar with exchanges controlled by electromechanical digital processors. Its importance to the war effort was such that the area, including Bletchley, where Colossus was located, was excused from power cuts to avoid interruptions to the valve heater supply, which would have increased the risk of faults.

This book, however, is not a history of accounting machines or of computers, but rather an account of how J. Lyons & Company Ltd became involved in the design and manufacture of a single commercial electronic computer, albeit the first in the world using programmed instructions to perform routine clerical tasks. The project was one of the most ambitious "DIY" projects of the 1950s; after all, this was a company with no previous engineering or electronic manufacturing experience, and whose roots were firmly established in catering and food manufacture. Nothing like it had been done before, and this considerable achievement helped to set in motion a flourishing industry which would have profound implications for the way in which business information would be stored and manipulated. The computer became known affectionately as LEO (Lyons Electronic Office), and its development was an act of faith by the directors of J. Lyons & Company Ltd. Credit must be given to them for their vision and boldness in funding such a speculative enterprise. At no time was the initiative threatened with cancellation, despite many technical difficulties and setbacks.

> It should be borne in mind that there is nothing more difficult to handle, more doubtful of success, and more dangerous to implement than initiating change. Innovation makes enemies of all those who prospered under the old regime, and only lukewarm support is forthcoming from those who would prosper under the new. Their support is indifferent partly from fear and partly because men are generally incredulous, never really trusting new things unless they have tested them by experience.

Niccolo Machiavelli, *The Prince* (1514)

CHAPTER 1

Company origins

The start of this story can be traced back to 1841, when two brothers, Samuel (1821–1873) and Henry (1832–1905) Gluckstein, arrived in England as immigrants from Europe. Samuel lodged with his aunt, Julia Joseph (1792–1868), in the poor Spitalfields district of London and married her illiterate daughter Ann (1819–1885) four years later. It is not known where Henry lived on his arrival.

Samuel and Ann Gluckstein had twelve children, two of whom—Isidore and Montague—would be key players in the development of Lyons. Thirteen years after arriving in England (1854), Samuel Gluckstein and his brother Henry, together with their cousin Lawrence Abrahams, started a small tobacconist and cigar manufacturing business from premises at 35 Crown Street, in the Soho district of London.

In 1864, the trio decided that the business arrangement between them should be put on a more formal basis, and on 15 October 1864 they formed a company which traded as Samuel Gluckstein & Company. During the same year they moved their business to 43 Leman Street in London's east end. Shortly after the Company's formation a good deal of family feuding started, allegedly as a result of the unreasonableness and overbearing nature of Samuel Gluckstein. The business quarrels, sometimes violent, became more frequent, and after months of legal wrangling the case was heard in the Chancery Court by Sir Richard Malins (1805–1882) on 25 March 1870, who, after hearing evidence, made an order that the business be dissolved and the assets divided between the partners.

In 1872–1873 Samuel Gluckstein started another tobacco business with his two sons, Isidore and Montague, and his son-in-law Barnett Salmon (1829–1897). The partnership conducted its business under the name of Salmon & Gluckstein, although the Post Office Directory of 1873 for 34 Whitechapel Road, the new business address, lists the occupants merely as Gluckstein, Samuel, cigar manufr. Samuel Gluckstein did not live to see his business prosper: he suffered ill health, and the years of family bickering and argument had taken their toll. He died of diabetes in January 1873 at the somewhat early age of 52 years. Isidore and Montague Gluckstein, now 22 and 19 years of age, respectively, were faced with providing for their mother, and others of the family. The rebuilding of family relationships was started, with unity being their main priority. To avoid becoming embroiled in another damaging family feud (the earlier quarrels had brought them all to the edge of bankruptcy), they had the wisdom or good advice, or perhaps both, to form a Family Fund based on equal sharing principles. This Fund would become the vehicle by which succeeding generations of the family would develop and recompense themselves from the business profits, which would become considerable and complex as the next century approached.

After Samuel Gluckstein's death the family was still relatively poor, and the success of the new tobacco business depended on hard work. The brothers faced intense competition from many other cigarette/cigar manufacturers, and the few staff they were able to employ made the cigars by hand, unlike other firms, which had converted to mechanisation. Imports, particularly from the Americas, were one of the greatest threats to the United Kingdom tobacco industry at this time. Freight charges were becoming more competitive, enabling tobacco products manufactured in other parts of the world to be shipped to the United Kingdom at prices that domestic manufacturers could not match. To meet this competition the brothers decided to diversify the business into the retail sector, opening their first retail tobacconist shop in about 1875 at 251 Edgware Road, London under the name of Barnett Salmon. Subsequently, the name was changed to Salmon & Gluckstein to reflect both family interests, and this seems to have been a most satisfactory arrangement.

By 1886 the families, having increased in numbers and improved their financial standing, had already concluded that their tobacco business, now amounting to shops as well as factories, although very large, was not enough of a challenge to occupy the ambitions and energies of the younger generations of the Salmons and Glucksteins. There seemed little potential for growth in the tobacco business. This was also a period of remarkable change, both at home and abroad; the Empire was at its peak and many grand plans and ideas took root in the final years of the nineteenth century. During this period, Montague Gluckstein's experiences at exhibitions in his travels around the country, in his salesman's capacity, brought home to him the dreary, unappetising state of catering. This caused him to consider the possibilities, and after some preliminary calculations he went to his brothers and other members of the family, and laid his plan before them. They showed little enthusiasm for his ideas. Their main concern was protecting the good name of the Company, which by now was well established. Above all they did not want it to be confused with some other trade, particularly catering, which they believed would have a detrimental effect on their business. Nevertheless, Montague Gluckstein must have been very persuasive—in that respect he took after his father. He argued his case and eventually won the family's support on the understanding that the name of Salmon & Gluckstein was not to be associated with the new undertaking and that a person be employed to deputise.

Having agreed this essential condition, Montague Gluckstein at once thought of Joseph Lyons (1847–1917), a cousin of his brother's wife Rose (1851–1908). Joseph Lyons had cultivated numerous important commercial friendships and had exhibition know-how—at this time he was running a market stall in Manchester. The idea of a catering concern appealed to Joseph Lyons and, as often happened in arrangements of this kind, in classic romantic style, the terms of business between them were agreed at a single meeting—said to have been on a train—and hand-written on a single sheet of paper. Joseph Lyons was invited to give his name to the new company, which he was happy to do, and in 1887 Isidore and Montague Gluckstein, Barnett Salmon and Joseph Lyons commenced trading as restaurateurs, refreshment and entertainment contractors, hotel proprietors, theatre show and music hall proprietors, general merchants and commission agents under the name of J. Lyons & Company, from the same address in Whitechapel Road as the tobacco company.

Laying the Business Foundations

The decision to start a catering enterprise in 1887 was fortuitous; it was, after all, Queen Victoria's first Jubilee and the potential catering opportunities would not have escaped the imagination of Montague Gluckstein. In every part of the Kingdom festivities and exhibitions were planned to celebrate the past successes of the Empire's soldiers and explorers, and there were high expectations for prosperity and enterprise throughout the land. Joseph Lyons plunged into the new-born catering venture with all his energy. He could talk convincingly and was a good organiser, qualities which helped him to secure the first important catering rights at the Newcastle Jubilee exhibition, with Montague Gluckstein managing the event. The two were determined to improve on exhibition refreshment facilities, which hitherto had received much criticism from exhibitors and public alike. Using his entrepreneurial talents and flair for the unusual, Montague Gluckstein had taken the important decision to engage the Blue Hungarian Band, led by Herr Barcza, to perform in the exhibition's refreshment hall, an unheard-of practice in Victorian society. The 3d pot of tea and music was an immediate success. Joseph Lyons introduced a shooting gallery, the first of its type in the world, where targets moved across realistic scenic effects. Now commonplace in fairgrounds and amusement arcades, albeit in inferior displays, they caused a sensation among the visiting soldiers, who were eager to demonstrate their prowess at weaponry to their accompanying ladies.

The Glasgow exhibition of 1888 followed, where the tea and music experience was repeated. The waitresses at this exhibition, all extremely attractive and dressed in Marie Stuart period costume, proved so popular that they were taken to Paris for the 1889 exhibition, but had to return when Lyons fell foul of French licensing law, and their misunderstanding of the service the girls were to perform!

No official documentary evidence for the period 1887–1889 has survived, and it must be assumed that J. Lyons & Company was a private company with the shares in the names of the founding members. The earliest records date from 16 March 1889,[1] when the company was first registered, the former unlimited company having gone into voluntary liquidation and the assets and contracts transferred (sold). The nominal share capital of the new company was £5,000, all issued in £1 shares and held by Joseph Lyons (1,249), Isidore Gluckstein (1,249), Montague Gluckstein (1,249), Barnett Salmon (1,249), Joseph Gluckstein (2), Abraham Joseph (1) and Julius Koppenhagen (1)—the new limited company was still very much a private company, with the majority of the shares held by the former partnership. It is noteworthy that the Articles of Association for the new company specified that the directors shall act without remuneration and would be entitled to hold office as long as each held capital of at least £1,200. The Articles also stated that Joseph Lyons should hold the office of Chairman for life unless he chose to resign, a clause that must later have been regretted by some of his partners; he held the job until his death in 1917 and there is evidence that by this time relationships had become soured. In fact his death was not reported officially to shareholders, as was customary, despite the fact he had held office for 30 years.

With several successful exhibitions and contracts to their credit, and Montague Gluckstein's growing reputation for shrewdness and business ability, it was considered an opportune time to raise further capital in the City to expand the business. This was achieved by a Special Resolution of Members (effectively Messrs Lyons, Gluckstein and Salmon) on 24 March 1894, when it was confirmed that the company be wound up voluntarily and reconstructed using the old company name. A "Notice of Consent to Take the Name of a Subsisting Company"—a device under Section 20 of the Companies Act 1862 —was the vehicle by which this was achieved. The reconstructed company was officially registered on 10 April 1894. The purchase price of the old company was £70,000, half paid in cash and half in shares: 8,750 each to Joseph Lyons, Barnett Salmon, Montague and Isidore Gluckstein. Edwin Levy (1840–1895), of whom little is known, took up 60,000 shares and was appointed a Director for a short period. One day after the new company was formed its registered offices were moved to newly acquired premises in Hammersmith Road, known as Cadby Hall.[2] The Directors had acquired the two-acre site for £10,050; it remained the Company's head office until August 1990, when they disposed of the last remnants of the property.

On 20 September 1894 Lyons opened the first of their famous teashops at 213 Piccadilly, the freehold of which had cost nearly £10,000. From the very first day it caused a sensation; the public were amazed to see the French style Louis XVI interior, with red silk panelled walls and elaborate chandeliers, marble tables, chairs instead of benches, and dainty china. On the outside the name J. Lyons & Co. Ltd was in pure gold leaf embossed on a white background, a style which would remain unchanged for more than 60 years. It is said that Montague Gluckstein chose gold because it was too expensive for others to imitate. The style, easily recognisable among the dark greens and browns of Victorian London, would prove to be a good choice.

In October 1894, Lyons secured a 99-year lease on a property near Piccadilly Circus and work was started to make way for the company's most prestigious project to date; the building of the famous Trocadero Restaurant. The lease was bought by private treaty and it sealed a particularly shrewd property investment, for in 1967 the Company disposed of its interests in the site, which included the Coventry Street Corner House, for £7,400,000.

The building of the Trocadero Restaurant almost bankrupted the company. Building costs soared to four times the original estimate, and a further £100,000 was required to complete the work. The overspend was a threat to the company's very existence and seriously affected its trading ability. Directors were under great strain and so serious was the heavy cost of development that no shareholder dividend was allocated in 1896. It is interesting also that only one teashop was opened between September 1895 and February 1898, compared with twelve during 1895 and eight in 1898; clearly, investment capital was not available. The financial crisis was distressing, and Edwin Levy, a very wealthy Director (stockbroker) who did not involve himself with the day-to-day matters of the Company, was approached by the other directors and agreed to take up debenture stock so that the Trocadero development could proceed. Unfortunately, his sudden death before the business could be concluded forced the company to call an Extraordinary General Meeting of shareholders in the incomplete Trocadero Grill Room. There was uproar when the need for further capital was explained. Eventually Montague Gluckstein, with the co-operation of other members of his family, was able to raise £100,000 by way of a loan to the company, with only £100 subscribed by the grumbling shareholders. Perhaps later, when trading improved dramatically, some of them might have realised that they had missed an opportunity.

Following the successful opening of the Trocadero Restaurant, other important catering contracts were secured, including the Franco-British Exhibition held at Shepherds Bush in 1908. It was the visitors' first impression of the all-white structure that soon earned it the nickname of The White City. For the British Empire Exhibition, held at Wembley in 1924–1925, Lyons employed many clerks and statisticians to control and monitor the vast catering facilities. Some lesser enterprises who had tendered for the business had suggested a form of subcontracting but the authorities wanted the catering plan in the hands of someone who could provide for a range of catering options. The contract was colossal and only Lyons could satisfy the exhibition organisers, with their plan to operate no fewer than 33 different restaurants scattered across the 400 acres of the exhibition. It was said that the contract was signed at 11.40 a.m. and by 12.30 p.m. the first pantechnicon van was seen making its way over the unfinished roads towards the exhibition grounds. All the restaurants were built by Lyons' own staff, who provided all the materials for the construction and kitchens. The 33 restaurants and cafes gave an estimated seating area of 10 acres, where 30,000 persons could eat simultaneously and in a single day more than 175,000 meals could be provided.

There is no doubt that the company had developed special skills in catering for large numbers. Their largest banquet ever, the Masonic Festival, held to mark the Freemason's Peace Memorial Fund and the raising of over £1 million towards the erection of the magnificent lodge in Great Queen Street, was staged at Olympia on 8 August 1925. Over 7,500 Masonic brethren sat down to 1.42 miles of banqueting table for luncheon. The tables were decorated with fresh flowers that had taken 45 florists 14 hours to arrange. They were served by 1,253 waitresses—known as Nippies—some of whom had been brought to London from across the country. A proportion of silver was borrowed from many of the Lyons' permanent teashops and it was arranged that all the borrowed articles should be cleaned and returned to their departments by 6 p.m. the same evening, just two hours after the lunchers had departed.

Apart from their exhibition catering activities, the company began to expand its food manufacturing processes, utilising a ready outlet for their products in the teashop retail counters, as well as through the thousands of small grocery outlets up and down the country. They undertook daily house-to-house supply of bread from their manufacturing steam ovens at Cadby Hall, delivering in the neighbourhood by horse-drawn vans and hand carts. Their contracts included one to supply bread to Buckingham Palace, for which they received a Royal Warrant, one of ten they were eventually awarded. In 1903 they first seriously turned their attentions to blending and selling packet tea, coffee and cocoa, although some tea and cocoa had been hand packed much earlier. A legendary reputation had already been established for a cup of Lyons tea in the growing number of teashops, more than 80 of which were in operation by this time. The Black & Green Tea Company was purchased in 1918 and during the same year a controlling interest was acquired in W.H. & F.J. Horniman, an established tea merchant operating from Manchester. The financial interest of Lyons in these two tea companies was primarily to increase its market share in the North of England, where Brooke Bond and the Co-operatives were in strong positions.

After World War I much modernisation was undertaken, to equip food manufacturing factories with mass-production machinery. Old methods of production were slow and inefficient, and could not satisfy the progressively increasing consumer demand. Lyons' products had a reputation for quality, and were viewed with the same affection that today's consumers have for the Marks & Spencer marque. In the case of bakery and ice cream products it became a tradition that orders received from an agent in any part of Great Britain would be delivered during the following day. This was possible because of the strategic location of Cadby Hall to Kensington Station. By now the company had diversified to incorporate hotels, laundries, printing works, wine cellars, and a carton and box making company which complemented the food manufacturing, catering and teashop businesses. A successful engineering works had also been established at Abbey Road, London to build and service the Company's vast commercial vehicle fleet.

Between 1909 and 1928 Lyons continued opening more restaurants, of varying styles, and acquiring property for this development, almost exclusively freehold or on long lease. In 1909 the Ceylon Tea Company was acquired, and this instantly brought several restaurants into the company, many of which were located in the provinces. These were quickly converted and pressed into service as teashops. During the same year, apart from opening the Strand Palace Hotel, the company opened the Coventry Street Corner House (known initially as The Corner House) to bridge the gap between the teashop and the speciality restaurant. This also was hugely successful. So much property was secured by Lyons that shareholders sometimes wondered whether they owned a property company operating in disguise as a caterer.

The Corner House was arranged on five floors, and was open day and night. During a 24-hour period over 25,000 meals could be served. Live music was played on four of the levels and the ground floor housed an extensive food hall where cooked meats, chocolates, confectionery, biscuits, wines, cakes and other company food items could be purchased. There were also de luxe hairdressing salons, a shoe-shine parlour, a theatre ticket booking office and a novel telephone bureau. This restaurant style, with its different standards on each level, was extremely popular, and before 1933 four were operating in London alone. To give some idea of the complexity of these establishments, the

Marble Arch Corner House employed some 700 persons, more than the average industrial undertaking of the period.

Since the initial occupation of Cadby Hall in 1894, the factory estate had been progressively expanded by the acquisition of adjoining properties along Hammersmith Road and Book Green, and eventually encompassed some 13 acres of diverse food manufacturing and administrative premises. The inability to extend the estate further seriously threatened the existence of certain vital departments and it was no longer a question of finding suitable alternative accommodation, but one of evolutionary expansion. In 1919 a 30-acre estate at Greenford, to the West of London in rural surroundings adjoining the Grand Union Canal, was purchased. By 1921 the first factory building was completed. The tea, coffee and other businesses were relocated and production quickly accelerated.

In 1925, 8,640 acres of virgin land were bought for £23,500 in the Mlanje District of the Nyasaland Protectorate (now Malawi). Here Lyons' staff developed a tea plantation using native labour, which started producing tea about 10 years later. However, the plantation at Lujeri was too small to satisfy the needs of Lyons (only 1,165,000 lb was produced in 1939), furthermore, it only produced one type of tea, and others were required for blending purposes. The major part of their tea stock was obtained at the London auctions and through Heath & Company, a buying agency based in Calcutta and acquired by Lyons in 1921, to satisfy their insatiable demand. For the home market, leaf tea was obtained from 5,000 estates and tea gardens world-wide to blend the many varieties sold. Packet tea sales grew phenomenally from 626,041 lb in 1903 to 37,296,636 lb in 1921.

In 1928 a new purpose-built laboratory was opened, replacing the inadequate premises that had been developed out of what was known as the Bio-Chemical Department. The laboratory applied science to food manufacture and became involved in all aspects of food production. Its objectives can be summarised as: to ensure the chemical and bacteriological purity of food supplied either through the teashops and restaurants or through the wholesale trade, to check the efficiency of all processes of food manufacture employed by the Company and to study new processes, new machinery and new materials, both raw and finished. In June 1949 a young research chemist, Margaret Roberts MA, BSc, joined the other 385 laboratory staff in the Physical Chemistry section, where she remained until her marriage in 1951 to a Denis

Thatcher. She did of course, in due time, become the Member of Parliament for Finchley and our first female Prime Minister.

By 1939 the company was operating 253 teashops from Blackpool in the North to Plymouth in the South, as well as more than twenty other large restaurant facilities such as the Trocadero, Corner Houses and speciality cafes. One hundred and eighty-seven teashops were trading in the greater London area, and by this time an additional 81 had opened and closed for one reason or another[3]. Such was the teashops' popularity that nine operated in London's Oxford Street alone. Since each teashop had an associated retail counter (Lyons called these front shops), it is not difficult to visualise the thousands of small separate transactions they generated. It was calculated that only a farthing profit was made on each of the 150 million meals sold annually from all teashops, and that only a decimal of a penny profit was made on each item making up the 75,000 tons per week of other goods sold through front shops.

With the need to control costs to fractions of a penny, it is not difficult to realise that the volume of paperwork and the consequent flood of dull routine processing of business transactions to keep this expanding enterprise ticking over was becoming an accounting nightmare. Furthermore, a small error in cost accounting could have a disastrous effect on profits. Of the total of 33,000 staff employed at this time, 1,500 were employed in accountancy and other statistical work, and an office block was specifically built to locate them. The outbreak of World War II caused considerable disturbance to trade, and despite steps that were taken to meet the altered conditions, the company's expansion plans were curtailed. Much of the clerical labour force, predominantly male before 1939, was conscripted to serve in the armed forces; 164 former employees (one a woman) lost their lives. The Company was prevented from transporting much of its produce to some parts of the United Kingdom due to restrictions on transport and fuel, and the production of ice cream was prohibited. However, they were still able to provide catering services and, among other contracts, were responsible for the catering at the United States Army Headquarters in Duke Street, London between September 1942 and December 1944.

The war years had created a labour shortage which continued well after demobilisation, and with the slow progress back to normality—food shortages were worse after hostilities ended than during the war years—the need to handle more repetitive clerical activity was again causing concern to the Lyons Board. In some parts of the business, notably the Corner Houses and teashops, self service had already been introduced in an attempt to overcome these difficulties.

However, clerical efficiency had been of concern to management for many years, and it was their introduction of efficient office methods, implemented long before the war started, that enabled them to take advantage of electronic automation when it came. The foundations for success were in place.

CHAPTER 2

Clerical efficiency endeavours

The complexity of business activity, largely as a result of strict control of the catering and manufacturing processes and the many thousands of individual business transactions to retail and other outlets, continued to create accounting problems, which became increasingly laborious. Constant efforts had to be made to prevent the offices from becoming swamped by paperwork. The increasing volumes of business and the need to contain overheads and improve productivity and information flow became more onerous. The millions of waitresses' bills alone had forced the Company into automation as early as 1896, when calculating machines were first used. By 1910 every waitress bill from every teashop was sorted into "before 3 p.m." and "after 3 p.m." business. They were despatched to Head Office, where clerks checked the totalling of each bill and calculated the average spending power to the nearest farthing for each establishment. For example, the daily average spend at the Piccadilly teashop for the month of March 1914 was 6¾d before 3 p.m. and 5½d after 3 p.m., compared with the Basinghall Street branch, which recorded 4¾d and 3¾d, respectively, for the same periods. It is surprising that the company fortunes were made on such modest income. Exactly why these detailed statistics were regularly recorded is not known, other than for comparative purposes, but the information enabled management to detect small variations of trading patterns at an early stage and, presumably, to take corrective action if necessary. The fluctuation of a farthing in one million transactions, for example, would result in £1,041 profit or loss. This detailed level of book-keeping was one reason why it was necessary to employ two clerical staff for each new teashop opened.

The teashop bills also served quite a different purpose; it was the practice of many of the waitresses to write on the reverse of the bill any comments made by the customers they were serving. These comments were carefully scrutinised by management and some, if they were complaints, would result in a detailed investigation, frequently by very senior staff, as to why a customer may have been sold a stale bun, for example. In such circumstances immediate remedial action was taken.

Reorganising for Efficiency

Lyons realised that the phenomenal business growth and the minutiae of clerical work this generated could, if not controlled, overwhelm them. In 1923 they decided to appoint five university graduates as management trainees to study this problem. (It was Lyons' policy to recruit graduates for fast-stream training for managerial roles before this practice was fully accepted by other parts of industry.) Among them was a Cambridge mathematics graduate named John Richardson Mainwaring Simmons (1902–1985). He reported to George Booth (1869–1959), the Company Secretary with responsibility for developing new accounting and office procedures so that the business could be run more efficiently. Simmons would eventually become Chief Comptroller (a title then used in Lyons to identify the person responsible for management accounts and other economic information) and later, in 1950, an Employee Director.

Soon after Simmons started work with Lyons he recruited another mathematics graduate, Thomas Raymond Thompson (1907–1976), who commenced his duties on 1 June 1931. He had started his career with Owen & Owen Limited in Liverpool, where he had been an assistant secretary. During the next 35 years these two brilliant individuals were together primarily responsible for developing the Company's office procedures; they would become the envy of many, copied by others, and would place Lyons at the forefront of clerical methods expertise. Thompson was always known by his contemporaries as TRT, unless one was subordinate—then it was Sir or Mr Thompson!

Although Simmons did not have absolute authority to impose his ideas on the various departments at Cadby Hall, his reputation for organisation and his aura increased, and he succeeded in obtaining the co-operation of many of his management peers, who could see the logic of his revolutionary ideas. He never raised his voice, was always polite, and was a good listener and very astute. If you ever missed one step in your reasoning with him he would quietly say, "I don't quite see how that follows", and if you had any sense you took the hint and retraced your steps. He could not be fooled by the complexity or technicality of an argument. One of his most disconcerting habits was to reply to an argument with "I hear what you say". It was his kind way of warning you either that you were wrong, or that you were not saying what you meant and had not convinced him. He also had a devastating and acid sense of humour. On one occasion he had called a meeting of managers for 9 a.m. All were gathered around the table at two minutes to nine, with Simmons in the chair, except one (who could never get up in the mornings), who burst into the room and said to Simmons "Sorry if I'm late, sir". "You're not late, Barnes," said Simmons in his usual quiet manner. "You merely prevented us from starting early!"

By 1935 Simmons and Thompson had replaced isolated groups of clerks in various factories, teashops and other locations by three main centralised clerical offices responsible for the trading and accounting records of the whole business.

The first office Simmons established was the Checking Department where, as the name implies, 450 clerks were responsible for cash control and checking the catering establishments' records, including every waitress bill produced. Each shop's receipts would be sorted into numerical and alphabetical sequence, normally by school leavers, and then passed to another section where the totalling was undertaken by more senior staff using Burroughs adding machines, the clatter of which was like a textile factory. The totals were checked against teashop bankings and discrepancies investigated. Since the waitress stubs were also retained it was possible to trace every waitress transaction from every teashop. The checks were sent to Cadby Hall in locked leather pouches and the Checking Department boys opening the bags in the morning soon learned what teashops were likely to have the occasional coin which had dropped from the till under which the bags were suspended. The teashop located at 396 Strand was said to be the most lucrative and their bag was sought out. Clearly, this was a labour-intensive task undertaken by clerks seated on benches in small cubicles reminiscent of the polling station booths of today.

The second office, known as the Stock Department (after World War II the Statistical Office), employed 400 clerks. This office maintained the stock records of the different departments of the company, such as raw materials, equipment and other inventory. Later, more elaborate departmental records were kept and the function that is now generally known as Management Accounting developed.

The third and largest office was the Accounts Department, where 600 clerks, of varying grades, were responsible for keeping the Company's trading accounts (sales and purchase ledgers) and for preparing the payroll. After the war, the payroll office functioned as a separate entity and groups within it were responsible for separate payroll units, for example, Bakery, Clerical, Tea, Works Services. The teashops payroll operated from Orchard House, Orchard Street, where Lyons occupied two floors.

The formation of this centralised clerical function, adopted for its practical advantages rather than as doctrinal policy, was a key factor in identifying accounting problems. It also provided the opportunity to create an environment in which research into their solution could take place.

The creation of these main offices made it possible for Simmons to provide consolidated financial information to members of the Board in weekly summaries known as White Books. Such information was by its nature historical, and no attempt was made to forecast the likely trend of the business. The compilation of the White Books, however, represented a major step forward in understanding the trading patterns at a comparatively short period after the event.

By 1934 the Checking Department had over 100 calculating machines at its disposal, and an additional 150 adding and book-keeping machines were in use elsewhere. To enable these to be used effectively Simmons had found it necessary to introduce, as early as 1928, a form of decimal currency for the internal accounting procedures of the company, and he thought that mechanisation was the only long-term solution to the costly and depressing employment of the human beings involved in this work. He later said, "The curse of routine clerical work is that, without exercising the intellect, it demands accuracy and concentration". Apart from the tedious aspects of the job, work started in the Accounts Office at 8.15 a.m. and at precisely 8.30 a.m., as one former employee recalled, "The Manager emerged from his office and walked down the 100-yard centre aisle of the large open-planned office, observing that everyone was hard at work. During this stroll it was forbidden for anyone to approach him; audience was by appointment only and strictly controlled by his secretary".

In 1936 Sir Isidore Salmon (1876–1941), Managing Director of J. Lyons & Company Ltd and son of Barnett Salmon, became President of the Decimal Association, a body which advocated the introduction of decimal coinage and the metric system of weights and measures. He considered this to be an issue of national importance and supported it strongly, using the shareholders meeting of June 1937 to launch a £50,000 fighting fund so that the Decimal Association could carry out a programme of education and, by gaining public support, convince the Government of the need for change. He and the more enlightened of his supporters believed that such a change would save the nation millions of pounds annually. Small wonder, therefore, that *The Times*, when reporting his speech Thursday 10 June 1937, chose the heading, "Sir Isidore Salmon's plea for decimal coinage".

The very next year, 1938, J. Lyons & Company Ltd reported their balance sheet in decimal notation and continued to do so until 1943, when they rounded entries to the nearest pound. In so doing, Lyons had hoped to persuade other companies to follow suit and so put added pressure on the Government. The start of World War II put a stop to this campaign.

To bring these and other changes about, Simmons established a business research centre in 1931 to study all forms of operating methods. Over a period of time this office developed structured and formalised methods of working, and gave much attention to the design and use of documents. A method of job grading evolved and a training centre was established, where all new clerical employees, from office boy upwards, trained in one discipline or other, depending on their job requirement, age and experience. A day release scheme operated for this purpose. These alterations simplified tasks, leading to increased productivity, and improved the flow of information through the organisation. The department that orchestrated these changes assumed the name Systems Research Office, a title which it retained until 1955, when it became known as the Organisation and Methods (O & M) Department.

In 1934 Geoffrey Mills (1910–1983), who had worked and qualified as a Chartered Secretary outside the Company, was recruited to manage and develop the department. He contributed greatly to the establishment of office procedures. In particular he published books and papers on the art of good document design and Lyons became leaders in this field. So successful were the Systems Research Office's techniques that other companies established similar departments and O & M, as it became known, soon became an acknowledged business discipline.

There were many examples of innovation. One worth mentioning is the study carried out in 1935 to reorganise the Wholesale Bakery Sales Invoicing department. Instead of copying the customer's order and producing the conventional invoice, delivery note, packing note and ledger posting copy for the account department, the customer's order itself was turned into the invoice by valuing it and then returning it to the customer for payment. A fairly simple thing to do, one might think, but the fact remains that nobody had previously done this. This turn-around document idea, itself novel, was soon accepted by many other organisations searching for office improvements. The technique rapidly gained acceptance and became widely used in many later computer applications developed by the Company. A further feature of this operation, suggested by Mills, was to record the office copy of the invoice on miniature film; it was a brilliant idea, although it may seem rather obvious today. The machine used for filming was a Recordak and its use in this way is believed to have been the first of any office system. It might be said, therefore, that Lyons invented microfilming for commercial record retention purposes.

Simmons and Thompson, with the full support of the company's Directors, continued to implement their revolutionary changes in office procedures, so that by the early 1940s a high level of efficiency in management accounting had been achieved, leading to improved management of the business. For many years, Lyons was the recognised leader of office management practice in Britain. Simmons and Thompson, always interested in improving management and office efficiency, became leading exponents in the development of clerical methods in the United Kingdom. Simmons also played a dominant role in the Institute of Administrative Management (founded in 1915 as the Office Machinery Users Association), joining in 1933. He was a member of its Governing Council from 1934 until 1968, Chairman from 1938 to 1950, President from 1944 to 1950 and honorary Vice President until his death. The Institute honours his 52-year membership record with an annual lecture in his name.

By the end of World War II Lyons had developed some of the most advanced office systems in Britain. Simmons and Thompson, who had been promoted to Assistant Secretary in April 1945 and to Chief Assistant Comptroller in December 1946, had by this time acquired a considerable reputation in office management matters and were well respected for their views; in today's parlance they might be described as Gurus or experts, even perhaps as consultants! They exerted considerable influence on all office matters within Lyons, and other companies sought their advice avidly.

From this power base and ideas reservoir, Lyons were able to carry out further clerical research, leading them eventually to automate the office in a way that would have profound implications for all businesses. Without the detailed background experience of their clerical operations the development of automated clerical procedures in the United Kingdom might have been delayed for many years and British industry might have turned to American technology.

Oliver Standingford, OBE (1913–1980), an Assistant Comptroller, who had first worked in the Stock Department in 1930 as a trainee manager, had his own ideas on how the Lyons' work could be automated and had conceived a plan to modify the existing accounting machines with an arrangement of automatic telephone equipment and magnetic records. He discussed these plans with W.J. Edwards (his father was a Lyons Board director 1934–1935), who was responsible for the electrical department at Cadby Hall. Both felt that the idea could be made to work, although by today's standards it would have been very slow. The outbreak of World War II prevented these plans from being studied further, but Standingford said later that he did give them further private consideration.

Technological Innovations

It is hardly surprising, therefore, that Lyons had been displaying an interest for some time in work being undertaken in the United States on electromechanical calculators and the like, though they had little enthusiasm for the punched card technology then being developed, which they felt would, at best, offer only a temporary solution. Contrary to their views, the punched card was rapidly gaining acceptance in office use on both sides of the Atlantic and, surprisingly, there was at least one punched card system operating in the company after World War II, in the teashops Wages Department. Because of the high turnover of staff, which affected the catering trade particularly, management considered punched cards to be particularly suitable as new or left staff could be inserted into the current employee card (database) pack. Regrettably, little is known of this operation and no reference can be found in historical documentation or other records of the company as to how or when the system was used, except that it was of Powers-Samas manufacture and operated at Orchard House.

Herman Hollerith, the pioneer of the punched card method of automation had, in 1890, competed with two other inventors, William Hunt and Charles Pidgin, to produce a sorting solution for the United States Bureau of Census in Washington. Hollerith's proposals won overwhelming acceptance and the Census Bureau used his equipment for the next twenty years. Hollerith had chosen the American dollar note as the basis for his card size. Using round hole punches, he set the standard for 80 column cards, which was subsequently adopted by nearly all other major punched card equipment manufacturers. This standard remains almost unchanged to the present day, even to the design of modern display terminals. With the introduction of faster electromagnetic mechanisms using brush feelers, a longer interval was required when sensing the holes, so some manufacturers introduced a rectangular hole. The same effect could have been achieved by making the round holes larger but this would have been at the expense of reducing the number of columns on a card.

The punched card industry continued to innovate until the 1940s, when there was a great upsurge in the electronics industry, much of it derived from experience gained during the war in government research establishments. This work had started in the early 1930s and progressed rapidly under the impact of total war during the 1940s. By 1945 one of the first electronic computers, ENIAC (Electronic Numerical Integrator and Computer), had been built by Professors J. Presper Eckert and John Mauchly, both Americans, working at the Moore School of Electrical Engineering, University of Pennsylvania, USA. The machine had been commissioned by the United States Army Ordnance Corps to calculate firing trajectories for the rapidly developing gun technology. ENIAC's completion in the autumn of 1945 came too late for it to make any contribution to the American war effort, but it continued to do useful work in ballistics and in rapidly developing fields such as atomic energy. The United States Army personnel for maintenance of the ENIAC were assigned to Captain Goldstine, and became effective on 1 June 1945, although the Army did not formally take possession of the machine until June 1946 when it passed acceptance trials. ENIAC had taken 200,000 man hours to develop at a reported cost of $750,000 and it contained no less than 17,468 thermionic valves, 7,200 crystal diodes and 4,100 magnetic elements, the checking of which took eight hours. The whole configuration consumed 174 kW of power, weighed over 30 tons and occupied an area of 1,800 square feet. Its major disadvantage was that each new computation required the resetting of plugged connections and switches, which in the worst situation could take several days to accomplish. Thus, even before ENIAC had been assembled for its first run, the benefits of a flexible stored program device had become obvious.

The ENIAC continued to work on ballistic and atomic energy problems at the Moore School until 9 November 1946, when it was dismantled and re-assembled at the Army Ballistic Research Laboratory at Aberdeen, Maryland on 29 July 1947. In the next few years, an additional $250,000 was spent on improving it. An immensely ambitious undertaking, ENIAC remained in service until 2 October 1955, when it carried out its last calculation.

Other developments followed, but it was not until 1951 that the United States could claim to have working, on a limited scale, a stored program computer. For a few brief years North American computer research lost direction, probably due in part to John von Neumann's (1903–1957) return to Princeton University and the departure of Professors Eckert and Mauchly from the Moore School in 1947, over a dispute on ENIAC patents, to form the Electronic Control Company.

The United States, however, soon recovered ground and captured much of the world computer market within a decade. This, perhaps, came about not because their machines were technically more advanced but rather because of their ability to identify marketing opportunities and to exploit them to the full.

The Trip to America

By 1947 some research work became declassified and reports started to appear in the press extolling these Electronic Brains, as the media liked to call them. These developments caught the attention of the Lyons management as they were about to despatch Thompson and Standingford on a tour of the United States and Canada to study and observe the latest work on electronic calculators. Before they left on their three-month tour, an article had appeared in a popular publication describing in broad terms the hitherto secret ENIAC computer. Thompson and Standingford suggested that this project should be included in their itinerary but this proposal met with some resistance from their business colleagues. After some debate, and with considerable wisdom, George Booth, then in his seventies, agreed that it should be included in the schedule, saying "Youth should be given its head even if the head contained unusual ideas". Booth's judgement was never questioned by senior management and no business decisions were ever taken without his approval.

Thompson and Standingford never did see ENIAC in action, as it happened; on the morning of their visit it was declared that the project was still secret. Later, as Standingford recalls, they were told that the visit had been cancelled because ENIAC was not working. This was not surprising: it had a reputation for unreliability, and Standingford reported that it was out of service for 97% of the time.[1] But Americans had said to him, "oh boy, that three per cent". Quite where Standingford obtained his information is not known but it was inaccurate. Bruce Breummer of the Babbage Institute, writing to Gail Pietrzyk of the University of Pennsylvania, says, "There was considerable discussion about the reliability of the ENIAC in the *Honeywell v. Sperry* trial. Nick Metropolis testified that there was one tube (valve) failure per day, and Ruth Teitelbaum said that there was rarely a day that it worked all day". Nancy Stern in her book, *From ENIAC to UNIVAC* (Digital Press. Bedford, MA), puts the mean time between failure at 5.6 hours.

The development of the ENIAC and von Neumann's paper on the stored program computer captured the imagination of the Lyons' executives, who, despite their disappointment over the visit to ENIAC, believed that the results of this research could be applied to solve many of the problems currently inhibiting the progress of clerical automation at Lyons. Ironically, during their 1947 trip, Thompson and Standingford learned from Herman Heine Goldstine (1913–1964), who was working with von Neumann at Princeton University, that a more advanced computer project, similar in nature, was taking place at Cambridge University. This project, known as the EDSAC (Electronic Delay Storage Automatic Computer), had been initiated by Professor Douglas Hartree (1897–1958) in 1945. Dr (later Professor) Maurice Wilkes followed it through after he had attended a course on electronic computers, sponsored by the Moore School in Philadelphia, between 8 July and 31 August 1946. Here, Delay Line Storage had been one of the topics of discussion.

Wilkes had joined the class two weeks before the end of the course and had missed an earlier visit to the ENIAC. However, he was given a private showing by Professor Mauchly and spent some time debating constructional details with him. Wilkes later recalled that both recognised that this stage of technology had passed and that any new computer development would need to take account of the stored program principle. When Wilkes returned from the United States the machine he built, the EDSAC, became one of the world's first working alterable stored program computers. Although he achieved complete success he has since confirmed that his project had been a crash programme. He had employed simple techniques, avoiding frills and the exploitation of technology. The architectural designs and decisions taken were his, including the bad ones, and he made no attempt to make the design more economic or elegant. It was this machine that became the basis of Lyons' automatic office.

During their study tour Thompson and Standingford also visited Harvard University, where they met Professor Howard Aiken (1900–1973), head of the Computation Laboratory. They were shown the Harvard Mark 1 computer. The Mark 1, which was not electronic but used magnetic relays, is said to have been the first machine to incorporate some of the principles of Babbage's Analytical Engine. Its hugely expensive construction, sponsored by International Business Machines (IBM), had taken five years to assemble. It measured over 50 feet in length and its collective conventional tabulating construction could calculate to 23 decimal places. For most of the time it was used for military purposes.

On return from their successful study tour of the United States and Canada, Thompson and Standingford visited Professor Douglas Hartree, Professor of Mathematical Physics at the Cavendish Laboratory, Cambridge, and Wilkes, Director of the Mathematical Laboratory, Cambridge. Close contact was maintained with the University and much friendly assistance and advice was given to Lyons by these two researchers

The Radical Proposal

On 20 October 1947 copies of Thompson's and Standingford's North American visit report, now lost, were submitted to members of the Lyons Board with a covering memorandum, from which the following is extracted:

We believe that we have been able to get a glimpse of a development which will, in a few years' time, have a profound effect on the way in which clerical work (at least) is performed. Here, for the first time, there is a possibility of a machine which will be able to cope, at almost incredible speed, with any variation of clerical procedure, provided the conditions which govern the variations can be predetermined. What effect such machines could have on the semi-repetitive work of the office needs only the slightest effort of imagination. The possible saving from such a machine should be at least £50,000 a year. The capital cost would be of the order of £100,000.

We feel, therefore, that the Company might well wish to take a lead in the development of the machine and indeed that, unless organisations such as ours, the potential users, are prepared to do so, the time at which they become commercially available will be unnecessarily postponed for many years.

Despite the radical nature of the proposal that Simmons and his team submitted, even it seems without a full cost analysis, they were successful in influencing the Lyons Board. After all, the two had considerable reputations in office management techniques with impressive past successes, and when they went to the Board with this notion to build an Electronic Brain they took it very seriously and regarded it as a perfectly reasonable proposition. In retrospect, it seems an extremely casual, but far-sighted, decision for a catering and food manufacturing organisation to have taken during this difficult post-war period, but, surprisingly, there was no resistance from any Board member to this radical idea.

On 11 November 1947, shortly after reading the report, a deputation led by Booth, whose support would have been necessary before Board approval, accompanied by Thompson and employee director Harold H. G. Bennett (1891–1978), visited Cambridge University and, without too many preliminaries, offered to donate £3,000 and the services of an assistant to the EDSAC project if in return guidance could be given on how Lyons could develop their own electronic calculator. Cambridge University viewed this gesture as most generous, since it came when the momentum of the EDSAC project was slowing from lack of funds, and they had no hesitation in accepting. By providing the donation, Lyons also hoped to accelerate the Cambridge development from which they would ultimately benefit. Two days after their meeting with Wilkes, Lyons forwarded their cheque and Cambridge University made an announcement on 2 December 1947 in the University *Reporter*, it being customary in those days to add the names of benefactors to the University's list. This thoughtful gesture pleased the Lyons Board enormously, coming as a complete surprise to them; the relationship between the two institutions became very warm and continued to strengthen.

Lyons' first concern, of course, was the commercial advantages that might be gained from the development of their electronic calculator. The machine, if it worked, could be used to run the business more efficiently than was possible by conventional clerical means. Work could be undertaken that had not previously been possible using conventional methods, either because it was too expensive, or because it could not be completed in the required time. Much of the business activity was geared to a response cycle of 24 hours or less (for example, baking rolls at night for sale the next day). The potential speed at which calculations could be made appeared awesome. Simmons also suggested that such a revolutionary machine might well be a prime factor in relieving the economic distress of the country, which was still suffering the aftermath of World War II; how Simmons planned to achieve this aim is now difficult to understand, but it certainly gave the company something to concentrate on since the fortunes of the teashops were beginning to fade. The new technological challenge acted as a boost to morale.

Simmons did not feel that Lyons should play a passive role, merely keeping in touch with developments and in due course acquiring machines as they became available, probably from American sources. Apart from the currency exchange controls then in force, such a role would not enable Lyons to have any influence on machine design and this they felt was essential if the problem of commercial clerical automation was to be solved successfully. After all, computer research until this time had been largely academic and directed towards solving mathematical problems, whereas Lyons' interests were primarily associated with automating routine commercial tasks, areas which many academics trivialised. This opinion is illustrated by Stuart Hollingdale's and Geoffrey Tootill's comments in *Electronic Computers*, describing the year 1946 as the end of the pioneering stage of automatic computer development. At this time no methods had been devised to use computers for business applications. Great advances were to be made after this date, and are still being made today.

Thompson and Standingford's report on their American visit sketched three alternative courses: first, to persuade Cambridge to follow a commercial computing path; second, to commission some large electronics firm or manufacturer of conventional business equipment to develop a computer for Lyons; or third, to develop a machine in-house.

Their involvement with the Cambridge staff had already convinced Lyons that the EDSAC team would not wish to redirect their research efforts to a more commercial bias. They were only interested in the academic and mathematical possibilities of the machine. It also quickly emerged, after exploratory discussions with electronic companies, both here and in America, that they also were unwilling to participate in what they considered a very speculative project, preferring instead to continue with their research or with the manufacture of their punched card equipment. IBM also, was approached, but their Chief Executive, John Watson, did not want to be deflected from their punch card manufacturing.[2] This indifference did not come as a surprise to Simmons since he had realised that any development of this kind would probably be prohibitively expensive and of uncertain outcome. Such a negative response did not deter Lyons' enthusiasm either: very naturally, they decided to proceed with the third alternative, to go it alone. This was not a difficult decision for Lyons, they were used to taking decisions of this kind and it fitted in with their management style. The idea was fully discussed with the Cambridge team and endorsed by them.

The Cambridge Connection

Soon after Lyons' donation to Cambridge University's EDSAC project, a member of the Lyons engineering staff, Ernest Lenaerts, started work under Wilkes at the University to help the EDSAC team and to gain practical experience of the new electronic technology.

Lenaerts had first been employed by Lyons, before the outbreak of World War II in a clerical capacity that he did not much like, in the Stock Department under Thompson. During the war years he served in the Royal Air Force (RAF), working on electronic navigation and radar counter-measures at Alexandra Palace. During this period he studied electronics, a field he was to be associated with for the rest of his working life. In September 1944, while the war was still raging in Europe, Lenaerts received a letter from George Booth, enquiring about his plans for post-war employment.

Lenaerts' period in the RAF had equipped him with a considerable understanding of theoretical and practical electronics, and he realised that much of the RAF work with which he had been associated would soon be turned to more practical uses. He wanted to continue this exciting work and did not see a future in returning to Lyons as a clerk, and said as much in his reply to Booth. He followed up this theme before demobilisation and wrote to his old chief Thompson, now Assistant Secretary, on 17 May 1945, listing various projects from which the company could potentially benefit. After discussions with others at Cadby Hall, Thompson realised that Lyons could benefit from Lenaerts' enthusiasm and fresh ideas, and offered him a position as a radio mechanic. He accepted and started work on 31 December 1945 for 2/7d per hour.

Lenaerts remained on secondment to Cambridge University for 12 months, during which time he improved his electronic skills, which he put to great effect when he eventually returned to Cadby Hall. When he arrived at Cambridge University plans for the EDSAC were still in a fluid state and many of the circuits, including the arithmetic circuits, had not yet been designed. During his stay he documented the work and problems that the EDSAC team were struggling with, writing no fewer than 45 letters to Cadby Hall. This initially concerned Simmons, who had sent Lenaerts to Cambridge University to help Wilkes in any way that he needed, and did not want him distracted from that main consideration. However, that said, Simmons on one occasion wrote, "Any notes or information would be very welcome", and reciprocated with some 45 letters to Lenaerts. By November 1948 Lenaerts had written a complete "Introduction to EDSAC" with comprehensive descriptions of binary arithmetic, the principle of delay line storage, the need for timing and gate pulses, the form of order code and examples of adding, subtracting and multiplication. He had learned his craft well.

Lenaerts admits he was sometimes out of his depth while working with the researchers at Cambridge, and frequently worked long hours to grapple with binary multiplication or other new techniques with which he was unfamiliar. His work was mainly associated with individual circuit pieces, such as the arithmetic circuits, and he was sometimes at a disadvantage, not having been given the overview plan. It was some time before all the pieces of the EDSAC puzzle came together and began to make sense.

While these significant developments were taking place Lenaerts had great difficulty in obtaining such mundane items as paper on which to write his reports. He received a letter from Edwards in January 1948, soon after requesting writing material, which simply said, "The position here is desperate and all we can supply you with is some carbon paper and two typist's note books. It would be best if you buy your own stationery locally and I will let you know if and *how* it is possible to reimburse you in this respect". (A few years later tons of listing paper would be pouring off the world's computer printers and disposing of it would become a problem!) The situation was so serious at times that some of Lenaerts' reports, which still exist, were written on the reverse side of bakery goods wrapping paper. Shortages of items, due to enforced deprivations during the war years, cannot now be properly appreciated and it is astonishing that this project succeeded at all, given the acute supply difficulties of everything at that time. However, Lenaerts meticulously reported to management routine details of the work in which he was involved, describing highly technical functions in layman's terms for the benefit of those at Cadby Hall. This was not always necessary as Simmons and Thompson, both fully qualified in mathematics, were intellectually capable of understanding some of the finer points Lenaerts made, and, indeed, sometimes questioned some of his logic. Lenaerts has been described as an "indefatigable diarist" and much of the archival data on the project to which I have had access was carefully recorded by him.

Building the Team

Several other appointments were made around this time, including that of Derek Hemy. He was the first member of the project team to have been recruited, even before Lenaerts was seconded to Cambridge, and he commenced his new duties in September 1947. Hemy first joined Lyons in July 1939 as a management trainee attached to the Checking Department. At the outbreak of war the Lyons' training schemes were suspended and Hemy was associated with several miscellaneous duties that gave him an insight into the operation of the Corner Houses, the Restaurants and the Hop Cellars. He joined the Royal Engineers (Chemical Warfare) in July 1940. When he returned to Lyons after demobilisation, earlier plans for him were changed and he joined the Systems Research Office, then managed by David Caminer, and worked under him on a number of O & M assignments between 1946 and 1947. In September 1947 Hemy was offered a job in the O & M Department of the newly formed Coal Board, but whilst considering this offer Mills informed him about the computer project that Lyons were poised to start, inviting him to join it. He immediately decided to accept this opportunity. This was fortunate for Lyons, since Hemy, under the astute management and guidance of Caminer, went on to establish some of the software techniques and standards for the historic machine that Lyons were about to build. He also became responsible for coding many of the first commercial computer programs to be written.

For some time Hemy continued as a member of the Systems Research Office under Caminer, who took a close interest in the computer project. On 1 May 1950, when it became necessary to form a larger programming team, Caminer and Hemy left the Systems Research Office and moved to the Head Office building where the computer was being built, and Caminer took charge of programming.

Caminer, recruited by Simmons in 1936, had also joined Lyons as a management trainee. After the statutory period of learning Lyons' methods he was put to work on management accounts to improve their method of compilation and to reduce the length of time it took to provide completed reports to management. His management style has been described by some as aggressive, and he was forthright in expressing his views. He set high standards and expected them to be met, but he led from the front and worked himself at least as hard as anyone else. He was a hard, but fair, taskmaster, and often took a strong stand to protect the interests of his subordinates.

The systematic discipline required by computers to solve problems was not new to Caminer. He had, with Simmons and Thompson, adopted this approach to improve many of the clerical tasks at Lyons, and computerisation was a natural adaptation of this discipline. It was, undoubtedly, the understanding of the nature and function of the various clerical processes that enabled Lyons to develop successful systems on their first computer. The approach was in accord with the views of Simmons, who held that it was necessary to define "the true requirements" of a process before proceeding to the study of the means available to meet them. This basic understanding of clerical procedures enabled Lyons to make use of computers successfully without any previous experience or knowledge of them: indeed, they regarded them as merely another tool to solve a particular clerical problem.

In September 1948, before the EDSAC project at Cambridge University had reached completion, Lyons decided to engage a qualified electronic engineer to advise them and to lead a small select team to design a computer. This had followed earlier discussions with Wilkes, who had visited Cadby Hall on 22 April 1948 to discuss, with the Lyons Board and others, the practical problems of building and programming a computer suitable for clerical procedures.

By now Lyons were sufficiently motivated and ready to proceed to the next stage. They placed an advertisement in the scientific journal *Nature*, during October 1948, for a qualified electronic engineer with experience of television circuit design and ultrahigh frequency techniques. Their advertisement gave no indication of the company or the task in hand, other than that it was a permanent post. It was answered by a young Cambridge University researcher, Dr John Pinkerton, who had previous knowledge that Lyons were about to embark on a project of this kind and, suspecting it was them, applied for the job. (Wilkes had alerted him to Lyons' plans some time previously.) Until now Pinkerton had not been involved in computers but, through a common interest in radio and radar, knew Wilkes and his work at Cambridge and the similar developments that were taking place at Manchester University and elsewhere.

He had entered Cambridge University to study natural sciences in 1937; the Government allowed him to continue his degree course at the outbreak of war in 1939, and from 1940 until 1945 he worked on radar research, initially at the Telecommunications Research Establishment (TRE) at Swanage and later at Malvern. After the war he returned to Cambridge University to research into ultrasonics while reading for his PhD.

Lyons had planned their interview with Pinkerton very thoughtfully; on 13 December 1948 he spent the whole day at Cadby Hall, during which time Lyons gave him a thorough understanding of the business and their unique clerical operations, arranging special demonstrations of some of these for his benefit. He was impressed with the care and attention Lyons had taken to prepare the interview and with their obvious commitment to this extraordinary project. After a long day, George Booth, who was the Director responsible for the total clerical operation, finally asked him, "Do you think you can build this machine?", to which he replied confidently, "Yes, I think I can make it, but whether it will be reliable I am not so sure". Lyons offered Pinkerton the position of Electronic Engineer that very day and asked what salary he expected. He suggested £800 per annum (despite the advertisement's maximum of £600); Lyons offered him £900 and confirmed the appointment. He started work on 17 January 1949 and, after clerical induction training, went back to Cambridge University to study the EDSAC. Pinkerton, then 29 years of age, became a Director of Lyons' subsidiary company, which was incorporated to manufacture computers, within a decade.

By the end of October 1948 Lenaerts had returned to Cadby Hall. Progress made on the EDSAC project was sufficiently encouraging for Lyons to proceed cautiously with the preparation for the construction of their device. A suitable area on the second floor of the Head Office building, known as WX block, was made available to the nucleus of a small technical team being assembled by Pinkerton. At Simmons' request Lenaerts provided some estimates as to the floor space that would be required for the machine. Based on the EDSAC (very cramped) experience, Lenaerts thought that some 820 square feet would be about right but this was a serious underestimate—it turned out that some 5,000 square feet were required. This was no fault of Lenaerts; he was very meticulous in everything he undertook. It was the bald fact that nobody had done it before and all estimates were based on the EDSAC. Lenaerts also provided some costs for preliminary work (three months) and advance provisioning, listing such items as oscilloscope (£140), benching (£10), four stools (£4), and small tools (£15). The total cost was £400, which included Lenaerts for 13 weeks. How such an advanced technical project could be undertaken with such casual and modest funding is quite staggering.

Earlier, in October 1948, Simmons had suggested making office space available for three separate machines. In his letter to Lenaerts at the time he said:

We shall clearly need the best part of two complete machines before we can trust any section of the office work to it, because of the possibility of breakdown, and it is probable that with improvements that will be made possible as a result of increased experience, we shall want to start building a third machine almost as soon as we have completed the second. In any event we shall probably under-estimate the amount of space required.

In the event, only one machine was built at Cadby Hall but his prediction on office space proved correct: only six months later more space was required for an experimental workshop that quickly took shape in the lodge of St Mary's College, a property in Brook Green, once a seminary, and now used as offices and forming part of the Cadby Hall complex.

Additional staff were taken on about this time, and in August 1949 Ernest Kaye was employed. He had obtained a Honours Degree in Engineering (BSc Eng) at Imperial College, London, where he had studied between 1940 and 1942. He joined the team from the General Electric Company (GEC) Research Laboratories at Wembley where he had been working in the communications section, on underwater homing torpedoes and later on pulse modulation and electromechanical relay systems. The project team required another qualified engineer with experience in pulse technology and relay circuitry, and Kaye brought much practical electronic experience to the team through having worked on similar problems at GEC from 1942 until 1949. Pinkerton, Kaye and Lenaerts were subsequently responsible for much of the early circuit design of the computer and in 1954 published a series of technical articles in *Electronic Engineering* that won them the Radio Industry Council's award for the best technical writing of the year.

Kaye was appointed Assistant to Pinkerton when he joined, somewhat to the disillusionment of Lenaerts, who had now been working on the project since 1 December 1947, when he first joined the Cambridge University team. He kept his disappointment very much to himself and it is greatly to his credit that he did not let it interfere with his work. Kaye was never aware of Lenaerts' feelings and both worked amicably together, always with the greatest respect for each other's expertise and experience. As Kaye later recalled, "There was fantastic team spirit from its inception to its final shutdown".

After the design phase had been largely completed Kaye assumed new responsibilities as procurement manager for all materials and subcontracting work. This was extremely important to the rapid completion of the project, and, as it turned out, could not have been achieved by the resources at Cadby Hall alone.

Raymond Shaw was recruited by Pinkerton in August 1949 as an electrical engineer primarily concerned with electronics. His responsibilities initially involved the testing of units before their assembly. He joined the team from Radio Electronics, a company he had returned to after active service in the RAF, where he had also trained as a radar mechanic (1943–1947) on pulse techniques, a skill that he put to use after joining Lyons.

Robert Gibson was appointed head of the Engineering Maintenance Section (in November 1956) after Shaw had left for Australia, and was responsible to Pinkerton for the training of engineers. In September 1958 he introduced training courses for commissioning engineers and in 1960 suggested advanced programming courses for potential senior programmers. In 1961 he gave the first programming course for the LEO III computer, where trainees were required to write a model program in the new computer language known as CLEO (Clear Language for Expressing Orders).

Gordon Gibbs was another young engineer employed as a junior electrical engineer and he specialised in the input and output mechanisms.

Jean Cox came from the Lyons' clerical department and served as secretary to Pinkerton. She became involved with circuit tracing in the early days of the project and was joined by Miss Plant.

Wally (Walter) Dutton, originally a Lyons electrician, transferred from another department and brought a sense of practicality to the mass of basic electrical engineering problems that the project team were faced with in the early days. Equally useful on the mechanical side was Arthur Clements, whose great adaptive talents help to solve many of the mechanical problems faced by the team. Both men, although contributing greatly to the early phases of the project, are regretfully seldom mentioned in the papers researched.

David Wheeler started in 1951 as a young engineer with Wally Dutton and grew up with the team. Between 1953 and 1956 Wheeler did his National Service and returned to Lyons, who by this time were manufacturing computers at Minerva Road, Acton.

The Programming Team

In parallel with the formation of the engineering team, the programming team that was its necessary complement was being built up. Leopold Fantl, from Teplitz Schoenau, Czechoslovakia, joined as Hemy's first programmer in 1950. Hemy described him as "A good mathematician, an outstanding programmer and an indefatigable worker with a great sense of humour". Leo, as he always liked to be known, came to Britain from Czechoslovakia on a Children's Transport in June 1939 and was due to have travelled on to Palestine, but Italy's entry into the war put a stop to that. He worked on the land as a general farm labourer, first in Kent and then in Devon, before joining the RAF in 1942, when he was 18 years old.

He joined Lyons as a trainee in the Labour Planning Department in March 1949, and in 1950 Thompson interviewed him and he joined the computer project team as Trainee Programmer. All this just 10 years after he arrived at Liverpool Street Station in London unable to speak a word of English!

Antony Barnes joined the programming team from the Statistical Office in November 1950 where he had been employed as a management trainee after serving as an Instructor Lieutenant in the Royal Navy. He rapidly became a very valuable and energetic member of the team, tackling a variety of work with considerable panache and great effectiveness. He was clearly destined for a wider field, and in July 1953 left programming to take charge of the increasingly important operations side of LEO. He was described as "A wizard at the console, altering programs in binary almost like playing an organ". In 1955 he accompanied Thompson on a six-week tour of the United States, visiting s computer manufacturers and users. In January 1956 he became the Administration Manager of the Design and Development Section, before becoming the Production Director of Lyons' manufacturing subsidiary, taking charge of the new LEO III composite Production Division.

John Grover joined as a programmer shortly after Barnes. In 1940 he had won a five-year engineering apprenticeship at the Royal Arsenal, Woolwich which was intended to produce BSc (Eng) graduates with practical experience. In 1943, before the completion of his apprenticeship, he volunteered for RAF air crew training and won his pilots wings in 1945, passing out as Student of Honour. In 1947, however, he decided not to pursue a long-term commission and joined Lyons as a management trainee working in the Sales Accounts Office. In 1950 Thompson invited him to join the LEO team, partly as an experiment and partly because of an earlier industrial psychology assessment of him as a potential management candidate. Hemy said of him:

He had a quiet manner which sometimes disguised his undoubted talents. At times he appeared to be slow in thought but this was the result of his think-

1. The American ENIAC computer. From left to right: Erwin Goldstein, Homer Spence, Elizabeth Jennings, and Francis Bellis. *Reproduced by kind permission of the University of Pennsylvania.*

2. Part of the EDSAC computer from which LEO was designed. It performed its first successful task on 6 May 1949. *Reproduced by kind permission of the Syndics of Cambridge University Library.*

3. Outside the mathematical laboratory, Cambridge University, in 1949. Back row left to right: D.W. Willis, L.J. Foreman, G.J. Stevens, R.S. Piggott, P.J. Farmer, P. Chamberlain. Centre row left to right: D.J. Wheeler, E.H. Lenaerts, J.E. Steel, R.B. Bonham-Carter, C.M. Munford, S.A Barton. Front row left to right: E.E. McKee, J.M. Bennett, B. Noble, M.V. Wilkes, W. Renwick, E.N. Mutch, H.M. Gordon. *Reproduced by kind permission of the Syndics of Cambridge University Library.*

4. Thomas Thompson. c.1967. *Reproduced by kind permission of the Institute of Administrative Management.*

5. Anthony Salmon. *Reproduced by his kind permission.*

6. Dr John Pinkerton. c.1960. *Reproduced by kind permission of J. Lyons & Co Ltd.*

7. John Simmons. c.1956.
Reproduced by kind permission of J. Lyons & Co Ltd.

8. Derek Hemy. c.1953.
Reproduced by kind permission of Leo Fantl.

9. Ray Shaw (left), David Caminer (right) and Gordon Gibbs (front). c.1953. *Reproduced by kind permission of Leo Fantl.*

10. (*above*). Raw Shaw (left) and Leo Fantl. c.1950. *Reproduced by kind permission of Leo Fantl.*

11. (*left*). Tony Barnes. 1962. *Reproduced by kind permission of Leo Fantl.*

12. (*right*). Wally Dutton (left) and Ernest Lenaerts. c.1952. *Reproduced by kind permission of Leo Fantl.*

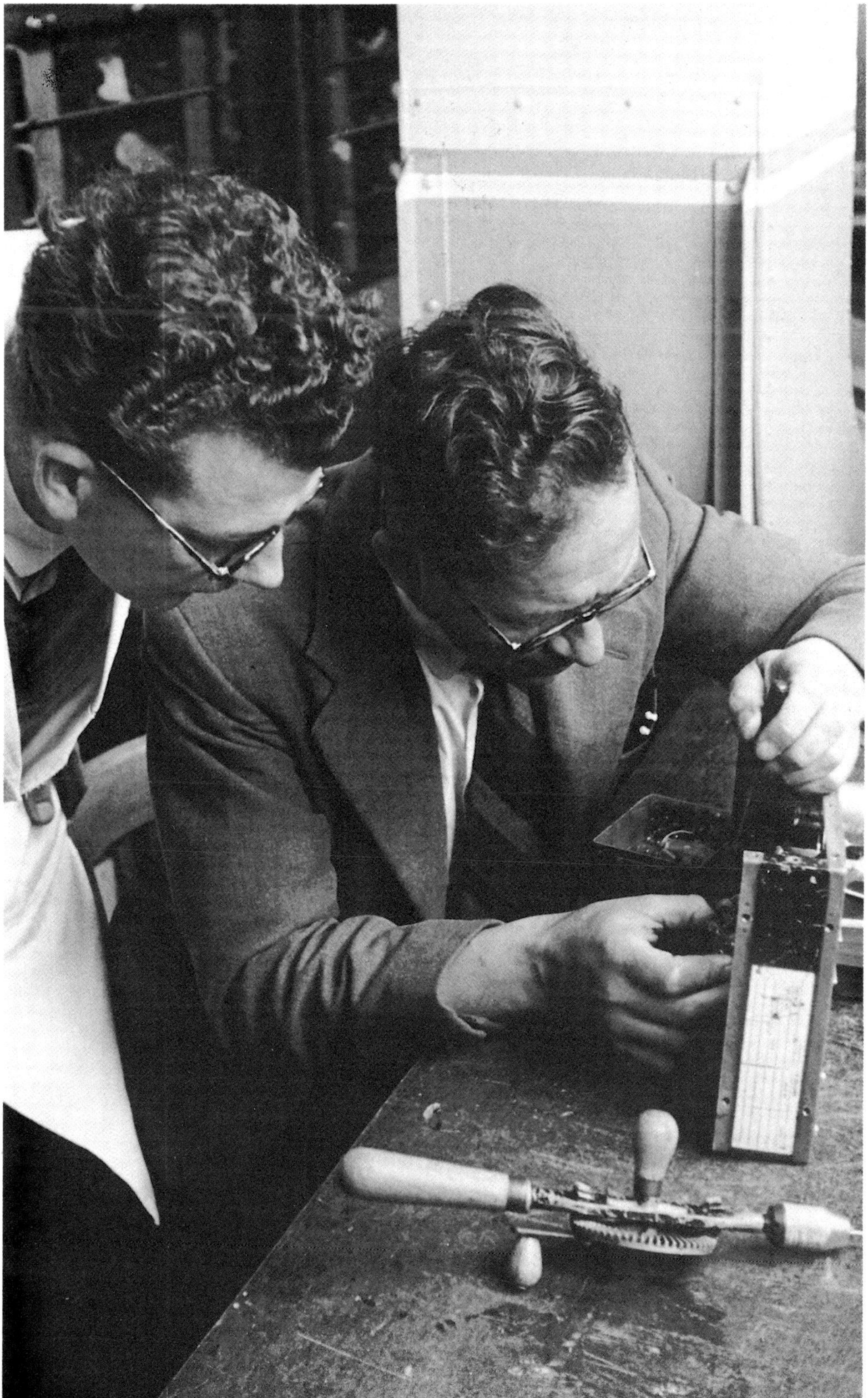

13. John Grover. 1954. *Reproduced by kind permission of Leo Fantl.*

14. John Gosden. c.1951. *Reproduced by kind permission of Leo Fantl.*

ing things through before he spoke out; his ability to produce original ideas without any preliminary flourishes could often be quite disconcerting. Once he had mastered the basics of programming (such as they were when he joined) his work was penetrative and thorough; he could always be relied upon to carry through any project with determination and imagination, and to great effect. He made a very full contribution to the success of the programming team and helped to generate the spirit and comradeship that sustained us through some very taxing times.

This team of five—Hemy, Fantl, Barnes and Grover—together with Caminer, who was responsible for the software team, worked together as an integrated unit. Between them they carried through all the early work to establish the programming techniques and disciplines that made possible the rapid development of a series of commercial applications over the following years. They established a natural rapport, not only among themselves, but also with Lenaerts and other members of the engineering team.

Another programmer from the early days was Mary Blood (now Coombs), LEO's first female programmer. She first started work for Lyons in the summer of 1951 as a temporary clerk after obtaining her BA Honours degree in French, with History, at Queen Mary College, University of London. Her first permanent position with Lyons was in the Statistical Office and she recalls that this was the first occasion when she had used a calculator to help cost the recipes of various company products. She was given the opportunity to attend a LEO appreciation course and aptitude testing in 1952, and was delighted to be offered an immediate job on LEO; after suitable training she worked under John Grover on the payroll programs. In 1954 John Coombs joined the LEO programming team from the regular army, and after a whirlwind romance married Mary Blood in March 1955. It was company policy in those days not to employ man and wife in the same department, so John was transferred to the Accounts Office.

Another woman who joined the team at a very early stage was Marjorie Coles; she may be considered the pioneer of data preparation and was responsible for the LEO data preparation department. She was transferred from the Accounts Office in 1951 where she was the supervisor of a large ledger posting group.

Another early programmer was Frank Land. Born in Germany, he came to Britain in 1939, and subsequently took a degree in Economics at the London School of Economics. After a year of research work, he joined Lyons as a cost clerk in the Statistical Office, where he kept accounts for the Provincial Bakeries and Laboratories. He was included in the company's 1952 trawl through the Lyons' offices to see who might be interested in becoming a programmer. After a week of aptitude testing he was offered a position as a trainee programmer and joined the team under the supervision of John Grover.

John Gosden joined as a programmer in October 1953, having studied mathematics at Cambridge University between 1950 and 1953. He was hired by Thompson and supervised by Fantl, who taught him a great deal about rounding errors. Gosden worked on many LEO I applications, including those for the National Physical Laboratory, Legal & General Insurance, Handley Page Aircraft, and Teashops Ordering, and it was he who prepared estimates and plans for a job to calculate the shortest distances between all pairs of railway goods stations on the United Kingdom rail network. This job, which ran largely at night, took six months to complete. In 1956 Gosden cleaned out all the remaining logical faults on LEO II/1 and a year later planned and directed the drum storage routines for this computer. He was also responsible for the input/output routines to handle magnetic tape routines, autochecking, alignment and restart control programs. He worked on the later master-routine facilities, interrupts to permit multi-programming working and programming languages of the later LEO III computer.

In May 1952 Ashley Peter Wood (always known as Peter) joined the team as operations supervisor, with Sid Jenkinson (who was engaged from Lyons' subsidiary company Normand Limited) as his deputy.

The software aspects of the computer project were started very much earlier than the hardware design, and the department's first objectives in October 1947 were to analyse the cost of clerical work in Lyons, to identify the nature of the clerical processes in the various departments, and to assess their homogeneity, the balance between data volumes and the amount of calculation, the time scale to which jobs had to be done, and the way in which data was originated. On that basis, rough estimates were made of the scope for savings. Then, nobody had much idea of what a computer was and the only available documentation was a bound programming manual for the Harvard Mark II machine, which was pretty much incomprehensible.

For two weeks during May 1948 Hemy was based at Cambridge to study programming methods. Although warmly welcomed by Wilkes and his team, he was disconcerted to be told that they lacked a programmer and had not been able to spare any time from machine design and development to consider programming. All Wilkes had was a fairly rough file of jottings.

After some very heavy sessions, Hemy managed to decipher some notes on a possible input routine that were included in the file. However, they appeared more appropriate to the mathematical applications for which EDSAC was being built rather than to commercial work. Nevertheless, this served to give him his first exposure to the problems of programming, and was a starting point for his work.

He then discussed with Ben Noble, the Cambridge team's first programmer, the way in which the various functions of the order code were to work, the machine language shape that orders would take and the addressing system. During these discussions, Hemy and Noble agreed that the idea of writing programs in machine language was absurd, and that since the machine could process the input data, it should also be used to translate programs written in a form convenient to the programmer into the binary form required; in this way the subject of initial orders (or synthesis instructions, as they were known in the early days), was first raised.

When Hemy returned from Cambridge he discussed his progress with David Caminer. He was anxious to continue working on the detail of programming and part of his time was spent on this. David Caminer showed greater interest in the broader aspects and pressed him to develop his ideas on how to design and construct programs, as opposed to their actual coding. Hemy explained to me that his first thoughts on this were to devise a form of charting, soon to be christened flow charting, and in this Caminer encouraged him. Looking back Hemy describes his first efforts as:

Grotesquely complicated and in the result a wasted effort since I soon abandoned the complications and instead devoted my efforts, as I should have done in the first place, to defining the purposes and uses of flow charts. The first function was to simplify the analysis of a process into logical steps, each of which might represent several orders, as an aid to structuring a program. Second, such a chart, by showing where and under what conditions choices were to be made and the processing that would result, would help in checking the logic of a program before it was written and could lead to better coding. Third, when a program had been written the chart would provide a guide and index to the coded orders.

Later, it was found that there were other uses for them, in that they formed part of the operating documentation and were of real value in program testing and in the modification of programs. Subsequently, as programming techniques developed, attention was given to simplifying the way in which flow charts were laid out, to ensure that the logical progression of the program was clearly shown. In practice, these stylistic improvements were found to produce more effective programs.

During the summer of 1948 David Wheeler of Cambridge, who had by then started work in the Mathematical Laboratory as a research student, came to Cadby Hall for vacation work and was of great help in developing early ideas on the techniques of programming. It should be noted that, then and for some years to come, the term "programming" was taken to include not only the writing of programs but also what might now be called Systems Analysis, Systems Design and Software Engineering. For a time even Operating and Data Preparation were not distinguished as separate functions. When LEO became operational separate units were set up for these activities.

It was fortunate that in Lyons the user/systems-oriented approach was already established and that Caminer and Hemy had been working in such an environment before the computer project started. The programming itself, however technical, was regarded as a means to an end: a technical tool for developing systems that were to be carried out on the computer. Caminer certainly took an interest in programming (he was interested in everything) but never actually turned his hand to coding; that was left to Hemy. Caminer, on the other hand, devoted a great deal of his time to specifying, charting, optimising, and desk checking logical programming sequences. He excelled in Applications Planning and System Design, and Hemy enjoyed his leadership, management and criticism, which was "rarely unfair and always helpful and constructive". So, in effect, both carried into the work on LEO the disciplines of systems work that had already been adopted as the norm.

From Calculator to Computer

The EDSAC computer and, following it, the Lyons machine, operated sequentially; that is, instructions were taken one at a time from the store and carried out one after the other in the main circuitry. In this respect, the computer was little more than a fast automatic calculator that could carry out a prolonged series of operations. It soon became clear that there were two characteristics that radically increased the power of the computer over the conventional calculator. These were the branch instruction and the fact that both data and instructions were held in the same form (a string of binary digits) in the same store.

To control the sequence in which instructions were executed there was a sequence register in the computer; as each instruction was carried out, the sequence register was incremented by 1. In the original EDSAC order code there was a function (function E), which enabled this sequence to be departed from. When an E instruction was selected and the accumulator contents were negative the instruction had no effect other than that 1 was added to the sequence register. But when the accumulator was positive the address part of the E instruction was transferred to the sequence register. In this way a program could, under numerically defined conditions, switch control to an alternative sequence anywhere in the store, either forwards or backward.

Two early examples were identified in the field of payroll (which was already being considered as a possible application). The first was a branch instruction at the end of the whole sequence of orders for calculating an employee's pay; this would cause a return to the start of the program to repeat the whole set of instructions for the next employee. This return would be conditional on the result of subtracting the identity number of the next employee to be dealt with from, say, 999 (a number larger than any employee's number). Thus a return to repeat the calculating sequence would occur each time the data for another employee was read. When the signal 999 occurred to mark the end of a department, the calculation sequence for processing an employee's data was not repeated; instead the operations required to end a department were carried out. The second would occur in the stage of the program that calculated income tax (PAYE). Sequences would be included in the stage for levying tax at the various progressive rates, and by subtracting the limit of each tax band in turn from an employee's taxable pay the computer could be directed to jump to, and carry out, the sequences appropriate to that employee's pay.

The second major factor was that data and program instructions were both held as binary numbers in the store. Since arithmetic could operate on the contents of any part of the store it could also be used on store locations that held instructions. Thus, a program could be designed to modify its instructions as it operated. This clearly had very wide implications that demanded prolonged study before the possibilities were fully realised. Again, an early simple example that was devised was based on the need to value, say, deliveries of various items according to their different prices. The item number and quantity of a delivery would constitute the input and would be stored in two fixed locations. A table of prices for all the products would be held in a sequence of locations so that an item number would constitute an index to the address of the appropriate price inside that table of numbers. The sequence of instructions to carry out the valuation would first tell the machine to transfer to the accumulator from the store (as though it were a number) an instruction that referred to the location number one less than the first in the sequence of prices. The second instruction would tell it to add into the accumulator the item number (from its input location) to increase the address of the instruction there so that it would then refer to the price for that item. The third instruction would then tell the machine to transfer the valuation instruction from the accumulator into the store as the next (fourth) instruction to be carried out. That fourth instruction would select the price of the item, to be multiplied by the quantity specified in the input data.

Another significant advance was made in the manner of storage addressing. In the first efforts to construct programs each instruction consisted of a function letter followed by an absolute address (the number of the actual store location to be operated on). Clearly, such an inflexible notation would have been unmanageable in a program of any size. When errors were found in a program that required the insertion of a few more instructions, the job of altering absolute addresses throughout the program caused by that change would be impossible. Hemy discussed this problem with David Wheeler when he was at Cadby Hall that summer on student vacation work, and their ideas developed towards a better notation. They decided that they would need to divide a program into manageable sections; now they might be called "procedures" but at Lyons they were called "stages" and at Cambridge, "open subroutines". (Terminology was not yet standardised and a variety of words were used by these early programmers.) They decided that where an instruction within the stage was to be addressed, its address should be specified by reference to the start of that stage. This would require the start of each stage to be marked, and the relative address to be ended with a suffix to signal that it was to be modified. This suffix was at first written as theta and later at Lyons as "18". On this basis the program (the Initial Orders) to read in and translate the written instructions, which was planned but not yet developed, would detect the beginning of a stage and record the address in which its first instruction was to be stored. Then, as the instructions of that stage were processed, any address marked as relative would have the starting address added to it to convert it into an absolute address. By this means the effect of amendments within a stage would be confined to that stage, and the difficulties reduced to a manageable level.

Early discussions had started on the Initial Orders (Synthesis Instructions) when Hemy visited Cambridge, and David Wheeler was very active in this field when he visited Lyons in the summer of 1948 and thereafter—in fact he was the leading spirit in their development and formulation. When the Initial Orders had been formulated and were in operation it was realised at Lyons that this idea could with advantage be extended: just as the suffix theta could be used to mark addresses as relative to a stage, in the same way (and using the same process) other suffixes could be used to mark addresses as relative to sections of the store allotted to various classes of data. A further facility was added to resolve the problems arising from references from one stage to another. For each cross-reference, both the instruction referred to and the instruction making the reference were given a cross-reference number, and during program input a directory was compiled in the store. After the program had been read, this directory enabled absolute addresses to be inserted into any instructions referring to other stages. By these developments the use of absolute addresses in a program was almost eliminated, and the task of the programmer was significantly simplified.

The first payroll program, completed in November 1948, was never intended to be an operational program, but was the first attempt at putting together a program for an application. It was undertaken to identify the difficulties involved, to validate methods that had already been established and to see what changes or improvements were needed. Hemy started writing this program in the summer of 1948, before ideas on splitting programs into stages had been fully developed, and it was consequently a single monolithic program. Since ideas on data preparation were still at an elementary stage, Hemy had to use a standard Creed paper tape punch for preparing the program. The method used was to punch the tape twice, compare the two versions visually and then doctor the tape with the fewer errors using razor blade and gummed paper.

This program could not yet be tested, since the EDSAC had not been completed. When EDSAC started work in 1949 it was agreed that there would be little point in Hemy taking the tape to Cambridge and trying to run it himself, because time on the machine was very strictly rationed. A queuing system operated, where program tapes were hung from a length of wire in sequence and were fed into the EDSAC machine as time became available. So, instead, Hemy sent his payroll program to Wheeler to run it through when he could find time. Eventually Wheeler telephoned to say that he had fed the tape into the machine and it had run for something like two minutes and had then stopped. No output had been produced and no other information was available.

There were several conclusions to be drawn from this exercise. First, there was a very pressing need to split the program into manageable units (stages). This is a conclusion that Hemy had already reached before the program was run. Second, there was a need to extend relative addresses to data; this had already been assumed, but was now confirmed. Third, better methods of testing were required, to give information about the progress of the tests so that when they failed one would not be left with the bald fact that the program had failed. Fourth, it was necessary to establish some form of modular testing so that individual stages of programs, where at all feasible, could be tested in isolation; the complete program could then be tested when its constituent parts had been well proven. Lyons distinguished between these two different phases of testing: they called the former "tests" (of stages) and the latter "trials" (of the whole program). Fifth, full documentation for programs and for tests and trials of programs was required, so that problems could be dealt with more easily as they arose.

It is of interest to note here that the approaches of the Mathematical Laboratory at Cambridge and of the Lyons team tended to diverge, as a result of their differing aims. The Cambridge team were concentrating on mathematical work and their approach was defined in an early classic book on programming by Wilkes, Wheeler and Gill, *Preparation of a Program for an Electronic Digital Computer with Special Reference to the EDSAC and the use of a Library of Subroutines* (Addison-Wesley, 1951).

In this work the distinction was made between open subroutines and closed subroutines. The open subroutines corresponded to what Lyons termed stages, that is, divisions of the program that usually followed sequentially one after another. A closed subroutine was a self-standing subroutine to carry out a mathematical function (one of the first to be developed was for division). Cambridge worked to build up a comprehensive library of closed subroutines to carry out the mathematical functions that might be expected to be required for a complete computation. A closed subroutine was so constructed that, when it was entered from another sequence, it returned control after its execution to the original sequence. The appropriate subroutines were selected for a given application, and what was termed a Master Routine was written, the sole purpose of which was to enter in turn the various closed subroutines that were required, and to control the sequence in which they were to be used to give the result. Thus, at Cambridge, with the exception of the Master Routine, open subroutines were rarely used.

At Lyons, on the other hand, it was considered that the routines of commercial work were too varied and too variable to allow this sort of approach. A few subroutines were used, particularly for controlling input and output operations, but it was concluded that the general use of closed subroutines for commercial work would be far too costly in operating time and would use extra storage. They therefore adopted what Cambridge would have called an open subroutine approach (stages).

It was decided early that a limit should be set on the size of each stage to make it manageable. The limit set at the beginning, that a stage should be somewhere between 32 and 64 instructions, was confirmed by experience and was adhered to. The coding sheets Hemy had designed, which allowed for 64 instructions, continued to be used.

There were two main constraints under which Hemy and his team had to work in developing programming:

> **1. Storage.** Although the Lyons computer had a store twice the size of that of the EDSAC, there were still only 2,048 locations, each of 17 binary digits, which had to hold all the orders and data that were to be used during the operation of a program. There were occasions where some numbers had to be held in double (35 binary digit) locations; EDSAC had been designed for mathematical work and had the capacity, as had the Lyons

machine, to deal with both single length and double length numbers. As a result storage space had to be used with the utmost economy. The payroll program as it was first used operationally occupied all but 5 or 6 of the 2,048 locations, and programmers had to hope in those days that the next budget would not introduce complications in tax structures that would call for additional instructions in the program.

2. Machine speed. The times taken for executing various types of orders varied widely but were always of the order of milliseconds (at least a thousand times slower than the present generation of computers).

Thus, programmers were presented with the difficult choice of economising on space at the cost of time or increasing the speed of a program by using more storage. This balance had to be assessed for each program, according to the particular requirements and circumstances of the application.

Diagnosing Program Faults

As ideas on programming were developing Hemy conducted regular sessions for Lyons management and staff, and compiled detailed notes. Simultaneously, the programming team did much work on developing programs and methods which would support program testing and program trials. They developed various ways of deriving information about the way the program was behaving that would give them the most helpful clues in diagnosing program faults. An early idea suggested by Hemy was that, when a program failed, the programmer should take photographs of each section of the store by using a combination of a camera and the control console switches. When he suggested this, Simmons asked whether he had a suitable camera, which he confessed he did not, so Simmons immediately offered his Leica camera for the tests. In practice, it proved to be unwieldy and it was obvious that something better would have to be devised.

Following the camera experiment a range of programs were produced that could be used, when a program failed, to print out the contents of specified locations of the store (or all locations if necessary), not only in decimal notation but also in sterling, binary and instruction format (such programs were later called post mortems or dump programs). Another type of program that was experimented with and used for some time was the interpretive program. This was a program that was fed in with the program to be tested and in effect aped the control mechanism of the computer itself: it was programmed to select in turn each instruction of the program being tested, to carry out the operation specified by that instruction and to print out selected data, either after each instruction or at specific points. Although it was used only occasionally it was of limited value because it was very slow; a program run in this mode was about 20 to 25 times slower in operation than one used directly.

Fantl was very active in the writing of test programs for the engineers. He remembers one particular test routine designed to identify the likely cause of a failure in any circuit. After extensive testing, Thompson decided to demonstrate this program to a group of VIPs. Lenaerts was commanded to remove a valve (what could be more convincing than that?), and nothing happened. The valve that Lenaerts had selected was in the addition circuit and Fantl had not thought to test addition circuitry. Thompson was not amused.

Programmers also developed a technique of hand-modifying programs that were in the store by using the control console buttons; an interactive method of trying program logic before committing it to paper. However, it was soon found that such methods, though useful, were also dangerous in that the changes so made were often not recorded.

The need for very full documentation was soon realised. First, an operating log was started, following Ernest Lenaerts' example in his meticulousness on the engineering side. A log book was kept in which every programmer who used the machine was required to enter everything he did in the minutest detail. It was useful to the programmers because when problems were encountered the log could be examined to see whether they had been caused by the programmers' actions rather than by errors in the program or data. This log was also of great value to the engineers because it often enabled programmers and engineers together to distinguish between programming, engineering and operating faults, and so save considerable programming, engineering and machine time.

The documentation for engineering test programs and for operational programs differed because the uses and users were different. Hemy recalls that no programmer ever liked having to work on the documentation of test programs. It was undoubtedly a boring job, and he admitted, "There were times when, if a programmer fell from grace I set him to work on the documentation of test programs, almost as though sending him to a penal settlement". The main effort was concentrated on the documentation of operational programs and for each program there was a complete flow chart showing how the stages worked together (the inter-stage logic), a flow chart for each separate stage (its internal structure), a coding sheet for each stage, storage charts, a specification of input and output and any necessary narrative notes.

All found the work of documenting tests and trials irksome, but accepted that it was essential. Details were set down of the objectives of each test or trial, the data to be used, the various cases to be tested, the results to be expected and a schedule of all the combinations of various cases that needed to be tested.

The formalisation of operating documentation started somewhat later; on the very early jobs, for instance the first Bakery job, the programmer who had written the program and who therefore knew it intimately (in that case, Tony Barnes and later John Grover), was responsible for its operation and could operate it from personal knowledge. When Lyons set up a separate Operations Section under Peter Wood it became most important to produce full documentation, which included the flow charts and complete instructions on how to operate the machine and on what actions were required at all points in the run and when exceptional occurrences or stoppages were met.

When an application was proposed and had been studied, a full definition of what that system would achieve, how it would work, the data required and the results produced, and the necessary clerical operations was set down. Its purpose was to provide a basis for approval of the system and a first specification for the development of detailed systems and programs.

When the application had been developed in some detail, the user documentation was produced. This specified to the user departments what was expected from them—the form of data they would have to provide and the check totals they would have to calculate from that data, the results they would get and the format of those results, and the subsequent handling that those results would require, with details of exception reports (reports of any anomalies that the program had discovered) and their treatment. An exception report would be printed by the payroll program, for example, where it was found that there was insufficient or inconsistent data; instead of printing the normal pay data on the payslip the program would print instead, in a different format, details of the data that it had received and an exception number indicating the nature of the error that it had identified.

In dealing with the user specification and with users at earlier stages in the development of an application, a major difficulty arose from the need to make users aware not only of how the computer would process the data, what results they would be given and how they should handle them, but also of what they would not get. There was always a real danger that users would assume that the machine could deal with any circumstance that had not yet been identified. This difficulty admits of no full solution, and can be described in words Pinkerton used on another occasion: "You are asking me to make a list of all the towns in China that I don't know".

In the early days the machine was by no means completely reliable and data preparation methods were rudimentary. It was clear that there was a need to ensure that correct data had been received, that it had been correctly punched and that the calculations based on that data had been carried out correctly. Among the checks that were used was the batch totalling of input, where the users pre-calculated totals of input items to enable comparison with totals compiled by the computer. Wherever possible, tests were made on the data to establish that the quantities read in were within tolerable limits; such tests were never considered at first and were only introduced after an embarrassing incident, which occurred during the early running of the teashop deliveries job. Bread rolls were to be ordered in units of one hundred, but one teashop manageress, who required one hundred rolls, ordered one hundred units, resulting in ten thousand rolls being printed on the delivery instructions. Over many years the loaders were, of course, intimately acquainted with the loading routine and teashop requirements and despatched what they knew to be the correct order. Soon after this *faux pas*, range and other checks were made on the data to ensure that it was consistent and did not fall outside the logical limits of what the computer could deal with.

Again, Hemy remembers a particular example on payroll that occurred soon after Lyons had started operational work; the program was asked to deal with an employee who had previously taken Territorial Army leave, during which he was injured, so his Territorial leave was followed by sick leave; as he finished sick leave he went on holiday before returning to work. Clearly, this was not a combination of circumstances that the designers of the system could have been expected to anticipate, but Hemy "was proud when, instead of a payslip being printed for that employee (which must have made nonsense), the employee was rejected as not computable and the input data was printed back on the payslip as an Exception Report".

A primary assurance of accuracy in all the programs consisted of a series of reconciliation accounts that were printed at the end of the job with, in each reconciliation account, a final line entitled Discrepancy. This was required to be zero. If it was not zero the results of the program were not released until the reason for the discrepancy had been found.

The job of calculating and printing these discrepancy accounts from the totals that had been accumulated in the store constituted an additional program of some size. The payroll program itself occupied almost the whole store, and no space was available for this final program. Therefore, when the end of the department was reached the reconciliation program was read in to replace the payroll calculation program, the totals for reconciliation being retained in the store.

Much has been said here of the technical developments and of the programming disciplines that were required and applied. What is less easy to describe is the spirit that animated the team. Throughout the early years of development, when there was so much to be done and so little time—particularly machine time—for doing it, responsibilities were willingly and unstintingly assumed and met, with little need for direction or control. Hemy later remarked about the period that "It is easy to remember much of what we did, but somehow easier still to remember the instinctive mutual understanding, the comradeship and the high good humour with which we all tackled it. I then knew what Nelson meant when he talked of his Band of Brothers".[3]

CHAPTER 3

Computer construction begins

The computer project team's initial objective was to construct a machine in the shortest possible time and to bring it into operational use as soon as possible. But this posed an enigma: until thought was given to clerical uses, it could not be decided how best to build the machine. On the other hand, until there was some definition of how the machine was to work, the best approach to clerical applications could not be determined. Thus, it became necessary for both engineering and programming teams to progress in parallel, each complementing the other's ideas. Once this essential ingredient was recognised, teamwork throughout the project was both close and flexible.

Because Lyons could not find a suitable contractor—many had poured cold water on their ambitious ideas—they decided that the control of engineering and constructional design should be exercised by their staff, using EDSAC as the basis of their machine. Cambridge University gave willing support to this decision, and throughout this period Wilkes and his colleagues unselfishly volunteered much information and advice that was of great value to the successful completion of the project.

Pinkerton's team adopted a pragmatic approach and did not allow themselves to be influenced by new ideas until they fully understood the design thinking behind the EDSAC. In this way, their design closely followed that of Cambridge. The engineers first tackled the problem of pulse generation and control of the pulses through the mercury delay tubes, where the instructions to the machine logic would be momentarily stored. Considerable experimentation took place to ensure that the pulses were reliable and of precise duration, much of this work being undertaken in the temporary St Mary's College workshop with equipment that had been bought and assembled largely from government surplus supplies. One of Lenaerts' first tasks was to analyse the EDSAC main control units and to determine how they carried out their function. This was a preliminary task to drawing up these circuits for issue to Wayne Kerr Laboratories, and was carried out with Kaye to enable him to gain an understanding of the subject. Much specialised test equipment was not readily available, at least not on the budget assigned to the project, and a second priority for Lenaerts was to design and build a raster oscilloscope, based on one already designed by the Cambridge researchers. He and others set about making this equipment themselves from a pot-pourri of parts, including old ex-War Department radar tubes. He designed a more powerful power pack for bench testing purposes and carried out work associated with pulse shaping and some of the early electronic circuits connected with gates, flip-flops and amplifiers. Separate machine parts were first made to work to specification; then, as time went on, they were assembled with other parts for further testing. Since the EDSAC was contrived to work in binary mode it was necessary to devise a method of converting and reconverting the machine's signals into a form suitable for clerical needs, decimal or sterling. Pinkerton later thought that this approach was probably wrong and in that he was probably right, but hindsight we have not, until events are history.

In May 1949 Standard Telephones were given a memorandum setting out Lyons' plans for their computer, and their views on the input and output requirements. Standard Telephones had recently installed a very large telephone exchange at Cadby Hall. During this project Lyons had heard that they were developing magnetic tape equipment for use with their teleprinters and had expressed interest in it. Standard Telephones Laboratories (STL), a subsidiary of the Standard Telephones Company (STC), were given a study contract to define the development work required to produce satisfactory input and output facilities for LEO. STL set up a team under an experienced telecommunication engineer of international standing, Esmond Wright, to carry out this work. He was said by Pinkerton to have had a very quick intellect, almost as quick as Thompson's. Lyons' required prototype equipment to be available in May 1950, as they intended to have the equipment in full use by December of that year. A sum of £1,000 had been authorised by Lyons, with a contingency of £500 towards laboratory development expenses. In October 1949 an internal STL memorandum, prepared by Wright, said that expenses incurred by STL and STC on gas tubes and their tape machine were between £20,000 and £25,000 and future development was anticipated to cost a further £7,000. Wright had arrived at this figure calculating that 194 engineer weeks were required. See Figure 3.1

Fig. 3.1 Esmond Wright's notebook calculation of the time required to design his decimal/sterling converter (input output device).

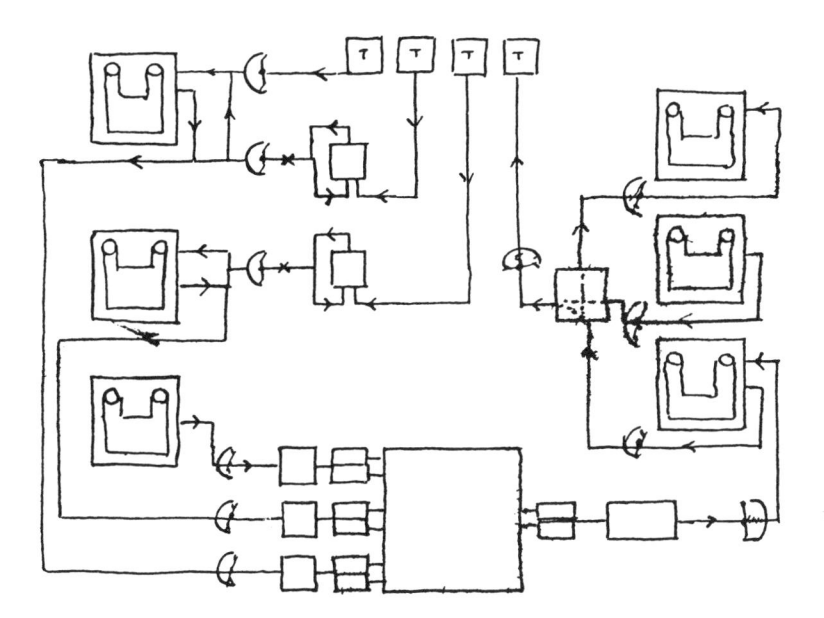

Fig. 3.2 Esmond Wright's initial notebook drawing for his decimal/sterling converter (input/output device).

EDSAC Succeeds

As the Lyons' project team was still being assembled and the preliminary work started, news came through from Cambridge University that the EDSAC had completed its first task successfully, the calculation of a table of prime numbers, so beloved of mathematicians.[1] The date recorded in the official EDSAC log was 6 May 1949 and the program, which ran slower as the prime number size increased, took 2 minutes and 35 seconds. The computation program was written by David Wheeler (now Professor of Computer Science, Cambridge University), who also introduced one of the world's first operating systems ("Initial Orders") so that the calculations could be carried out. These instructions have since been recognised as a brilliant piece of programming.

After Wilkes' euphoria had abated he telephoned the EDSAC news to Simmons at Cadby Hall, who immediately passed a note to the Board, who were in session at the time, asking them to consider formally whether the computer project could proceed in view of the good news. Within a few minutes he received a message from the Chairman, Harry Salmon (1881–1950), that they were fully committed and that the building of the machine should continue. Management's belief in their project had been vindicated and, fired with enthusiasm, work on the Lyons' calculator, for that is how it was referred to, slipped into top gear.

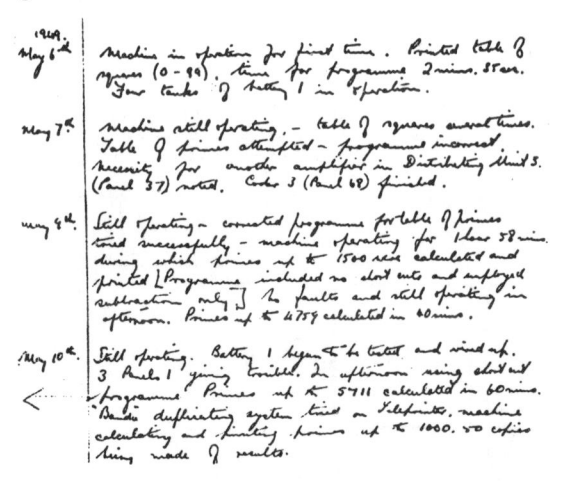

Fig. 3.3 The EDSAC log of 6 May 1949.
By permission of the Syndics of Cambridge University Library.

LEO is Born

In August 1949 Simmons first suggested the name "LEO" for the Lyons' machine and from this, some three weeks later, he suggested that the department undertaking the development and eventual running of the machine should become known as Lyons Electronic Office (LEO). The acronym closely expressed the objectives of the project, namely: it was inspired and funded by Lyons, it was to be Electronic and, if it worked, would greatly improve Office procedures. It is not known whether Simmons had called the device LEO after Leo the lion (Lyons). Such an association is apt but may have been coincidental.

Meanwhile, the work continued using the original slow speed input and output; this had now been supplemented by the addition of a second paper tape reader (photoelectric) and an output punch that allowed some ability to handle data to be carried forward (see later in this chapter). Although many programs were being written to use the facilities to be provided by STL, much of the work was tested on the limited equipment then available.

Early in 1950 the proposals drawn up by STL, after their preliminary study, were accepted and an agreement was reached on how these should be incorporated with LEO early in 1951. STL's proposals were that they should provide data preparation and verification equipment to record data on magnetic tape, which would then be read at higher speed into equipment, using their newly developed gas trigger cathode tubes, to carry out the conversion to binary in preparation for high speed input to the computer. Similar equipment for the recording, reconversion and printing of output was suggested. During the year a range of programs were planned and written to test and use the STL equipment and it was intended, when possible, to carry out operational work by this means.[2]

As the STL equipment became available considerable time was spent in testing and running the programs. Early trials were unreliable, and delays in the delivery of usable equipment were increasing. There were continuing difficulties with the STL tape transports (one used for input and one for output), but a more serious problem was associated with the electronic gas trigger tubes that had been designed to provide a trigger circuit. The operation of these tubes was totally unpredictable, a problem that appeared insoluble. The story goes that whenever a fault occurred, the STL engineer removed the offending gas trigger tubes from the suspect unit, put them in his apron pocket, and then reinserted them again, randomly from his pocket, and asked the LEO staff to try the operation again. This seemed to indicate that the STL engineers had no more faith in their equipment than the LEO team!

Pinkerton and the Lyons management became seriously concerned that the STL developments might fail to achieve an acceptable level of reliability, and that LEO might consequently be left without the means of handling commercial work as had been planned. To add to these difficulties the working relationships between STL and Lyons were becoming strained on the question of patents; STL felt that Lyons had no patentable invention, and consistently delayed any agreement on the grounds that they, themselves, had a right to some of the patents. Lyons refuted these claims and the problems remained unresolved.[3]

A Change of Plan

Clearly, if, as seemed probable, the STL developments failed to produce an acceptable solution to the input and output requirements for LEO, then another solution must be found without delay. The requirements were re-examined and revised in the light of the experience that had been gained in the use of the computer, and a survey of possible alternative input and output equipment was carried out. Photoelectric paper tape readers which operated at high speed were thought to be one component of the solution, but there remained the major problem of carried forward output, data to be carried forward from run to run (the database) and the transfer of data to and from the computer at high speed concurrently with the input and output operations.

Pinkerton, in consultation with other members of the team, decided to use conventional punched card equipment to meet these needs, making use of the buffering systems that had already been developed. The paper tape readers were obtained from Ferranti Ltd, and the British Tabulating Machine Company agreed to supply tabulators, card readers and card punches for attachment to the computer. The tabulators were rather special in that they were designed to print the figures 10 and 11 together as one character, to handle the peculiar UK requirement of 10d and 11d sterling notation of that time. It is somewhat ironic that punched card equipment was now to be used in view of Simmons' long standing doubts about its future; in the longer term its replacement by magnetic tapes and other storage devices could be said to have justified his view.

The major task now facing Pinkerton was the complete design, construction and testing of the equipment by which these devices could be connected to the computer to operate reliably and at the required speed. At the same time, a range of programs had to be adapted to suit the new computer pattern. These activities went forward under the designation of consolidation, to avoid discouraging the STL staff, who were still working earnestly to improve the performance of their equipment.

This change of plan put considerable strain on the whole team and their efforts redoubled. The maniacal pressure and pace did not get them down and in many respects they managed to maintain their sense of fun. This was helped by occasional invitations to "coming out" dinners for the banqueting waitresses. The courses at these events were not planned as good things to eat, but as difficult things to serve! The trembling girls, for whom this was the final graduation performance before being thrown to the Lyons' banqueting services, were given flat trays of frozen lumps of ice cream swimming in a pool of tinned peaches with an extremely slippery syrup, which they had to serve with a fixed smile, while chasing the ice cream around the syrup. A daunting assignment for the girls, but for the guests a form of light relief and an excuse to let off steam that helped them to keep their sanity.

Gradually, the machine began to take shape, but the team had to retrace their tracks several times when they were confronted with technical problems.

The process of testing a new computer or any complex electronic assembly is now well understood, with models, simulators, and even other computers being employed for the task. By contrast, Pinkerton's team were in a continuous learning cycle. As time passed, they introduced more ingenuity and their test methods evolved. Programmers were also very active, and new instructions to simplify the manipulation of clerical and arithmetic functions were discussed and designed through the collaboration of Lenaerts, Kaye and Hemy.

The method of feeding the control instructions, called Initial Orders, to the machine was essentially an electromechanical one, using a Strowger switch (a rotating switch used in telephone exchanges), which had been pioneered at Cambridge. This allowed the insertion of just 25 instructions into the store, and it became something of a competition to design an order sequence within this limit. Wheeler became a leading exponent in this field but Stan Gill (who had joined the Cambridge team in October 1949 from the National Physical Laboratory, where he had worked on the ACE project), Hemy, Fantl and probably others were also involved in attempts to compress the Initial Orders within the compass of 25 instructions. The first attempt took over 40 instructions. This total was gradually reduced; Hemy at one point got it down to 32, then Wheeler did better, reducing it to 27. During the last desperate efforts to reduce it further, Wilkes managed to obtain a second Strowger switch and the competition stopped, since 50 instructions could now be accommodated.

Manchester's Mark I Computor

While the Cambridge University team were delighted with their EDSAC success, it was not the world's first successful running of a stored program computer. The Royal Society Computing Machine Laboratory at Manchester University lay claim to this record, having run their stored program computer on 21 June 1948, on their Mark I computor (sic), one year earlier than Cambridge University. This is also well authenticated and was reported in the scientific journal *Nature* on 25 September 1948 and in the *London Illustrated News* on 25 June 1949. The Cambridge triumph, however, was the first successful running of a program on a complete computer with a working input and output that printed its results in decimal; a fine point, perhaps, but nevertheless an important one.

Whereas the Cambridge team had used mercury delay lines as their method of storage, the Manchester team had used the Williams cathode-ray tube memory. This method of storage had been invented by Professor Frederick Calland Williams (1911–1977) while working at the Electro-Technics Department at Manchester University, and was universally known as the Williams tube. The Williams tube was used, under licence, by IBM in their 701 and 702 computers and by the Princeton University team working on the Institute of Advanced Study Computer. American research into electromagnetic storage had been less successful than British, and for some years the Americans were having to pay royalties to the National Research Development Corporation, a government body set up to advise on and support developments in British industry. From time to time it was necessary for them also to represent industry in litigation on patent infringement. By the end of 1956 Professor Williams and his collaborators had generated 81 computer patents, and Professor Williams would continue with other aspects of electrical engineering, particularly in linear induction motor design. He was knighted in 1976.

The Manchester University machine had been designed primarily to test the soundness of the Williams tube storage principle and to permit experience to be gained before embarking on the design of a full-size machine. Their prototype machine had a very small storage capacity of 32 words, each of 32 binary digits, a token computing circuit for subtraction only, and input and output facilities of the crudest kind. For example, all results had to be read off the monitor cathode-ray tube as light dots, which could then be translated into figures by the operator. All program instructions had to be entered manually from a set of switches, after which the machine could be started to undertake the required operation. It was a slow, tedious task with input and output stages being principally manual.

EDSAC, on the other hand, used automatic input by punched paper tape and a teleprinter output device, a technically more advanced and efficient operation. The Manchester University machine, or to give it its full title, the Manchester Automatic Sequence Controlled Calculating Machine, sometimes called MAD-M (Manchester Automatic Digital Machine), was an equally ambitious and successful project, leading to the commercial development of the Ferranti Mark 1 computor (sic), installed at Manchester University, and later the different and much acclaimed Atlas computer. In one respect MAD-M was more advanced than the EDSAC: its memory could be accessed directly, whereas the EDSAC used a sequential method that was inherently slower. Both storage types, however, were soon to be replaced by ferrite core memory.

LEO: Design Features

The logical design of the Lyons' machine closely resembled that of the EDSAC but it differed in construction, had twice the memory size and had several notable features. During LEO's construction many modifications and enhancements were made to the circuitry and other units, where this would improve the performance or the reliability of the various assemblies. To enable rapid replacement of the units if they became defective, a modular design for the machine became essential.

Some 228 separate electronic units were housed in 21 racks, each having the capacity for 12 units. Pinkerton prudently allowed spare positions for additional units, which Lyons thought rather extravagant. As time passed, his caution was proved correct. The racks were locked into position by knurled finger nuts, to make servicing and replacement easy. Each self-contained unit comprised some 25 thermionic valves (with space for additions if required) and other electronic components. A facility was provided for circuit testing and each panel was powered, wired to racks and fused separately. The interconnecting wires were screwed down (Cambridge soldered theirs), and the use of plugs was avoided since Pinkerton, and Wilkes for that matter, lacked faith in their operation. The equipment generated much heat which, if not controlled, could adversely affect machine stability. To reduce this risk, cold air was blown in at the bottom of the electronic assemblies by a common duct linking all the racks and extracted by a fan at the top in a similar fashion.

The whole machine used 5,936 valves, with a further 300–400 in the auxiliary equipment.[4] Many valves used in the calculator were of the types then commonly used in television and radio; others were more specialised. Much of the early equipment was assembled from components obtained in London's Lisle Street, where some inexpensive government surplus shops traded, and it was not uncommon for an engineer to dash out and purchase a particular valve because one had failed during a machine operation and there was not a spare readily at hand. When it came to expenditure Lyons were well schooled, and erred on the side of caution: one job first allocated to Wheeler (the Lyons' employee) was to strip down ex-War Department surplus units, which could be obtained inexpensively, to recover their components. Later, such inventory was obtained from more orthodox sources such as Mullard, the General Electric Company and the Telegraph Condenser Company Ltd, since the reliability of some components gave cause for concern. Contrary to common belief, the Cambridge University team did not use surplus supplies for their machine. Almost all their equipment was new and readily available from normal trade sources or from a government store to which the University had access. The exception to this was the gift and use of many surplus valves from the Ministry of Supply, who had been charged with disposing of them; purchasing these through normal trade sources would have increased the development costs of EDSAC considerably, since most of the valves at the time would have cost between five and six shillings each.

The delay line storage, or memory, was similar to that used in EDSAC, but with some improvements in the control of the frequency of the clock pulses. (See Appendix 13 for a fuller explanation of the operation of the calculator.) The store, twice the size of EDSAC's, comprised 64 tubes (Cambridge called them tanks to avoid confusion with thermionic tubes), each 5 feet 4 inches in length with a 1-inch bore, and filled with mercury weighing half a ton. Wheeler (of Lyons) was responsible for cleaning and refilling the mercury delay tubes, which involved emptying the tubes, cleaning them with methylated spirit and then, by gravity feed, refilling them; all this was carried out without any special safety procedures. Wheeler's responsibilities extended to the early start-up of the computer in the morning so that the valves could warm up and the machine be ready for use when other staff came in. Pinkerton once promised him one shilling for every defective valve he could find before the start of the day's work.

A total of 2,048 orders or short numbers could be held in the memory at any time. There were an additional 16 tubes kept as spares in case of failure. All were housed in thermally insulated containers under the floor (called coffins by the project team because of their shape), and fans aided air circulation so that the temperature of the mercury was kept constant. To prevent accidental switch off a safety device was fitted to the fan units.

The operational control of the machine was carried out from a console, from which the machine could be started, slowed, single-stepped through individual program instructions, stopped and restarted. Several monitoring oscilloscopes were grouped on the control console to allow the contents of the store to be examined in detail. Programming and engineering staff had available on the control desk of the computer switches and buttons that enabled them not only to see, as a visual display of dots and 1s, the contents of any part of the store, but also to alter the contents of any storage location. Programs could be tested and manipulated in this way (today's parlance would call this interactive programming) but the process was very expensive in machine time, error-prone and left no record of what had been done.

Another feature that was developed and found to be very useful was an audible speaker. This speaker, wired to a waveform in the central control circuits, generated a noise, the frequency and tone of which

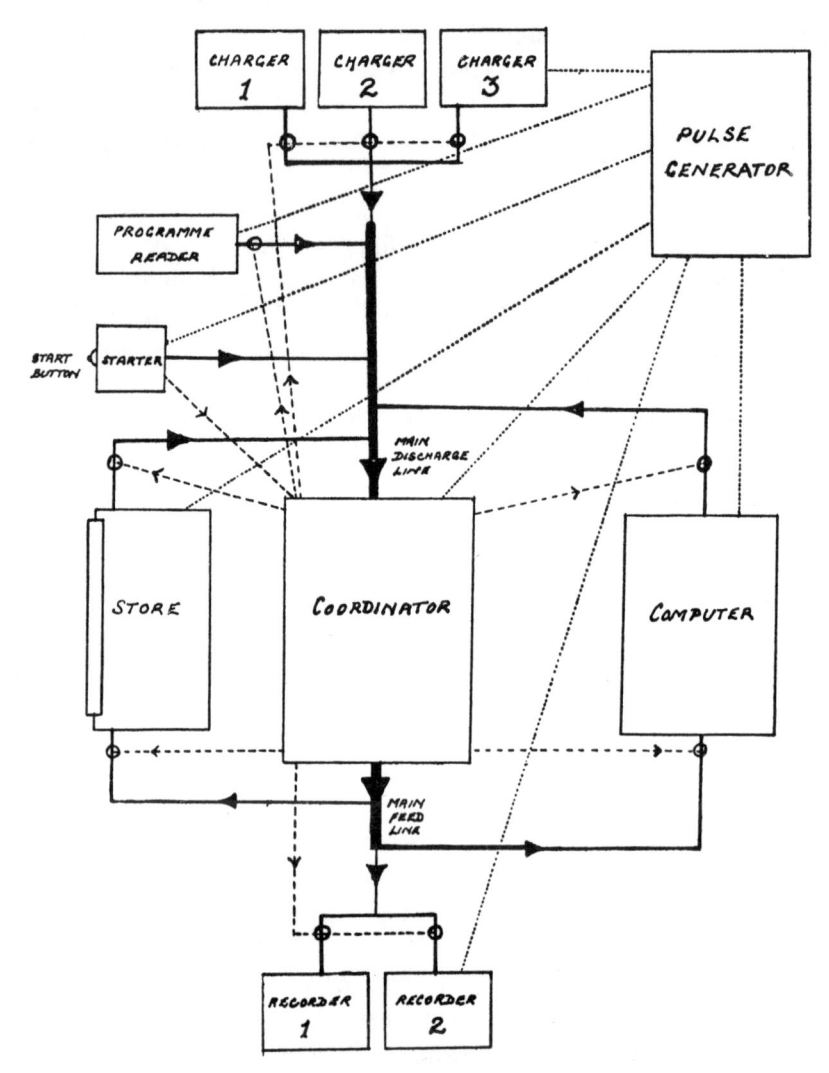

Fig. 3.4 A schematic diagram of LEO as it appeared in *The Layman's Guide to LEO* in 1952. Terminology had, clearly, not developed; the chargers were in fact magnetic tape units for inputting information whereas the recorders were intended to record information onto magnetic tape for subsequent input. *Reproduced by kind permission of J. Lyons & Co Ltd.*

depended on the sequence of instructions being carried out. Every program had its characteristic rhythm and it was possible to detect alteration of this rhythm, as happened, say, in a program loop (program error) or premature program stop. This audible feature was carried through into the design of the later LEO II and LEO III machines and was used, unofficially, by programmers to generate computer music, Colonel Bogey's march being one of the better arrangements on LEO III.

The British Broadcasting Corporation (BBC) made a more dramatic use of this sound feature in 1956–1957. Hemy recalls the screening of Quatermass 2, a popular science fiction television series, in which a mad Welsh mathematician used a computer to calculate the orbit of some unknown body that was flying about the heavens. He immediately recognised that the sound emitted from the BBC contraption was that of LEO doing weather forecasting for the Meteorological Office. Hemy was probably the only person watching (with the exception perhaps of the Meteorological Office programmers) who realised how the sound had been made and only then because he had taken the weather forecasting programs (which the Meteorological Office were writing) under his wing and knew their characteristic rhythms. He remembered that the BBC had visited Lyons two or three years before and had made recordings in the LEO computer room: perhaps the first occurrence of computer piracy! Such ingenuity undoubtedly led to the development of the electronic organ and other musical instruments widely available today as consumer products.

The power supplies for the calculator were large by any standard, and W.J. Edwards, manager in charge of the electrical department at Cadby Hall, gave much advice on this. The total power consumption of the machine was 30 kW. Three-phase rectifier assemblies provided +250 V d.c. and -250 V d.c. There were two +250 V supplies, the first, a 30 Amp. supply for general high tension requirements and the second, a 2.5 Amp. special purposes (high tension for flip-flops and amplifiers) where better smoothing was required. To prevent surges, which sometimes occurred on the national grid, from affecting the calculator, a voltage controlled alternator of 12 kW was installed in the basement, driven by an electric motor operating from the mains supply. Diesel generators were installed on site in case of mains power supply failure. A main requirement of the power supply was the need to raise voltage slowly on all valve heaters to minimise failure due to thermal shock.

Built into the supply was a system of interrupts designed to switch the supplies on and off in the correct sequence and to facilitate fault finding.

Many skilled trades staff employed at Cadby Hall were fully utilised to help in the calculator assembly. Electricians, engineers, plumbers, carpenters, draughtsmen, and work-study and office specialists were all involved to a greater or lesser extent.

Thompson's Inspirational Leadership

During the construction period Lyons went to great lengths to brief managers and other clerical representatives of the progress being made, but the calculator assembly area was out of bounds to most staff, some of whom had unkindly dubbed the device TRT's folly. Throughout, Simmons took a keen interest in all aspects of the design and assembly and frequently visited the construction area.

Much of the inspiration for the development of the project came from Thompson: Pinkerton, writing in *Computer Bulletin* in 1986, said:

He had the quickest intellect of anyone I ever met. On occasions, he would become almost incoherent as his ideas struggled to find expression. Sometimes, when trying to persuade him of the value of some new approach, one would meet a momentary resistance, but, if you were right then in a second or two his attitude would switch, your idea was seized on and elaborated in ways beyond anything that had occurred to you and it became a strain to keep up with his fresh thinking. He maintained the enthusiasm and set the intellectual and management tone of the LEO project from its beginnings.

Undoubtedly the project would not have been the project without him, but some said that Thompson was sometimes the victim of "fixed ideas and self-deception". It is said that he positively overflowed with ideas of all sorts; some were acute, many ingenious, some incoherent or clearly wrong, as on one occasion in 1950–1951, as Hemy recalls when:

Thompson was expatiating to some visitors on how he had conceived the idea of the use of input and output buffers (these were shorter mercury delay tubes and associated circuits) to improve the operational efficiency of LEO. Lenaerts, from his very meticulous records, could confirm that he had written to Thompson a year or two before, giving him full details of proposals for input and output buffers; he had heard about these in a presentation (by Americans) which he attended when still at Cambridge.

Another incident, typical of Thompson in a way, was recalled again by Hemy. For the first demonstration to outside visitors (a senior management group from Ford) of the payroll program, Hemy had agreed with Lenaerts that if trouble hit the machine Lenaerts would signal him [Hemy] and he in turn would notify Thompson and ask him to continue talking, to give Lenaerts time to fix the machine. Of course, Murphy's Law operated and Hemy got the signal from Lenaerts just before Thompson was due to announce the start of the payroll run. To Lenaerts' horror Thompson stood up and announced to all those gathered that a fault had been discovered and that we should sit and wait to see how quickly it would be fixed. Lenaerts worked wonders and five minutes later the machine was back in business. Thompson took this line despite knowing that another fault at rehearsals the previous day had taken two hours to clear!

Many of Pinkerton's contemporaries have said he seemed the ideal man to cope with this outflow and there were many occasions, I am told, when he adroitly steered Thompson on to the right course.

Boat Builders Help

Despite the skills and experience Lyons could muster from their staff, it became necessary to subcontract the more specialised work, particularly in the area of electronic circuitry and machine tooling. In July 1949, Wayne Kerr Laboratories Ltd were awarded the first contract and were commissioned to produce panels of electronic circuits to Lyons' specifications. They also built the first arithmetic units. They were contracted to build a variety of electronic assemblies and, since costs had become a sensitive issue, their work was closely monitored by the Lyons cost accountants, who checked each assembly, assessing the individual component requirements and even measuring the wire used, to the nearest inch, which the Wayne Kerr staff thought highly amusing. However, their units were expensive and not totally satisfactory and Wayne Kerr were eventually replaced by Camper & Nicholsons Limited (the yacht builders).

Camper & Nicholsons had just started a subsidiary company known as C & N (Electrical) Ltd. This new subsidiary had been established to provide contract employment to keep their electricians occupied during slack periods of boat building. They made some trial units under the careful supervision of the Lyons project team's staff. Kaye later recalled, "The Camper & Nicholsons work turned out to be highly professional, the units themselves being beautifully engineered and wired; besides, the units they produced were competitively priced and a happy relationship developed with them". C & N (Electrical) Limited, despite their unorthodox boat-building background, became the major subcontractor to Lyons for this type of electronic circuitry work.

Wayne Kerr did not fall completely from grace and were later asked to quote for the construction of the control console. However, their proposal was politely rejected on cost grounds. Instead, Lyons supplied a reject naval radar console that had been obtained from Standard Telephones & Cables Ltd, at scrap value, and contracted Wayne Kerr to modify it. The console, considerably out of true and fabricated from ¼-inch steel plate, required much machining and hand work to enable the electronic panels, manufactured by Camper & Nicholsons, to be properly fitted. As a final refinement Lyons required an ex-RAF clock, which had been obtained from the Gamages' department store in Holborn, to be fitted to the front of the console. Wayne Kerr embellished this by fitting a chrome bezel but after delivery of the console to Cadby Hall, which involved hauling it up the outside of the building by winch, the clock ceased to function; Lyons promptly returned it to Gamages for replacement and a second clock, of a different type, was readily supplied.

A second contract was awarded in October 1949 to the Coventry Gauge & Tool Company, who were specialists in high precision engineering. Their expertise was required for the construction of the mercury delay tubes, the length of which had to be controlled to tolerances better than 1,000th of an inch in 5 feet. Subsequently some work was done on delay tubes at the Lyons engineering works at Abbey Road, London.

In Search of Reliability

Lyons realised at an early stage that the completion of regular routine clerical tasks to a fixed schedule would demand a very high standard of reliability of the machine. The 6,000 or so valves and other delicate components occupying approximately 5,000 square feet of floor space had to be put right quickly if a breakdown did occur. At one stage some 50 or so valves per week were being replaced.[5] This level of usage could not be sustained, and measures were taken to improve reliability, as 47% of machine failures were due to defective valves.

To help the engineers, both in routine testing of the computer and in the diagnosis of faults as they occurred, Lenaerts suggested that a set of programs should be designed to test specific functions of the machine. He discussed this requirement with Hemy, and as a result the first range of test programs were produced. As experience of their use grew, and as new types of fault were discovered, these programs were modified and supplemented. Through close co-operation between engineers and programmers, the range of test programs and their usefulness steadily increased.

At an early stage of machine and circuit testing a source of unpredictable interference was found to be associated with stray signals emanating from the fluorescent light fixtures on the ceiling directly above the machine. These had the effect of causing spurious unwanted pulses to enter the storage units. Later, the card readers and tabulators with their electromechanical design caused arcing in the mains supply, which had to be dealt with by suppressors.

The designers recognised that if component failure could be predicted or anticipated then engineers could devote their efforts toward preventive rather than corrective maintenance, and so reduce the likelihood of faults occurring during operational work. A system of marginal testing evolved, and during routine maintenance periods, lasting about one hour each day, the machine was made to operate outside its design limitations. The idea of marginal testing, first used at Cambridge on the EDSAC, was to cause the machine to operate outside its design limitations in order to detect the gradual deterioration of performance of individual circuits before they reached the point of failure. An alternating voltage was injected into the most vulnerable 350 circuits throughout the machine, each of which could induce a malfunction if the voltage was large enough. In preparing the marginal test structure the various voltages were so proportioned that under the standard test conditions each circuit was driven to approximately the same fraction of the breakdown point. Thus, it was possible to increment the marginal test voltage gradually at all points simultaneously. If the standard value could not be reached without inducing a failure as indicated by the performance of the machine during a test program, then it followed that one or more circuits must be nearer failure than on the last occasion a test was carried out.

A particular feature of the marginal test arrangements was the partitioning of sections and subsections so that individual marginal circuits could be rapidly located by analytical procedure. Thus, although there were some 350 different testing points at which margins could be applied simultaneously, it was possible to find the one offending circuit in a matter of minutes. Later the marginal test features were further improved by increasing the number of points tested.

The use of this technique, in conjunction with the diagnostic programs that the software team had progressively developed, enabled components and circuits likely to cause failures to be identified in advance. Suspect units could be replaced or adjusted, and thus it was found that the machine operated more reliably under operational conditions. These tests were applied daily to all electronic circuits and mechanical parts, and, with other changes, they had the effect of improving the reliability to acceptable levels, with only occasional random failures.

It eventually became necessary to employ a full-time valve tester, who meticulously maintained records of all valve functioning. New valves received from suppliers were rigorously tested for 50 hours and returned to the factory if their performance deteriorated. About 1.5% were rejected in this way. Used valves were also removed from the calculator at regular intervals and similarly tested. The first valve testing machine, designed by Lenaerts, had a most ingenious arrangement of a commutator and vibrator. On the first run it seemed very impressive: valve after valve was rejected. However, it soon became obvious that, in the way it was then working, it was not a valve tester, but a valve destroyer. After Lenaerts had moderated the vibrating device it became a very effective instrument.

These rigorous testing procedures helped to identify any valves that were beginning to show signs of fatigue, and these could be removed before actual failure occurred. Knowledge and statistical data was also accumulated, leading to improved preventive maintenance procedures. The additional valve space that had been made available on each panel to allow for modification or enhancement of the system was put to effective use.

Machine failures were categorised into three main groupings. The first group consisted of failures due to the gradual drift in component

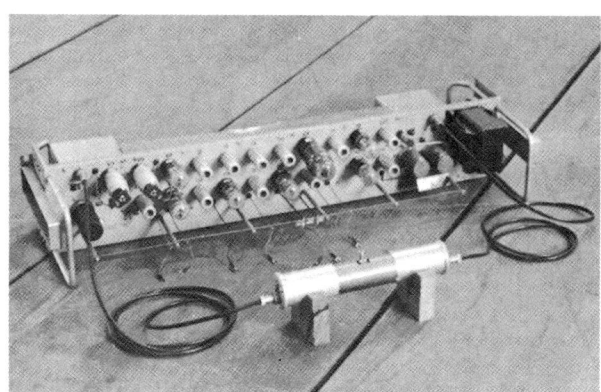

15. (*above*). Experimental mercury delay tube on the bench in St Mary's College (Cadby Hall) in 1949. *Reproduced by kind permission of J. Lyons & Co Ltd.*

16. (*left*). A mercury delay tube wired to its electronic assembly for testing. June 1950. *Reproduced by kind permission of J. Lyons & Co Ltd.*

17. One of the 228 separate electronic assemblies which made up LEO I. They were secured into 21 racks and were wired and fused separately. The loops at each end were not only used as handles for easy removal but protected the delicate valves when up-ended to work on the underside. *Reproduced by kind permission of J. Lyons & Co Ltd.*

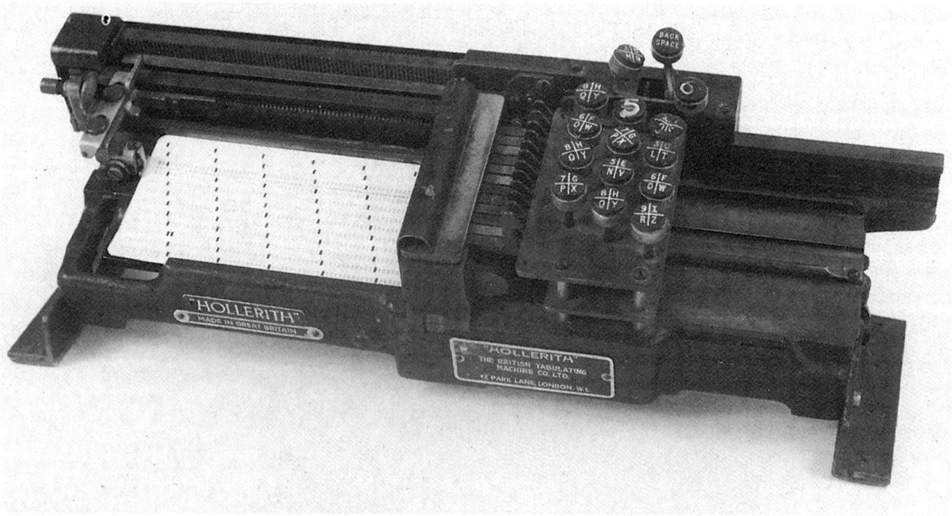
BACK SPACE
"HOLLERITH"
MADE IN GREAT BRITAIN
"HOLLERITH"
THE BRITISH TABULATING MACHINE CO. LTD.
17 PARK LANE, LONDON, W.1.

18. (*top left*). A Hollerith card punch used for single card preparation. They were first used in 1901 in the United States and by Lyons until 1965. Telephonists at Lyons used these to record teashop orders by telephone. *The author*

19. (*bottom left*). A group of 16 mercury delay tubes, sometimes called tanks or lines to avoid confusion with valves, in their thermally lagged 'coffin'. A box containing the electrical matching sections is on the trestle behind. *Reproduced by kind permission of J. Lyons & Co Ltd.*

20. (*right*). Gordon Gibbs (left) and Ray Shaw looking at a circuit diagram. February 1950. *Reproduced by kind permission of J. Lyons & Co Ltd.*

21. (*below*). Racks in position with part of the cooling (exhaust) trunking assembled. This photograph, of the partly assembled LEO, was the first seen by the directors and it was submitted with report No. 7 on 3 July 1950. *Reproduced by kind permission of J. Lyons & Co Ltd.*

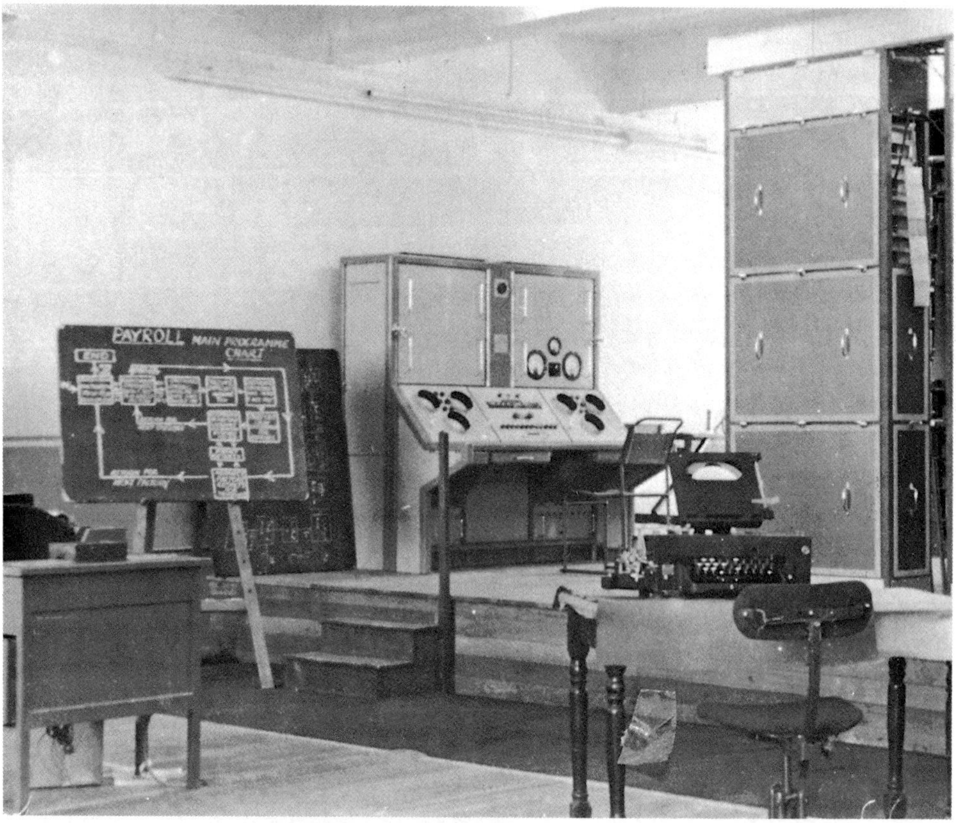
PAYROLL MAIN PROGRAMME CHART

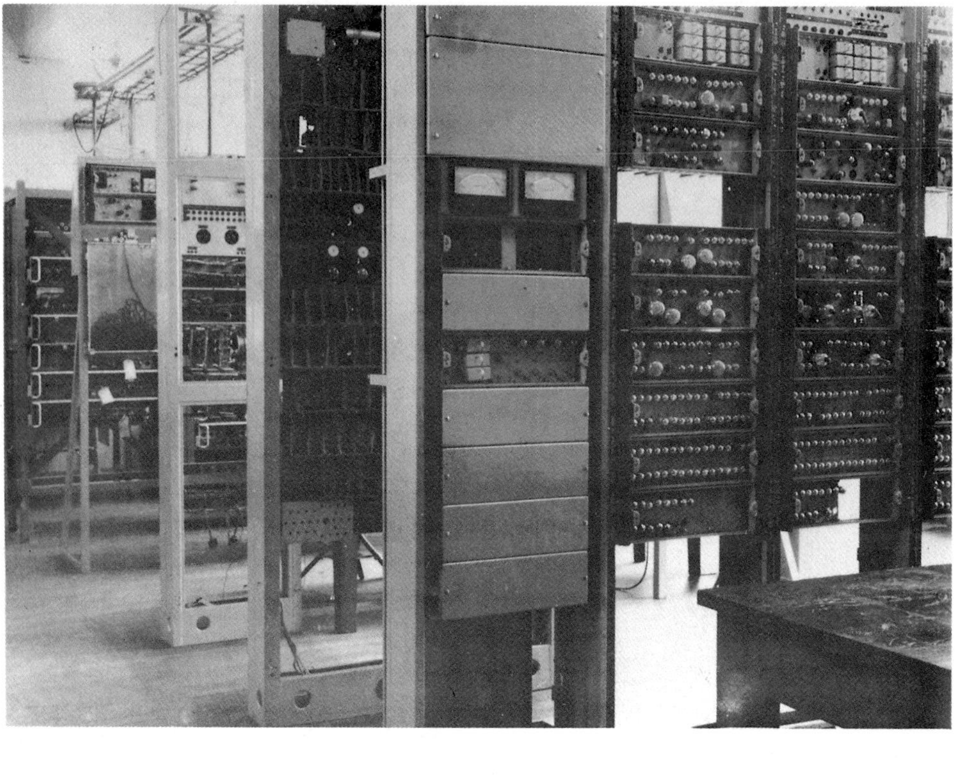

22. (*top left*). The scene set for a pseudo demonstration of payroll to directors, office managers, supervisors and representatives of the clerical committee on 8 March 1950. *Reproduced by kind permission of J. Lyons & Co Ltd.*

23. (*left*). A general view of the STC decimal/sterling binary converter. c.1953. *Reproduced by kind permission of ICL*

24. (*above*). A close-up of the STC magnetic tape units. The date chalked on the right tape chamber is 9 July 1953. Engineers were unable to bring them to reliable operation and they were removed in August of the same year. *Reproduced by kind permission of Leo Fantl.*

25. (*right*). The Ferranti 5-hole paper tape reader. c.1953. *Reproduced by kind permission of Leo Fantl.*

26. (*above*). A view of LEO I looking up towards the engineers console. The mercury delay tubes were housed under the raised floor and at the extreme left can be seen a slow teleprinter and a 'home-made' paper tape reader. 1953.
Reproduced by kind permission of Leo Fantl.

27. (*left*). Wally Dutton checking circuits late at night. Long hours of non paid overtime was the norm for all the team.
Reproduced by kind permission of ICL

28. (*top right*). A general view of the completed LEO I in 1953. The machine was finally closed down in January 1965 after 12 years of continuous use.
Reproduced by kind permission of J. Lyons & Co Ltd.

29. (*right*). A view of LEO Is power distribution panel. An auxiliary operators console is now in place and additional card read/punch equipment has been installed. Late 1953 or early 1954.
Reproduced by kind permission of Leo Fantl.

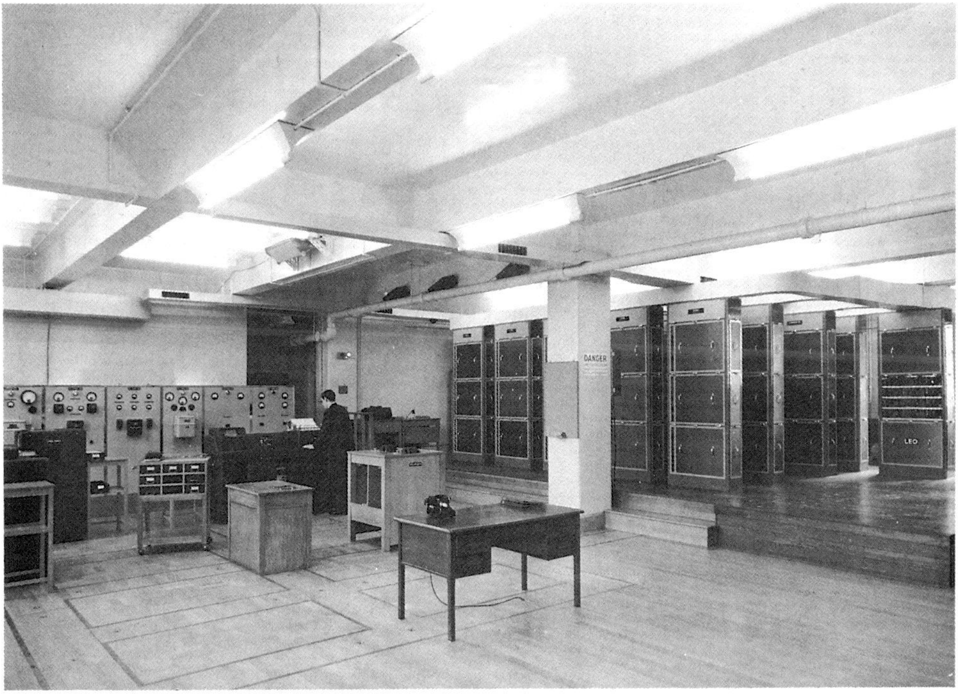
DANGER
LEO

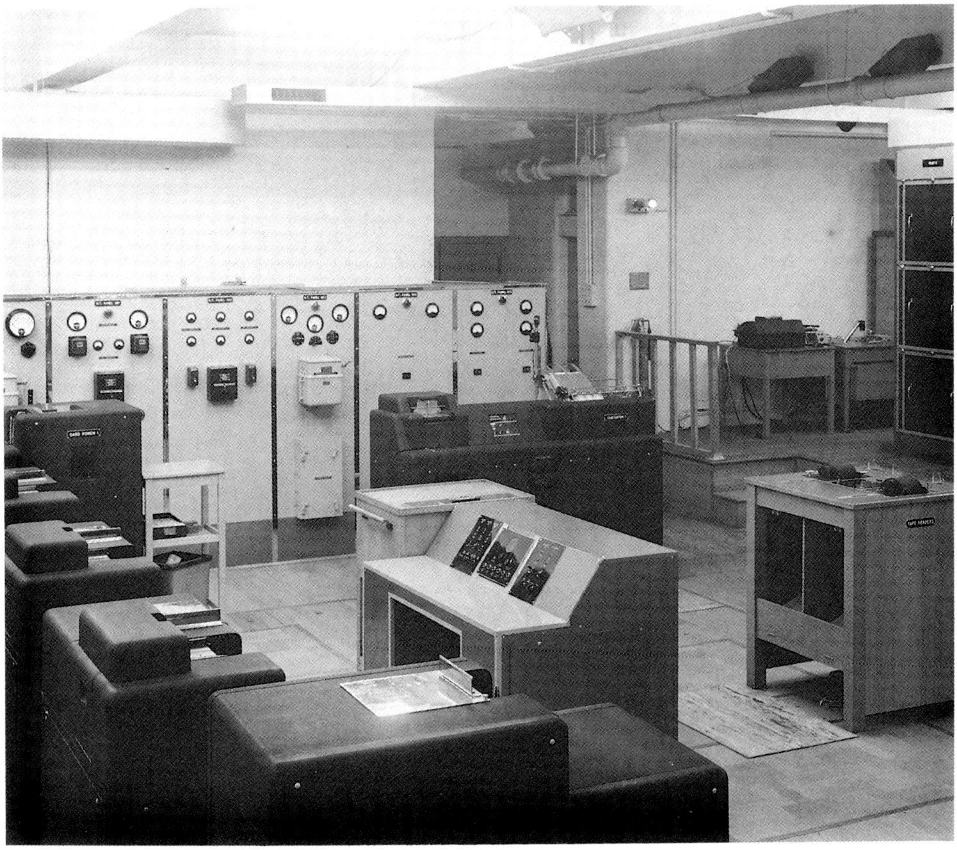

30. The engineers and support staff responsible for building LEO I. Back, left to right: Gordon Gibbs, Jean Cox, Wally Dutton. Front, left to right: Raymond Shaw, Ernest Kaye, Miss Plant, Dr John Pinkerton, David Wheeler and Ernest Lenaerts. The part played by the software designers, not shown in the photograph, has never been fully recognised; the project of course would not have succeeded without them. *Reproduced by kind permission of J. Lyons & Co Ltd.*

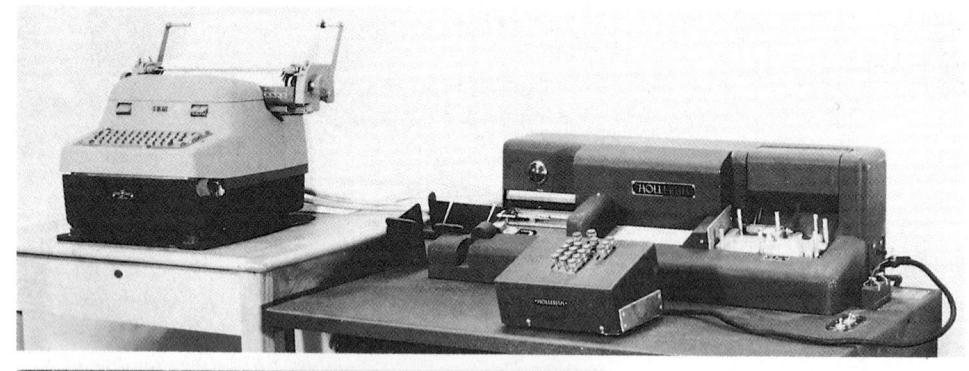

31. An auxiliary printing device, prepared for LEO 1, comprising card reader and IBM electric typewriter. *Reproduced by kind permission of ICL.*

32. A Creed paper tape punch and comparator (numeric only) used on LEO II. *Reproduced by kind permission of ICL.*

characteristics, and these were generally detected during routine maintenance when the machine was operated outside its design tolerances.

The second group of failures were those that were described as catastrophic, where either complete machine failure or sufficient failure for it not to be usable occurred. Such failures could be caused by component failure, open circuits, failure of insulation in capacitors, or simply by a blown fuse.

The third group of failures, and those most difficult to detect and repair, were classified as intermittent faults. As the word implies, such failures occurred at unpredictable times, sometimes with many hours between one failure and the next. These faults demanded careful attention, since their treatment depended upon the type of work being processed. If the results of the job were fully checked by the program, or could easily be verified, then it might be decided to spend only the minimum time in trying to locate the fault, and instead to continue with the job, since a fault of this type could often be expected to deteriorate until a clear failure resulted that was easily identifiable. On the other hand, some work (such as the De Havilland application described later) was not self-checking or verifiable; in such cases the work could not proceed until the fault had been found and rectified, and more engineering time would be devoted to its investigation.

The failure of peripheral devices, which were mainly of electromechanical construction, was rather easier to deal with, and simply a question at most of duplicating the devices. When they became defective it was more obvious where the fault was located and the offending equipment could easily be disconnected and repaired while a substitute allowed continued operation. Mechanical faults, though easy to find, are by their nature usually difficult to fix, whereas electronic faults are normally difficult to find but somewhat easier to repair, perhaps just by the replacement of a valve.

The initial machine form adopted for LEO followed that of EDSAC regarding input and output facilities; input as punched tape read by a mechanical reader operating at up to seven characters a second, and output printed by a Creed teleprinter at five characters a second. From initial surveys carried out in 1947 and 1948 by Hemy, it was evident that these facilities would be insufficient for the commercial tasks that were planned. The overall speed of the computer had been reduced because computing was inhibited while the teleprinter or paper tape reader was operating; this was necessary to avoid the mess that would have arisen had another character been output (or input) before the first one had been dealt with. Clearly, considerable thought would need to be given to defining the facilities required for commercial work and their development.

A further problem emerged as work progressed and the first programs and data were produced. The data to be fed to the machine obviously had to be error free, and data preparation equipment was needed that would not only enable the accuracy of the data to be ensured, but could also be operated efficiently at acceptable speeds. This problem, of immediate concern, had to be resolved satisfactorily and in 1948 a standard Creed keyboard punch was obtained for experimentation. Unfortunately, the codes produced from its keyboard differed from those required by the computer, and the first step was to obtain a set of key caps that were fitted over the keys; each key then produced the correct code, but the keyboard layout was, to say the least, idiosyncratic. Engineers soon cut a new set of combination bars and restored the keyboard to normality. The accuracy of punching was determined by producing two separate tapes, superimposing them and correcting any error by gummed paper or razor blade. Although this method proved to be surprisingly accurate, it could be no more than a temporary expedient. Consideration was urgently given to the selection of equipment for the perforating operation, and to deciding how the data should be checked.

Considerable attention was devoted to the selection of paper tape perforating equipment, the main contenders being Creed of Britain and Siemens of Germany. The Siemens equipment was already in use, for other purposes, at the offices of the *Daily Mail* and *Daily Express* but Lyons had some difficulty in obtaining technical information. When this eventually arrived, it required translation, by Fantl, from German to English. For seven months the Lyons team experimented and discussed ways of adapting the perforating equipment for use with their calculator. Special characters were required and modifications to the coding bars in the standard equipment became necessary. Eventually, Pinkerton considered the Creed equipment the most adaptable and a decision to use it was taken.

A method of data checking that became known as verification was devised. This was accomplished by cleverly linking together a keyboard, a tape reader and a tape punch. When the source information from documents had been converted to 5-hole paper tape (it was found that approximately one mistake per 700 characters keyed was made during this process) it was placed in a tape reader which was incorporated in the verifier (this equipment was originally referred to as a comparator). A second operator rekeyed all the original data on the keyboard of the verifier and the signal so produced was compared with that from the reader. If the two signals agreed, the appropriate character was punched on a second paper tape, but if they disagreed the machine would lock and a visual check could be made to determine which operator had made the error. The correct character could then be confirmed and punched, and the process continued. The final verified paper tape would then be used as input to the calculator and was considered to be error free. In theory, it was possible for both keypunch operators to make the same mistake and this did occur occasionally, particularly if a figure had been badly written and interpreted similarly by both operators. In practice, this occurred so infrequently (once or twice per million characters punched) that such errors were considered acceptable.

These measures allowed work to continue with the development of programming techniques and applications. Meanwhile, the input and output facilities that would be required in the final configuration were being considered by both teams. Not only was it necessary to increase speeds considerably, but it was apparent from the studies already carried out, and in particular from the work on payroll that Hemy had done, that the machine would need to be given facilities to handle more than one stream of input and of output. Thus, in payroll work three types of input data could be distinguished: current data, such as the hours worked for each employee, which needed to be originated for each run; permanent data, such as an employee's tax code and rate of pay, which could be presented in the same form from run to run; and brought forward data, such as tax paid to date, which would have to be output from one run to be used as input to the next run. In the same way, at least two types of output had to be dealt with: in the payroll job, payslips and data to be carried forward to the next run. It seemed from the survey of other applications that this categorisation of input and output would hold good for almost all the work envisaged; it was therefore agreed to adopt the aim of providing the computer with three input and two output channels, operating at higher speeds.

This by itself was not considered sufficient to meet the perceived needs; it would be necessary to provide a means of allowing computing to continue during the input and output processes. Some form of buffer storage seemed necessary to enable rapid transfer of batch information into or out of the computer while another batch was being read or printed. A further problem had been identified because of early programming work: the conversion of decimal and sterling numbers into binary (or the reverse) would be very expensive in computer time on commercial work. The software team suggested that the incorporation of conversion facilities into the input and output units would, if feasible, relieve this problem and the idea was given full consideration. After a number of false starts the logic was eventually designed, primarily by Lenaerts, and diagrams were supplied to Wayne Kerr in May 1953 for them to build the units.

Meanwhile, systems and programming work had proceeded on the development of several applications, and the engineering team had been making considerable progress in establishing the computer itself on an operational basis. One great difficulty was the allocation of machine time to both engineers and systems staff, and much of the program testing was carried out during evening and night working. Although Caminer was able to compensate their efforts to some degree by way of overtime payments, these fell well short of actual time worked: had he attempted to recover the full costs for them there was a great danger that management would think that the whole team were inept and incapable of doing their jobs. There is no doubt that the whole LEO team worked incredibly conscientiously, putting their personal and family relationships under great strain.

LEO had by this time gained some modest reputation, and during a visit to Cadby Hall on 15 February 1951 HRH Princess Elizabeth (now Queen Elizabeth II), was shown LEO carrying out a simple test program. On 17 April of the same year, demonstrations were given, for the first time, to the Lyons Directors, presumably to show them how their money was being spent and to encourage them to invest further capital to remove the machine deficiencies, which had by now been identified and were largely associated with the STL tape drives. Until this time the Directors had only seen the calculator spread over the floor and under it, and must have wondered at times whether it would ever work.

The project was not without influential supporters, and one of the family champions was Anthony Salmon, Director. He had been given responsibility for the LEO project in 1953 and his active interest in all matters associated with it helped to secure management commitment and the necessary flow of funds. It was he who arranged for his co-Director, Geoffrey Salmon (1908–1990), to host a party at the Trocadero Restaurant on 16 May 1951 to congratulate the LEO project team on the progress so far, a thoughtful morale-boosting exercise in view of the difficulties experienced with the STL tape system. Later, with other influential members of the Lyons Board, he played an important part in promulgating LEO to other large business enterprises, thus performing an effective marketing role, and occasionally his connections in industry were sought to apply pressure on difficult suppliers whose electrical products were sometimes less than satisfactory.

Some later visits to LEO, that Thompson was inordinately fond of organising, provided a source of light amusement to the LEO team. These demonstrations normally took the form of an initial talk by Thompson that took place in a little room on the top floor of WX Block, followed by a demonstration of a job run on LEO, which was on the second floor. The "stage management" was left to Wally Dutton, whose job was to prepare the lecture room with blackboard and easel (no flip-charts then), to arrange for tea to be supplied at 4 p.m. and finally to clear the lecture room after all was over—a job that he frequently forgot to do and for which Thompson had taken him to task more than once.

Now, all this would have been fine if only LEO had been more reliable and less erratic in its operation. Thompson was aware of the machine's unpredictability and did not want to bring his guests down from the fifth floor only to find that LEO had broken down again, so he fixed a set of signals between the lecture room and the computer room. It was arranged that when the machine was operating satisfactorily a green board would be placed in the window of the computer room within sight of the lecture room, but when it was not working, as often happened, a red card would be displayed as a signal for Thompson to fill time with further talk.

On one occasion he was giving a presentation to an influential group of people from a large insurance company and was extremely anxious that everything should be seen to run without a hitch. As fate would have it, on this particular day LEO was being difficult and Thompson saw, to his dismay, when he looked from his fifth floor window, a red card in the computer room window; he bravely went on talking and ad libbing (I am told he was never lost for words) until at last the green card was displayed. As the group were about to leave the room for the visit to LEO the door handle came off in Thompson's hand.

He was stranded on the fifth floor in an office without a telephone and he started to panic. He tried to attract the attention of staff working on the floor below, while a more enterprising member of the insurance company, with the aid of a penknife, managed to unscrew part of the handle assembly. The party made their way down to the computer room on the second floor. Of course, by this time LEO had broken down again and Thompson immediately suggested going back upstairs for some more tea. By now the blackboard, tea and other items had been removed promptly by Wally Dutton, who for once had been scrupulously efficient and had cleared the room, believing that the talk and demonstration were over.

This threw Thompson into more panic but after some telephone calls he managed to restore some credibility to his reputation. The group eventually got their tea and a visit to the working LEO, and subsequently wrote a charming letter to Thompson saying that they were pleased to see that simpler mechanisms than LEO, such as door handles, could also go wrong!

The First Job is Run

During 1951 the development, programming and testing of the Bakery Output Valuation application, known as Bakeries Valuations, was carried through under the direction of John Grover, and the first complete run providing full and accurate results was achieved on Wednesday 5 September 1951, the same day that little Mo Connolly, at 16, became the youngest winner of the US Tennis Championship. The job had been selected and specified by Caminer and initially programmed by Barnes under the direction of Hemy, but Grover had built on this experience with subsequent amendments and enhancements, producing the full documentation and operating instructions. The unreliability of the STL equipment prevented the task from using magnetic tape regularly and it was modified to use punched paper tape input and output, with hard copy results printed on a slow teleprinter. With this change it was boldly decided to undertake the weekly valuations again on 30 November 1951 and, as a matter of pride and determination, to present the results to the Statistical Office every Friday morning thereafter. Failures of input and output equipment, thermionic valves and dry joints combined to make this a hazardous task and it sometimes took 10 hours to complete the 20 minute job. It was the engineers and programmers who saw the job through, because there were no operations staff at that time. Grover recalls that Thursday evenings, in particular, did not exist from a social point of view for the few who tended this job for many months—some said that they cannot remember any night being particularly social, bearing in mind the amounts of overtime being worked.

One aspect of the job was the accumulation of grand totals for all the bakeries; the need to restart from the beginning at each machine failure was frustrating and very time wasting. Consequently, the idea of dumping Totals to Date was implemented for the first time ever on this job. This procedure enabled a restart to be made at the beginning of the bakery in which the computer failure had occurred, rather than at the very beginning. Dump and restart would become a standard feature for LEO systems and was adopted generally throughout the industry. This very first job, known by the code "P1" (program one), was the world's first routine commercial application, albeit at a speed very much slower than intended.

If LEO was to fulfil the role envisaged by Simmons and was to become an acceptable business machine, high speed input and output facilities were essential. This fact was not only demonstrated by the Bakeries Valuations job but was also brought home when Jim Bentz, one of the old school of Lyons clerks engaged in some LEO project costing work, was invited to attend a demonstration of LEO. He surprised everyone by giving the correct total of a column of figures in pounds, shillings and pence before the computer managed to print it. The slow speed of the teleprinter had completely nullified the electronic speed of the circuitry. Jim had done the calculation in his head!

Bureau Operations Start

The progress of LEO now began to come to the notice of others in industry and Government. The Ordnance Board sought and were given facilities to carry out ballistic computations, a task for which the machine was admirably suited. Hemy met with the Ordnance Board's representatives, who were occupying offices in Charles House, Kensington, quite near to Cadby Hall. Their Dr Boulton had been on a programming course at Cambridge and had been working on some ballistic calculations. Hemy worked with him to prepare programs for the work and to structure the necessary program tests. After a few days they punched up a program and verified it, ran their program on LEO and compared the result with specimen trajectories that had previously been computed by Boulton on a desk machine. Both were pleasantly surprised that the results produced were identical. This activity was the first recorded bureau job run on any United Kingdom computer and was eventually to lead to a new service industry that flourished from the 1960s. The Ordnance Board's work was shrouded in secrecy but it was revealed some time later that the calculations Boulton's programming team were performing were associated with the trajectories of the Black Knight missiles, which incidentally failed to achieve the great expectations the Government had of them. Lyons received a payment of £300 from the Ordnance Board for this work.

A very much larger and more complex mathematical job was later undertaken for De Havilland. This had particular problems, too, for it required secrecy and only afterwards, when Hemy had left Lyons and started working with EMI, did he learn that he had been involved with the Blue Streak rocket. There was some signing of the Official Secrets Act and the computer area was literally enclosed with red tape when the De Havilland job or anything else of a sensitive nature was run.

The calculations that were carried out on LEO for De Havilland were simulations of the guidance system under operational conditions, which included taking account of noise in the system. This noise was represented in the computing by the injection of random numbers at intervals. Hemy thought that it would have been helpful to have been able to discuss the mathematical processes with Fantl. However, Fantl, of Czechoslovakian birth, would not have passed the security vetting; whereas Hemy had already been cleared more than once when working in Signals Intelligence during World War II. Fortunately for Hemy the De Havilland mathematicians were very understanding and explained the processing required in intelligible terms that enabled him to write the program piece by piece and test it against known results. De Havilland required the integration of many simultaneous differential equations using the Runge–Kutta method; Hemy had no knowledge of this method nor even of the two after whom it was named.[6] He humorously referred to them as "Those two gentlemen", and Fantl was of great help in introducing him to them and explaining their methods. What Fantl could not see, because of security, were the printed results.

While running these highly complex calculations LEO suddenly started to go terribly wrong, and the results produced were not as predicted. No fault could be found, either on the engineering side or with the software. Naturally, the engineers were convinced it was a programming problem, which Hemy was hoping to heavens it was not. Lyons sought the assistance of Cambridge, and Stan Gill spent about a week with Hemy and others. After a week or so he had located the problem. It was a machine fault; the machine was suffering from what was described as pattern sensitivity, a condition caused by the subtle deterioration of valve performance causing a loss of pulse. Hemy found that in his test calculation, used for checking the machine's operation, the multiplier register happened to contain a number that included a succession of consecutive 1s and because the valves in the circuit had wandered off specification the last 1 in this sequence was missing. As a result the multiplication was in error. The machine test programs were supplemented to check for pattern sensitivity and the stable door was bolted.

A further satisfied customer was the Meteorological Office, who did a lot of work using their programming team. Their interest had been aroused when Frederick Henry Bushby returned from Cambridge University, having attended a course on the EDSAC, and as Mavis Hinds records in the *Meteorological Magazine* (1981), "There was lively discussion on the merits of applying the first calculations to the behaviour of a textbook model cyclone rather than to the irregular disturbances of a real synoptic chart". By the end of 1951 Bushby and Hinds were actively using the Lyons machine. For this early program the machine took 3 minutes to read in the program and data, 1 minute to do the calculations and another 1½ minutes to print the results, compared with manual methods that would have taken 4–5 hours. Fantl and Hemy gave a lot of their time to the Meteorological. Office staff, to help and advise them in any way they could. What Hemy remembers about that job in particular was that Dr Reginald Sutcliffe CB, OBE, FRS (1904–1991), who was then Head of Forecasting Research in the Meteorological Office, said one day how satisfied he was with the work they were doing; he then remarked "If only we had a machine of ten times this power, we would have the problem cracked". That is a remark that the Meteorological Office have been making at about four-year intervals ever since, and are still making; they currently utilise the most powerful computers in the world to undertake the vast number crunching models they have developed to aid weather forecasting and for research into possible climate change. These modern machines are capable of processing tens of millions of instructions per second compared to the seven hundred per second of LEO. It must be acknowledged, however, that weather forecasting has improved immeasurably during the past decade or so, largely as a result of improvements in the speed of machines and their ability to handle large mathematical equations and data.

As the facilities of LEO were enhanced by the addition of card punches and readers it became possible for the Meteorological Office team to produce 24-hour forecasts for an area covering Europe and the north-western Atlantic Ocean. Data for two levels in the vertical and horizontal network of 18 × 14 points, about 260 km apart, were used in the calculations. The two partial differential equations of the Sawyer–Bushby atmospheric model were solved by an iterative process. These equations gave rates of change of temperature and pressure with time, thus enabling a forecast to be made of the state of the atmosphere an hour later. Twenty-four such steps gave a 24-hour forecast. There were serious problems with computer storage space, and so much memory was overwritten that information had to be punched out on cards for each time step and then read in again for the next step with part of the program instructions. A 24-hour forecast took about four hours of computing time. One earlier occasion for which a forecast was attempted (albeit after the event) was for the serious east coast floods of 31 January 1953. The computer model predicted even more calamitous floods than those that actually occurred.

During 1951 a program had been written and tested to reproduce the tables issued by the Inland Revenue for the weekly calculation of income tax. Early in 1952 it was decided to use this program to give the computer an extended reliability trial by setting it to calculate the tables for the full year. The test ran continuously for over 59 hours, and during this time 51 hours of useful work were completed. The LEO team was modestly proud of this effort, but it was recognised that 87% efficiency fell some way short of what would be needed to meet the aims of the project, and that further effort was needed to improve LEO's reliability.

During 1952 work continued on the STL tape equipment and many programs designed to use its facilities were run, with very mixed results. Simultaneously Lyons' consolidation work for alternative input and output methods was advancing, and by the middle of the year a Ferranti photoelectric reader was in use. This was very much more reliable than the one originally built by Lyons, which, because it used many glass plates, soon became dirty and was unreliable. Soon after, agreement was reached with British Tabulating Machines on the equipment to be supplied by them, and in October Pinkerton secured Lyons management's agreement to the additional expenditure of £20,000 to build the proposed alternative input–output interface.[7] It now appeared likely that standard card and paper tape devices, rather than STL's magnetic tape units, would be used for operational work on LEO, and the preparation of programs for that purpose took up much of the effort of the team. Work continued on programs using the STL equipment for some time yet, and it was not until 1953 that the STL project was eventually cancelled.

The First Computerised Payroll

The first full-scale trial of the payroll system was carried out on 1 January 1953, using the STL equipment. It enabled much of the program that would be used operationally to be tested in full. Also a parallel version for use with Lyons' own input–output devices was being prepared, although this could not be tested until the punched card machines were delivered and working with the computer. These machines were delivered in May and June and were soon coupled to the computer; comprehensive testing of the equipment and full program trials could then be vigorously pressed and experience in using the complete configuration was built up. LEO now had two 5-hole paper tape readers which could operate at 120 rows per second, fifteen times the speed of the original reader. A line printer operated at 100 lines per minute, but was only capable of numeric notation 0–11, compared with the original teleprinter of just five characters per second and a card reader that enabled binary information to be carried forward from run to run at high speed. The input–output operations fed short mercury buffer stores to enable computing to be carried out simultaneously. Sterling to binary conversion (and vice versa) was not carried out in the input–output channels, as had been originally envisaged, but the computer was provided with automatic conversion functions to replace the programmed sequences that had previously been necessary and had been so expensive in computing time.

By 24 December 1953 the whole machine had been working satisfactorily for several weeks, the payroll programs had been exhaustively tested and weekly runs were started using operational data, although it was decided to continue with the manual system in parallel for a time.

This date marked the inauguration of the world's first computerised payroll, and in fact the first regular full clerical task to be undertaken on a programmed computer. A party was held in the senior management dining room at Cadby Hall to celebrate the official completion of the project, although further improvements were still to be made. A more formal celebration dinner to mark this event was held at the Company's prestigious Cumberland Hotel at Marble Arch on 27 May 1954, when the whole LEO project team were entertained by Lyons' Chairman Montague Gluckstein OBE (1886–1958) with cabaret by Shirley Abicair and Howard de Courcy.

The project had taken almost five years, more than twice the time the Cambridge University researchers had taken to build the EDSAC. About 18 months of this period were spent on designing, testing, and installing on site the units that had been manufactured by Wayne Kerr Laboratories and Camper & Nicholsons' subsidiary. The rest of the time was spent in designing and testing input and output circuits, which had proved more difficult than first thought, and in finding ways of making the machine reasonably reliable. In fact, LEO never was very reliable; the mean time between failures was 6–10 hours and there was a good chance that it would fail every eight hours. This was mitigated by the elaborate testing features, which enabled engineers to remedy faults without delay and thus keep the inoperable time to a minimum.

The Lyons Bakery staff payroll, numbering 1,670 employees in January 1954, continued to be processed on LEO in parallel with a manual operation until 9 February 1954, when it was decided that LEO was sufficiently reliable to allow manual operations to be discontinued. A task which had taken an experienced payroll clerk 8 minutes was now carried out in approximately 1½ seconds. This was somewhat better than Hemy's and Thompson's earlier calculations had suggested. Hemy had calculated in 1949 that to complete a payroll program of 18,000 persons, a rate of processing equal to 3 seconds per person was required. The designers had improved on this by 100%. Beside the production of payslips, the programs could provide a range of other employment information which would have taken many hours to produce by conventional clerical methods. The task had been made harder by the need to convert £.s.d notation into binary form, for the machine to handle, and then to reconvert the answer back, in numeric form only, to £.s.d for the payroll office. This was both an engineering and a software problem. Decimalisation was not introduced for another 17 years (1971).

It was suggested in February 1954, in a prepared answer to a question from staff, that LEO would eventually be doing the work of some 200 to 400 clerks; but it was emphasised that this was a misleading idea since LEO would not only be doing some existing clerical work but would ultimately be undertaking new work that could not be done, or was too expensive to be done, manually. In the event no staff were made redundant as a result of the initial introduction of LEO, apart from a handful of part-time clerks.

A Quiet Revolution

Lyons had been sufficiently confident of their machine to invite the press corps to a demonstration of payroll on 16 February 1954. LEO also made an impact in Government circles for it stood by on budget day in 1954 ready to re-calculate the Pay-As-You-Earn (PAYE) tax tables on the basis of the budget measures; as it happened there were no changes that year and LEO was not required. However, LEO stood by again in 1955, and got to work after the Chancellor's speech to Parliament. By 10 p.m. the same evening the first set of tables had been despatched to the printers; and by 7.45 a.m. the following day the whole job had been completed; work that would have taken many clerks (using accounting machines) many weeks to complete. Both Land and Fantl had been responsible for the program coding and testing, which had been carried out under a heavy security screen.

Although a quiet revolution had begun, there was no showroom razzmatazz. Lyons did not see much virtue in publicly claiming technological firsts. Much research was being undertaken by others at this time, and Lyons feared that their work would be copied before patents could be properly registered. As it happened, a computer patent for LEO was first filed in August 1950 (known as the main case) and this was followed in 1951 by six other specific patents but none was brought to a satisfactory conclusion. After much effort and expense the patents were abandoned on 13 September 1956, when the Patents Office cited an application that had been filed in 1948 by the Raytheon company for their computer, which bore remarkable similarities to LEO. Their two articles described, in very general terms, a computer in which input data is on tape, and is transferred to one of two mercury delay lines used in turn, before being transferred to the internal memory of the calculator; a converse arrangement was used for output. Thompson accepted that this feature appeared to be exactly the concept of the loader and unloader devices used in LEO and although he undertook to have the matter considered further, no interpretation of the disclosures of the two Raytheon articles could be found which avoided this conclusion. He accepted the Raytheon computer as anticipation of the broad idea of the LEO inventions even though no progress had been made in construction. However, in 1951 Lyons had not anticipated this outcome and by 1954 their sights were already set on bigger things.

The initial payroll volumes were deliberately kept to approximately 1,700 employees until a little more operational experience of the young LEO could be gleaned. As the months passed confidence grew and more work was loaded on to the LEO computer. Engineers and programmers alike had built better than they had dared to hope, and LEO had lived up to its expectations. The project had taken longer than anticipated, nearly five years, and the total cost to date, including research, was officially stated as £150,000, some £50,000 more than budgeted. In one of the early training manuals, a figure of £75,000 was mentioned as the cost of hardware but this cannot be substantiated. It is likely that the project far exceeded this figure.[8]

LEO was not alone for long. The American General Electric Corporation installed their UNIVAC computer late in 1954 and this has frequently been called, especially by Americans, the first business computer. Other American manufacturers would soon follow, and in the same year IBM announced their commercial data processing system for business use, incorporating cathode-ray tubes and magnetic tape for storage.

To put the LEO event into historical perspective, it is worth mentioning that 1954 saw the end of food rationing and the general easing of the controls that had been introduced in the United Kingdom during World War II, with meat the last item freed; Roger Bannister (later Sir) ran the first four-minute mile; the French, under the command of General Christian de Castries (1902–1991), were defeated at Dien Bien

Phu (Vietnam); America exploded its second hydrogen bomb at Bikini Atoll; the British Petroleum Company was formed from the previous Anglo-Iranian Oil Company; and Oxford won the 100th boat race. Not only was it a time to celebrate the inauguration of LEO, 1954 was also the Company's jubilee year, it having commenced trading on 10 April 1894 with an authorised share capital of £120,000.

In this sixtieth year too, the Chairman, Montague Gluckstein (1886–1958), decided to mention the LEO project for the first time in his speech to the shareholders on 5 July, at the Trocadero Restaurant. He said:

Developments of a different kind have been proceeding in the Lyons Electronic Office or, as we have named it, LEO. Large scale electronic computors [sic] have been built on both sides of the Atlantic, but they are designed for calculations of a purely mathematical and scientific character. We felt that it should be possible to design one primarily for commercial needs and utilise the very high speed at which these instruments work to avoid the arithmetical drudgery of much clerical work. Thus LEO has been built. It has already reached the stage where it has taken over some sections of our clerical work. It is also capable of all types of mathematical and scientific calculation and is doing, and will continue to be available for, much work of a varied character for other organisations.

All this had been accomplished with no more than a dozen very dedicated staff whose collective annual salaries were probably no more than £20,000. Most importantly, LEO returned inspiration and hope to all levels of Lyons' employees, placing them in the van of technological achievement when other parts of the business were still recovering from the austerity of wartime Britain. It was a considerable boost to morale and this feeling of achievement percolated to the highest echelons of the business.

The dawn of office automation had arrived and the feeling at the time can perhaps best be described by quoting from Coleridge's "Rime of the Ancient Mariner": "We were the first that ever burst into that silent sea".

CHAPTER 4

Full computer manufacture

Having been freed from his other Lyons duties in April 1950 and with the success of the prototype machine (LEO I) behind them, Thompson turned his attentions to the building of the next machine. Reliable as LEO I was, Simmons prudently decided that full loading should not commence without a second machine in place to act as stand-by. A catastrophic breakdown could have had serious consequences for the business, and of course staff had to be paid promptly week by week. As Simmons commented, "They could not be kept waiting because an interesting experiment had failed". Furthermore, Lyons had always planned for more than one machine, possibly up to three. If the company were to maintain the momentum of improved clerical efficiency and effectiveness, which by now was clearly achievable, it must ensure that research and development continued. Outline proposals for building LEO II were submitted by Pinkerton on 4 May 1954, followed in July by the Board's approval and general policy instructions. This decision had been expected by the project team and such was their confidence that material had been stockpiled since March 1951 as a safeguard against the continuing shortages.[1]

The development of LEO II followed intrinsically the same design methods as had been used on LEO I, but several changes were made in the light of experience with building and running the earlier machine. The arithmetic unit of LEO II comprised 16 registers compared with only 3 in LEO I. Provisions for arithmetical and transfer operations between registers to eliminate the need for frequent transfers to and from store during calculating sequences were incorporated. The store cycle speed was improved to nearly four times that of LEO I; this was achieved by making the mercury delay tubes one quarter of the length of those of the first machine and narrowing the store pulse width to a quarter of a microsecond. In today's parlance, LEO II used 250 nanosecond pulses (a nanosecond is one thousand millionth of a second). The idea of shortening the mercury delay tubes to improve performance had first been suggested by Lenaerts on 19 August 1953, even before LEO I had been officially completed. These two measures significantly increased the operating speed of LEO II.

Further significant changes were made in storage architecture, including the use of ferrite core storage, which increased its capacity to 8,192 words. This feature did not appear on the first production machines but was incorporated only on the last four LEO II computers; they were technically known as LEO IIc, the "c" indicating core storage. The other main features which set the LEO II's apart from the previous model was the use of Decca (type 3000) magnetic tape backing storage and the incorporation of transistors in the magnetic core control circuits. This enabled LEO II to be operated as a parallel instead of a serial machine and thus improved speed. The transistor had been invented in December 1948 by William Shockley (1910–1989), John Bardeen (1908–) and Walter Brattain (1902–1987) while working at the famous Bell Laboratories in the United States. (Shockley, born in London, shared the Nobel Prize for physics with his colleagues in 1956.) Transistors had been commercially available earlier but were only now becoming an economic alternative to the thermionic valve. In fact, Pinkerton and Caminer visited the manufacturing plant of the Radio Corporation of America (RCA) in March 1958 to see the latest developments in semiconductor design, but despite the transistor's appeal valves continued to be used in the co-ordinator, arithmetic and input–output circuits of LEO II. Microprogramming was also introduced for the first time, a technique developed by Wilkes, and this enabled a more sophisticated instruction code to be used.

The Samastronic Printer

At this time some peripheral equipment manufacturers began to make their presence felt; realising at last that computers would become a lucrative market for their mechanical skills, many showed intense interest. Lyons had been particularly interested in the work being undertaken by Bull in France (who joined forces with Honeywell) and the Powers-Samas Company, whose historical background was in punch card equipment. Bull had developed a computer line printer with a full numeric and some alpha capability. The alpha characters S, O, I and G were created from the numerals 8, 0, 1 and 6, and were acceptable compromises; the full stop and hyphen sign were also available and the maximum printing speed was 150 lines per minute. Powers-

Samas had developed in their factory at Croydon, a printer which could produce 60 different characters at printing speeds of 300 lines per minute in 140 print columns. As well as the full alphanumeric characters, fractions, asterisk, ampersand, plus, minus, colon, comma and brackets were all possible. The Powers-Samas Samastronic achieved character generation by using a needle stylus assembly to create a pattern of small dots in the form of the required character. It was considered a major breakthrough in printing technology (much the same technique is used in the dot matrix printers widely used in offices today) as up till then computer tabulators (printers) could only present results in numeric form; quite unsuitable for most commercial work. Lyons found that the printers were difficult to maintain, because of their engineering complexity, and constant attention was needed to maintain the mechanism responsible for character shaping. It was realised from the onset that the quality of printing would need to be sacrificed for the additional speed the printer offered. In 1962 a study was undertaken, and on examination a sample of printing from the machines in use was found to be unacceptable. Generally the top copy was readable in that there was rarely any doubt as to what characters were intended. On carbon copies, however, the legibility varied considerably depending on how the machine had been set up and on the amount of use it had. Engineers spent an inordinate amount of time on this problem and eventually sought Lenaerts' ingenuity. He soon developed a technique of great benefit to the engineers. His solution was to invent a special character, which became known as the Lenaerts Character: it used the stylus assembly in the worse possible way so that in practice characters would be presented in the best possible formation.

The Samastronic printer was optional on the LEO II machines from about 1958 but Powers-Samas built few of these devilishly complicated devices, and, despite its name, the printer contained no electronics. They were not a commercial success and the financial crisis they created was one of the factors that led to the merger of Powers-Samas with the British Tabulating Machine Company (BTM) in 1959.

Magnetic Drum Storage

Another major development at this time, which Britain can claim to have initially led, was the magnetic drum store. The magnetic drum consisted of a rapidly rotating cylinder with a magnetised external surface on which data could be encoded by way of read/write heads floating a few millionths of an inch above the surface of the drum. This computer related device had been invented by Dr Andrew Booth of Birkbeck College, University of London and was first used in 1947 on the University's Automatic Relay Calculator (ARC) that had been developed for the British Rubber Producers Research Association. The calculator used 800 high speed Siemens mechanical relays; the nickel-plated magnetic drum had a capacity of 256 numbers of 21 binary digits, a modest capacity compared with today's technology. The ARC was followed by the Simple Electronic Computer (SEC), using thermionic valves instead of relays. This is now accepted as having been the first fully electronic machine with magnetic drum storage.

Manchester University were the first to use magnetic drum storage commercially, incorporating the technology on their Mark I computor (sic) in 1951. For recording information it offered greater scope and flexibility than magnetic tape, since tape had to be searched sequentially, whereas the magnetic drum store could be randomly accessed at far greater speeds. It therefore offered greater potential for system designers.

Ferranti also developed a magnetic drum (type 1009) device with 64 tracks on which 16,384 words could be encoded. The LEO II machine allowed for up to four of these magnetic drums to be attached as optional features providing a total backing storage of 65,536 words, each of nineteen bits. There were many difficulties associated with the early drum technology; some of a mechanical nature. On one occasion, in February 1958, while under evaluation in the LEO factory, overheating caused the read/write heads to score the recording surface of the drum so that it became totally unusable and consequently had to be replaced; since delivery of these devices ran into months the availability to users was somewhat delayed. Thompson, surprisingly, did not think that drum backing storage, or indeed any backing storage, was a necessity, and according to Caminer, did not understand it. The early use of drums on the LEO II machines was probably deterred by his attitude, which was shared by Simmons.

The Computer Manufacturing Subsidiary

By the mid-1950s, the LEO project had begun to generate much interest in business circles. In February 1954, Television Newsreel and Paramount News carried news items on LEO. Representatives from many large and well-known companies came to see LEO, to talk to its designers and to marvel at the operations it could undertake. A special viewing gallery was built to enable visitors to have a better view of the operating floor. In later years it became fashionable for companies to place their computers at ground level, with large glass windows, so that the public could see the equipment; they hoped that this would convey a subtle message of modern efficiency. Concern for security has completely reversed this trend and now machine rooms are locked away behind a plethora of security devices, with access granted only to a privileged few. Indeed, the very survival of some businesses depends totally on their use of computers.

To maximise the commercial opportunities, which became increasingly obvious with each new group of visitors, the Lyons Board decided to form a company to manufacture, sell and lease electronic computers and to provide other associated services. This was a major departure from their core business of catering and food manufacture, but a natural decision for Lyons to take. They had, after all, previously diversified into other non-food activities such as vehicle assembly, carton manufacture, printing and laundries, to avoid being dependent on others for their supplies, and the decision to create a computer manufacturing subsidiary was seen as an opportunity to exploit their unique office expertise and make money.

In September 1954, through their solicitors Bartlett & Gluckstein, Lyons applied to the Registrar of Companies to find out whether they could use Leo Calculators Limited or Leo Limited as a name for a subsidiary computer company. The name Leo Limited was not available for registration, so arrangements were made to form the subsidiary under the title of Leo Calculators Limited, presumably because LEO had been called a calculator for so long. In the Company's Memorandum of Association one objective listed was: "To carry on business as manufacturers of and dealers in all forms of electrical or automatic computers and office machinery and automatic control equipment of

Full computer manufacture 101

THE COMPANIES ACT, 1948.

COMPANY LIMITED BY SHARES.

Memorandum of Association

— OF —

LEO ~~CALCULATORS~~ COMPUTERS LIMITED

1. The name of the Company is "LEO ~~CALCULATORS~~ COMPUTERS LIMITED".

2. The registered office of the Company will be situate in England.

3. The objects for which the Company is established are :-

    (A) To carry on business as manufacturers of and dealers in all forms of electrical or automatic computers and office machinery and automatic control equipment of any kind.

    (B) To carry on business as shop and office furnishers, upholsterers, woodworkers, electrical manufacturers, engineers, metal and alloy makers, refiners and workers, paper and cardboard manufacturers safe makers, cabinet and furniture manufacturers printers publishers and stationers.

    (C) To manufacture, import, buy, sell, exchange, clean, erect, instal, repair, alter, remodel, let or take on hire or otherwise deal in any plant, machinery, material, article or thing capable of being made, used, or sold in any of the businesses or trades aforesaid.

    (D) To carry on any of the above trades or businesses in any part of the world and to undertake, fulfil and execute any agency of any kind whether connected with the above trades or businesses or not and to carry on any other trade or business which in the opinion of the Company may be carried on advantageously in connection with any of the other trades or businesses aforesaid.

1.

Fig. 4.1 Leo Computers Ltd—Memorandum of Association.
By kind permission of J. Lyons & Co Ltd.

any kind". Clearly, this clause was incompatible with the word "calculator" in the Company's title and on 11 October 1954, instructions were given to solicitors to modify the title to Leo Computers Limited.

This new name was subsequently approved by the Company Registrar; a name more in keeping with the machine's true capabilities and trend in terminology of that period. Leo Computers Limited (registered number 540140) was incorporated on 4 November 1954 with a share capital of £100, and the event received wide newspaper publicity. The Company's first directors (Anthony Salmon, John Simmons and Thomas Thompson) were appointed on 16 November 1954. On 16 April 1959 a further issue of £249,900 ordinary shares was made, bringing the total share capital of the Company to £250,000, and on 9 June 1959, at a meeting of directors, Dr John Pinkerton, David Caminer and Anthony Barnes were appointed additional Directors of the Company. By 1960 Leo Computers Ltd were employing 439 staff, 7% of whom were classed as management.

The Wider Context

By this time the upsurge in office technology had begun to accelerate rapidly, with many new companies introducing their particular models of equipment, although few British computer manufacturing companies could demonstrate sophisticated configurations to the same extent of Lyons; they had after all been using real computers (machines controlled by stored software instructions) to carry out clerical tasks since 1951 and could talk with some authority on the subject. Nevertheless, in December 1955 when Thompson returned from his second United States visit he warned that the lead in office automation was in danger of slipping from Britain. He and Barnes had visited IBM at Poughkeepsie in New York State, the Westinghouse Company, the General Electric Company, the Bureau of Census in Washington, Harvard Computational Laboratory, the Bank of America and several other influential companies, and they could not help but be impressed with the progress being made and the technical excellence of the equipment.

His comments were not always complimentary, and on his visit to the Defense Department (Supply and Logistics), Pentagon, Washington DC, itself an achievement bearing in mind the security surrounding that place, Thompson made the following comments:

Judging from the number of Colonels of the Army, Captains of the Navy, other high ranking officers, and even higher ranking civilian personnel who advise or direct them, who are involved in trying to use electronic computers for controlling the supply needs of the forces, there must be at least the equivalent of a division of men and women involved in this operation.

There is one UNIVAC in the Pentagon, not really in use, and there are many computers on order. There seems to be ample evidence that they have no real idea of organising a job for the computer. Everyone seems to be bluffing everyone else. Wing Commander Belcher of the RAF, who is taking the place of a United States Lieutenant Colonel in the Pentagon, alone seems to have realised that they do not yet know what they are doing. He told us in advance what he thought of the position and it was amply brought out in all our conversations.

Thompson was more complimentary about his visit to the Harvard Computation Laboratory, Boston. Their original Mark I electro-mechanical computer was still doing useful work after ten years, but Thompson had really come to see the latest Mark II version. All input and output to the computer took place via eleven magnetic tape machines. The program and data were recorded on magnetic tape before transfer into the machine, which impressed him. For their main backing store Harvard had chosen a magnetic drum that had 10,000 available locations. Twenty-five program orders could be held on a single track of the drum's surface and each order could be executed in 1.3 milliseconds. The computer was contained in an air-conditioned chamber twenty feet in length, thus allowing anyone to walk about inside the chamber. Students spent one year working on the computer as part of a Master's course in Electronic Computers.

Thompson could not help being impressed with the amount of money some companies were investing to bring automation to their clerical operations. Their individual computer budgets greatly exceeded that of the LEO project in total, and many companies were involved. The Metropolitan Life Insurance Company in New York, for example, had invested in a million dollar UNIVAC computer to undertake just one job, actuarial statistics.[2] They were processing IBM punched cards that had been used as part of another operation. The actuarial job was said to have had 100 separate steps and to have taken sixteen man years to program and test. When undertaken manually the same job had taken 198 people and 138 punched card machines; computerisation had reduced this to 84 people and 18 punched card machines. It took four years to recover the computer and planning costs.

Several million dollars had been spent by the Bank of America at San Jose, San Francisco for their computer. The bank had sponsored the development of a device known as ERNA by the Stanford Research Institute, a special purpose machine designed to deal with payments and withdrawals in connection with 32,000 accounts. Very much an experimental device of immense size, it worked on the principle of wired-in programs.

At International Business Machines, Madison Avenue, New York, Thompson saw the IBM 702 and IBM 650 computers being used by customers to test their programs. Customers were allocated half an hour each and were expected to operate the machine themselves, although if necessary, an experienced IBM operator could be called upon for advice. Thompson thought the IBM 702 computer, which used the Williams tube principle for storage, very compact. The later IBM 705 machine impressed him even more, particularly IBM's use of core storage and magnetic tape, which he had not seen before. The tapes, which he saw in full operation for the first time, had an automatic rewind facility actuated by a photoelectric sensing mark at the end of the tape. He discussed the use of computers for office work with IBM's Vice President, who expressed his opinion that payroll could not be done economically on automatic computers and confessed frankly that their Poughkeepsie payroll was not economic. General conversations with the supervisory staff on the computer floor suggested to Thompson that they were lacking in knowledge of the equipment and its use. Thompson also visited the IBM workshops at Poughkeepsie and saw the production lines of the IBM 704 (mathematical) and IBM 705 (data processing) machines. Many were being made simultaneously and he was told that orders for over 100 had been taken for both models. He believed that IBM were gearing up production rapidly to develop a very large new section of the company.

From his United States visit, to both users and suppliers, Thompson came to the conclusion that the American effort appeared still to be concerned with scientific work but realised that the large commercial companies he visited had the cash and enthusiasm to develop at a rapid pace and that LEO's commercial lead in the United Kingdom could soon be threatened. He was less impressed with the way in which the American computer users were designing their procedures. These were heavily influenced by orthodox punched card philosophy, which resulted in feeding data through a series of computer runs and keeping intermediate records that, with correct use of automation, should not have been recorded at all. This approach resulted in the need for more computer processing to complete a given clerical task, but this seemed the method preferred by the Americans. By the late 1950s, the American competition had become increasingly effective; their introduction of reliable well-designed equipment and the availability of the FORTRAN scientific programming language to customers in 1957, and later the commercially-oriented COBOL, proved to be decisive factors in their success.

LEO II: Development and Marketing

Meanwhile, the task of developing and marketing LEO II continued and by 1955 many genuine commercial enquiries had been received at the offices of Leo Computers Ltd. At one time, a Lyons confectionery regional sales manager (Henry Levy) was employed to cold call on prospective clients but Caminer said this was not a good idea; the individual did not learn anything about computers, although he had a likeable personality. The first official sales representative, J.C. Masters (formally an assistant secretary with Armitage & Rigby Limited), was employed on 9 July 1956. However, this was not a successful undertaking and on 25 September 1958 the marketing and consultancy divisions were merged under the management of Caminer. Experience had shown that the only effective way to market computers at the time was through the consultants who understood the customer's needs. Masters continued to be employed in a lesser but perhaps more important capacity in customer relations. Geoffrey Mills, previously responsible for the O & M office, training and other personnel schemes at Lyons, was appointed on 11 August 1958 to assist in the marketing and personnel function. It was a role that did not suit his character and he did not enjoy it. Nevertheless, he embarked on a vigorous advertising campaign, using the services of Voice & Vision to prepare publicity material and Public Relations Ltd for brochures.

Although LEO had been exposed to wide publicity and Lyons enjoyed a fine reputation in office systems, the marketing and selling of computers proved very difficult. There was considerable reticence by the customer and much debating took place before a formal order was eventually placed. Potential customers had little understanding of computer technology or of the potential of the machines. The long-term uncertainties of replacing conventional and familiar systems with automatic processing were, for many, extremely difficult. The generation of managers of the late 1950s were far more cautious and had less capital at their disposal than the more adventurous types of pre-war Britain. When faced with investment on this scale it was normal to obtain competitive quotations, but because other computer manufacturers had not yet established themselves this option was not available. Even if it had been, the matter of selection would still have posed difficulties, since few were computer literate and they did not understand the subtle intricacies of software, operating systems and electronic technology. To management of that period the question of the future was all-important. Would such machines play as important a role in industry as Lyons and others would have them believe? Even when they had made this first difficult decision potential customers needed to know, in some detail, what was involved in the installation and operation of the equipment. Would it be reliable? What would be the purchase and running costs? Could space be made available? How could the investment cost be justified? What additional staff and training would be necessary and were there any latent drawbacks? How would unionised labour react? And so on. Not least, of course, was the growing competitive threat from across the Atlantic, where in particular, IBM offered rental terms for their computers.

For many this appeared a more sensible approach since there seemed little financial risk. Purchasers were much troubled by the question of obsolescence and anxious not to enter a commitment that might tie them to an out-of-date system. The Americans were, and continue to be, masters of marketing techniques (although there are now signs that Japan is gaining control of this discipline). They invested heavily in document preparation, in contrast to the literature available for LEO, and they had a knack of inventing jargon which at the time captured media attention. In some competitive situations, Lyons found it necessary to study the target company's office procedures to convince them of the benefits a LEO computer might bring. This expensive preliminary work, largely provided without charge, seemed appropriate at the time and no doubt encouraged some companies to develop confidence in their ideas. Indeed, some tenders were won on this basis, but the success was not always due so much to the merits of LEO as to the

Lyons consultants being able to define their customers needs and specify remedies.

Enquiries came from all sections of British industry; some of the more famous of that period included Stewarts & Lloyds Ltd (steel manufacturers), English & American Insurance Company, the South Eastern Gas Board, the National Coal Board, Ford Motor Company, Kodak Ltd, Imperial Tobacco Company, British Road Services, the Ever Ready Company, Legal & General Insurance Company, Commercial Bank of Scotland, British Transport Commission, De Havilland Propellers Ltd, Alliance Assurance Company and many government and research establishments. Parliament too was conscious of the progress being made in office automation and on 20 December 1955, Commander Maitland MP, asked of the Chancellor, R.A. Butler (1902–1982):

In view of the advances towards automation made by Messrs Lyons in their use of the electronic device named LEO, details of which are in his possession, will he consider the possibility of using similar methods in the Treasury and the Civil Service generally to enable the Nation's business to be carried out more expeditiously and more economically?

Butler's reply was:

Several electronic computers are already in use within the Civil Service for mathematical work, and less elaborate electronic apparatus is used in some departments on clerical work. The scope for further use of electronic computers is continuously studied by the Organisation and Methods Divisions of the Treasury and other Departments. (*Hansard*, 20 December 1955).

Caminer's consultancy team were extremely active at this time and they did not confine their canvassing to the UK; countries as far away as Brazil and Australia were seen as potential markets. They were frequently commissioned by companies to undertake full system studies, resulting in program specification and equipment orders. Several government departments did in time place orders for the LEO III machines, including the Board of Trade, Customs and Excise, the Inland Revenue and the Post Office, who became the largest customer, ordering several machines over a period. Their largest job was telephone billing, the revenues from which were worth £3,500 million per year to the Post

Office. With so much money being invoiced, this job became critical to the organisation and the unions soon learned that withdrawing a relatively small amount of labour, which they frequently did, could cause havoc to the Post Office cash flow.

On 1 July 1956 the Lyons staff who up till this time had worked on LEO were formally transferred to Leo Computers Ltd and by 10 November 1956, the new company had taken occupation of premises at 38–42 Minerva Road, London. This site would become the development, design and production facility. For about two years previously some staff had been at Olaf Street, Shepherds Bush, where electrical circuits had been manufactured and where the LEO II prototype was built. The new Minerva Road premises consisted of 26,400 square feet of floor space with just 6,200 square feet devoted to the computer shop. The other space was allocated to training, drawing, wiring and testing, design, development, and other office support facilities. Later, in 1961, an additional adjoining site (24–30) was taken on a 21-year lease.

With so much interest now being generated in the LEO computers it became necessary to recruit and train more staff at all levels. An ambitious recruitment campaign was initiated, supported by advertising and the production of a booklet entitled *Openings in Leo Computers Limited*. This booklet described the three main business classifications of Leo Computers Ltd: the first involved the development, production and sale of electronic computers; the second, advising customers on all aspects of the application of computers and the subsequent preparation of jobs for a computer; and the third, the carrying out of commercial, mathematical and scientific computations as a service to industrial and commercial concerns and to government departments as a service bureau.

For these activities the company needed engineers and physicists in the research, design and operating division, while mathematicians and others were required for the marketing and programming divisions. Full-time training was provided for all staff. There were two basic engineering courses, the Preliminary Electronics Course, lasting eleven weeks, followed by the Computer Engineering Course that lasted a further fourteen weeks. The full twenty-five week course was taken only by those trainees not already versed in electronics. The syllabus for the preliminary course consisted of alternating current theory, thermionics, semiconductors, and electronic circuitry, while the advanced course covered computer principles, computer logic, input and output systems, power supplies and the theory of programming.

The programming and operating course lasted five weeks, spent partly in the working environment. The syllabus for this less demanding course included the fundamental characteristics of computers, the principles and practice of coding programs, the use of input and output facilities, the way the coded program is put together and entered into LEO, and devising a model job and running it on the computer.

The qualification requirement for design and development engineers specified a university degree in electrical engineering or physics. For programmers and consultants the official requirement was a good education to at least General Certificate of Education (GCE) A level standard, including mathematics, although many programmers were eventually taken on without this. A university degree was often the preferred qualification, particularly for the more senior positions, and often mathematics with honours was required.

Operational engineers were required to be educated to GCE A level standard in mathematics and physics or to have a Higher National Certificate (HNC) qualification. Computer operators were required to be educated to GCE O level standard, with at least a pass in mathematics.

The selection process was a lengthy one. Preliminary interviews were held to determine suitability of the candidate for the position applied for. Some interviews were held in London and others at universities during the spring term. Those candidates who satisfied the preliminary requirements were given aptitude tests designed to determine their mental and logical abilities. Following the aptitude test a further interview would take place, normally on the same day, covering in more detail the job requirements, employment conditions and aspirations of the applicant.

One of many persons selected through the University Appointments Board was John Aris, now Director of the National Computing Centre, Manchester. After reading classics at Oxford University, he was recruited as a LEO programmer and worked on a variety of software applications, eventually becoming a senior consultant and English Electric-LEO Sales Manager for government departments.

At the request of Mills, a series of appreciation courses were held for the Lyons management. From the business community in general a huge appetite developed for information on computers and how they could be used for both clerical and non-clerical work. Consequently, Pinkerton, Caminer, Thompson and others were in great demand at meetings, seminars and the like, to talk and give papers on a variety of computer-related subjects. On one occasion Dr John Pinkerton gave a talk on the BBC programme *London Calling Europe*. Mary Coombs also participated in a BBC programme but in her case the interview was conducted in French for the European Service. These activities provided good publicity and helped fuel the continuing interest in clerical automation from which Lyons ultimately benefited, but they also became a drain on the limited resources of Leo Computers Ltd.

In July 1957 Lyons took delivery of the first LEO II machine and it was soon pressed into service, ironically in the very building that had been built some twenty years earlier to accommodate the increasing numbers of clerical staff. The decision to install the machine in that location was not automatic. Serious consideration had been given to siting the second machine outside London on security grounds, one reason cited being the fear of atomic explosion. High Wycombe was one area considered. At one time too, Simmons had suggested siting the original teleprinters for LEO I (before tabulators were used) at the remote factory estate in Greenford, some 20 miles distant from Cadby Hall. It is difficult to know how he expected these to operate although it would have been theoretically possible using the established Post Office telex network. With the benefit of hindsight, his idea can be seen as quite revolutionary: a remote workstation. Clearly, the benefits of having both machines in one location outweighed the security risks; mutual backup, for example. It is interesting, however, that such matters were considered and discussed at such an early stage; those involved must already have been aware that the business could come to depend on these machines. The LEO II/1 computer, although much improved on its parent, was still very much subject to continuing development and experimentation, and for practical purposes it was necessary to have it located close by.

External Work

With the same readiness to recognise valuable business opportunities as had been shown in the past, the management of Lyons wasted no time in trying to turn LEO II to profit. Not only did Lyons encourage external companies to send their development staff to Leo Computers to work under the experienced direction of Caminer's senior project managers, they also undertook regular computer bureau work for many companies. Some of this work was of an *ad hoc* nature, which generated revenue, and some of a more permanent type such as regular payroll processing. In fact, as early as 1954 Lyons had produced terms on which "Leo Calculations" were to be carried out. The calculator charge would be £50 per elapsed hour, the services of a programmer in advising or becoming involved in the trials was £2.00 per man hour, and in the event of perforated paper tape being required a charge of 10/- per hour would be made. There were the normal exclusion and charge clauses for failed work. The high machine costs contrasted with low labour cost, quite the opposite of present day costs. Some of the companies participating in this kind of activity wanted to benefit from improved efficiency as quickly as possible while awaiting delivery of their computers, while other, less adventurous, clients wanted to experiment without the full financial commitment of setting up their own data processing installations.

One notable job run on the LEO computer, later the subject of a documentary film, involved the payroll processing for the Ford Motor Company whose main plant was situated at Dagenham in Essex. By 1958 Lyons were processing over 21,000 weekly-paid Ford employees on their LEO computers as well as their own large payroll and those of Kodak Ltd, Tate & Lyle Ltd, Greenwich Borough Council and many others. Payroll was seen by many, Lyons included, as an expensive but necessary overhead which contributed nothing to the profitability of the business and seemed to take increasing numbers of staff to manage.

A great variety of other jobs were processed. One of the longest ever undertaken was for the British Transport Commission. LEO had been programmed to find the shortest distance from each of the 7,000 stations and goods depots on the UK rail network to every other, so that freight charges could be calculated. To simplify the task, the 7,000 stations and depots were reduced to 4,000 groups. The job had to be completed by a specified time and, in order to fulfil commitments, the computer was utilised for 168 hours per week with computer operators working a three-shift pattern totalling about 1,000 hours. This foreshadowed the fuller exploitation of the equipment: it would not be long before this unpopular shift pattern became the norm for LEO and for many other computer installations run by commercial companies. The distancing job for the British Transport Commission, undertaken mainly at night, was finally completed on 3 May 1957, LEO having undertaken 16 million distance calculations, which would have taken 250 man years to compute by conventional clerical methods. Work carried out for the Ministry of Defence, in calculating shell trajectories was even more onerous for the computer, involving over 110 million calculations.

Before long the two LEO computers in use at Cadby Hall, LEO I and LEO II/1, were fully occupied and were running twenty-four hours a day, processing work for the various Lyons departments and for the expanding bureau operation. With the capacity exhausted on the Cadby Hall computers, Lyons decided to provide a full dedicated computer bureau service from offices in Queensway, London, and in May 1959 commissioned LEO II/5 (the fifth production machine) with full supporting facilities, such as programming and data preparation, an increasing revenue source. The LEO II/5 configuration, more advanced than the earlier production machines, boasted ICT card punching equipment, a Samastronic printer, Ferranti magnetic storage drums, Decca magnetic tapes, type 3000, of a wholly different design from those experimented with earlier (but which were also very troublesome), Ferranti photo-electric paper tape readers, and improved Creed paper tape punches.

The new offices, on the upper floor of the famous Whiteley's Department store, immortalised in the film *My Fair Lady* when Professor Higgins bought Eliza Doolittle's Ascot dress there, were named Hartree House, in memory of the late Professor Hartree of Cambridge University, who had given so much early support and encouragement to the Lyons Board during the late 1940s when they first contemplated building an electronic computer. HRH the Duke of Edinburgh visited the Minerva Road factory and new offices on 22 March 1960. For the occasion, the programming office had been decorated and seating arranged so that the Group Leaders were best placed to answer any questions—alas to no avail! HRH wanted to speak to the not-so-accessible people: he was so interested in the work being carried out, both at the factory and offices, that his departure was delayed by 20 minutes, and not before the machine suddenly burst into a chorus of the Sailors Hornpipe while computing the payroll for the Army and Air Force Officers; quite unprepared, HRH asked the senior operator, "How did you get that machine to make those noises?"

The bureau business, essentially the selling of computer time, was soon copied by companies who had invested large sums of money in their own computers and saw this as a lucrative way to recover some of that investment. Other companies formed service bureaux themselves for the sole purpose of selling machine time and, like the Lyons subsidiary, eventually encompassed programming and consultancy services. It was the start of a flourishing industry that continued well into the 1980s and is still active today. The Lyons charge for undertaking bureau work in 1958 was £30–£35 per elapsed hour, although this was subject to haggling.

The First Order

The first order received in the United Kingdom for a LEO commercial computer came on 3 February 1956 from the cigarette manufacturer W.D. & H.O. Wills Ltd and was subject to the delivery with it of the new alphanumeric Samastronic printer and the first Ferranti magnetic drum. It was not coincidental that the order came from a tobacco manufacturer. Several of the Lyons directors, including Anthony Salmon, still had business relationships with some of Wills' directors and as recently as 1946 Wills had written to the Salmon and Gluckstein families notifying them, out of courtesy, that they were about to change the name of their former Salmon & Gluckstein company to the House of Bewlay.[3] These high level contacts were used to invite the Wills Board to a demonstration of LEO at Cadby Hall. Anthony Salmon believed that the Wills directors might not necessarily understand the demonstration too well and so a rather exclusive luncheon was prepared to compensate. The visit was considered so important that no expense was spared; even the claret and port was brought into the dining room 24 hours beforehand so that it would settle and be in the best of condition.

Technical difficulties with the Samastronic printer and drum storage delayed installation of the Wills machine, which had been designated LEO II/2. Meanwhile, a further order was taken and delivery of this proceeded normally and so Stewarts & Lloyds Limited, of Corby, had the distinction of being the first company to take delivery of a LEO computer in May 1958; LEO II/3. It had been purchased for £125,000. Their management had been aware of the potential benefits of computerisation and had instigated studies as early as 1955. In December of that year they produced a detailed payroll specification which they circulated to a number of computer manufacturers, including Leo Computers Ltd. The first eight months of 1956 were "a phase of digestion, elucidation, collection of more detail, modification of requirements and consideration of the final proposals", as Stewarts & Lloyds Ltd put it at the time. The LEO proposal was accepted in principle and a formal agreement was concluded, by which Leo Computers Ltd were to program and prove, on live data, a section of the Corby payroll. The final edition of the job specification was available by August 1956 and by the end of the year Leo Computers Ltd had completed the programming work. To the disappointment of all, some technical problems manifested themselves on the LEO II equipment and the demonstration run could not be carried out until May 1957. In the event Stewarts & Lloyds Ltd found the delay a hidden benefit as it allowed them to reorganise their wages department, carry out what training they could and prepare the necessary operating manuals and procedures.

When the payroll demonstration was given, on 19 May 1957, it took the form of a parallel run, with the results obtained from the computer being compared with those produced by the manual operation for 520 blast furnace employees. This process was continued for five full weeks, and in November 1957 a further 500 employees' salaries were computerised. The complete payroll of Stewarts & Lloyds was transferred to the LEO II/3 computer by May 1958.

The machine was used for a variety of clerical jobs—warehouse invoicing of supplies, stores accounting, pension fund records—and for scientific work such as stress calculations for high-pressure pipe systems. It had a long and reliable 13-year history, eventually closing down on 23 June 1971.

The first Electronic Computer Exhibition and Business Computer Symposium was held at Olympia from 28 November to 4 December 1958. It had been sponsored by the Electronic Engineering Association and the Office Appliance and Business Equipment Trades Association. HRH the Duke of Edinburgh was Patron of the exhibition and symposium, the first to be held in Europe. Forty-two exhibitors were represented, including, of course, representatives from Leo Computers (Stand Number 27), who shuttled guests between the Olympia exhibition hall and Cadby Hall, where LEO I and II could be seen in full operational use.

The exhibition attracted many well-known companies including Elliott Brothers, English Electric Company Ltd, Ferranti Ltd, Siemens Edison Swan Ltd, Standard Telephones and Cables Ltd, National Cash Registers, EMI and, on a stand farthest from the main entrance, IBM United Kingdom Ltd. On 1 December 1958, the first day of the symposium, Neil Pollock, MBE, Manager of the O & M Department of Stewarts & Lloyds Ltd, gave a talk on payroll and production applications. Twenty-three other speakers followed him over the three days of the symposium, from companies such as Fords, Boots Pure Drug Company, National Physical Laboratory, HM Treasury, Imperial Chemical Industries, British Railways (Western), Glaxo Laboratories Ltd, and the National Coal Board, and the scientific correspondent of the *Financial Times*.

The exhibition was well attended and was subsequently deemed a total success. For Lyons the interest shown in their LEO computer was beyond expectations, with regular informal visits made available to those who wanted to see a computer being used commercially on real work at Cadby Hall. Some visits eventually paid off and Leo Computers Ltd were successful in manufacturing eleven LEO II machines; of these, two were used by Lyons and the other nine were sold to leading United Kingdom businesses of the period. Each configuration was unique and machines were assembled to users' requirements. In those days production line methods were comparatively informal and Leo Computers Ltd were receptive to configuration modifications during production, allowing users to incorporate the latest technological developments into their configurations as they occurred and before delivery. As a corollary of this, maintenance documentation needed to be almost bespoke for each site.

The LEO II machine delivered to the British Oxygen Company (BOC) in 1960 never worked to their management's satisfaction. This is hardly surprising; they were so impressed with Frank Land's presentation that they decided to buy a machine without really knowing what to do with it. Although the hardware was satisfactory, the programs had been badly specified, and Mary Coombs, who headed the team of programmers on the project, felt they were doomed to disaster from the beginning. She had thought that the BOC planners had been too ambitious in their plans for statistics and that they had not considered the sheer volume of paper these would produce, quite apart from the machine running times. Their requirements had made it necessary to design complex programs, which the staff working on them were never able to debug completely. The machine stood idle for much of the time, with little operational work, and eventually BOC traded it in for the later LEO III model. The LEO II continued to give good service in the expanding bureau operation that Lyons had set up in Hartree House. A list of companies who took delivery of LEO II machines appears in Appendix 5.

Experimenting in Automation

Interestingly, Lyons themselves did not adopt the policy that was followed, almost as a convention, by later users of computers. Instead of proceeding to use computers to handle the whole of their accounting work, they wisely decided to experiment with three main areas of the business to decide whether they could be automated and, if so, what effect this automation might have not only on office efficiency but also on business management.

Payroll had been the first full-scale application to be carried out; this had originally been chosen as the first subject of study, not so much for its accounting content, but because its requirements were precisely definable and performance could be measured accurately. Thus, if payroll could be undertaken successfully it would not only yield savings on a job that called for increasing staff, but would also establish that LEO could be deployed, with confidence, on other routine clerical work. As the volume of payroll work carried out on the computer steadily grew, it was readily accepted that the use of LEO on other office tasks would yield similar benefits. This success would soon be found to raise its own problems.

Management was keenly interested in putting LEO to work on applications that contributed more directly to the conduct of the business, with the intention not only of reducing labour costs, but, more importantly, of increasing the efficiency with which the business could be run. After very considerable thought, management boldly decided to select, as the second main application for LEO, the processing of teashop orders. This involved the replacement of the finely tuned clerical system that lay at the heart of the business. The efficient functioning of the teashops, the food production unit and the vast delivery fleet at Cadby Hall depended largely on the successful running of this job.

Every day each teashop, of which there were about 200, submitted its orders for goods to Cadby Hall for delivery the following morning. Thus, within 24 hours the total requirements for several hundred items had to be notified to the manufacturing departments and delivery instructions prepared to enable the goods to be made, assembled and loaded sequentially overnight for delivery to the shops for the start of the day's trade.

The existing system had been developed to a high degree of efficiency to provide a reliable means of processing the vast amount of data at low clerical cost. It was a simple system that had been honed with all the design skills that Lyons had developed between the wars to obtain the greatest efficiency at the least cost.

It was considered that this application would provide a searching test of the extent to which LEO could be used not merely as an instrument of clerical cost saving but as a true management tool. The study was started in 1953, even before payroll had been put into full-scale operation, to ensure that when it succeeded a further advance could be made without delay.

The study soon confirmed that the existing system was economic and that there was little, if any, opportunity to make savings on the scale of payroll. However, a close examination of the teashops, the despatch department and the factories, along with discussions with management, revealed that although the existing system satisfied the logistic needs of ensuring that the goods ordered were provided to the teashops on time each morning, there were some problems and difficulties that might well be solved by using a computer.

In dealing with the mass of data submitted each day (over a hundred items ordered by each teashop) the system provided for the operational needs, but it could not, at any reasonable cost, simultaneously produce any management reports in significant detail. Thus, although the total value of deliveries to each shop and the total demand for each line were known, it was not possible to detect and report any significant changes in ordering patterns or trends in trading, nor was any information available that would enable the performance of the shops to be monitored. Such information was available only, if at all, after the event, by the subsequent analysis of records, which involved considerable cost, without enabling management to intervene in events to affect their outcome.

Because of the time constraints of the system the shop manageresses had to carry out the time-consuming job of entering their requirements on the pre-printed order sheets early in the morning of the day before the goods were required. Not only did they feel that a better judgement could have been made later in the day, but they considered that this task came at a time—the start of trade for the day—when their attention should have been directed to the management of the shop. A further problem that became apparent in the shops was the level of wastage (goods unsold at the end of the day). This, it was clear, had led to widespread under-ordering, for it was observed that many lines were sold out long before the shops closed.

In the consideration of these problems and possible ways of meeting them in a new computer system, another factor was significant; it had been noted that in originating their orders manageresses often referred to the previous week's orders. Further investigation confirmed that the order quantities for a shop followed a repetitive pattern, with variations to allow for weather changes and special circumstances. The new system, therefore, was planned to work on the basis of monthly standing orders from the shops; this would reduce the time spent by manageresses on originating orders, and would not distract them during the busy morning period.

Clearly, the use of a static standing order alone would have been too inflexible, so it was decided to give manageresses and management the means of submitting changes each day; management could modify the standing order if weather or other circumstances required and manageresses could add or delete their variable requirements. Since the processing of the information would be much faster in the new system, these changes would not need to be submitted until the afternoon before delivery. To speed the processing the changes were to be submitted by telephone to operators who would punch them directly on to punch cards and check their accuracy by reading the card contents back to the manageresses. These changes would then be processed against the standing orders, which might also have been modified, held by LEO to produce the production, loading and despatch schedules needed to supply the shops in time for next morning's breakfast trade. A weather correction factor was also introduced, which enabled Head Office to increase or reduce teashop orders by a percentage factor. Later, management learned that the same facility could be used to modify the standing order when the availability of products was affected by production shortfall: an ingenious and unforeseen mechanism to control allocation.

It was now possible, based on the standing orders, to provide management with timely reports identifying any significant changes in the trading patterns to be expected in the next month. Facilities were also incorporated in the programs to enable management to specify the levels of significance to be applied, to avoid the presentation of excessively detailed reports. Further similar but briefer reports based on the changes were produced daily.

This application was the first pseudo on-line commercial system to be run on a computer: LEO constituted an integral part of the daily operation to supply the teashops. Moreover, it provided management with information that allowed them to take action on the basis of knowledge of what was planned before it became history. LEO was now being used as a management tool, not just as a clerical processor, and the teashops job was the forerunner of integrated data processing, before that phrase was coined.

However, the time constraints of this job were severe and the computer was not infallible, so the system had to be supported by a manual fall-back method to be used in the event of failure. Thus, in practice, higher overall costs than those of the previous manual system were incurred, both because of the need for backup and because extra punch operators were needed. Although it was true that the new system provided management information of significant value, and the shop manageresses found that it relieved them of a considerable burden, LEO had originally been regarded as a means of reducing clerical costs and the management responsible for the teashop operating budget refused to accept any additional cost over that of the old system. In addition, some manageresses did not take kindly to the new method of computer ordering. They were eligible for bonus payments if their takings tallied with the value of goods ordered when returns were taken into account. Since the computer held the retail price of each item sold in the teashops it, too, could produce this information, which had the effect of reducing some bonus payments. The accuracy of the computer was challenged on at least one occasion, but a manual check by the Audit Office confirmed that the computer was 100% accurate, much to the displeasure of the manageress, and that it could henceforth be relied upon. Simmons and his O & M staff were convinced that the application was successful and that the extra cost was well justified. So, to avoid damaging morale, the excess cost was absorbed in the LEO budget; in time, as clerical salaries increased, the cost difference diminished and the subsidy was discontinued.

Tea sales had grown dramatically and contributed substantially to group profits and it was not surprising, therefore, that the third area that the Company addressed was the analysis of tea stocks. This was a weekly job that maintained a detailed control over the company's unblended (bulk tea in the warehouse) tea stocks, which consisted of many grades and classifications. It controlled the issues of tea from the warehouse to the factory and compared the actual average cost of producing a blend, such as Orange Label or Quick Brew, with the standard budget cost. The computer was used to find the optimum blend at the best price, a process that involved a mass of calculations.

It would not have been possible by conventional clerical means to analyse and manipulate a similar volume of data and to have modelled such comprehensive strategies in the time at the disposal of management. In addition, the analysis of historical information provided the marketing and sales departments with new information, particularly in identifying the subtle consumer trends that took place after the war in the different regions of the country.

Not all jobs computerised on the early LEO machines were successful. An early sales ledger/invoicing application for Lyons Catering Industries, known as L22—LEO's 22nd job—was returned to a manual operation to avoid complete loss of control. For twelve months, ledger clerks had struggled desperately to get to grips with the computerised results, but the inflexibilities of design defeated their attempts. Stationery design, in particular, received widespread criticism from users, who found the information unintelligible to varying degrees. The lack of any facility to deal with alphabetical notation on printed output resulted in much numerical coding; this caused many queries and was a great hindrance to efficiency. The problem was partially solved by providing the clerks with clear plastic overlays, a form of template, which had field descriptions etched onto them so that the numeric printout could be interpreted. (Such devices were used for other computer jobs such as payroll.) The number of lines on an invoice frequently exceeded the limits allowed for in the computer programs; this again increased the number of queries to intolerable levels. Accounts could only be opened on one run per week, where previously the manual operation had permitted this to happen at any time. Despite the

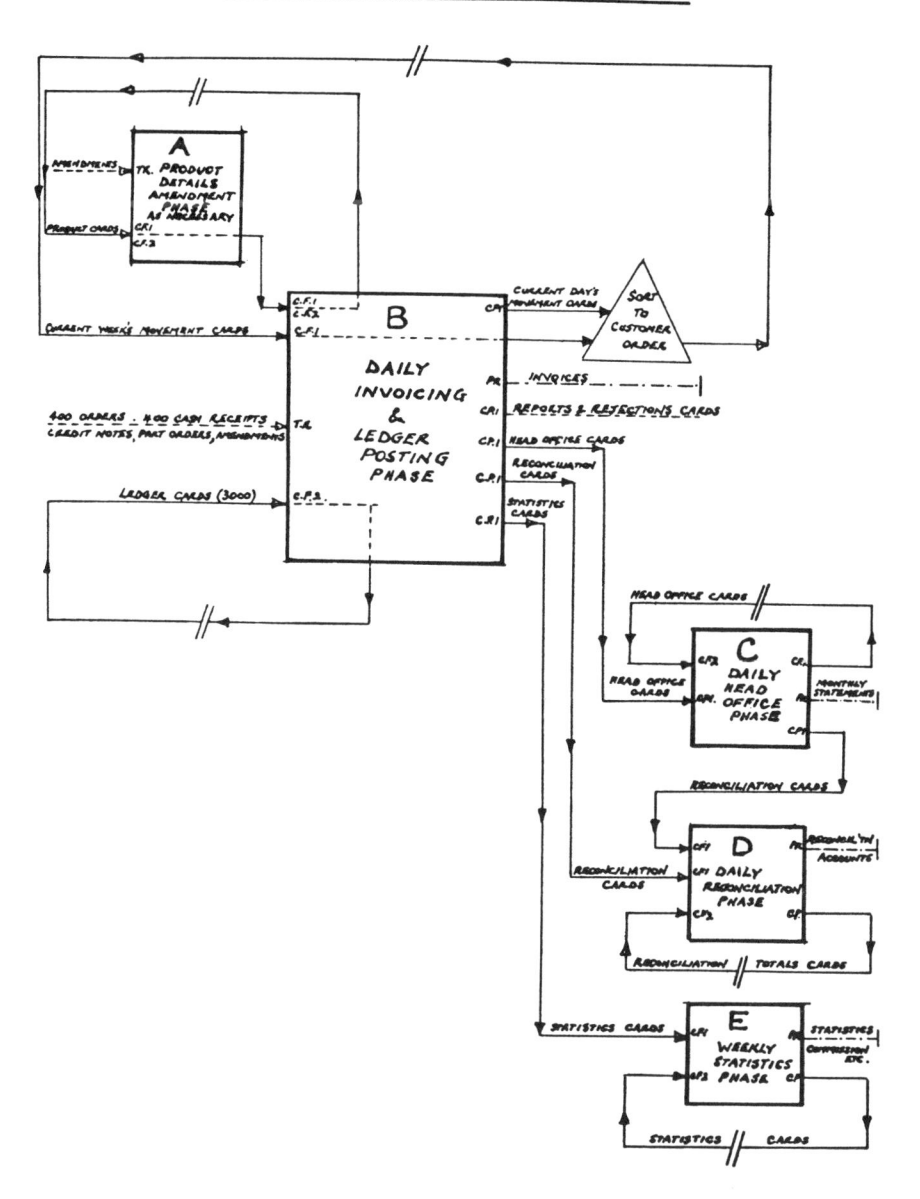

Fig. 4.2 Part of the system flow chart of the disastrous L22 job.
By kind permission of J. Lyons & Co Ltd.

enormous strain placed on the sales ledger office the dogged staff maintained control of monies owed, but the return to a manual operation, notwithstanding the costs so far involved, was deemed essential. The job had been fundamentally misconceived but its failure was not entirely due to this. There was also a strong element of passive resistance from some staff, almost to the point of effectively sabotaging the operation; in part this arose from their not being involved in the design. Fortunately, such failures were rare and in this instance the problems arose mainly from the over-ambitiousness of the system designers and their lack of understanding of the clerical procedures in the first place.

Some departments, as they became computerised, also exhibited a mild degree of hostility. This was largely the result of the rapid pace of automation and because there had been insufficient co-operation between the computer teams and the line departments in deciding what jobs should be computerised, or how computerisation should be approached. Some older Lyons' managers considered the new breed of computer experts too academic and too cavalier in their attitudes towards user department problems and needs. This meant that many managers developed an in-built aversion to computers that was difficult to overcome in later years. Some held the view that too much emphasis was given to attaining technical progress as opposed to meeting management's needs. On the management side, the traditional barriers were difficult to dismantle.

During 1961 there was a period of consolidation within Lyons while the company considered carefully the progress that had been made to date in the use of automation. Originally, automation was conceived as the method that would relieve the repetitive and uneconomic nature of clerical work, and this it did very successfully. The success of the teashop and tea stock analysis jobs also demonstrated convincingly that the power and versatility of the computer could also be harnessed to improve management decision-making, although some managers still harboured doubts on this score. Despite early concerns, the more informed realised that LEO was not just another tool to improve clerical efficiency, as the calculator and punched card had done in a previous era: it was a device by which top management themselves could better control the business.

The First Multiprogramming Computer

LEO I had by now been working for ten years (1951–1961), or a little less if the first two or three experimental years are discounted. It could not work for ever, and Lyons felt that at best fifteen years would be a prudent life cycle. LEO II/1 was already in use and this would become fully loaded when the first machine was retired.

By 1961 Leo Computers Ltd had completed the development of the next generation computer, known as LEO III. It was one hundred times faster than LEO I and for the first time an operating system, known in LEO as the Master Routine, was used to control its sophisticated features. LEO III bore little resemblance to its predecessors, other than in name, and when first shown could claim to be the only truly multi-programming computer commercially available. Well ahead of its time, it incorporated many new features, some of which would be adopted throughout the computer industry. It was a fully transistorised business computing system capable of undertaking up to 13 jobs simultaneously, although in practice rarely more than three jobs were run concurrently.

This job sharing capability, known as time sharing, was derived from the use of interrupt commands written into a program, which could enable the machine to divert its attention to another program if the first program had to pause for data transfer or another peripheral action to take place. (The word "peripheral" in this context means a peripheral device such as paper tape reader, card reader, printer or any other connected facility.) To prevent the information used for one program corrupting that of another, reservations could be specified by the users to allocate storage space for a specific purpose; additionally, each area of the store was automatically tagged for use by only one concurrent task. LEO III had been designed to handle the commonly-used numerical notations such as decimal and sterling, and even tonnes, hundredweights and quarters could be accommodated. Information could be read into the computer from a variety of devices: the more commonly used were punched cards, punched paper tape, magnetic tape and later mark-reading machines such as Lector and Autolector. Peripheral devices were connected to assemblers by physical connections known as routes; there were up to eight routes on each assembler so that eight devices could be serviced simultaneously from each assembler. The connection from the assembler to the computer was called a channel. An input assembler sought access to the store when it had obtained one word from a peripheral device, and would automatically obtain a further word when its existing contents had been discharged into the store. Similarly an output assembler sought access to the store for another word when the processed one had been successfully discharged to an output peripheral device such as a printer. In this way the channels operated autonomously in parallel with the central processor.

Each part of the system made demands for access to the store. The Store Access Control unit resolved the possible conflicts between these demands; by providing automatic priority, it ensured that those units that had the most urgent need obtained most rapid access to the store. The system was so organised that an input or output channel would never be kept waiting for longer than the connected peripheral unit would tolerate. Priority was given to the faster devices such as magnetic tape drives.

The execution of instructions in the computer was controlled by the Co-ordinator, as in LEO I and LEO II. This unit initiated and interpreted in turn each instruction of a program and sent controlling signals to the arithmetic registers and to other parts of the computer to achieve its execution.

Another innovative feature of the LEO III machine was its use of microprograms. These were permanently installed algorithms that governed fundamental machine operations; they had been used in the EMIDEC 1100 computer in 1957–1958 and before that on the Cambridge machine that succeeded EDSAC (EDSAC 2). The sequence of steps required for each instruction, for example the addition of £.s.d or yards and inches, was defined by the pattern of wiring of a magnetic core plane in the co-ordinator. This was a flexible and highly efficient system, as planes could be built to control the automatic execution of complex procedures that would have taken much longer to execute by normal programming techniques. A typical LEO III would be equipped with ten microprogram modules, although the exact number would depend upon the particular applications for which the computer was intended. All peripherals were connected to assemblers that, on the input side, would take blocks of data and assemble them into words of 48 bits. These words were then passed to a store access control that routed them to the magnetic core memory. On the output side the reverse process applied. In the LEO III range of machines the memory consisted of up to four modules of 4,096 words of core storage.

The modular structure of the LEO III system enabled it to be adapted and developed into a family of machines. Components were interchangeable and the replacement and change of units could be carried out with the utmost speed. The family was developed into three models: the standard LEO III, LEO 360 and LEO 326. The three different store units had co-ordinator cycle times of 13.5, 6, and 2.5 microseconds, and the three arithmetic units had cycle times of 34, 12 and 5 microseconds. By installing the 2.5 microsecond processor and the 5 microsecond arithmetic unit, LEO III became the LEO 326, the fastest model in the range. The LEO 360 and LEO 326 were extended to allow up to eight divisions of storage and up to fourteen channels for the concurrent operation of one peripheral device per channel in parallel with the operation of the arithmetic unit. The increased speed of the faster models was achieved by improvements in the wire matrix microprogram assembly; condensing alphanumeric information for output to magnetic tape; removing all non-significant zeros; merging and sorting items from two sets of data into a single combined sequence; locating the information relating to a particular item in a stored table; converting data from one scale to another; and the provision of floating point arithmetic, although not initially, for mathematical work. A new random access disc file unit was made available for the two faster model machines, a single unit comprising 16 or 32 disc planes giving storage for 29.5 or 59 million characters with access times of 230 milliseconds and a peak transfer rate of 120,000 characters per second.

Magnetic tape, the usefulness of which had finally been proved beyond doubt on the later LEO IIs, was now the established backing storage medium, enabling more sophisticated system design of the type envisaged by Simmons and Caminer. Data could be stored, retrieved and interfaced with other external computer systems with much greater ease, and the integration of different systems began to develop. The magnetic tape units used on the LEO equipment were of American manufacture, their technology having now made an impact in the United Kingdom market. Both Ampex and Potter systems were used.

The line printers, too, were of American design and make, and were supplied by the ANelex Corporation. The printing mechanism was simple, consisting of a steel drum 4 inches in diameter and 16 inches long. The total length was made up of eight separate sections, each 2 inches long, with a full 64 character set mirror etched on its circumference. The drum revolved at high speed and print was obtained by hammers that were activated electromechanically against the inked ribbon and paper that passed between them and the print drum. High quality print of up to 1,000 lines per minute could be produced and it was possible to obtain a maximum of 160 characters across the width of the page; by comparison most current line printers can only provide for 132 print positions. Paper movement was controlled by a loop of 8-track perforated metallised tape attached to the movement mechanism. This could be altered by the operator to enable a variety of printing formats to be used. Up to five copies of stationery could be handled through the printer.

Pinkerton and Lenaerts had visited the ANelex Corporation in June and July 1961 and reported that their production arrangements were very efficient and well equipped. The majority of parts were made on hand tools in their workshops and offices in Boston and during their visit no mass production facilities were in evidence. Lyons were concerned, however, that ANelex would place their United Kingdom business with an agency who might be a computer manufacturing competitor. It was suggested to ANelex that Lyons would be prepared to take on an agency themselves but ANelex did not think that sales of 25–30 machines during 1961 and 1962 would warrant the setting up of such an organisation. In fact they felt that if an agency were placed in the hands of a computer manufacturer this would be likely to restrict sales to competitor organisations in the UK.

LEO III also had the capability of supporting up to eight concurrent data communication channels through Marconi paper tape conversion devices. These devices, known as Marconidata H6000, could transmit data to and from paper tape over normal Post Office public or private telephone circuits at 62½ characters per second. They worked with Post Office Datasets (modems) of a type known as 1A, but these communication facilities were not widely used; electronic communication in the early days of LEO had not yet been properly established.

Programs for LEO III were written in a language devised to express in simple terms the procedures to be carried out to do any job. This job language was independent of the computer's code of instructions, and when a program had been set down it could be translated into the computer code automatically using a special suite of programs known as a Compiler. This new CLEO (Clear Language for Expressing Orders) language brought about a dramatic improvement in program development since less skill was required in its use. The acronym

CLEO is said to have been suggested by Robert Gibson (Maintenance Training) in November 1960, although John Gosden, who helped to develop CLEO, also lays claim to this idea.

The first LEO III machine (LEO III/1) was delivered and successfully installed at Hartree House on 15 April 1962. After installation, and for some months to follow, irksome problems manifested themselves with the peripheral equipment, particularly the Ampex magnetic tape drives. By September the equipment was achieving only 72% availability:[4] this was 14% less than LEO I, now ten years old, was achieving at the same time. Many of these problems were of a mechanical nature and had not revealed themselves before. They were due to the fast running of the equipment. Brake shoes on the magnetic tape equipment deteriorated quickly, causing tape slippage and misalignment. The oxide coating on the magnetic tape itself caused a build-up of particles on read/write heads leading to read/write malfunction. Tape spools had a habit of falling off the model FR300 tape drives, a problem that was rectified in the later TM2 models. Engineers, too, were inexperienced and it was several weeks before they became fully proficient at adjusting tape, card and printer peripherals. It was suggested at one of the many management meetings (13 July 1962) that other users were able to operate similar card readers successfully and that Lyons' troubles were due to a lack of engineering knowledge, which could have been improved if they had visited some other card installations instead of undertaking development themselves. Up to 106 hours every week was allowed for these malfunctions, as well as for maintenance, modifications and software testing, leaving only 62 hours per week for operational work.

These setbacks obviously had an effect on the successful completion of computers in the production cycle and deliveries began to fall behind schedule. Most serious were the delays to the program testing of clients' software, which had not been anticipated or allowed for in the development schedules. Taking advantage of the increase in storage size, some programs were very large, with insufficient modularity, so that when a machine fault occurred long reruns were necessary to restore it to the point of failure. This exacerbated computer scheduling, causing delays to following or dependent jobs. Some customers became so infuriated they attempted to claim for loss of business because of the delay.[5]

These problems could not have come at a worse time: other manufacturers were beginning to make an impact in the United Kingdom market and the delays had an adverse effect on sales of both machines and service work. The magnetic tape difficulties eventually resulted in post-design work, including the fitting of voltage stabilisers and a reduction in operating speed to 120 inches per minute. The circuitry boards were also improved and a decision was taken to gold plate the connectors at the socket ends of these and replace all Ampex sockets by a new type, thus improving signal quality. Apart from the design and electrical difficulties of the Ampex tape equipment, more practical problems were manifesting themselves, and a condition known as cinching (sometimes termed pack slip) was occurring. Quite simply, the magnetic tape was being incorrectly rewound in the various computing tasks and as a result became damaged, making the information unreadable in subsequent operations. Cooling fans located in the magnetic tape cubicles were also failing at an unacceptable rate, and, because these units employed high energy vacuum tubes, overheating became a problem.

One interesting feature of this machine was the modification carried out to the input and output assembler and to one of the Ampex magnetic tape units to enable the machine to read the magnetic tape from the ICT Pegasus 2 computer. This facility was provided at the request of Shell Refining Company so that data could be automatically copied to LEO form in readiness for the LEO machines they were soon to order. Apart from the different logical arrangements and layout of data on the tape, the main novelty was the different type of read/write head and track spacing arrangements.

Despite the difficulties, all was not gloom. The first LEO III bureau work was carried out in September 1962 for the textile company Courtaulds, which involved the take-on of their first preference stockholders and the production of the account and transfer records, although not without incident. Due to a combination of program errors and a misoperation, some 800 payments were overlooked and a special computer run had to be undertaken to incorporate these.

Going Further Afield

The first sale and installation of a LEO III computer outside the Lyons group occurred 6,000 miles away in Johannesburg, South Africa during May 1962, and was a more successful and happier event. As long ago as 1959 Leo Computers had considered the possibility of export orders and had correctly concluded that if progress were to be made in this direction it would be necessary to establish an overseas office. It was agreed that the South African and Australian markets showed most promise, and in South Africa, Johannesburg was chosen since this was the centre of the gold mining industry and near to the Government Offices at Pretoria. They were able, of course, to make use of the already established Lyons South African Subsidiary. Thompson made a trip to South Africa in May 1960 and his itinerary was well planned. Arrangements had been made for him to lecture to the Computer Society of South Africa, the Chartered Institute of Secretaries, the Transvaal Society of Accountants and the National Development Foundation, before going on to Australia.

As a result of his trip, Leo Computer Services (Pty) Ltd was established, on 20 June 1960, with share capital of R960,000. This was a subsidiary jointly owned with Rand Mines Ltd (31.25%), Central Mining Finance Ltd (6.875%), Transvaal Consolidated Land and Exploration Co. Ltd (6.875%) and Leo Computers Ltd (31.25%). It was to this company that the South African machine was delivered. Fantl had been instrumental in the tender to Rand Mines Ltd in 1959, which was for an in-house bureau, intended to process the administration functions for the Rand Group and to offer bureau operations to other outside concerns as well as becoming a marketing agency for LEO computers to South and Central Africa. The tender was successful and signed by Caminer in May 1960, but Lyons were committed to send out a Bureau Manager with the machine. Fantl's wife had died tragically in an accident that year, and, with his customary insight, Caminer felt that a change of scene would be good for Fantl, who agreed to go. The computer was air freighted to South Africa on 18 May 1962 on a KLM DC7f aircraft via Kano, on a charter contract price of £9,821. Air transport was chosen for three main reasons: first it was felt that less damage would occur to the equipment, second there would be a saving on staff salaries, and third there were savings of £2,000 in bank interest charges. Fantl left for Johannesburg on 2 June 1960.

A brand new building was put up for the machine at 36 Anderson Street, Johannesburg and recommissioning work started on the afternoon of 22 May 1962. Rand Mines had guaranteed their staff that no one would be made redundant because of the computer and, in support of that policy, anyone interested was interviewed for positions with LEO. Fantl put all the more promising candidates through the LEO appreciation course, which lasted a whole day. After the first year he had tested over 1,000 applicants. Not everyone, of course, was accepted—many had come along out of curiosity. Fantl records that three of the successful persons who joined that year (Barbara Chelius, Bob Day and Faith van Rooyen) still work in the Rand computer office.

The installation of the LEO computer was undertaken by Tony Morgan and Arthur Clements, both experienced installation engineers who had worked for Leo Computers since 1957. The first computer programs were very difficult and at one stage Fantl did not think that the machine could handle all the work; a not uncommon initial situation in computing circles. After much tuning and refining he was not only able to handle all the Rand Mines Group work but also that of other groups as a bureau operation including Cape Asbestos, Union Corporation and Anglo-Vaal Group, who between them owned some 56 mines.

The next LEO III order came from the Dunlop Rubber Company and was only secured after frantic telephone calls. Lyons had worked hard with the Dunlop team, over a long period of time, helping to specify their business requirements, and had received a letter of intent for a LEO III configuration. Twenty-four hours before the order was expected to be signed, however, the Leo consultants learned that IBM were on the verge of securing the contract by devious business means. Now, it so happened that the Dunlop Chairman was Sir Edward Beharrell, a cousin of Anthony Salmon, and after private telephone calls were made to his home, by the Lyons Chairman Sir Norman Joseph, Beharrell promised to investigate the matter. The IBM decision was reversed and Lyons eventually won the business. The relationship between Lyons and the Dunlop company did not suffer, in fact one of Lyons' managers, Peter Herman, joined Dunlop to take charge of their data processing and Dunlop went on to place another LEO III order three years later.

The Master Plan

At this time Lyons gave considerable thought as to how they should proceed in their continuing use of computers, Caminer by this time had

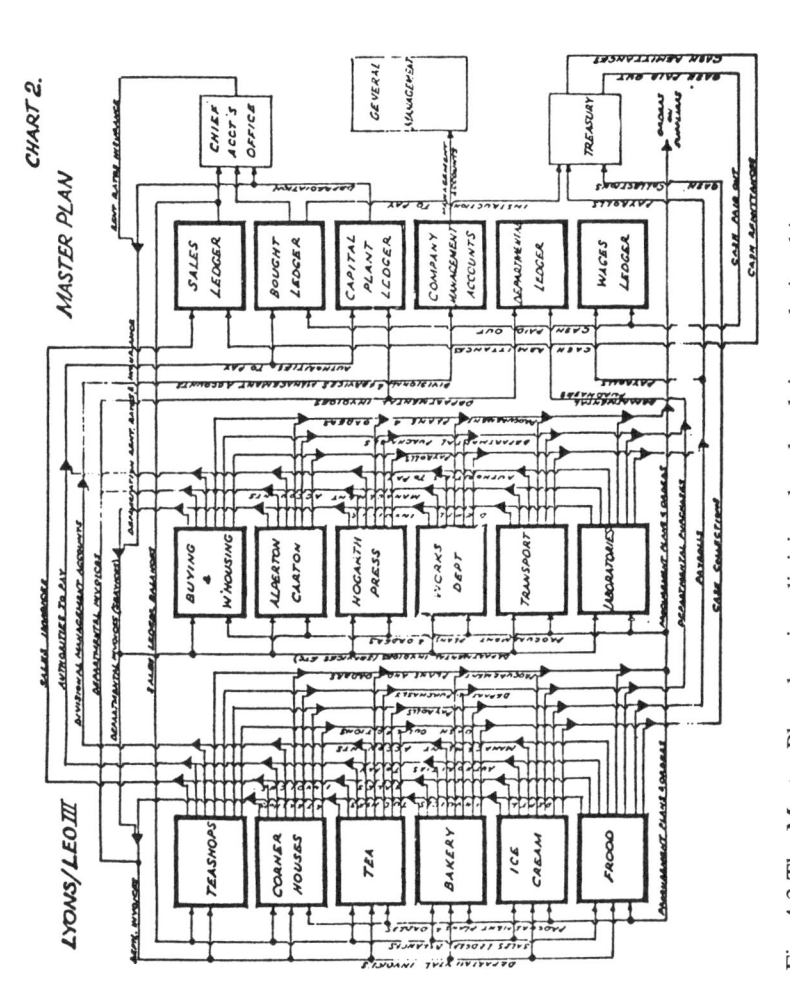

Fig. 4.3 The Master Plan showing divisional and task interrelationships.
By kind permission of J. Lyons & Co Ltd.

had been transferred to take up the full marketing responsibilities within Leo Computers Ltd. The result of their consideration, led by Simmons, was the creation of what became known as the "Master Plan". This plan was not merely to install yet another computer but rather to carry out a series of interrelated divisional business applications, linked together by the use of the computer. The project was ambitiously designed in three stages that would take three to five years to carry out and cost £1 million (initially £500,000).[6] To offset this considerable expenditure Simmons was convinced that savings could be made in clerical labour and servicing of stock within the divisions. In the Divisional Comptrollers and Management Accounting Offices alone, 1,800 clerks were employed at a cost in excess of £1,350,000 p.a. An unknown number were employed in other areas of the Company. The plan, submitted by Simmons in April 1961, comprised three separate proposals.

The first suggested that a study be undertaken to investigate possible applications for a new computer, the LEO III. The second proposed that Lyons should plan to install a LEO III computer and have it operating by 1963. The third and final proposal was for Lyons to continue to computerise business tasks until a fully integrated system had been accomplished with all linkages (see Figure 4.3). It was the first attempt at what would now be called a Management Information System, although of course in the early 1960s the use of information databases was not fully understood, nor had they been developed to any significant extent. Simmons published a book in 1962 entitled *LEO and the Managers*, in which he set down his ideas. Some said, rather unkindly, that his book had a manager blind spot, in that it took no account of the manager's view of LEO. The so-called Master Plan discussed in his book was primarily the idea of the O & M Department, with little or no input from line managers.

The first part of the plan, the study to investigate possible applications for a new computer, was completed in December 1961. This study, undertaken by the O & M Office, identified several possible new computer applications, which, if implemented, would show considerable clerical economies. Seven of the new clerical applications studied identified savings of more than 500 jobs.[7] The savings from these alone were sufficient to recover the capital cost of the project and the preliminary and operating costs involved; this would amount to just over £500,000 over the 4-year period of the project.[8] The cost of a clerk was taken as £500 per annum, but a higher value was used in calculating the clerical needs for the new computer system since higher grade clerical staff would be required.

The feasibility of the new computer project and the cost reductions that would result from it depended to a very great extent upon the development of new equipment that would reduce the cost of handling the huge volumes of data involved. Optical page readers were still at the experimental stage but Leo Computers had worked intensively on their development and were confident that they could fulfil their place in the new systems under consideration.

By June 1962 orders for 13 of the new LEO III machines had been taken from customers outside the Lyons Group for delivery over the next two years, each being the result of close study by the LEO consultants. With each costing between £150,000 and £350,000, depending on model and configuration, the value of these orders exceeded £3,000,000. The Lyons Board discussed the prospect of another machine on the basis of seven new jobs and agreed to place an order for a LEO III on 21 December 1961. They did not take delivery of their LEO III/7 machine until 31 March 1963, at a cost of £277,000 and it went into operation during early May, with document readers following in mid-May. The first pioneering jobs planned for LEO III/7 were two Ice Cream jobs known as Sales Records and Operations Control (L301 and L302) but both of these were delayed by over a year because of a merger of ice cream businesses and subsequently became very much larger than first anticipated. However, other rationalisations in the Tea and Bakery Divisions gave rise to greater volumes of computer work and the losses arising out of the Ice Cream job were more than compensated for by the other work. Thus, Lyons proceeded at great speed to implement their Master Plan, with the computerisation of seven new applications encompassing twelve separate Operating Divisions and Service Departments with their complicated interlinking financial systems.

An appraisal report suggested that substantial clerical savings could be made by computerising Tea Sales Records. The report showed that the cost of routine clerical work associated with the distribution and sales operation could be reduced from £1,200 a week to £480 a week using the LEO system. The difference, £720 per week, amounted to £37,000 in a full year of operation.

Similarly, the Bakery Rounds Sales Records identified a possible saving in clerical costs of £960 per week, or £50,000 in a full year, and Ice Cream Sales Records showed a potential saving of £80,000 a year. All the systems studied offered the possibility of considerable savings in clerical labour alone, without taking account of the further savings that would result in the automatic feeding of business transactions into the accounting programs. Over the next four or five years the Lyons programming department worked intensively on the Master Plan and the programming office was considerably enlarged.

The Master Plan was to be carried out by systems development teams assigned to each of the four trading Divisions of the company: Bakery, Ice Cream, Teashops and Central Accounts. Senior O & M managers were responsible for planning the necessary business information flows and clerical procedures within the total strategy, and specified what results had to be produced. A senior programming manager in each team was responsible for designing file structures and processing logic.

Some 50 persons were employed on the Lyons systems development and maintenance tasks by the mid-1960s, not including operators and other support staff. Whereas the responsibilities of programmers, operators and engineers had by now crystallised, a need for new staff positions was identified, for example, magnetic tape librarian, job assembly clerks and query clerks for handling the error rejections from automatic document handling machines (see Chapter 5). Lyons had at least by then moved on from serried ranks of attractive young ladies bashing away at paper tape and card punch keyboards.

At this time Simmons recognised that the work which was about to be undertaken would affect the great majority of managers throughout the Lyons organisation. This work should be seen as a personal service, not as being provided by an impersonal master. He proposed, therefore, the establishment of a LEO Divisions Service Manager responsible for maintaining a link with those managers providing data to the computer or entitled to receive results from it and dealing with any queries or problems that would arise. The person appointed to this task was Joe Wilmott (1910–1993).

The development teams collaborated to try to ensure that the Master Plan went ahead as rapidly as possible across all the Divisions. The approach was that each major application would be installed in one or two Divisions and then, when successfully operational, the basic logic and procedures would be modified comparatively quickly for use in the remaining Divisions. So the Tea and Bakery teams concentrated on order processing, invoicing and sales statistic systems; Ice Cream took production, stock control and distribution control; the Central Accounts team concentrated on payroll and ledger systems. The decision on priority and team allocation was dictated partly by the size of potential immediate benefits to the business and partly by the need to redesign some older LEO I and LEO II systems. Payroll and Tea Original Stocks were, for example, high priorities for transfer from the older machines: the Bakery rails job, in contrast, was allowed to fade away with LEO I because of the shift in business from rail to road delivery.

It was a time of great excitement and challenge, with the Master Plan seen almost as a Holy Grail, the equivalent of today's integrated information system. With hindsight, the seeds of failure had already been sown. The design concepts behind the Lyons Master Plan demanded processing power that even the advanced LEO III, with its high speed input and output peripherals, could not deliver. There was a particular problem with the rapid access to large amounts of data. The magnetic discs and tape transports of the time were not up to the task (in any case Lyons did not use magnetic discs on the LEO machines) and as for terminals on managers' desks, they were not even a gleam in the eye. So systems were delayed and, when finally in place, struggled to meet business timetables or failed to satisfy unrealistically high expectations.

The pioneering nature of this early computing was to cause some difficulties in the development of computing applications in later years. Because the work was new, senior management, at each stage of development, took vital decisions without being able to foresee all the problems that would arise. There were discrepancies between the objectives of the computer specialists and those of the line managers. These conflicts were exacerbated by communication difficulties, as the language of computers was too new for some general managers to comprehend. Some advanced systems did reach an operational stage but as the 1960s passed the Master Plan faltered and faded, and the magic was gone. It remains still, a memorial to the imagination of Simmons, its author.

The sale of computers continued during this internal Master Plan phase but the computer subsidiary was successful in manufacturing a total of only fifty-nine LEO computers despite the phenomenal efforts of the marketing team. Of these, four were exported to Australia, two to South Africa and three to Czechoslovakia. Tenders were prepared for Poland and Brazil but these were not successful. For the Australian market, which Lyons thought had good potential, a subsidiary company was formed (Australian Computers Proprietary Ltd) and Peter Gyngell was appointed General Manager. Through this offshoot two machines were delivered to Shell Australia and one each to Tubemakers Pty in Sydney, a subsidiary of Stewarts & Lloyds, and the Colonial Mutual Life Assurance Society, whose offices were at 330 Collins Street, Melbourne. The cost of Colonial Mutual's machine was £240,754 (sterling) plus an additional amount for taxes, duty, shipping and installation. The Colonial Mutual company had made its entry into electronic computers in May 1958 when they installed a Powers-Samas punched card computer to handle a variety of office work, and in so doing became the first life office in Australia to use a computer. This initial machine, although restricted to accepting information and putting results out in punched card form, nevertheless enabled the company to move from mechanical manipulation of punched card information to electronic data processing.

Their LEO III machine was delivered in September 1964 and was soon put to work by a small group of nine system analysts and programmers under the direction of Peter Murton, who is still with the company. The first job designed for LEO was the processing of the main policies that enabled actuarial valuations to be made on several valuations on different bases before declaring the surplus in any year. Policy renewal and billing, agents' commission and payroll were added, and the systems themselves became dependent on each other. By 1973 a 2½ year conversion was completed and the Society transferred their systems to a Burroughs B6700 computer using disc files and video terminals that were not available on LEO.

The Shell Group in Australia installed two LEO III machines after a comprehensive study of six other manufacturers. Their first machine, LEO III/15, was handed over by the Managing Director of J. Lyons & Company Ltd, Sir Samuel Salmon (1900–1980), to the Shell Directors in August 1964 at their Melbourne offices; the configuration had cost £A235,434.

After the handover the machine played a few bars of Waltzing Matilda and then worked on four programs simultaneously. Among those present at the ceremony were Sir George Paton and Dr Louis Matheson, vice-chancellors of the Universities of Melbourne and Monash, respectively, Dr Frank Hirst, President of the Victorian Computer

Society (now the Australian Computer Society), and Mr Allan Spowers, CMG, DSO, MC (1892–1968), Chairman of the Colonial Mutual Life Assurance Society.

An extract taken from Shell's computer study of July 1962 which recommended the LEO equipment reads:

Leo Computers have established an excellent reputation in the U.K. for successful installations of computers and have been known to refuse to supply where they considered that the chances of success were not good. The people we have dealt with here have impressed us more than representatives of any other company, and we know that a similar impression has been registered with other potential users with whom they have had discussions.

The report submitted by Leo Computers was by far the best of any, confirming the already favourable impression we had gained of local personnel. Its content demonstrated imagination, as well as computer knowledge and hard work.

The first Australian delivery, however, was made in 1963 to Tubemakers of Australia Ltd, a company whose major shareholder was Stewarts & Lloyds. They built a new computer facility at Botany, a suburb of Sydney, to house it. The manager in charge of the computer facility at this time was Alex Mackie and he was assisted by Alan Corbett (Operations Manager), Barry Baird (O & M Manager), and Graham Smith (Chief Programmer); Graham Smith now lectures in computer studies at the University of New South Wales. As well as being used for Tubemakers' own work the LEO III/8 was also used, initially, by Leo Computers Australia as a service bureau providing a range of services during the evening and night when the machine was not required by Tubemakers. Under these arrangements the bureau provided all Tubemakers' operations staff for many years. The Tubemakers LEO III computer was taken out of service in 1977, with 87,279 hours on the hours-run clock, and sold as scrap to the maintenance engineers, who shared in a metal recovery project. This was the fate of so many of the computers of this era; gold and other precious metals used in some of the components at the manufacturing stage increased their scrap value considerably.

The first Czechoslovakian machine was delivered to the State Railways, Vypocetni Laborator Dopravy (VLD), the second to the Klementa Gottwalda Steelworks (NHKG), and the third to the office of Social Security, Ustredi Duchodoveho Zabezpeceni (UDZ). These machines were used for more than ten years and Jiri Petru, Data Processing Department Manager at the Klementa Gottwalda Steelworks, claims that the LEO era was the most successful in his company's automation history. Between May 1966 and the end of 1977 the LEO machine was engaged in many commercial and scientific tasks, 24 hours a day, providing computer services for the steel mill, rolling mill, tube mill and engineering plant. The machine was very reliable and the Czechoslovakian engineers, who had been trained in Britain, could cope with every eventuality. Both user departments and management were very satisfied with the machine's performance and capabilities, and when it was decided to replace it, it was broken down and its parts used by the other Czechoslovakian LEO users. One LEO III computer was even shown at the Prague Exhibition in 1966 and another at the Moscow Exhibition of 1967; this maintained Lyons' tradition of attending—though not now for catering—international exhibitions.

The General Post Office (GPO) placed the largest order for LEO III machines, ordering fourteen to undertake telephone billing and other clerical tasks in their National Data Processing Service (NDPS) centres throughout the country. In 1968, after production of LEO computers had stopped, it had to be restarted to satisfy the GPO's urgent need for more machines, a request that could hardly be denied. Her Majesty's Dockyards were also a large user of LEO III equipment and took delivery of four machines that were installed in separate dockyards throughout the United Kingdom. A comprehensive list of companies who took delivery of the LEO III machines appears in Appendix 8.

There are many stories about the system testing, installation and commissioning of the machines from Minerva Road. Surprisingly, there were no formalised procedures or instructions for testing the equipment. A Senior Commissioning Engineer was responsible for the complete process, from the initial switch-on in the factory to final acceptance at the customer's site, and the success of the operation depended on his skill, experience and ingenuity. Other test engineers reported to him, and his team was assembled in the factory to work with him and gain experience after their formal training. In the later stages of the system testing phase, which normally lasted three or four weeks, a team of Commissioning Operators were let loose to run a multiprogramming suite of programs for factory acceptance. The final stage of the testing procedure was the running of the customer's own programs, during which time it was essential that the machine did not fail. These final trials lasted about a week. The author remembers that during 1966 when he attended the last day of trials for the second Lyons machine, LEO III/46, the heavens opened and it poured with rain. After a short time rain started pouring though the roof of the rather old buildings, flooding most of the production area and the machines under test. Some buckets and other strategically-placed receptacles saved the day and the trials were completed satisfactorily, although most machines suffered considerable wetting, fortunately without sustaining serious damage.

Due to the multiple pitched roof construction (with guttering between) and given the vagaries of the British climate, flooding occurred more than once. Apparently when this occurred industrial heaters, hair dryers and other forms of LEO ingenuity were used to dry machines out so that production and testing could be continued with the minimum of delay. Only towards the end of the production days at Minerva Road were the premises waterproofed and air conditioned. It was always difficult to justify to visiting customers why they needed to invest in special clean, air-conditioned premises when the production facilities were less than satisfactory. The normal ingenious explanation was that the machines were being tested in the worst possible conditions so they were sure to work in the recommended favourable operating environment! The truth was that in the early days investment in such equipment was prohibitively costly, and space was at a premium; when the project eventually went ahead it was a major logistical exercise to free the area in two phases and keep the manufacturing and testing process going. At the high point of production in 1967, ten machines were being dealt with, eight in the factory and two on customers' sites.

Some early machines were installed in temporary accommodation while awaiting the construction of customers' computer rooms. One of the more bizarre temporary locations was that of LEO III/4, destined for London Boroughs Joint Computer Committee at Greenwich, which cost £312,000. It had been installed in a temporary home in the Board Room of the old Licensed Victuallers Alms Houses building in Asylum Road, Peckham. Surrounded by the debris of the walls that had been partly demolished to get it in and with no air-conditioning, the machine had to be switched off frequently and the skylights opened to allow it to cool.

CHAPTER 5

Further automation improvements

The transcription of information from original commercial forms into a medium that can be read by machine accounts for the greater part of the manual effort associated with electronic data processing. Moreover, because this work is undertaken manually, stringent methods have to be adopted to ensure the accuracy of the transcribed data; for LEO this work was undertaken by a large keypunch and verification department, and a major project under consideration by Lyons just prior to the time of the author's engagement (1964) was the automation of data input.

For a long time it had been recognised that the most efficient method of gathering data would be to arrange for it to be recorded at the outset in a form that could be understood by machine. Not only would this speed up the handling processes by eliminating the transcription stage, it would also result in a reduction in administration costs.

Broido's Tabulator 7

This approach to data entry, known simply as single entry, had been a vision of Lyons for many years, and their quest for a machine to read pencil entries from source documents had started before World War II. During 1941–1942 clerical labour became acutely scarce, because of the war effort, and Lyons became excited about a little known machine, the Tabulator 7, which had been developed by Daniel Broido (1903–1990) while he was working as Managing Director and Chief Engineer for Olding Developments Ltd, a subsidiary of Jack Olding & Company of Hatfield. Broido, born in the Siberian town of Kirensk while his parents were in exile for their political beliefs, was educated at the Technical University Berlin, where he obtained his degree in mechanical engineering. He worked for the General Electric Company (AEG) and then for Rotaprint in Berlin, who sent him to London in 1934 to work at their London office, after which he joined Olding Developments Ltd. He took out British nationality in 1946.

Broido's Tabulator 7 invention had been designed to read printed or hand-marked restaurant checks or tickets and he considered it an ideal device for reading the many thousands of waitresses bills generated in the two hundred or so teashops Lyons were operating at that time. He approached them with his idea. Essentially the same arrangement could be used for the automatic analysis and tabulation of other marked documents such as payroll time cards, meter documents and the like. It was the first fully automatic optical mark sensing machine of its kind, and its design incorporated three basic elements: a paper feed mechanism, photoelectric registers and a printing mechanism. Sales slips could be read through the machine at 7,200 per hour and the information on them (amount of cash, number of customers and other details), represented by marks in certain index areas of the tickets, would be accumulated, verified and compared with the hash total which had also been entered by the waitress. Any discrepancy between the two would be reported. The machine could also count the number of tickets read

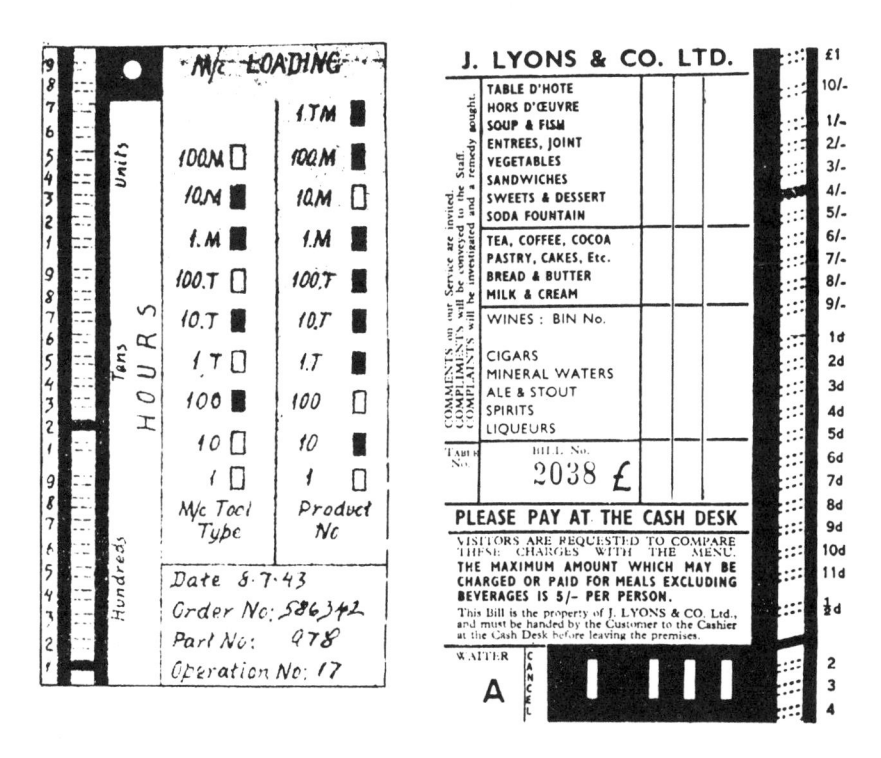

Fig. 5.1 Broido's waitress check design, July 1943.
By kind permission of Daniel Broido.

and any reference number(s) for batching or control purposes. Later, in his patent specification (No. 551,025) diagrams for Tabulator 7, Broido used a copy of a Lyons teashop bill in his submissions to the Patents Office. See Figure 5.1.

Preliminary discussions with Broido indicated that his machine could be adapted for reading teashop checks and, encouraged by their early assessment, Lyons decided to install a prototype Tabulator 7 machine at Cadby Hall to test the device further, particularly the marking process. They had two main objectives in mind: first, they wanted to satisfy themselves that the teashop waiting staff could adapt to the technology and cope with the new method of bill preparation in a busy teashop environment. Second, management needed copper-bottom guarantees that the machine was reliable enough to enable them to dispense with the manual arithmetical task of dealing with the many thousands of slips created each week. Their evaluation was very thorough, as always, and a variety of paper qualities, such as were available during World War II, and pencil types were tested, even Broido says, toilet paper. Approximately 100 staff from the capital's teashops were trained for the field trials, and to the managements' surprise they adapted to the new method of marking with little difficulty.

However, while the staff training and marking trials were considered a success, the machine itself proved to be unpredictable and less than satisfactory; at this early stage of technology the optical reading mechanism was not reliable enough although the principle itself was sound. By 1945, because of continuing labour shortages and in an effort to improve productivity, Lyons had taken the radical decision to replace the famous Nippy waitress with self-service counters in their teashops, and the need for check mechanisation disappeared.

Nevertheless, Broido continued working on his inventions. In 1950 Olding Developments was sold to the British Tabulating Machine Company and all his inventions and patents were transferred to them. He became one of their development engineers and continued working on all types of optical reading devices, becoming a pioneer in this field, with over 100 patents to his credit.

By now Lyons had turned their attentions to the development of the LEO computer and by the mid-1950s, with the increased speed and sophistication of equipment then emerging, again turned to finding a method to do away with the formidable barrier between the machine and users, and to improve the process of submitting data to the computer. In June 1956 Thompson recruited Broido as Chief Mechanical Engineer, to be responsible for all mechanical aspects of LEO, and he worked very closely with Pinkerton on the development of the LEO II computer, first at Olaf Street and then at Minerva Road.

The Development of the Document Reader

From early 1959 it was felt by some that there was a need for a document reader to speed up the process of getting information to the computer, which was becoming faster as developments in technology occurred. Others were less convinced and had doubts as to whether there was a need for such a device and whether it could be commercially viable.[1] One of the main stumbling blocks was to design a form which would meet the requirements of all parties, bearing in mind that if the document reader were to be commercially successful it must meet the needs of other computer users. Pinkerton agreed to make a specification of the equipment which could be provided, indicating what limitations there would be with regard to paper size and printing requirements, but was not convinced that Hogarth Press (the printing subsidiary of Lyons) would be able to provide documents to the required accuracy. His specification and report were completed by August 1959 and were accepted in principle. He had estimated that £1,000 would be required to develop a prototype which, amazingly, would read a double-sided document. Before starting the work, however, he sought the views of George Stevens and others in the Lyons organisation to test out his ideas. This exercise was completed by September 1959, and, subject to a way being found to obtain accurate registration on document printing, the £1,000 was approved. Pinkerton and Broido together worked on a document reader design, but as with the earlier pioneering work on LEO I and LEO II, progress was slow. Both had a very busy schedule, and in addition to his UK duties Broido was asked at this time to explore the German market for potential computer sales.

Broido was described by Pinkerton as "A most ingenious engineer" and his talents as a salesman were equally impressive. With the LEO III marketing feedback beginning to show encouraging signs in the United Kingdom, Broido and Land persuaded Thompson that LEO should have a presence at the 1960 computer symposium in Dortmund, Germany (both spoke fluent German). Both had previously been invited to give lectures on the LEO computer at the Dortmund Society for Technology and Economics but these had generated little interest; IBM had a stranglehold on the German computer market and exhibited a much higher profile, making it almost impossible for smaller, less well known, companies to make any impact. It was a disappointing exercise which did not please Thompson.

In the following year, 1961, Broido approached Thompson again, suggesting this time that LEO should be exhibited at the first British Trade Fair in Moscow. He put forward the idea that the eastern European market showed greater potential, as it had not been influenced by IBM, who still viewed eastern Europe with a measure of hostility. With the 1960 disappointment still fresh in his mind Thompson did not think it was such a good idea and refused to give it further consideration. Undeterred, Broido went there on his own initiative, and in his own time, acting as an interpreter for a consortium of companies who were being represented. He made many important contacts and was vindicated when a large EMIDEC 2400 computer was sold from the British stand.

The following year Thompson changed his mind, and appointed Broido sales manager for eastern Europe. He was subsequently directly responsible for the sale of three computers to Czechoslovakia to the value of £1,050,000, the single largest export order in the history of LEO. His fluent command of Russian and German (he also had a working knowledge of Polish, Czech, Slovac and Serbian) was a major factor in his winning over the eastern European customers.

Apart from the computer sales to Czechoslovakia, he travelled widely in Russia lecturing on computers; at one notable event he gave a lecture to 500 students of Minsk University. This was followed the next day by an attendance of 700 students and by 800 the next; word had got around that an Englishman, who spoke Russian, was lecturing on computers!

Despite this considerable achievement Broido did not receive any commission for his efforts, which did not finish when he left the Trade Fair for home. He was responsible as interpreter for all the Russian and east European staff who subsequently visited the United Kingdom, including those being trained. He was also solely responsible for translating all the LEO technical manuals into Russian and was very critical

33. A section of improved electronic units racked in LEO II. *Reproduced by kind permission of J. Lyons & Co Ltd.*

34. (*above left*). The LEO II/1 computer installed at Cadby Hall (Elms House) in 1957. At the console is Kathleen Keene and adjusting the tabulator is Peter Wood. LEO II/1 was discontinued in 1967 after a long productive life. *Reproduced by kind permission of J. Lyons & Co Ltd.*

35. (*above right*). This Hollerith tabulator, with its duplicate to the left, was installed at Stewarts & Lloyds, Corby in 1958. *Reproduced by kind permission of ICL*

36. (*below*). A general view of Stewarts & Lloyds LEO II/3 computer, installed at Corby in June 1958. This was the first LEO machine to be installed outside of Lyons. *Reproduced by kind permission of J. Lyons & Co Ltd.*

37. (*above left*). The Samastronic print head assembly. Despite its name the printer had no electronics. It was unreliable and for maintenance engineers a mechanical nightmare. *Reproduced by kind permission of ICL.*

38. (*above right*). The Ferranti magnetic drum, type 1009, used on the LEO II computer. *Reproduced by kind permission of ICL.*

39. This LEO II/2 computer was the UK's first order for a programmable electronic computer placed by W.D. & H.O. Wills Ltd in February 1956. However, lateness of delivery of the Samastronic printer and Ferranti drums delayed installation until September 1958. *Reproduced by kind permission of J. Lyons & Co Ltd.*

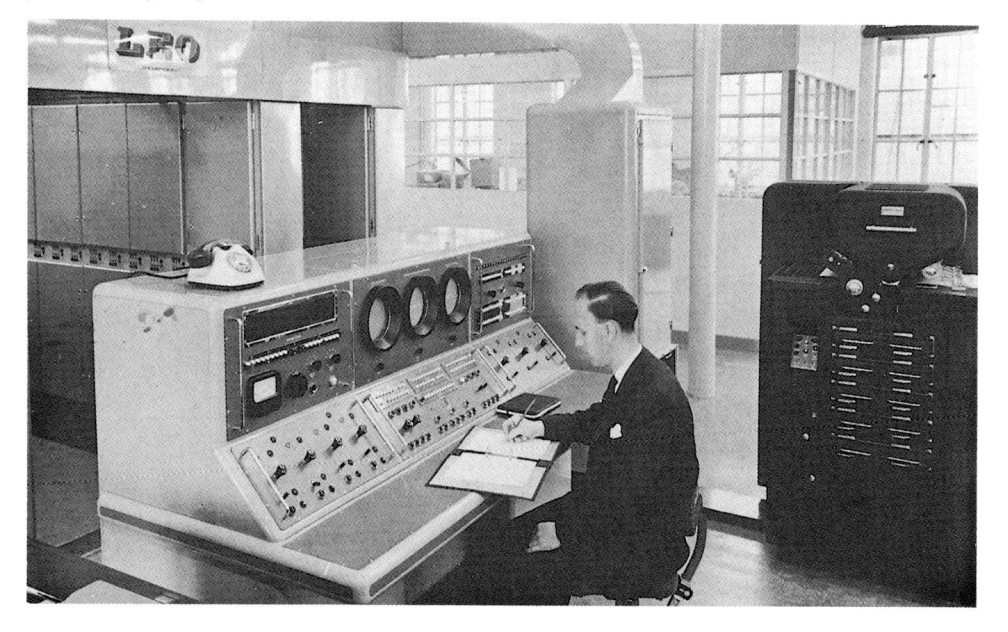

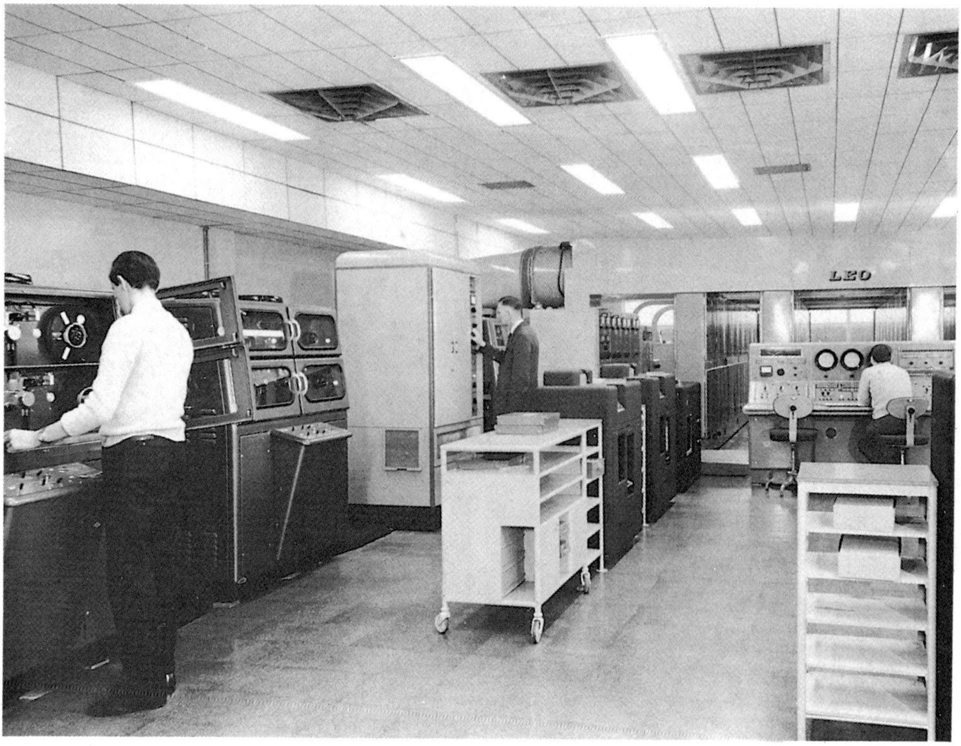
LEO

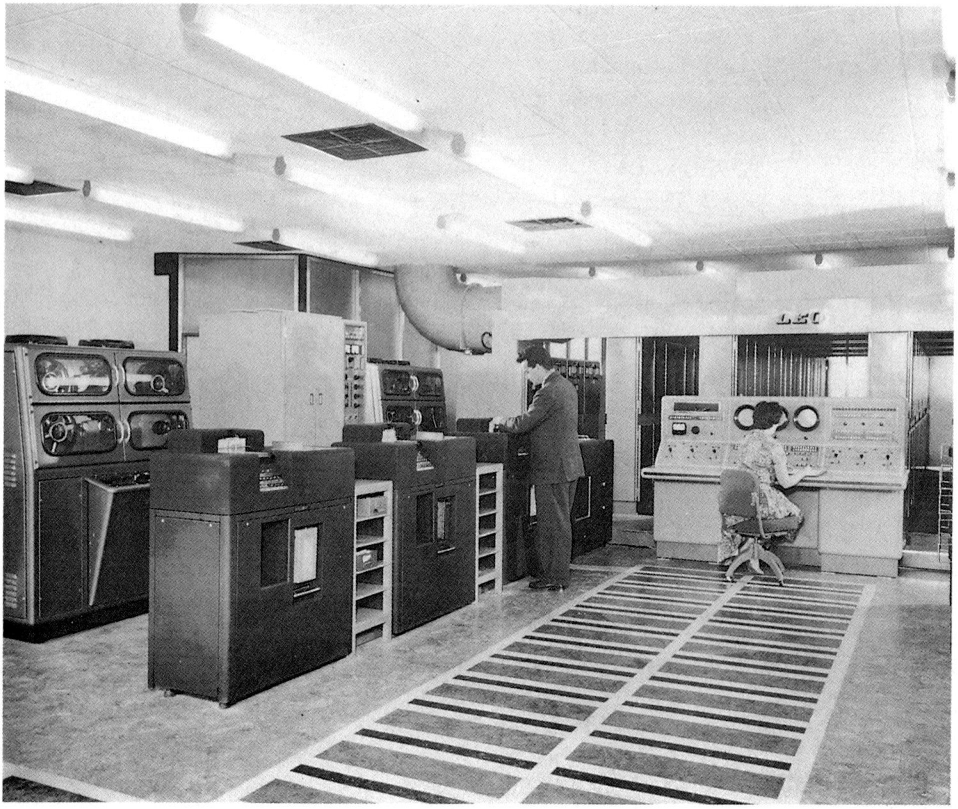
LEO

40. (*left*). The British Oxygen Company's LEO II/7 computer at Edmonton, London in February 1960. This was later traded in for a LEO III computer and LEO II/7 was used by Leo Computers Ltd as a second bureau machine. *Reproduced by kind permission of J. Lyons & Co Ltd.*

41. (*bottom left*). The LEO II/5 bureau machine at Hartree House in July 1959 with Decca tapes and Ferranti magnetic drum. *Reproduced by kind permission of J. Lyons & Co Ltd.*

42. (*right*). HRH the Duke of Edinburgh visiting the LEO computer works at Minerva Road on 22 March 1960. Isidore Montague Gluckstein, Chairman, J. Lyons & Co Ltd, and Anthony Salmon (*right*). *Richi Howell Photography.*

43. (*below*). LEO III/2 in the works during April 1962 prior to shipping to Rand Mines in South Africa. George Manley, manager of system test, has his back to the camera. This was the only LEO III computer to be clad in the works. *Reproduced by kind permission of Tony Morgan.*

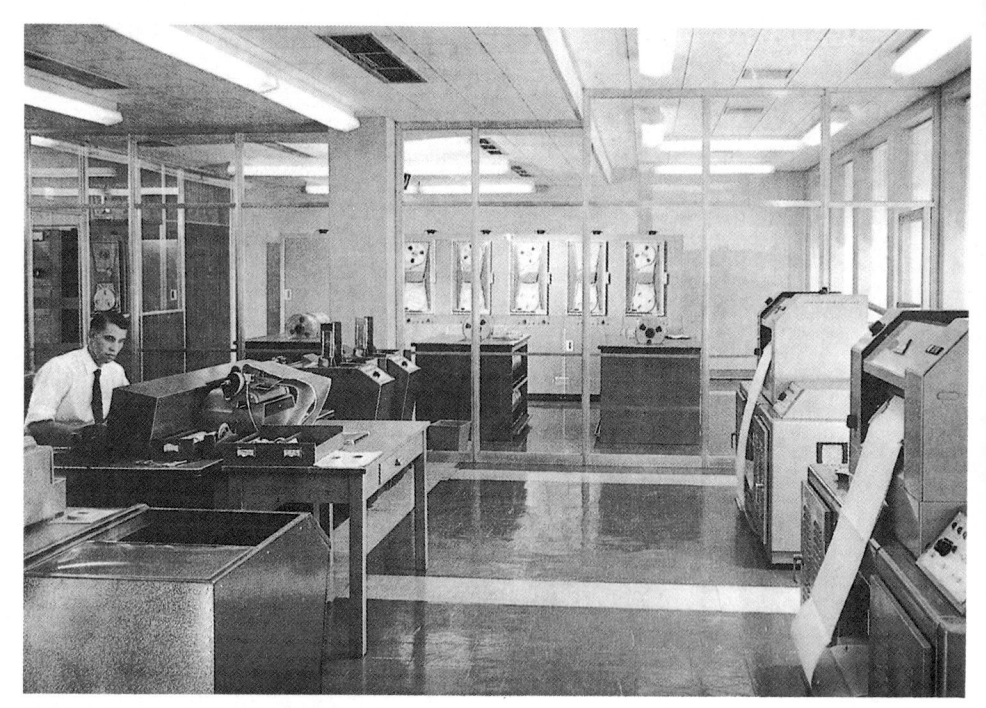

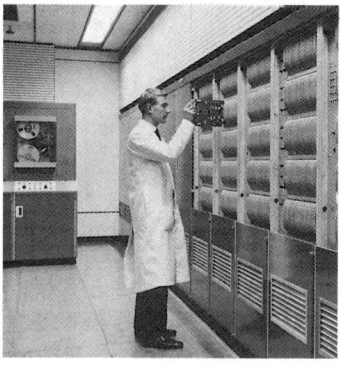

44. (*top*). The LEO III/2 computer installed in the Anderson Street offices of Rand Mines, Johannesburg. At the console is Brian McCook. May 1962.
Reproduced by kind permission of Rand Mines Ltd.

45. (*above*). This photograph demonstrates the classic modular design of the LEO III computer.
Reproduced by kind permission of J. Lyons & Co Ltd.

46. (*left*). The comprehensive engineers control console of the LEO III computer. The contents of the store could be displayed in the small cathode tube—a carry-over from the LEO I and LEO II design. The marginal testing facilities are incorporated into the left centre panel. The switches on the lower right panel could be used to make program changes interactively and the operating console could be switched to this position. *Reproduced by kind permission of J. Lyons & Co Ltd.*

47. (*top*). The LEO III/1 bureau machine at Hartree house with one of the first ANelex printers. April 1962. *Anthony Blake Photography.*

48. (*above*). A single Discfile unit used on the LEO III computer. Up to eight units could be attached. *Reproduced by kind permission of ICL.*

49. (*left*). The LEO III/1 computer being craned into the Whitely's Building in Bayswater on 15 April 1962. *Reproduced by kind permission of Peter Cuthbert.*

50. (*above*). The new ANelex printer shown here attached to LEO III/27 in 1965. The operator is changing the format control tape used to control the various stationery and printing requirements. *Reproduced by kind permission of Freemans Ltd.*

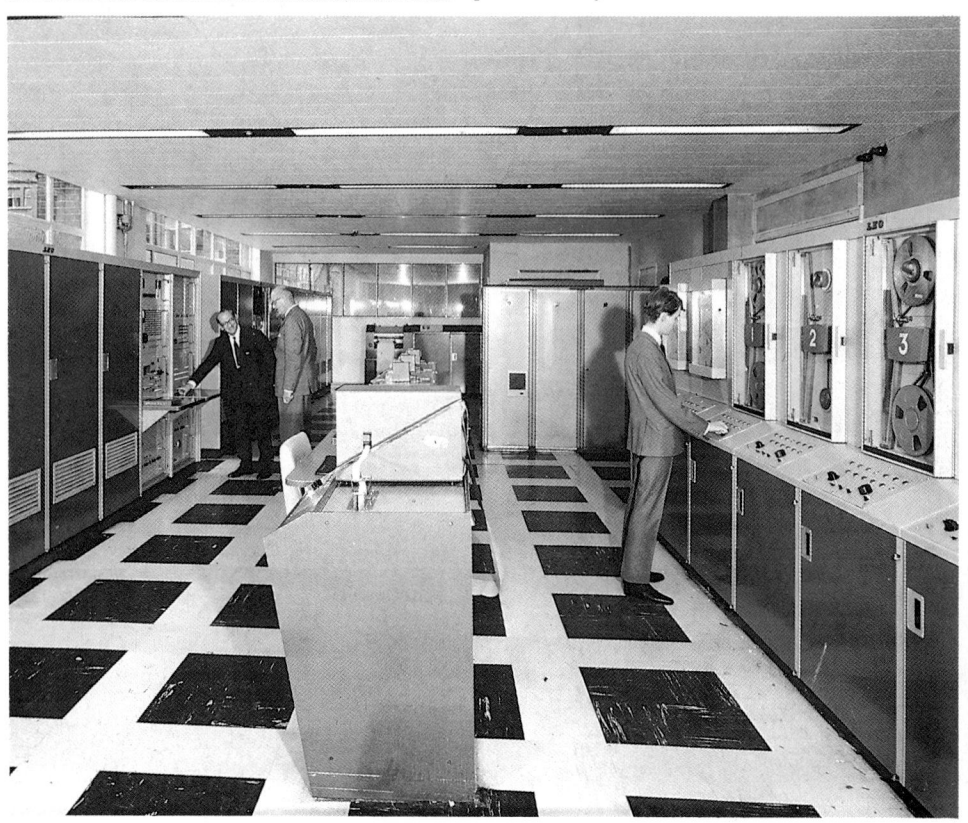

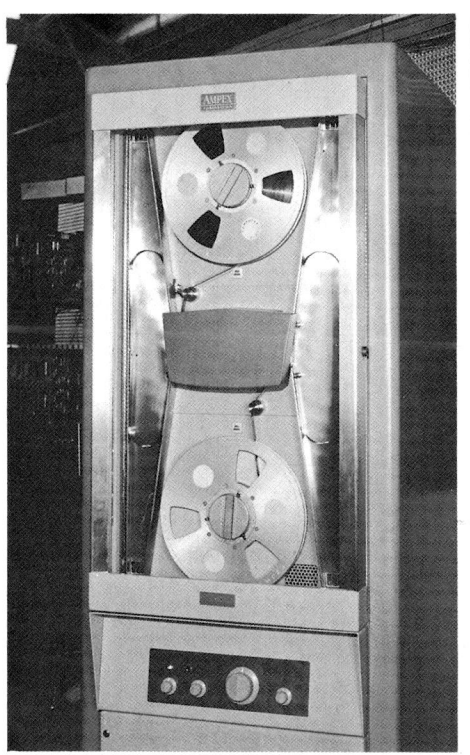

51. (*left*). Lyons' own LEO III/7 computer at Elms House in 1965. *Reproduced by kind permission of J. Lyons & Co Ltd.*

52. (*top left*). A single Ampex tape unit. These initially gave many teething troubles. c.1962. *Reproduced by kind permission of ICL.*

53. (*top right*). A LEO III micro programme module of 1964. *Reproduced by kind permission of ICL.*

54. (*right*). An Elliott, D4/23, paper reader operating at full speed. May 1962. *Reproduced by kind permission of Rand Mines Ltd.*

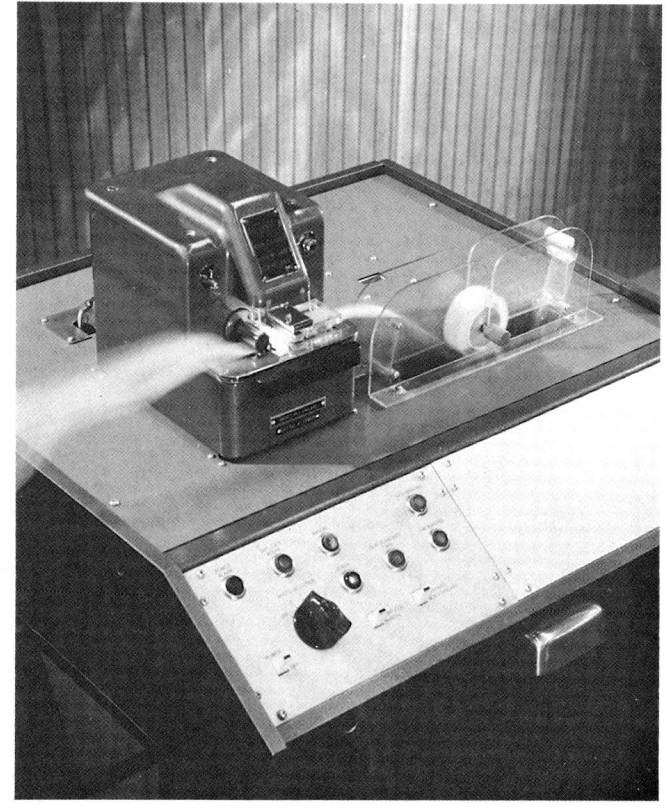

H.A. CHALMERS PTY LTD.
74 STANLEY ST
MELBOURNE
30-4211
3
D DRIVE
PTY. LTD., CARTAGE CONTRACTORS

55. (*top left*). Delivery of the LEO III/20 computer to Colonial Mutual Life, Melbourne. September 1964. *Reproduced by kind permission of Colonial Mutual Life.*

56. (*bottom left*). Commissioning of the LEO III/20 computer at the Collins Street offices of Colonial Mutual Life in September 1964. When the machine was replaced in 1973 it had registered 37,225 hours on the 'hours run' clock. At extreme right is Owen McKenzie, Systems Consultant, English Electric-Leo Computers (Australia). *Reproduced by kind permission of Colonial Mutual Life.*

57. (*above*). This building, belonging to Tubemakers Australia, Botany, Sydney, was specially built to house their LEO III/8 computer which was delivered in 1963. *Reproduced by kind permission of Tubemakers of Australia Ltd.*

58. (*below*). The LEO III/8 computer room of Tubemakers Australia, a subsidiary of Stewarts & Lloyds. *Reproduced by kind permission of Tubemakers of Australia Ltd.*

59. (*left*). Keith Cocks (left), Company General Manager, with Neil Lamming (centre), Managing director of ICL Australia, and Alex Mackie, Tubemakers Australia DP Manager at the closing down ceremony of LEO III/8 in 1977. *Reproduced by kind permission of Tubemakers of Australia Ltd.*

60. (*centre*). This panoramic photograph shows Shell (Australia) Group Chairman, Lewis Luxton, formally accepting their first LEO III computer in August 1964 from Sir Samuel Salmon, Managing Director of J. Lyons & Co Ltd (extreme right seated). *Reproduced by kind permission of Shell Australia.*

61. (*bottom*). A typical small LEO III data preparation department. This one is Tubemakers Australia and from left to right are: Lyn Beecher, Lesley Merry, Margaret Christy, Delma Masterton and Kathy Gray. 1963. *Reproduced by kind permission of Tubemakers Australia.*

SHELL 🐚 TIMES

VOL. 3 NO. 7   A MONTHLY NEWSPAPER FOR SHELL GROUP STAFF IN AUSTRALIA AND THE PACIFIC ISLANDS   AUGUST 1964

'LEO' PLAYED 'WALTZING MATILDA'

62. (*top*). The LEO III/41 computer used by the Czechoslovakian steel makers, Nova Hut, at Ostrava. 1966. *Reproduced by kind permission of Nova Hut.*

63. (*above*). A conference celebrating the installation of LEO III/41 in 1966 at Nova Hut, Ostrava, Czechoslovakia. David Caminer is third from left and on his left is Sir Gordon Radley, Managing Director of English Electric Ltd. The banner reads "Through the most efficient way by means of computing technique". *Reproduced by kind permission of Nova Hut.*

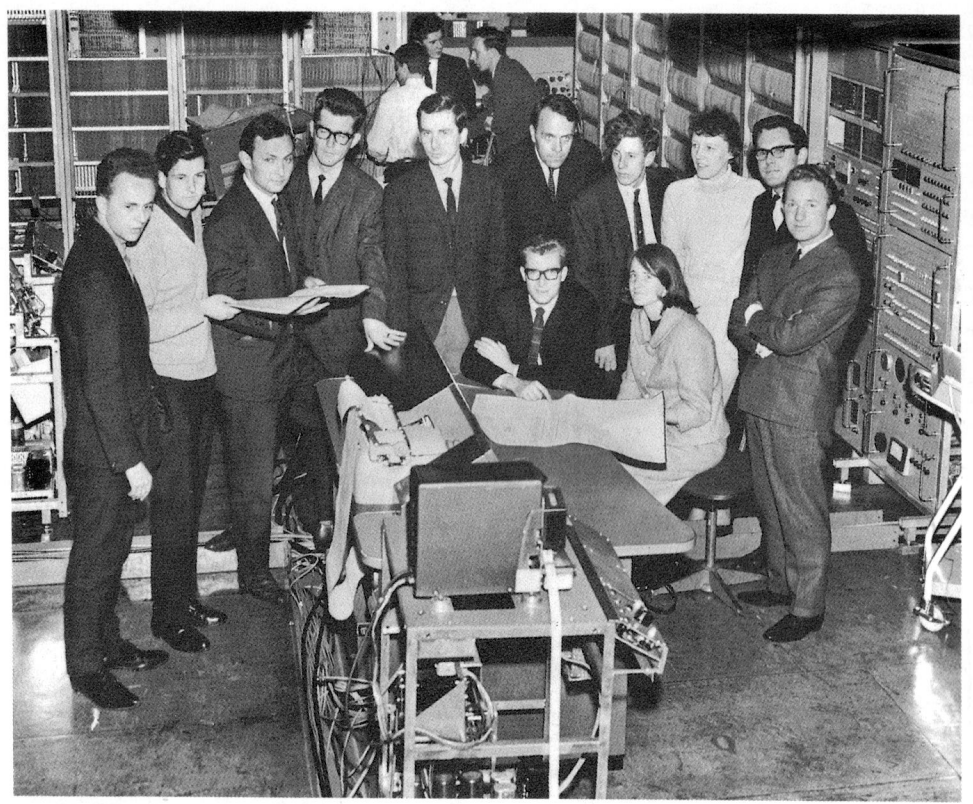

64. (*top*). Czechoslovakian engineers from the Vypocetni Laborator Dopravy (Railways Laboratory), Prague undergoing training in readiness to take delivery of the LEO III/93 computer at the Minerva Road LEO works in 1965. *Reproduced by kind permission of Tony Morgan.*

65. (*above*). Daniel Broido, seated right, at a signing ceremony for one KDF7 and two LEO III computers valued at £1,050,000. Prague 27 September 1965. *Reproduced by kind permission of ICL.*

66. (*top right*). Preparation for a LEO III documentary film being made by Kratky Film Praha in 1967. Probably the first film made of western technology by an East European country. *Reproduced by kind permission of ICL.*

67. (*right*). The National Savings LEO III/36 centre at Lytham St Anne's. 1966. *Reproduced by kind permission of National Savings (Bonds and Stock Office).*

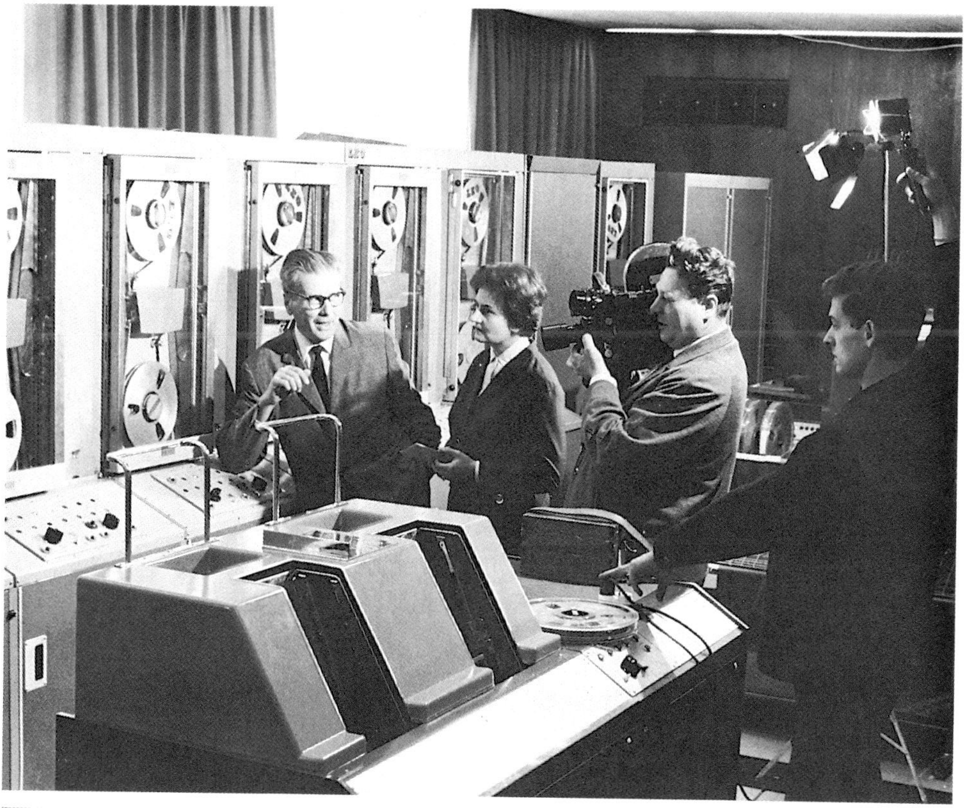

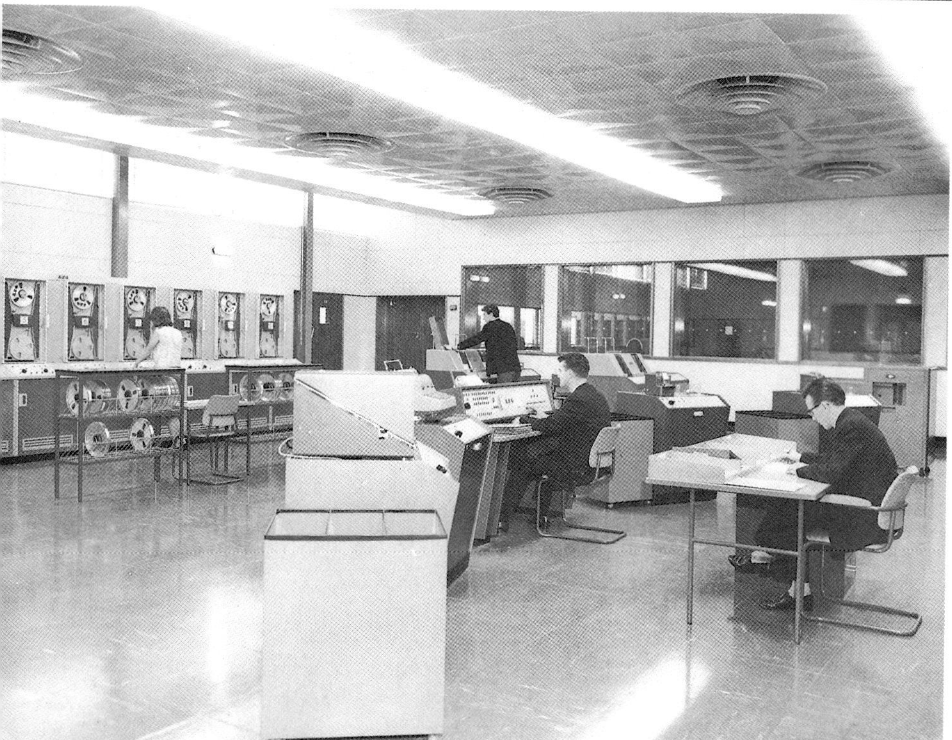

68. (*top*). One of the many LEO III computers operated by the Post Office. This one shows Charles House, Kensington. Originally badged LEO III/90 it was renumbered III/39 and sold to Ever Ready Ltd in 1965. *Reproduced by kind permission of British Telecom plc.*

69. (*centre*). This machine, LEO III/27, was installed in the mail order company Freemans Ltd in South London. It processed over 16 miles of paper tape every day and was said to have the largest data preparation department in Europe. 1965. *Reproduced by kind permission of Freemans Ltd.*

70. (*above*). This LEO III/4 computer was installed at Greenwich and provided resources for six London Boroughs. It was officially opened by George Woodcock, secretary of the TUC, on 26 March 1965 two years after it had been in service. *Reproduced by kind permission of Greenwich Council.*

of the poor translation services available to industry. His wife also supported him actively, frequently entertaining the eastern European technicians and other guests, outside normal working hours, during their stay in Britain. Later, Thompson joined him on his visits to eastern Europe and he received considerable support from other members of the LEO staff, particularly during the big exhibitions in Moscow, Poznan (Poland), and Brno (Czechoslovakia), where LEO III computers were assembled after transportation from the United Kingdom by road in two house removal lorries. Nevertheless, Broido carried a very considerable responsibility and workload, which ultimately resulted in him having a breakdown in Moscow; thankfully, he made a full recovery.

Meanwhile, Pinkerton had his hands more than full in designing the LEO III, and was grappling with numerous problems associated with magnetic drum and tape attachments to the LEO II machines. Leo Computers were short of good mechanical and design engineers, and work which could have been carried out by others was falling on Pinkerton with the inevitable consequence that it fell behind schedule. Despite all this a prototype document reader was built and was ready for field trials by April 1960. These were not allowed to start, however, until a second backup machine was made available. This posed a problem because the experience gained in making the prototype reader indicated that the optical and mechanical components should be redesigned if it were to be successful. This would have meant taking away design effort from the LEO III, which was not permitted. Several months passed without much progress being made and in January 1961 Thompson suggested that, without interfering with the LEO III effort, the document reader should produce 5-hole paper tape so that it could be tested on the LEO II/1 computer without risk. The prototype was used in this way, and the trials were encouraging. Work started again on a modified reader for completion by the end of July 1961 in order that it could be demonstrated at the Electronic Computer Exhibition at Olympia in October of that year. Further problems and delays occurred and the reader was not in a sufficiently reliable form before the start of the exhibition. Although exhibited, it was not seen as a working model. The delays were causing some concern to both the Leo Computer and Lyons staff and it was agreed that a full-time mechanical engineer should take charge.

Caminer, in his marketing role, reported encouraging signs in July 1962 for the future of the document reader, which became known as Lector, and he thought that the electricity industry might be able to make use of it for reading their meter documentation. Design work continued and the idea of providing automatic form input was considered as a further enhancement. Pinkerton recognised that for the machine to be a business success it must be capable of interworking with computer printers (reading documents previously produced on computer line printers) as well as dealing with those documents created from normal clerical procedures. He found it necessary, therefore, to consider the printing mechanism and capabilities of the ANelex printers, which had been planned for LEO III, and other factors such as paper quality and opacity had to be addressed. Apart from the subtle changes in specification which Lyons made from time to time (the O & M office, too, were very much in the experimentation stage), the whole design process was complicated since the document reader's performance could be directly influenced by other factors which themselves had not been properly evaluated and tested. All these difficulties meant that the first machines were not available, and only then in a hand feed mode, until April 1963, just in time to coincide with the delivery of the Lyons' LEO III computer, the installation of which had been dependent on the availability of Lector to enable the early economic handling of the large volumes of data which were planned.

The business application which Lyons selected as the subject of the first experiment using the Lector document readers was the bakery salesman's order form (see Figure 5.2), on which were recorded details of products to be delivered to dealers by rail. Quantities of goods ordered were recorded by clerks on the document by drawing horizontal marks, with pencil or black pen, through the appropriate guide boxes. Marks could be made in more than one box in each horizontal line to record a quantity that was the sum of two or more of the separate values. For example, the value 10 would be indicated by drawing horizontal lines in the boxes of the columns headed 2 and 8. A cancellation was achieved by filling in the box completely and an amendment by first making the appropriate cancellation and then entering the correct figure.

The specially designed documents were hand fed through the feed mechanism of Lector, under a bank of photoelectric cells which interpreted the pencil entries and automatically produced the corresponding

E/21 BAKERY RAILS ORDER FORM

DEALER'S NAME

JOURNEY NUMBER

DEALER'S NUMBER

ITEM No.	DESCRIPTION		UNIT	PRICE	QUANTITY ORDERED 1 2 3 4 5 6 7 8 12 24 48 96
1	KUP KAKES	×3 Chocolate			
2		×3 Lemon	ctn.	9d	
3		×3 Orange			
4	COCONUT TOASTIES ×3		ctn.	9d	
5	CHOC ROLLS ×12	C.V.F.	ctn.	3/-	
6		Jam			
7	MILK CHOC ROLLS ×12	C.V.F.	ctn.	3/-	
8		Jam			
9	COCONUT LAYER CAKES		ea.	2/3	
10	LARGE SWISS ROLLS	Raspberry	ea.	1/8	
11		Apricot			
12	TARTS	×6 Jam (Assorted Flavours)	ctn.	1/6	
13					
14		×6 Lemon	ctn.	1/8	
15		×6 Almond Bakewell	ctn.	1/9	
16		×6 Blackcurrant	,,	1/9	
17		×6 Treacle	,,	1/4	
18	INDIVIDUAL PIES	Apple			
19		Blackcurrant with Apple	ea.	7d.	
20		Apricot			
21		Strawberry & Apple	ea.	7d.	
22		Variable			
23	SPONGE CAKES ×8		ctn.	1/6	
24	GINGER CAKES		ea.	1/6	
25	ROUND CAKES	Madeira	ea.	1/6	
26		Fruit Madeira	,,	1/9	
27		Fruit Cherry	,,	1/11	
28		Plain Madeira	ea.	2/-	
29		Cherry	,,	2/6	
30		Banquet (Duchess)	,,	1/6	
31	HOSTESS CAKES	(Cartoned)	ea.	2/6	
32	MACAROONS	Coconut (2 × 5)		2/6	
33	NEW CORONET CAKES	Chocolate	ea.	2/-	
34		Variable			
35	SPONGE SANDWICHES	Princess	ea.	2/6	
36		Raspberry Jam	,,	2/-	
37		Choc. Flav. Filled	,,	2/-	
38		Jam & Van. Fld.	,,	1/6	
39	KUT-A-KAKE	Countess	piece	1/9	
40		Madeira	,,	2/-	
41		Dark Fruit	,,	1/9	
42		Fruit Cherry	piece	2/9	
43		Sultana	,,	2/-	
44		Cherry	,,	2/9	
45	LARGE SWISS ROLLS	Choc. Sponge Van. Filled	ea.	1/8	
46		Princess			
47		Choc. Flav. Filled			
48		Walnut and Vanilla Flavour Filled			
49	KUT-A-KAKE	Festive (Pack of 3 pieces)		6/9	
50		Fiesta ,,		6/-	
51		Gaiety ,,		6/9	
52		Chocolate ,,		6/9	
53	JOLYROLS ×6	C.V.F.			
54		Jam			
55		Choc. Flav. Filled		6/-	
56		Princess			
57	SPONGE CAKES ×4		ctn.	10d.	
58	DUNDEE CAKES		ea.	8/6	
59			,,	12/6	
60	CADBY ROLLS	Choc. Sponge Van. Filled	ea.	1/8	
61		Variable			
62	SLAB CAKE	approx. 4 lb. Dark Fruit (S'd)	slab	7/-	
63		,, 4 lb. Kensington	,,	9/-	
64		,, 5 lb. Genoa	,,	13/9	
65		,, 4 lb. Madeira	,,	8/-	
66	BATTENBERGS ×3			6/-	
67	JUNIOR JOLYROLS ×4	(CARTONS OF 6 JAM)		4/-	
68		(CARTONS OF 6 C.V.F.)			
69	NIPPY FANCIES ×3	(BOXES OF 6)		6/-	
70	BARGATTO ×3	White			
71		Chocolate		5/3	
72		Variable			
73					
74					
75					
76					
77					

DELIVERY REQUIRED — MONTH / DAY

FORM Number

Fig 5.2 Bakery rails order form.

formation on a 7- or 8-hole paper tape punch at a rate between 120,000 and 200,000 characters per hour; a plugboard determined the layout of columns and characteristics of form layout, thus making the reader very flexible. The paper tape so produced was subsequently used as input to the computer, via a normal paper tape reading device, without the need for any manual intervention in preparing data. The speed of Lector, about 1,400 forms per hour, was approximately thirty-two times faster than conventional hand punching. Furthermore, no special skills or training were required, either of the persons preparing the original documents or the operators of Lector, other than general guidance.

Lector proved to be an extremely successful device within the O & M office at Lyons and its use was extended to payroll and other appropriate systems. The effect of using Lector had a dramatic effect on the timing of the daily business activities, improving their completion time by some three or more hours, and considerable economies were made in the data preparation department. In practice, very few errors were introduced by Lector and the machines could be used by anyone. Operations staff, not keypunch trained, frequently lent a hand to prepare the paper tape by hand feeding forms to the machines.

From Lector to Autolector

Despite the success of Lector Lyons did not regard this as a complete solution, and before it was operational work had already been started by Pinkerton to automate the feeding of forms. He had known of a company called Parnall & Sons Ltd and had forged a relationship with them in 1962. Parnall had been established in 1820 by Henry Geach Parnall (1802–1881) and traded primarily as scale makers and shop fitters, for which they had a considerable reputation. William Parnall, son of the company's founder, was an accomplished innovator. One of his more ingenious inventions was the Dial Weigh scale. The success of his device prompted Avery Weighing Machines Limited to buy the Parnall Company to secure the patents on the invention, which, as they rightly considered, had huge potential and was further developed and exploited by them. Parnall continued their shop fitting activities; the bronze shop-fronts and display cases at Piccadilly Circus underground station, the exterior canopies at the Savoy Hotel and the Shakespeare Memorial Theatre are all examples of their work.

During the late 1950s under the Managing Directorship of Stanley Thompson, Parnall became involved in designing cheque sorting equipment for a large London bank. The machine used a magnetic recognition system known as FRED (Figure Reading Electronic Device) that had been developed at EMI in the 1950s and used experimentally on their EMIDEC computers. The bank decided, after evaluation, to adopt instead an American design based on the E13B standard, a more appropriate sorting code, which left Parnall somewhat exposed.

Following this disappointment, Parnall experimented with other paper handling equipment and turned their attentions instead to mark reading machines, a development which was given high priority by a number of moderately sized companies of the period. Following Pinkerton's discussions with Parnall on 29 January 1962 it became apparent that their machine, as it stood, was not suitable for the needs of Lyons, and initial specifications were prepared by Pinkerton so that Parnall could adapt their device. This led to a partnership being formed by which Parnall would develop a new paper feed and optical scanning system and Leo Computers Limited would be responsible for the electronics. The machine became known as Autolector LEO-Parnall, the name being derived from that of the earlier Lector.

The relationship was good and both sides worked hard to overcome the many difficulties, which were different to those experienced on the Lector project. Pinkerton visited Parnall's offices on a number of occasions. A machine gradually evolved which caught the imagination of Caminer and others, and in September 1962, during the development phase, a decision was taken to operate Autolector in an on-line mode, in the way planned, but not implemented, for Lector. This involved the design of a new input assembler for the LEO III computer and a senior engineer was assigned to the task. By 1964 most of the design difficulties had been overcome and Autolector was installed at Cadby Hall and connected on-line to the LEO III/7 computer.

Autolector had been designed for large-scale data processing, reading documents at speeds of up to 24,000 per hour and recording the marks directly on magnetic tape. Considerable flexibility in document design was provided and the machine could read handwritten and computer-produced hyphens. Forms were read at a constant rate, irrespective of

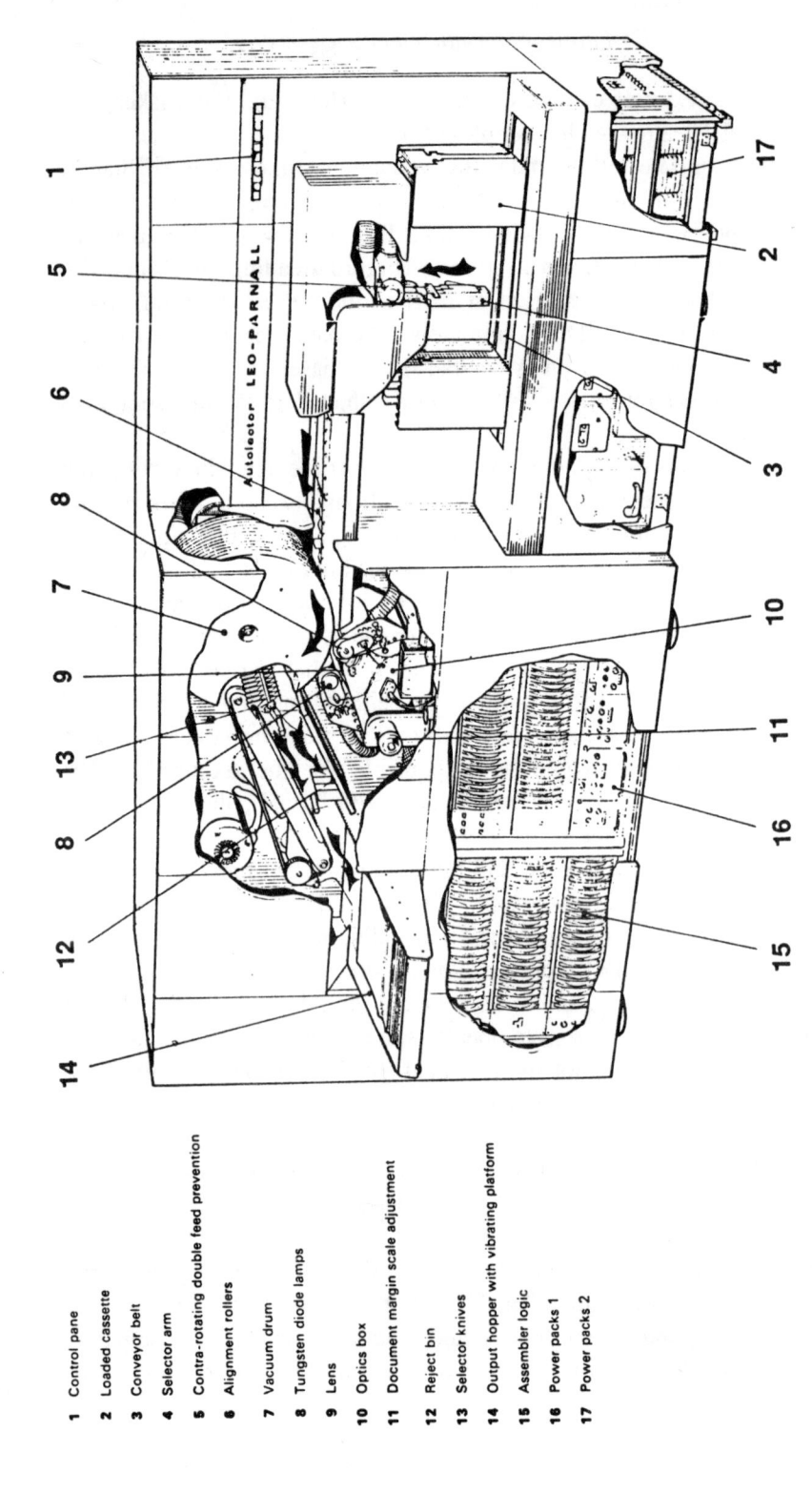

1 Control pane
2 Loaded cassette
3 Conveyor belt
4 Selector arm
5 Contra-rotating double feed prevention
6 Alignment rollers
7 Vacuum drum
8 Tungsten diode lamps
9 Lens
10 Optics box
11 Document margin scale adjustment
12 Reject bin
13 Selector knives
14 Output hopper with vibrating platform
15 Assembler logic
16 Power packs 1
17 Power packs 2

Fig. 5.3 Schematic diagram of Autolector.

the data content, small forms at 400 per minute, large forms at 270 per minute. A typical batch that might be received in the daily post could consist of 2,000 tea order forms with an average data content of 100 characters per form. Punching and verifying the total 200,000 characters would have taken two keypunch operators, one punching and one verifying, 20 hours to complete, assuming a keypunch rate of 10,000 characters per hour (8,000 characters per hour was normally used as the maximum rate achievable other than in short bursts). Autolector could read the same 2,000 forms in under 10 minutes, or 120 times faster, and it was estimated that it could do the work of 200 keypunch operators.

Autolector forms were selected individually from cassettes by a rotating belt pick-up and carried by alignment rollers to a vacuum drum, where they were held smooth and flat for reading. After reading, the forms were picked off the drum and passed to the output bin, or to a rerun bin if the machine had rejected them for any reason. The main features of Autolector were the thirteen silicon photovoltaic cells, supplied by Ferranti Ltd, and the revolving drum, which, with its clever vacuum feature, held the documents in place while passing them across a lens, directing an image of the form across the reading cells. There were twelve data cells that scanned the information area of the form, controlled by a thirteenth timing cell. This timing cell was triggered by the scanning of preprinted timing marks on the right-hand edge of the document.

No time was wasted in bringing the payroll and order entry systems on to Autolector and its success was entirely due to its ability to handle, reliably and economically, large input requirements with speed. The impediment of the keypunch department was removed, thus improving the timing of some applications by 24 hours. The machine appeared to have huge potential, particularly in the business areas of order gathering, time sheets (payroll), market survey, billing, stock control, meter recording, production control, material handling, and piecework recording. The Government was the largest user of Autolector, installing four machines which were attached to the LEO III computers in Her Majesty's Dockyards at Portsmouth, Devonport, Chatham and Rosyth. The equipment was used to analyse the various dockyard labour activities from which job costings by ship and project were produced. The analyses of these activities were reconciled with payroll, although the payroll attendance was not derived from the job costing data.

Autolector and its predecessors were the forerunners of the highly sophisticated optronic reading systems of today that are still commonly used for the scanning of football pools and other coupons. Their use revolutionised computer systems design at Lyons, and in 1967 a second machine was delivered to handle the growing demand and also as security. Although there was a clear need for machines of this type, their cost, £20,000 compared with £7,500 for Lector, deterred many users from investment, and the success of the project was limited. It was dealt a final blow when the Avery Board, who owned Parnall, instructed the Parnall management to disengage from this business venture and confine their business activities to shop fitting. By this time the merger of Leo Computers Ltd and the English Electric Company, discussed more fully in the next chapter, had occurred and no doubt management were occupied with consolidating a product strategy. The relationship between Parnall and Leo Computers also became a little soured because Pinkerton would not allow Parnall a free optical patent licence, which he felt may be used to Leo Computers' disadvantage.

In the early stages of using mark reading machines poor print quality (not clerical marking) frequently caused an unacceptable level of document rejection. Such documents had been produced from a previous computer run and it was found that the placement and registration of hyphen marks, a character used by Lyons to indicate data, were often inaccurate or badly printed. The hyphen marks were sometimes a little to the left, sometimes to the right, and sometimes too high or low, in relation to the preprinted timing marks on the special stationery used to control the photoelectric reading cells within Autolector. This condition was nearly always the result of bad paper alignment during the printing stage or because the line printers had wandered from specification without this being noticed by operators. Continuous use of hyphens on the left—or right-hand side—of the form tended to cause wear on the printer hammers in those positions most frequently used.

Bad phase adjusting also created a condition known as ghosting, which had the effect of superimposing a second character almost in the same position as the first but slightly above or below the original, causing a blurred character (one can get the same effect with a manual typewriter if a heavy touch and/or a new ribbon is used). These problems and the need to improve the output speed of information from the computer led to an investigation, resulting in the use of a non-impact printer, which addressed both the quality and speed requirements. To the operators it brought relief from the incessant pounding of print hammers, since acoustic muffling was not provided to the standards of today.

Rank's Xerographic Printer

Simultaneously and coincidently with the development of Autolector, Rank Precision Industries Ltd, a subsidiary of the Rank Organisation Ltd, had been working on a revolutionary electronic printing system that led in 1958 to the introduction of their Xeronic printer. This high speed computer output printer used the principle of xerography to obtain its results. Xerography, a photoelectrical process invented in 1937 by an American, Chester F. Carlson (1906–1968), derives its meaning from two Greek words meaning dry writing (*xeros*, dry and *graphein*, to write). It is not a chemical process, nor does it employ liquid inks, but depends on the photo conductive properties of a light sensitive element called selenium.

The same principle is used in the ubiquitous photocopiers to be found now in all offices and high street print shops. Without light, selenium acts as an insulator and can retain an electric charge on the surface, but when illuminated it conducts and the charge dissipates rapidly. In xerographic printing an electrically-charged black thermoplastic graphite-like powder, called the toner, is normally cascaded over a selenium-coated revolving drum. This adheres only to the uncharged parts of the drum's surface; the image forming toner is then transferred to paper and is permanently fused on by a heat process which literally melts the toner to the paper; a relatively simple principle with few mechanical components.

The process was brought to Britain in 1956 when the Haloid Company of Rochester, New York and the Rank Organisation formed Rank-Xerox Ltd to manufacture and market xerographic equipment in Britain for sale everywhere except North America. The Anglicisation of the British equipment fell to the recently formed Central Research Laboratories of Rank Precision Industries Ltd. Their Dr Nyman Levin (1906–1965), Chief of Research and Development, and Keith Huntley, said to be the thinker of the Electronics Laboratory, firmly believed that there was a real need for a high speed computer output printer and that the new Haloid xerographic process would make such a machine possible.

In March 1958 Huntley demonstrated an experimental device that could print one figure (6) and one letter (E), and he claimed that the two big problems, writing the character on a cathode tube and printing from it, had been overcome. He was confident that the problems that remained were somewhat minor in comparison. It is interesting to note at this juncture that the first production line automatic copier, the Xerox 914, so named because it made copies up to 9 inches by 14 inches, was not delivered until 1960 (1961 in the UK).

It was obvious that with only eight months to go before Britain's first electronic computer exhibition at Olympia Rank Precision Industries would be unable to complete their development in time to exhibit a full working machine. They had already concluded that it was far too important a milestone in the development of electronics in Britain for this machine not to be represented and decided, therefore, to exhibit an unfinished prototype, to enable visitors to the exhibition to gain some idea of the potential of xerographic printing and at the same time to give them an opportunity to gauge user reaction.

Before Dr Nyman Levin could put on display this first major achievement of the Central Research Laboratories of Rank Precision Industries, he was asked to leave industry to become Sir William Penney's (1896–1964) deputy at the Atomic Weapons Research Establishment at Aldermaston. Therefore, in August 1958, Dr Nyman Levin handed over as Chief of Research and Development to his life-long friend, Dr Arthur Tisso Starr, who continued the work at Rank Precision Industries. Dr Starr, who was an expert on radar and electronic filter systems, had been recruited from Plessey's subsidiary company, Cottage Laboratory Limited, where he had been working on underwater detection and sonic research for the Government. He had, incidently, previously worked with Pinkerton during the war years, both at TRE Swanage and at Malvern, and they knew each other very well.

In September 1959 Ian D. Brotherton, who was a Technical Manager at Plessey, joined Rank Precision Industries as a Technical Sales appointee, working under the Managing Directorship of Thomas Law. Brotherton soon formed the opinion that the £70,000 budgeted to bring the Xeronic printer to the market was greatly underestimated and calculated that a figure of £300,000 would be more realistic.[2] He had concluded that selling a printer of this sophistication could not be done without a proper software, engineering and servicing organisation to support it. After consultations with John Henry Davis (1906–1993), Chairman and Chief Executive of the Rank Organisation, his revised budget was approved, but only after he had agreed to a three-year employment contract to carry out his plans. The main business activity of Rank Precision Industries at this time was the supply of film and cinematograph apparatus and it was decided to form a new subsidiary company, Rank Data Systems Ltd, which would be wholly responsible for the development, production and sale of the Xeronic printer. With the new subsidiary established, Brotherton created a professional production, marketing and sales team. To enable effective marketing of the printer in Europe, subsidiary companies were formed in France, Germany, Italy, Sweden and Denmark with their own technical support staff.

It was originally intended to sell the printer to some of the main computer manufacturers of the period and Rank Data Systems worked closely with Ferranti (Orion computer) and AEI (1010 computer) to perfect software which would allow the printer to work as a normal peripheral device, on-line to their respective computers, which it was eventually able to do. This approach had been taken because the printer could work at much faster speeds than the computers of the period, and also because the magnetic tape technology was still unreliable and the technicians felt this might be a hindrance to Xeronic's reliability. This on-line approach was not a total success, the main difficulty being the division of responsibility in respect of the software. Plans to make future machines work in this way were soon dropped. Instead, the Xeronic printer was made to work as an off-line device and, apart from the Ferranti and AEI machines, all others worked in off-line mode with the magnetic tape forming the interface boundary between computer and printer. Because of early technical difficulties the Ferranti printer was never used operationally. Rank Data Systems bought it back, modified it and resold it to another customer. The AEI printer did go into on-line operational use at RAF Hendon.

During the 1950s and 1960s there was an underground of knowledge within the computer industry and Lyons were aware of the work going on at Rank Data Systems. Indeed, Keith Huntley had already carried out some earlier exploratory discussions with most of the United Kingdom's computer manufacturing community. However, it was during the Electronic Computer Exhibition which was assembled at Olympia,

London in November–December 1958, that Lyons were able to see for the first time the Xeronic prototype printer. Although it was not fully developed, it was sufficiently impressive for Lyons to realise its possibilities in relation to their plans for automation. By July 1962 Lyons had more or less decided to install the Xeronic printer in preference to a conventional line printer, but Thompson felt that there were bound to be teething troubles with this approach which could delay the use of the LEO III computer. Following this statement Pinkerton visited the Ministry of Pensions in Newcastle-on-Tyne to see the Xeronic printer attached to their EMIDEC 2400 computer. He was impressed with what he saw and was keen to explore the possibility of using the same printers in appropriate LEO installations. He suggested to Thompson that perhaps Lyons should install one. Although Thompson was unenthusiastic he did go along with the idea for more information, and John Aris, who had started as a programmer in September 1958, was asked to undertake a study. His report, completed by August 1962, suggested that more research was required, some certainly by Rank itself, and that in any event Lyons could not depend on Xeronic alone and would certainly still require ANelex printer(s). Pinkerton kept a close watch on developments and appointed a senior engineer to take charge, with Broido to help and advise on any mechanical questions. A programmer was also assigned to investigate programming and systems problems with a view to suggesting how they might be overcome. Pinkerton also suggested that as soon as a Xeronic printer was operating anywhere Lyons and Leo Computers representatives should arrange to spend some time observing the day-to-day running and maintenance. By 1964 most of the system and engineering problems had been resolved and Lyons took delivery of their Xeronic printer in mid-year.

While the principle of xerography was used for the actual printing process, Rank Data Systems used an elaborate electronic method to generate characters. Together, these two processes resulted in a linear paper speed of 40 feet per minute. Input to the character generation logic was by 7-, 8- or 9-bit magnetic tape with normal computer parity checks and for this purpose the system had its own tape units of a type similar to that in use on the host computer. The Lyons printer which was delivered in 1964 (ordered 1962) had two Potter tape units to minimise the time of moving from one tape to another and to provide some measure of security in case of failure.

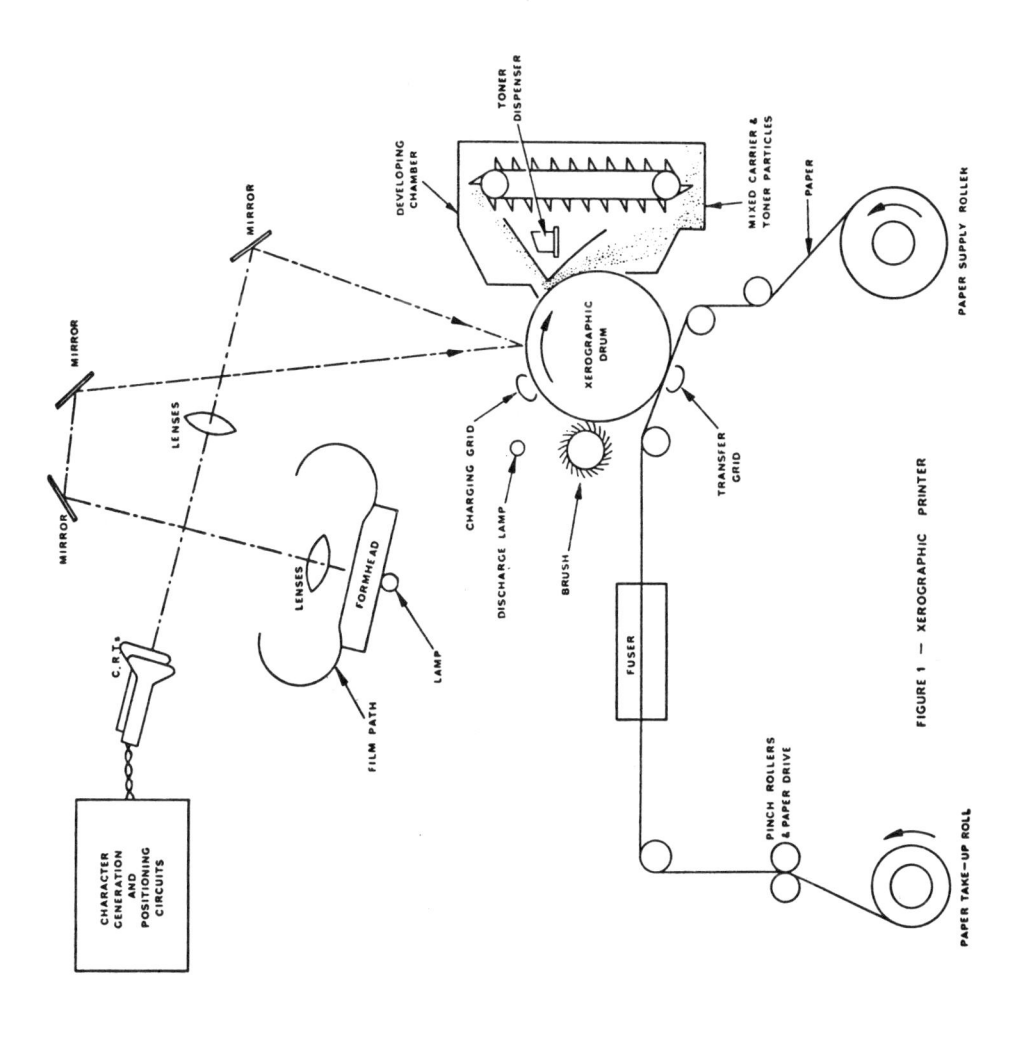

Fig. 5.4 Schematic diagram of Xeronic printer.

The signals from the magnetic tape unit were read a block at a time into the printer's own ferrite core memory. These signals consisted of the printable data, together with commands inserted at appropriate places by the edit program in the computer. The stored signals in the core memory were decoded as printable characters or commands, the former being displayed on cathode ray tubes and the latter to control the various functions of the printer. Because the characters were generated electronically it was possible to produce them in virtually any styling and even in foreign alphabets such as Arabic or Russian, and almost any mathematical or scientific symbol could be generated. Lyons had specified a special enlarged hyphen character that was to be used on forms subsequently read by the Autolector. Contrary to some speculation, Chinese was never developed.

The characters which were displayed on the two cathode ray tubes were projected via an optical system on to a light sensitive selenium-coated revolving drum. Simultaneously, a second image of the form outline held on a film negative was projected through a magnifying lens on to the same drum so that the variable data from the computer was superimposed on the form outline to produce the complete document. This feature gave the Xeronic printer great versatility: it allowed the system designer considerable freedom in specifying form layouts, with both horizontal and vertical addressing of information, and permitted a change from one form type to another merely by inserting the form number in the appropriate program command; in this way up to 32 form outlines were available for immediate selection without the loss of printing speed or the need to change stationery. Further groups of 32 form backgrounds could be obtained if a new film negative were inserted, a process that took only a few minutes. A repeat facility was incorporated which enabled a complete form to be repeated up to seven times without the need for repeating it on the magnetic tape. Tape positioning features also allowed the tape to be searched to any predetermined point as may be required to rerun output. Finally, perforations could be added to the printed documents during the printing stage to aid document dissection at a later stage if required.

Characters were generated at a rate of 4,700 per second, giving a constant printing speed of 2,888 lines per minute. This was nearly three times the speed of conventional line printers of the time but somewhat slower than the 5,000 lines per minute that had been the aim of the Rank designers.

The stationery used was plain untreated paper in reels some 2,700 feet in length and 26 inches wide. Three forms of average size could be printed side by side. A special paper guillotine, manufactured either by R.D. Thompson & Company Limited or Böwe, was used to cut the printed rolls both vertically and horizontally, with the cutting blade being controlled by a photoelectric cell triggered by a mark previously printed on the paper. Thus different sizes and types of forms could be printed in one print run without changing stationery or the guillotining set-up; each roll of paper kept the printer fully occupied for one hour.

The printer formhead (the mechanism for positioning the film strips) had a dual unit comprising two similar film positioning mechanisms side by side. Two identical film negatives, each approximately three feet in length, were inserted and used alternately. In this way the next document would be ready for printing when the previous document had been completed and no time was lost in the mechanical process of form selection. To minimise wear on the film strips, air was forced between the film and the projection gate whenever a fast drive was engaged so that the film was supported on a cushion of air, out of contact with the gate(s). If necessary a microfilm camera could be attached, enabling a record to be kept of printed documents. This became less of a requirement when microfiche records could be produced directly from magnetic tape.

The Xeronic printer was by any standards expensive and final delivery cost was dependent on user requirements. As an example, Lyons paid £90,000 for the printer that was installed in 1964.

The advantages of xerography over conventional computer output printers were threefold: first, there were no rapidly moving mechanical parts; second, the photo conductive surface was only used as a temporary carrier of the image and could be reused repeatedly (in the Xeronic printer the process was made continuous); and third, the toner forming the image was transferred to unprepared plain paper, with a consequent saving in preprinted stationery.

Many of the computer applications that Lyons developed required the production of special documents which, after being delivered to the various user departments and marked up by clerks, would be returned to the computer department as next week's input via Autolector. Initially, small blemishes were found on some of the returned documents and investigation showed that these had been produced during the printing process several days earlier. These marks were sometimes recorded as bogus data when the documents passed through Autolector. If undetected, as they frequently were, they subsequently caused real concern, with potentially serious consequences, particularly in the payroll application where, for example, they could have the effect of incorrectly recording additional pay. Naturally, staff seldom complained of this phenomenon! In practice this overpayment was nearly always detected in a subsequent external audit check, which Lyons employed outside their computerised systems, but the fact that it had happened at all threw into question the credibility of the whole process. Spurious marks on the company's product order forms were equally annoying and although not detected by audit involvement in the same way, did involve manual intervention, and subsequent cost, to correct records and return goods which had been wrongly delivered. The problem was not difficult to identify and was associated with the printer's selenium-coated drum. Because the drum was used in a continuous process, its surface suffered from exceptional wear and tear as well as from operator or engineer accident. Any small blemish made on its surface had the effect of creating a small mark, of the same size, on the printed page but not necessarily in the same vertical position because of the drum's circular movement. This problem was alleviated by frequent drum replacement, an expensive but necessary precaution, and to help to improve print quality it became necessary to incorporate a quality control procedure after the printing and guillotine stages so that visual and measuring checks could be made on sample print runs. Any print which was deemed unacceptable by the quality control procedure was rerun after corrective action had been taken. Despite this additional checking process some bad forms did manage to pass through, and operations staff soon learned that the sensitivity controls on the document reader could be adjusted, with great care, so that most of the bogus marks would pass unrecorded.

The development of the Lector, Autolector and Xeronic printer made it possible, for the first time, for a single document to be used for both input and output. This combination of automatic document reading and xerographic printing technologies was unique to Lyons, as far as is known. The Systems Department skilfully used both machines' capabilities to great effect and some applications that had been envisaged when LEO I was in development began to be realised. There was a considerable saving in stationery costs, and designers could modify their ideas without the need for expensive stationery stock write-off.

The Tea Sales order form used by Lyons was exploited to the full, and this unique turn-round document is worthy of special mention. Orders for some 120 tea, coffee and grocery products were taken by salesmen calling on customers on a preset monthly, fortnightly or weekly call cycle. Some 1,500 of these orders were received daily by post and were processed by a LEO III system that generated delivery instructions, invoices and sales statistics. A major function of the LEO III programs was to print, by way of the Xeronic printer, a supply of order forms for each salesman for use in the following cycle, each form tailored to the customer's unique buying pattern. These forms were posted direct to the salesmen's home addresses with pre-addressed envelopes in which to return them.

The basic design of the order form was that found on a standard Autolector input document. The timing marks were printed down the full right-hand edge, the computer-produced customer number at the top, the characteristic "soup bowls" as a guide for marking, and the customer's name and address, call day, terms and product descriptions were printed down the left-hand side. Further information was entered to enable the order form to be used by Lyons Tea management as a pro-active sales and marketing tool, not just a cost-effective and accurate way of feeding data to the LEO III computer automatically. This more imaginative use was obtained in three ways.

First, only those products that the customer had ordered at some time during the previous three salesman calls were printed on the order form. This avoided burdening the salesmen with a multi-part document, which would have been necessary to accommodate the full range of items, and it highlighted those products for which a repeat order could be expected. This method of customising each order form greatly complicated the program logic, which had to keep a separate list for each customer.

Second, by the side of each product description the quantity ordered on each of the last three sales calls, and the number of cases still to be sold if the sales target was to be achieved were entered.

The third feature was the automatic inclusion, for a specified period, of new products or products subject to special promotion, either for all customers or for those meeting defined criteria such as size of shop or past pattern of business. There was, of course, a procedure by which a salesman could enter details of a product that was required but did not

162   LEO: the first business computer

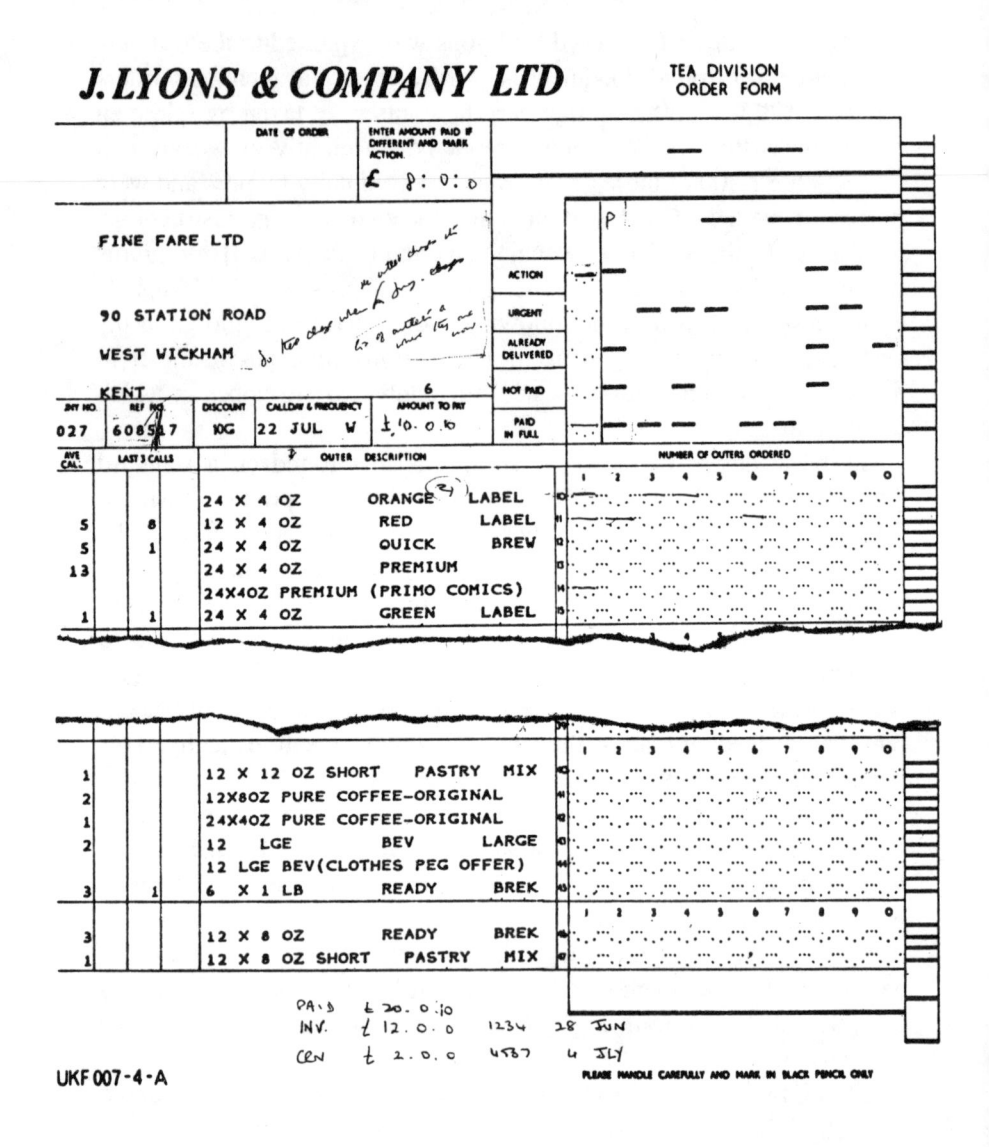

J. LYONS & COMPANY LTD
TEA DIVISION ORDER FORM

		DATE OF ORDER	ENTER AMOUNT PAID IF DIFFERENT AND MARK ACTION		
			£ 8:0:0		

FINE FARE LTD

90 STATION ROAD

WEST WICKHAM

KENT

handwritten note: do two days week of 5 days. charge. As I rather a wee 1 tg. and now.

					ACTION	
					URGENT	
					ALREADY DELIVERED	
				6	NOT PAID	
INV NO.	REF NO	DISCOUNT	CALLDAY & FREQUENCY	AMOUNT TO PAY	PAID IN FULL	
027	60857	10G	22 JUL W	£10.0.0		

AVE CAL.	LAST 3 CALLS		OUTER DESCRIPTION		NUMBER OF OUTERS ORDERED 1 2 3 4 5 6 7 8 9 0
5	8	24 X 4 OZ	ORANGE	LABEL	
5	1	12 X 4 OZ	RED	LABEL	
13		24 X 4 OZ	QUICK	BREW	
		24 X 4 OZ	PREMIUM		
1	1	24X4OZ PREMIUM (PRIMO COMICS)			
		24 X 4 OZ	GREEN	LABEL	

					1 2 3 4 5 6 7 8 9 0
1		12 X 12 OZ SHORT	PASTRY	MIX	
2		12X8OZ PURE COFFEE-ORIGINAL			
1		24X4OZ PURE COFFEE-ORIGINAL			
2		12 LGE	BEV	LARGE	
		12 LGE BEV(CLOTHES PEG OFFER)			
3	1	6 X 1 LB	READY	BREK	
3		12 X 8 OZ	READY	BREK	
1		12 X 8 OZ SHORT	PASTRY	MIX	

PA.D   £ 20.0.10
INV.   £ 12.0.0   1234   28 JUN
C&N   £ 2.0.0   4587   4 JLY

UKF 007-4-A   PLEASE HANDLE CAREFULLY AND MARK IN BLACK PENCIL ONLY

Fig. 5.5 Modified (decimal design) tea order form.
By kind permission of J. Lyons & Co Ltd.

Further automation improvements 163

BAKERY SALES RECORDS   INDEPENDENT STOCK CHECK ADVICE

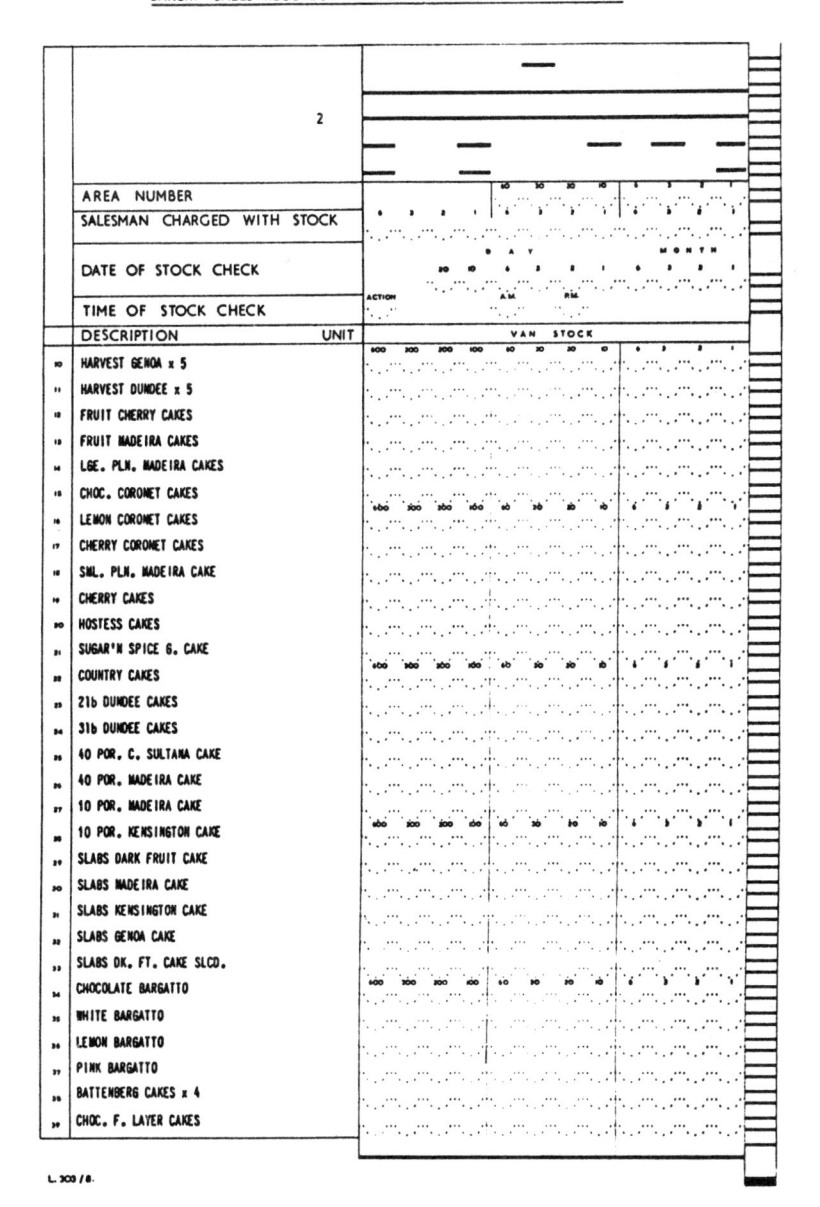

	DESCRIPTION	UNIT
10	HARVEST GENOA x 5	
11	HARVEST DUNDEE x 5	
12	FRUIT CHERRY CAKES	
13	FRUIT MADEIRA CAKES	
14	LGE. PLN. MADEIRA CAKES	
15	CHOC. CORONET CAKES	
16	LEMON CORONET CAKES	
17	CHERRY CORONET CAKES	
18	SML. PLN. MADEIRA CAKE	
19	CHERRY CAKES	
20	HOSTESS CAKES	
21	SUGAR'N SPICE G. CAKE	
22	COUNTRY CAKES	
23	2lb DUNDEE CAKES	
24	3lb DUNDEE CAKES	
25	40 POR. C. SULTANA CAKE	
26	40 POR. MADEIRA CAKE	
27	10 POR. MADEIRA CAKE	
28	10 POR. KENSINGTON CAKE	
29	SLABS DARK FRUIT CAKE	
30	SLABS MADEIRA CAKE	
31	SLABS KENSINGTON CAKE	
32	SLABS GENOA CAKE	
33	SLABS DK. FT. CAKE SLCD.	
34	CHOCOLATE BARGATTO	
35	WHITE BARGATTO	
36	LEMON BARGATTO	
37	PINK BARGATTO	
38	BATTENBERG CAKES x 4	
39	CHOC. F. LAYER CAKES	

Fig. 5.6 General purpose Autolector form. This one is for Bakery Van Stock. *By kind permission of J. Lyons & Co Ltd.*

appear on the order form, and for submitting orders where the forms were lost or damaged.

Though a "soup bowl" in any position could be interpreted by an application programmer to mean whatever business logic required, the entry of numbers was their normal use and this led to a problem for the design team that nicely illustrates the challenges of pioneering.

With twelve "soup bowls" in each row, the temptation, as originally adopted was for a straightforward binary approach in which marks would be interpreted from right to left, signifying 1, 2, 4, 8, 16, up to 2048 (the value of each position being double that of the previous one), the method allowing values up to 4,095 to be entered on one line. Regrettably, no forms of this design have survived. This approach, however, was found to be totally unacceptable to the salesmen, payroll clerks and others who had responsibility for completing the forms and so an alternative solution was adopted. Instead, the form was modified to create 10 columns and a decimal approach was used, with any combination of numbers used to create the required amount (see figure 5.5). An earlier analysis of tea order forms indicated that 98% of forms could be dealt with in this way whilst the other 2% could be dealt with by exception reports. (The computer remembered how many lines had been originally printed and thus questioned any additional which had been added.)

The tea order design was not suitable for all applications and other systems, such as payroll, had their own unique marking rules. Some systems used a general design (see figure 5.6) whereby the marking area was divided into hundreds, tens and units. This allowed up to 999 to be entered on one line: if a system required higher values, two lines of the form could be allotted. The four "soup bowls" for each decimal position were not labelled 1, 2, 4 and 8 (10, 20, 40 80, and 100, 200, 400 and 800) but 1, 2, 3 and 6, (10, 20, 30, 60 and 100, 200, 300 and 600) since this combination allows each value from 0 to 9 to be marked with a maximum of two dashes, whereas the pure binary labels need three dashes to enter the value 7.

By 1966 the LEO III/7 machine was fully occupied, running on three shifts with little or no capacity for additional work. With some way to go to complete the Master Plan, a second, more powerful LEO 326 (LEO III/46) was installed alongside the older machine; this greatly improved the operational schedules and provided faster test facilities for the team of programmers. This second machine, heavily discounted by their subsidiary company, had cost Lyons £189,814, with annual engineer maintenance of £14,482 for three-shift working.

Even when the main computers were working 24 hours a day the capacities of the Autolector and Xeronic printer were such that they could meet the needs of the two computers fully, with considerable spare capacity. Both reader and printer were only occupied with operational work for something like 5 hours in each 24. Most input was carried out during the morning and the corresponding printing during the evening and night shifts. For security, two Autolectors were installed, one allotted to each machine, but because of the high capital cost (£90,000), only one Xeronic printer was used. This sometimes led to delays in printing if prolonged machine faults occurred. Occasionally, the accumulated printing backlog would take a full 24 hours, or longer, to clear. At these times several miles of paper could be printed in one session. This new technology did from time to time cause some anxious moments when machine failures lasted for several hours.

An even greater risk posed by the Xeronic printer and not initially realised by the management was from fire. The printing process used a powerful heating element, the fuser, to melt the toner into the paper. The paper was kept moving fast enough to prevent it being exposed to the heat long enough for it to reach burning point (451 degrees Fahrenheit). Flame traps were included in the Xeronic printer to prevent the spread of any fire that might occur in the fuser, but this gave a false sense of security. At 2 a.m. on 12 July 1967 a combination of circumstances resulted in the paper catching fire. The blaze quickly got out of hand and almost destroyed both computers in use at the time. The action of staff and the prompt arrival of the fire services prevented a total loss of computerised records, machinery and possibly the building itself.

The investigation following the fire revealed that the printer contained a few inflammable components which, when added to the plentiful supply of combustible material, such as tinder dry paper trimmings, constituted a real fire hazard. Automatic room extinguishing facilities, such as Halon gas, were not widely used in computer installations at the time, and the portable extinguishers proved totally inadequate to deal with the fire that quickly developed. Fortunately, when constructing the computer room Lyons had wisely chosen fire resistant materials and had the good sense to treat all timber floor joists with a special fluid, making them fire resistant.

Both computers were damaged by heat, fumes and smoke. The older LEO III was more seriously damaged, as this was nearer to the printer, being installed in the same air-conditioned room. So intense was the fire that the printer castings buckled, resulting in its total destruction before the fire was brought under control.

Shortly after the fire alarm had first been raised, the computer management and the Lyons' Works Services staff, who worked 24-hour shifts because of the food factory operations, were soon on the scene and a plan was formulated to deal with the situation. The computer maintenance engineers brought the LEO III/46 computer into operation by 10 a.m. the following day but because of the smoke and particle deposits several long failures occurred during the next 48 hours. The LEO III/7 machine was more seriously damaged and was to remain out of action for several weeks. It became necessary to dismantle wash, test and replace every circuit card within the machine. Lyons' laboratory staff, usually concerned with the amount of fat or water in food products, were called upon to suggest a cleansing fluid for the delicate electronic components. They suggested a method of immersing each circuit card into a special liquid and using ultrasonic vibration to dislodge the persistent soot particles. This was a slow and tedious, but effective, process. Nineteen computer engineers were drafted in for the cleaning up operation and several other specialists were used away from the site. Despite the considerable efforts of the engineering staff Lyons decided against publicity when the machines were finally brought back on-line. All realised that had the machine been of IBM or other American make it might have been replaced almost overnight. This point might have been seized upon by the press and it was thought that such publicity might have an adverse effect on future LEO III sales.

The replacement of the Xeronic printer was a more serious problem as all the computer programs that required volume printing had been designed for its use. They could be switched to conventional line printers only with major changes that would have taken many weeks to complete.

The high capital cost and the need for specific customisation meant that the manufacturers did not keep machines available for immediate delivery, but they were made to order, with delivery taking up to 12 months. Fortunately, at this time a new Xeronic printer was awaiting

Further automation improvements 167

delivery to a Government Ministry and arrangements were made for it to be redirected to Lyons in view of the seriousness of the situation.

Considerable effort was required to take out the old machine, modify the new one and install it. The printer weighed 1½-tons and walls had to be demolished to effect the installation speedily. The normal six-week commissioning period was condensed into just 72 hours by a very dedicated engineering crew who worked continuously until the operation was complete.

Despite everyone's efforts it was not possible to process the Lyons work on the one computer, particularly as it was now periodically faltering, making it necessary to rerun programs frequently. With the close co-operation of the National Data Processing Service (NDPS) it was possible to transfer some work to their LEO III computers under a previously negotiated mutual stand-by agreement. This arrangement continued for several weeks and in this way an almost regular service, at least in those applications on which the business depended heavily, was maintained. Under the same arrangement Lyons made use of the NDPS's newly installed Xeronic printer until their new one had been commissioned. That compatible computer equipment was available so close to their offices was convenient for Lyons, and for a Xeronic printer also to be available was incredibly fortunate.

This incident, together with the less than satisfactory reliability of the printer, must have helped in its eventual demise. Although discrete transistors had been used in its design from the outset Rank Data Systems could achieve an operational efficiency of only 80–90%, and the printer's complicated engineering design made it very expensive for all but the largest computer installation with high volume output. Each machine was specially built to the customer's requirements, taking account of the computer system with which it would be used and any special user requirements. As the 1960s passed and electronic computers became more reliable with the use of integrated circuits, Rank Data Systems, after a feasibility study, found it necessary to redesign their printer to match the new performance requirements. From studies made by Brotherton's team in 1965, they calculated that if the character generation could be undertaken by software, and a microcomputer was used instead of expensive circuitry, a substantial cost reduction and improvement in reliability could be achieved.

The single-product vulnerability of Rank Data Systems had long been realised by its management, and in 1965 Brotherton put forward a plan to market other manufacturers' optical mark reading machines alongside their planned Mark VI Xeronic printer. During the spring and summer of 1965 a series of discussions were held with the Philco Corporation of America with regard to marketing their General Purpose Print Reader, a device that could read typewritten and handwritten numbers. The machine had been developed to read the United States Zip codes (postal codes) for use by the American Post Office. The negotiations were protracted owing to Philco's own marketing problems in the United States and the failure to secure an exclusive European marketing licence. At the same time Rank Data Systems had discussions with Recognition Equipment Inc. of Dallas, Texas, the only other manufacturer of satisfactory optical page reading equipment, but they required in return the right to market the Xeronic printer in the United States, a condition which Rank Data Systems could not agree to in view of the Xerox association.

Several events caused Rank Data Systems to abandon these plans. The United Kingdom computer companies began to merge, so their numbers diminished, narrowing the marketing opportunities. Faster and more reliable line printers were becoming available and it was possible to install two or three of these for the cost of the Xeronic printer, with the added flexibility of being able to print different jobs at the same time and having the security of backup in the event of failure. The other devastating event was the decision by the Xerox Corporation in the United States to pursue the manufacture of a similar printer themselves. As it happened, the Xerox venture was not a success but by this time the Rank Organisation had decided to cease manufacture of the Xeronic. The last machine delivered was to GCHQ in Cheltenham. This machine was capable of creating over 1,000 different characters. Rank Data Systems continued to provide engineering support for the few users in the United Kingdom and Europe until 1977.

CHAPTER 6

End of an era—a new beginning

At the start of the 1960s British industry had been less eager than some of its competitors in the United States and Europe to adopt the electronic computer as an aid to commerce or production. By the summer of 1960 only about 250 computers were in use in the United Kingdom compared with over 1,000 in Europe and many more in the United States.[1] Added to this, Lyons found themselves with several operational problems. First, they were finding it increasingly difficult to fund, from the reserves of their core catering and food businesses, the research and development of their computer subsidiary, with all that entailed. The revenues from the limited sales of their LEO III machines were barely covering the production and marketing costs, and any scant profit was totally inadequate for the continuing research budget. Leo Computers was running at an operating loss and, without regular injections of cash from the parent company, would have been insolvent. An operating loss had been made on six of the eleven LEO II computers manufactured between 1957 and 1961 and subvention payments to the value of £430,000 from other Lyons' subsidiaries became necessary. (See Table 6.1.) By 1962 Leo Computers Ltd bank overdraft was over £1 million with an additional £1 million owed to other creditors.[2]

The main reason for this under performance was the difference in price quoted for machines and the actual costs ex-factory, and the apparent inability to reconcile these. This may have been due to the lack of a proper accounting function, for it was not until 20 June 1960 that the first accountant was appointed.[3] Another significant factor was the lack of control or realistic charging rate for their senior consultancy work, much of which was devoted to designing their clients' office systems, for which they received little or no revenue. This detailed involvement on the LEO II marque was necessary, though expensive, but the management were wrong to believe it needed to be continued for the LEO III models. The emergence in the 1960s of competitive domestic electronic companies engaged in computer manufacture dramatically reduced LEO's share of a market that was estimated to be worth no more than about £5 million a year.

Table 6.1 Leo Computers Ltd—Trading Information

Year End	Profit/Loss £	Less Tax £	Less Subventions £	Net Profit/Loss £
31.03.1955	No information for this year			
31.03.1956	3,344	3,075	nil	269
31.03.1957	(9,768)	172 refund	nil	(9,596)
31.03.1958	(5,672)	1,421 refund	nil	(64,251)
31.03.1959	(117,628)	nil	100,000	(17,628)
31.03.1960	(116,475)	nil	100,000	(16,475)
31.03.1961	13,902	nil	nil	13,902
31.03.1962	258,060)	nil	230,000	(28,060)
30.09.1962*	(182,171)	nil	nil	(182,171)
Totals	(732,528)	1,482	430,000	(304,010)

Source: English Electric merger January 1963. Figures in brackets represent losses.
* Six months only.

Table 6.2 Sales by Value of all UK Manufacturers of Electronic Computers

Year	Home Market	Export Market
1957	2,894,500	987,700
1958	4,243,700	1,023,200
1959	5,572,000	2,090,200
1960	5,895,000	2,301,100
1961	9,687,100	1,261,600

Source: Central Statistics Office of the Ministry of Supply.

Competition made it more difficult to sell the LEO III and a reduction in selling price from £249,000 to £227,000 in 1960 shaved profits even further.[4] In May 1961 Caminer suggested to his management that in order to sell computers it was essential to have a substantial reputation in the electronics field, and he was deeply concerned about the growing Honeywell threat to the UK market.[5] Honeywell being well respected in the process control business. Compared with IBM and ICT, LEO's maintenance quotations were high, which tended to cast doubt on their basic reliability.[6] With so much of the LEO equipment subcontracted or bought in and modified, Lyons' electronic experience became questionable. In 1954, when Lyons had first decided to launch their computer manufacturing company, only two other United Kingdom companies, Ferranti and Elliott Brothers, could compete with them. These companies were both targeting the scientific market and, at that time, could not provide the commercial requirement for input and output attachments. Even at this early stage, however, Lyons realised that some machines becoming available were technically more advanced than their own, such as Elliott's fully transistorised machine, but they felt they still had the competitive edge. They progressively found themselves in fierce competition with Ferranti's Orion computer, which was not only faster in store access and arithmetical operations than their own LEO, but considerably cheaper: similar equipment quotations for the LEO III came out £100,000 more expensive. The Orion machine used a binary code on magnetic tape, which resulted in more dense packing. Also, the gap between blocks of information was smaller on Orion than on LEO III. Ferranti were also thought to be further advanced with their operating routine and autocode facilities, and in addition to all this they were able to supply the Pegasus, Mercury, Atlas and Sirus machines for specialised engineering and scientific work. The excellence of Lyons' job planning ensured they were frequently one of the last two competitors in each case, but in the final event customers were buying what they considered the most competitive deal, and there was no comfort in coming second.

The inability to deliver to time was also a source of annoyance. Their suppliers, Decca for tapes and Ferranti for magnetic drums, were having technology problems themselves and this had a knock-on effect. It must be said also that the LEO team were seriously under-resourced, particularly with regard to research graduates, and at one time Anthony Salmon questioned whether Leo Computers were over committed in their operation.[7] All this developed at a time when many large industrial undertakings were beginning to give serious attention to their computer requirements.

By the early 1960s the number of United Kingdom and other computer suppliers had increased, with Electric and Musical Industries, English Electric, Standard Telephones & Cables Ltd, Associated Electrical Industries Ltd, British Tabulating Machine Company, International Computers & Tabulators Ltd (BTM/ICT), Burroughs Machines Ltd, De La Rue Bull Machines Ltd, Honeywell Controls Ltd, International Systems Control Ltd, Monro Calculating Company Ltd, National Cash Register Company Ltd, Packard-Bell Computer Corporation, and Remington Rand Ltd joining the two previously mentioned. It is not surprising therefore, that many potential buyers of computers regarded Leo Computers as some kind of amateur operation competing for business against the well-established electronic firms. The *Journal of the Office Management Association* reported in 1957, perhaps unfairly, that "A potential computer user needs to have some confidence in his own judgement if he is to buy his computer from a teashop". Leo Computers Ltd was the only electronic computer manufacturer without a pedigree associated with electrical or mechanical manufacturing, and, incidentally, was the only company in the entire industry whose sole business was the manufacture of computers. It is not surprising that some journalists questioned the wisdom of buying from them.

More serious perhaps, was the threat from America, where great advances had been made in computer technology. American research and development budgets had been on a scale far in excess of those in the United Kingdom and as a result their products were well engineered, well packaged and superbly marketed. Their strong domestic base enabled them to enter the United Kingdom market, and this they did relentlessly. Not only were the American systems technically superior in some respects, many of them were more economically priced. Although some machines were not comparable in performance terms with the LEO IIIs their lower price made it easier for management to justify capital expenditure. Some companies chose a cheaper and less sophisticated machine, even though it failed to meet their complete processing needs. Some UK divisions of large America multinationals were also persuaded to buy American equipment, if only to maintain a degree of compatibility between data processing centres.

In October 1960, IBM launched their 1401 system. For some time this was a computer with only limited capabilities but its low cost and rental terms allowed many of IBM's customers to replace, with little change in system, their existing ageing tabulating equipment. This provided the first step, for many companies, to full data processing status. Many of these companies subsequently migrated to other IBM models as they became available and remained loyal to the IBM marque for many years.

Until 1951 IBM had not marketed their equipment in the United Kingdom. Instead they had an agreement with the British-based Hollerith Company, giving Hollerith manufacturing and marketing rights within the United Kingdom and Commonwealth. They considered their interests would be better served if they manufactured and marketed under their own name, and in 1951 cancelled the agreement with Hollerith. The severance terms specified that IBM would allow Hollerith the right to continue the use of existing, but not future, IBM patents. Thus IBM established themselves in the United Kingdom, opening their first factory at Greenock in 1951 and their first sales office at Park Lane, London in the same year. By 1955 the IBM company, which had started as a consortium of manufacturing companies, was sponsoring American television games, helping to endorse its high profile and technological know-how with the American viewing public; their dominance of office automation had begun.

Perhaps the most fundamental mistake which British industry made at this time was underestimating the American challenge. There was a sense of arrogance in some quarters, and developments in laboratories and universities did not find their way into the world of commerce quickly enough. As an example, the experience gained on the Colossus code breaking machines of World War II was not made available to industry for nearly 40 years, under the guise of secrecy.

Lyons, clearly, did not have the resources for expensive research and marketing follow-through and by the late 1950s only had half-a-dozen researchers working on LEO III, whereas IBM's research and development staff were numbered in hundreds; a pattern repeated throughout most of the America manufacturers of that period.

Preliminary research by Barnes, in July 1961, showed there was a market for a less expensive LEO III machine, which, if designed carefully, could reduce price entry level by £20,000 Any new machine, he thought, should be compatible with the standard LEO III so that the magnetic tapes would be interchangeable. It would be a binary machine with an add time of 27 microseconds but with fast convert and reconvert action to compensate for the loss of the built-in mixed radix working. The assemblers would be the same as those used on the standard LEO III but with only five input/output channels. Most significantly, it would not be designed to operate in a multiprogram fashion but would run only one job at a time. His studies indicated that the machine could be available for delivery in September 1963. The intention was to offer industry an integrated range, to enable Leo Computers to compete in those cases where large organisations require central and peripheral computers able to communicate with each other. He also felt that Leo Computers should depart from numeric identification and that the new machine should have an identity of its own, even going so far as to suggest registering the name. He suggested LEO Minerva, the origin of which almost certainly stems from the address of the manufacturing plant in Minerva Road. Barnes probably did not realise the profoundness and brilliance of the name he had suggested since Minerva, in mythology, was the goddess of wisdom who sprang forth from Jupiter's head (in this case Barnes'), fully armed for combat; ready to take on the world, so to say!

However, his idea failed to generate sufficient interest with his co-directors and as a consequence was put on the back burner. Plans were laid, nevertheless, for a LEO IV and during 1962 a great deal of design work was carried out at Minerva Road.[8] Progress was slow and the project petered out as other events developed.

Disposal of Computer Interests

By 1962, the Main Board Directors were already embarked on other business plans more in keeping with their traditional food and catering businesses, and had realised that Leo Computers Ltd could not survive as an independent manufacturer. The management, too, had recognised they had seriously underestimated the pitfalls of becoming involved in high technology products and were clearly unable to compete on equal grounds with the major electronic giants. They decided therefore, to merge their computer manufacturing business with one or more similar British electronic equipment manufacturers. This they felt would free some of their investment capital which could be put to more profitable use.

This theme was echoed in discussions with Lazard Brothers, Lyons' merchant bankers, who coincidently were talking to the English Electric Company at the time on partnerships to enlarge their own Data Processing and Control System Division. Lazard's advised both English Electric and Lyons to put together a consortium of companies to fight off the IBM challenge which by now had become quite hostile, with IBM frequently using scare tactics about the vulnerability of Leo Computers. The Lyons and English Electric management agreed to hold their meetings at the Strand Palace Hotel to avoid any speculation arising from either party being seen in their counterpart's offices. Anthony Salmon and Sir Gordon Radley (1898–1970), an English Electric director, jointly toured Europe and had preliminary talks with Olivetti, Phillips, Siemens and Bull with a view of encouraging them to join a computer consortium but these talks were not successful. Lyons did not think that the Leo and English Electric companies alone were sufficiently large to mount a challenge to the Americans and were reluctant to proceed on this basis, but expediency, and the lack of alternatives, made it necessary to consider a Leo/English Electric merger seriously. Discussions were friendly and both companies worked hard together but both were conscious that the business community might conclude that the Leo company was failing, which would undermine the client base and jeopardise any potential business in the pipeline. English Electric, in particular, required that a statement be made to the effect that Lyons would remain associated with the new undertaking, that each would have three directors on the Board of the new company (English Electric had the right to nominate another), and that Anthony Salmon would continue to be one of them. At all times it was understood that the changes would take the form of a merger and Lyons would be committed to a new manufacturing consortium.

This arrangement was adopted and on 8 February 1963, J. Lyons & Company announced they had agreed with the English Electric Company to merge their computer businesses at home and abroad. To give effect to this merger the issued share capital of Leo Computers Ltd was increased to £2,000,000, of which Lyons and English Electric would each hold 50%. On 1 April 1963 a change of name was recorded, and Leo Computers Ltd became English Electric Leo Ltd. Sir Gordon Radley was appointed Chairman, and Anthony Salmon Vice Chairman.

English Electric gave assurances that all their computer activities would be carried out through the new company, except insofar as the work carried out by their almost wholly-owned subsidiary company, Marconi Wireless Telegraph Company Ltd. This work was specified as being in connection with air navigation, air traffic control for both civil and military purposes and equipment forming part of a communication system. Such assurances were embodied in the merger agreement. Lyons did not give a reciprocal assurance because they were advised it would be contrary to the provisions of the Restrictive Practices Act; English Electric were happy to accept Lyons' verbal assurance on this.

The publicity, jointly issued at the time, announcing the merger of the two company interests, said:

The English Electric Company had long been one of the acknowledged dealers supplying computers for scientific, educational and industrial purposes. They had been successful in marketing over thirty of their scientific based KDF machines which had evolved from their earlier DEUCE computers. Leo Computers Limited had been equally prominent as a manufacturer and supplier to industry and Government departments. The merger of the two interests constituted a powerful combination of research, development and production resources equipped to meet a large range of computer requirements of commerce and Government.

The merging of both company's activities was soon established and by 1 May 1963 the marketing, production, engineering and bureaux functions were integrated. In General Notice 1/63 (1 May 1963) it was announced that Thompson was to head the marketing activities, with responsibility to establish:

A powerful and effective sales force, to determine the detailed requirements of future customer applications and, in the commercial field, to provide specialist training courses.

He was assisted by Caminer and Donald Kilby, who came from English Electric. Pinkerton and Colin Haley were responsible for product research and planning.

The production functions and their associated services were co-ordinated to keep costs of manufacture to a minimum consistent with maintenance of the high quality demanded. Barnes was given the task

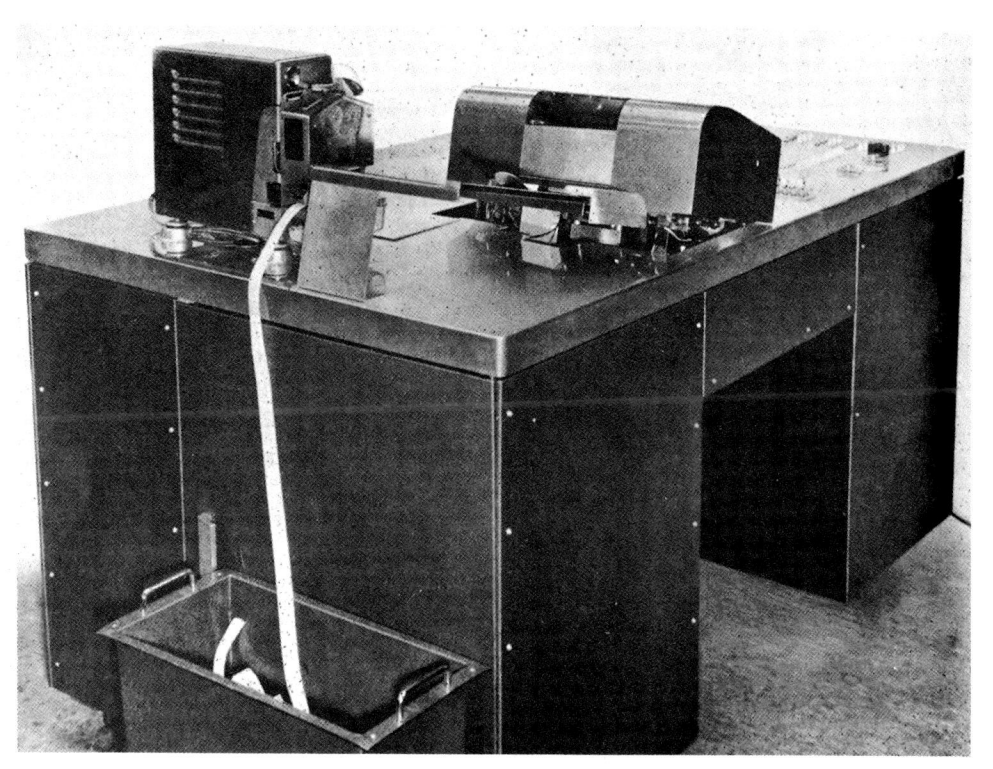

71. The prototype document reader designed by Dr John Pinkerton and Daniel Broido to read full-scap stationery. c.1959. *Reproduced by kind permission of J. Lyons & Co Ltd.*

72. The mark II document reader which became known as Lector. c.1963. *Reproduced by kind permission of J. Lyons & Co Ltd.*

73. A Kimball Tag reader with paper tape output. Tags were read at 150 per minute. *Anonymous.*

74. The Autolector, one of two used by J. Lyons & Co Ltd. Only nine machines were manufactured, four were delivered to HM Dockyards. 1966. *The author*

75. (*left*). The machine which led to Autolector under trials at Parnall, Bristol. This machine, which has a remarkable resemblance to Autolector, was designed initially to read football coupons. The period is believed to be the late 1950s. *Reproduced by kind permission of Stanley Thompson.*

76. (*above*). J. Arthur Rank talking to Ian Brotherton (left) at the first Electronic Computer Exhibition at Olympia in November 1958. *Reproduced by kind permission of Ian Brotherton.*

77. (*top right*). The assembled, but as yet non working, xerographic printer hastily prepared for showing at the first Electronic Computer Exhibition in November 1958. *Reproduced by kind permission of Bill Dunlop.*

78. (*right*). Rank's prototype xerographic printer under trials at their Shepherds Bush works. c.1957. *Reproduced by kind permission of Bill Dunlop.*

79. (*above*). The xerographic development team from left to right: K.C. Huntley, Dr A.T. Starr, R. Robertson and W.C. Dunlop. 1958. *Reproduced by kind permission of Bill Dunlop.*

80. (*below*). Bill Dunlop making adjustments to the cathode tube assembly which is placed above the Copyflo unit. *Reproduced by kind permission of Bill Dunlop.*

81. (*right*). The xerographic printer formhead. The cathode tubes are placed above the film optics. Two film strips are located in their respective carriers. From this position light sources, from the cathodes and film strips, would be projected by prisms onto to the selenium coated drum of the Copyflo unit below. *Reproduced by kind permission of Bill Dunlop.*

82. (*bottom right*). The Commercial Union Insurance offices in Exeter where this Xeronic printer is photographed. The Böwe guillotine can be seen to the left. *Reproduced by kind permission of Commercial Union Insurance Ltd.*

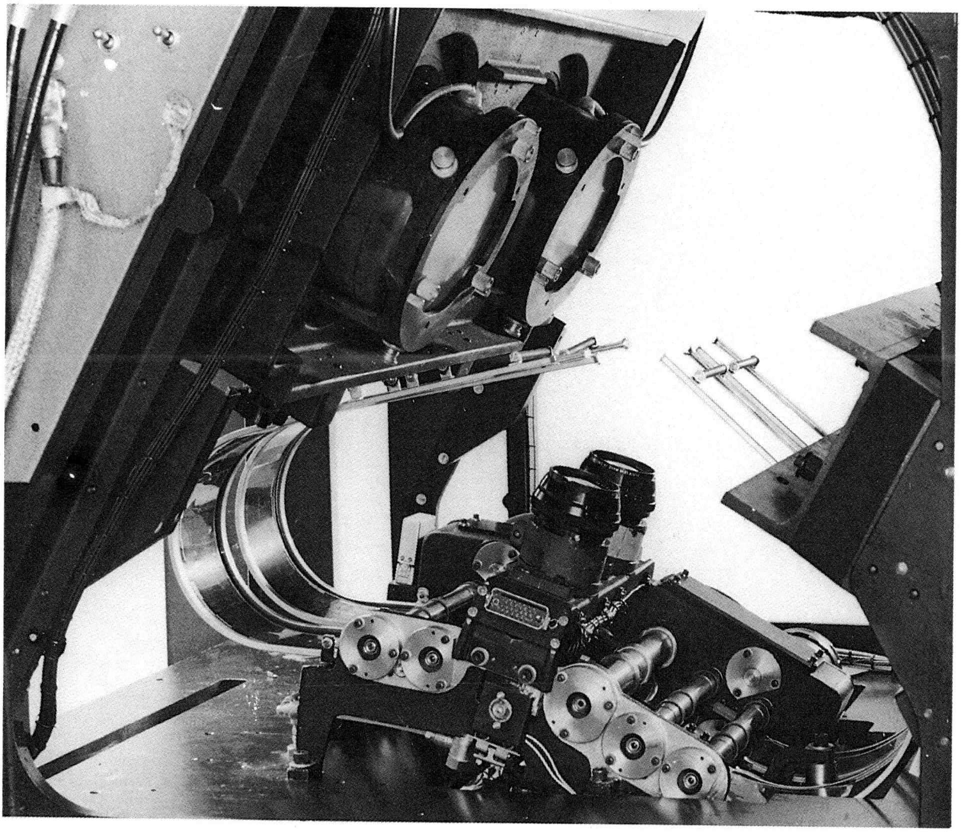

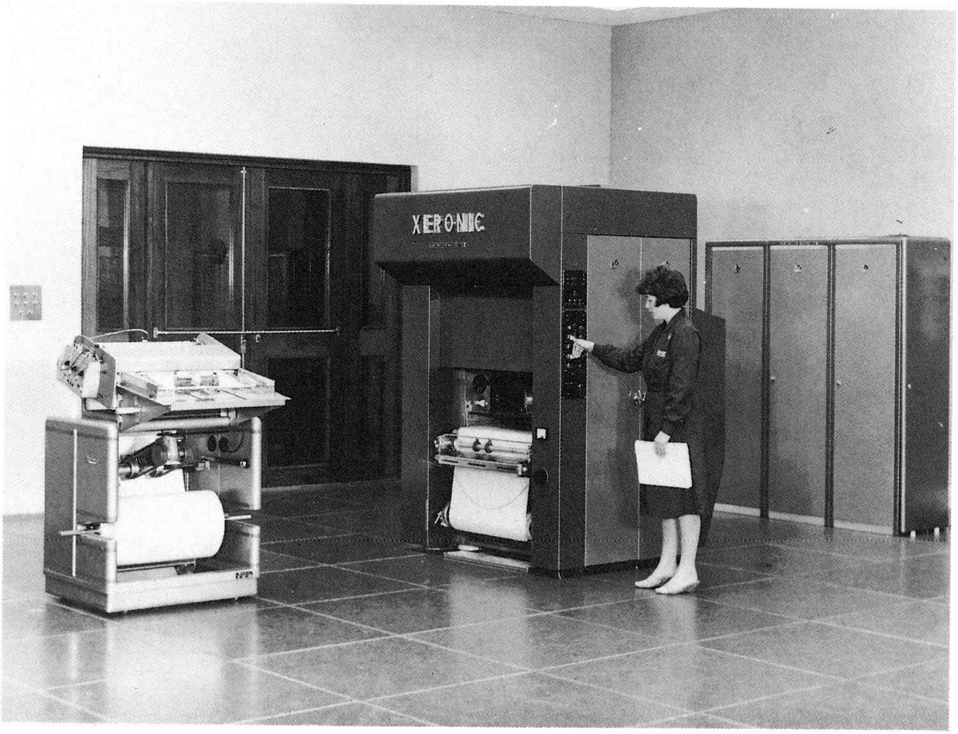
XERONIC

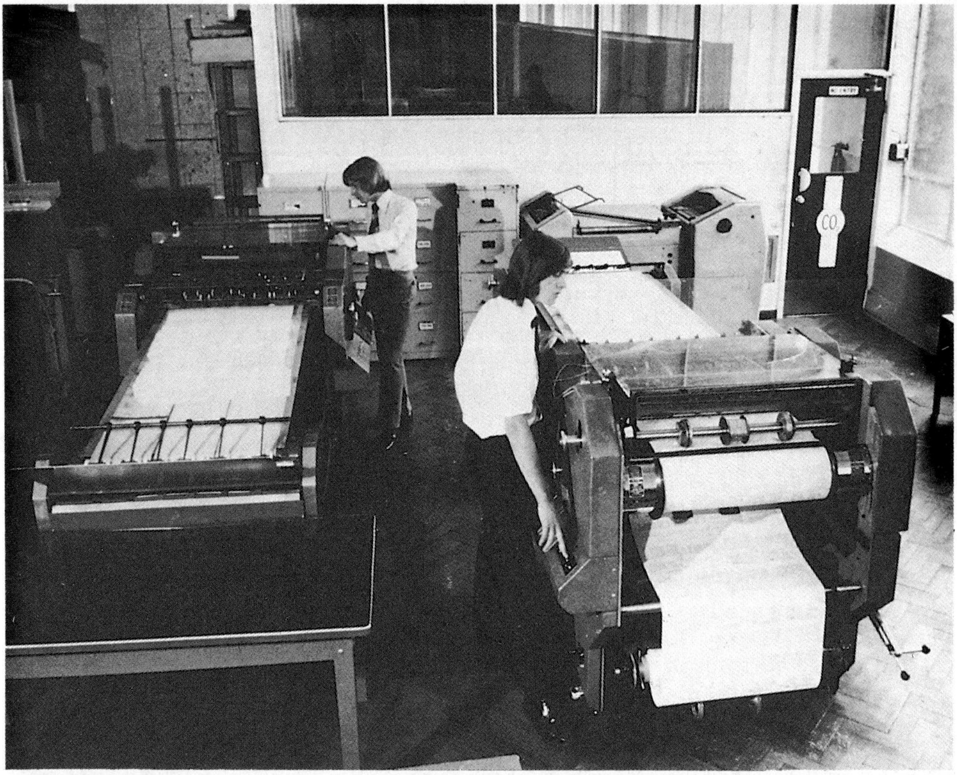

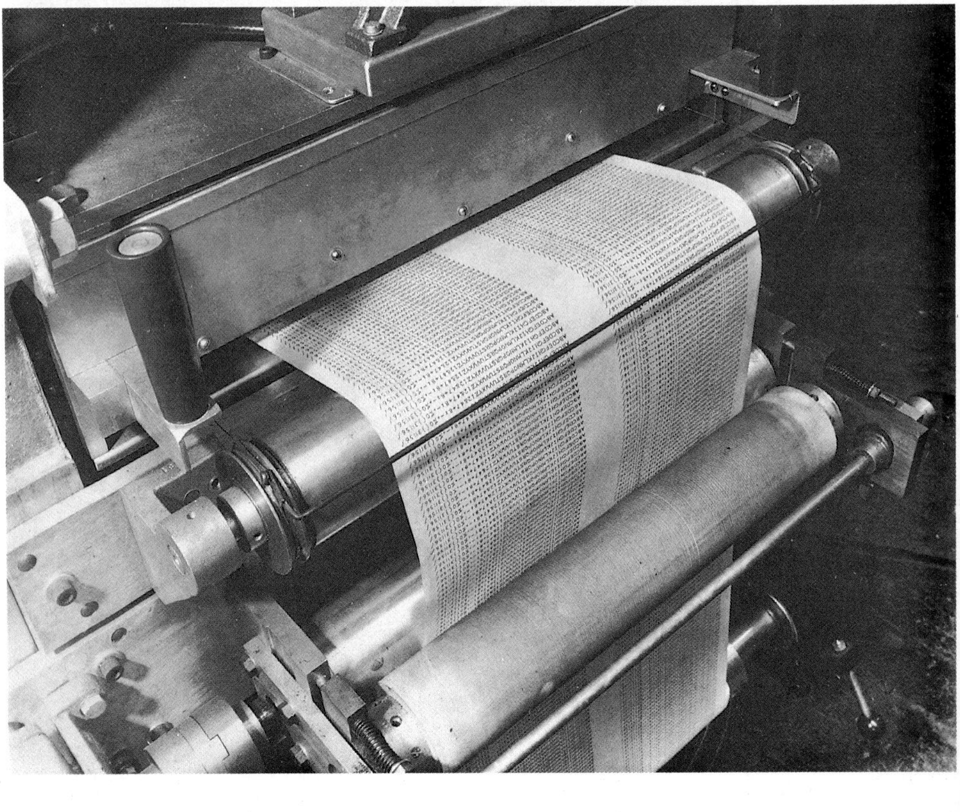

83. (*left*). The two Thompson guillotines used for cutting rolls of printed Xeronic stationery at Lyons. One roll equals approximately one hours printing. 1967. *Reproduced by kind permission of J. Lyons & Co Ltd.*

84. (*bottom left*). The printed paper as it exits from the fusing process. Any stoppage of this process required the immediate removal of the fuser unit (see vertical handle) to prevent fire. This photograph was one of a series taken in 1967 to establish how the Xeronic fire at Lyons started. *Reproduced by kind permission of J. Lyons & Co Ltd.*

85. (*right*). The side view of the burnt out Xeronic printer. 2 July 1967. *Reproduced by kind permission of J. Lyons & Co Ltd.*

86. (*below*). The scene of the LEO III/7 computer room on the morning after the Xeronic printer fire. 2 July 1967. *Reproduced by kind permission of J. Lyons & Co Ltd.*

87. Some of the engineers involved in bringing LEO III/7 back into service after it had suffered damage resulting from the Xeronic printer fire. 1967. *Reproduced by kind permission of J. Lyons & Co Ltd.*

88. A collection of power units from the dismantling of the Inland Revenue's LEO III/25 computer in 1975. *Reproduced by kind permission of Adrian Green.*

of integrating the production centres in London (Minerva Road) and Kidsgrove, where the main English Electric site was located.

The field engineering departments of both the English Electric computer division and Leo Computers were fully merged by 20 May 1963 under the management of Derek Royle. His responsibility was the provision and direction of a maintenance service for data processing equipment supplied to customers and to the service bureaux, the provision of supporting technical services, the final acceptance of equipment ex-works, and the installation and commissioning of Kidsgrove equipment on the users' premises. Royle was supported by Charles Ashby (Group Engineer, Operations) and Jack Richardson (Group Engineer, Support).

The computer bureau at Hartree House, already established and providing a wide range of data processing facilities to industry, was made the responsibility of Clifford Robinson. The new consortium considered this to be an important operation enabling its customers to carry out program writing and testing before taking delivery of their own machines. Moreover, the bureau was an important revenue source, which provided cash flow as well as a centre where products could be shown to best advantage; a working environment.

By July 1964 the agreement made between English Electric and J. Lyons & Company was causing some embarrassment to the English Electric management. It transpired that the restriction on the English Electric group—from operating independently—hampered computer development, particularly Marconi's development which, it was said, if they were free to go ahead, would be to English Electric–Leo's advantage. To overcome these obstacles it was originally proposed that a company comprising of members interested should be formed to act as a management/consultative committee for the two companies. Whilst this was a real step forward, solving some of the problems, the task of the company would not be an easy one where decisions on fringe matters were concerned, and there were plenty of them.

Instead, at Anthony Salmon's suggestion, and after refinement by both sides, it was agreed that English Electric–Leo Computers Ltd and Marconi should merge and come under one management and not three as would have been the case if the original English Electric proposal had been adopted. Having regard to the relative sizes of the two companies concerned, it appeared that Marconi should absorb English Electric–Leo. This meant that English Electric had to make an exchange with Lyons of shares in their own company for Lyons' holding in English Electric–Leo. The consequence of this would mean that Marconi would be in complete control with responsibility for the work in hand and the staff of English Electric–Leo. There followed meetings to agree the price of shares and on 2 October 1964 the following announcement was made:

The English Electric Company has agreed to purchase J. Lyons & Company's shareholding of 1,350,000 Ordinary shares of £1 each in English Electric-Leo Computers Limited for £1,856,250 which will be satisfied as to £1,350,000 in cash and as to the balance by allotment of 210,938 Ordinary shares of £1 each in English Electric at an agreed value of 48s.0d. per share.

The net profits for the current year to 26 December 1964 of the computer company attributable to the shares being acquired are expected to be approximately £320,000 before taxation.

Lyons have achieved their main purpose of developing computers to meet the requirements of their own business, and the consideration agreed approximately covers Lyons' total expenditure on the Leo computer project since its inception. Lyons intend to retain the English Electric shares for the time being. Mr Anthony Salmon, a director of J. Lyons & Co. Ltd, will remain on the Board of the computer company.

The effect of this change in share ownership is that English Electric-Leo Computers now becomes a wholly owned subsidiary within the English Electric Group, which enables the resources of English Electric's principal electronic subsidiary company, The Marconi Company Limited, to be applied to English Electric's computer activity.

The results of the merger of the 1 April 1963 of English Electric's computer business with Leo Computers Limited have been very satisfactory.

At the same time The Marconi Company has built up very considerable resources in the development of high speed on-line computers essential to Marconi's fields of air defence, navigation and control and telecommunication data transmission.

These resources together with Marconi's capabilities in such fields as micro-electronic devices development will now be available to the computer company and thus ensure that The Marconi Company is fully engaged in the computer business.

The shareholding in English Electric-Leo Computers Limited which is being acquired will be transferred to the Marconi Company, and the computer company will be known as English Electric Leo Marconi Computers Limited. Sir Gordon Radley remains Chairman and Mr W. E. Scott continues as Managing Director. The Marconi Company will be represented on the Board

The price Lyons received (£1,856,250) was less than had been expected; they had hoped for £2,000,000 to fend off any allegations from stockbrokers that they had lost money on their investment.[9] Whilst Lyons were not slow to extricate themselves from the computer "black hole" in 1964 it was not their intention to divest themselves of their computer commitment when they *first* (1963) formed their alliance with English Electric.[10]

The investment of £150,000 to build LEO I had, by 1964, turned into a total investment of £2 million, most of which, it is said, was recovered by the sale of Lyons' interests in English Electric–Leo Computers. At the outset, Lyons had not contemplated manufacturing computers for sale outside the group, but once LEO I came into operation in 1954 the market potential had become apparent. In the words of one executive, "We deluded ourselves that this could be a money-spinner".

The Death of LEO I

For Lyons, this period marked the end of seventeen imaginative years of technological achievement, during which time they had played a direct and important role in the development of the commercial computer industry of the United Kingdom. They had been instrumental in helping many large and famous companies both at home and abroad, to convert part of their clerical operations to computers and in so doing had made them more productive and cost-effective.

At 6 p.m. on Monday 4 January 1965, after a full day's work and 14 years of continuous service. The original LEO I computer was quietly closed down. Thompson, who had been part of the design team from the beginning, said in a farewell speech to press and other dignitaries: "The machine had seeded a great industry". Indeed it had. Nobody could have predicted the rapid growth of the electronic computer industry and the increments in computer power this was to bring. The LEO era is looked upon affectionately by all those people who were part of it, however modest their contribution. The author has never heard anyone talk unfavourably about those times, despite the many technical difficulties and social hardships the staff endured. The period generated an atmosphere of camaraderie that continues today in the

LEO Computer Users Association, which holds a reunion dinner every four years.

Parts of LEO I, specifically two half-adder units and two short delay tubes (one mercury filled), and one of Mary Coombs' coding sheets were donated to the Science Museum, London, where they are now on display. LEO II, installed in 1957, continue operating until 1967, when it too was decommissioned. The disposal of this machine was less ceremonious than that of LEO I. Sadly, there were no press releases, only a farewell drink in a public house for the few operators and engineers who had nursed the machine through its last moments when with full dignity it was finally switched off. Attempts were made to find a final resting place for the world's second commercial computer, but its size was such that museums could not find space, nor were they enthusiastic. It was sold as scrap metal to a company called Trading Post Limited in April 1967 for £500, their interest being the valuable mercury in the storage delay tubes and the gold plating that was used in electric relays and contacts Dismantling started on 10 April and was completed by 22 April 1967. Later, it was learned that some parts were used as theatrical props in a BBC television science fiction series, an ignominious end for such a unique assembly of electronics.

On 21 March 1967 English Electric–Leo–Marconi Computers Ltd changed its name to English Electric Computers Ltd when it absorbed the interests of Elliott–Automation Ltd; this company had been formed from a merger in 1957 between Elliott Brothers (London) Ltd, an old-established instrument manufacturing company, and Associated Automation Ltd.

By now English Electric were faced with the problem of concentrating their development on either the LEO machines or their KDF 9 (Kidsgrove Data Fast after their production centre). In the event they adopted a completely new system developed by Radio Corporation of America (RCA) and known as System 4. The System 4 range of processors was claimed to be the first family of computers in the world to use micro-integrated circuitry. This new generation of equipment was far more advanced than either the LEO or KDF 9 machines, and was more akin to the IBM System 360, which IBM had announced on 7 April 1964, and was regarded by many as one of the most significant success stories of the century.

On 25 September 1968, a Government-sponsored merger of English Electric Computers Ltd and International Computers and Tabulators

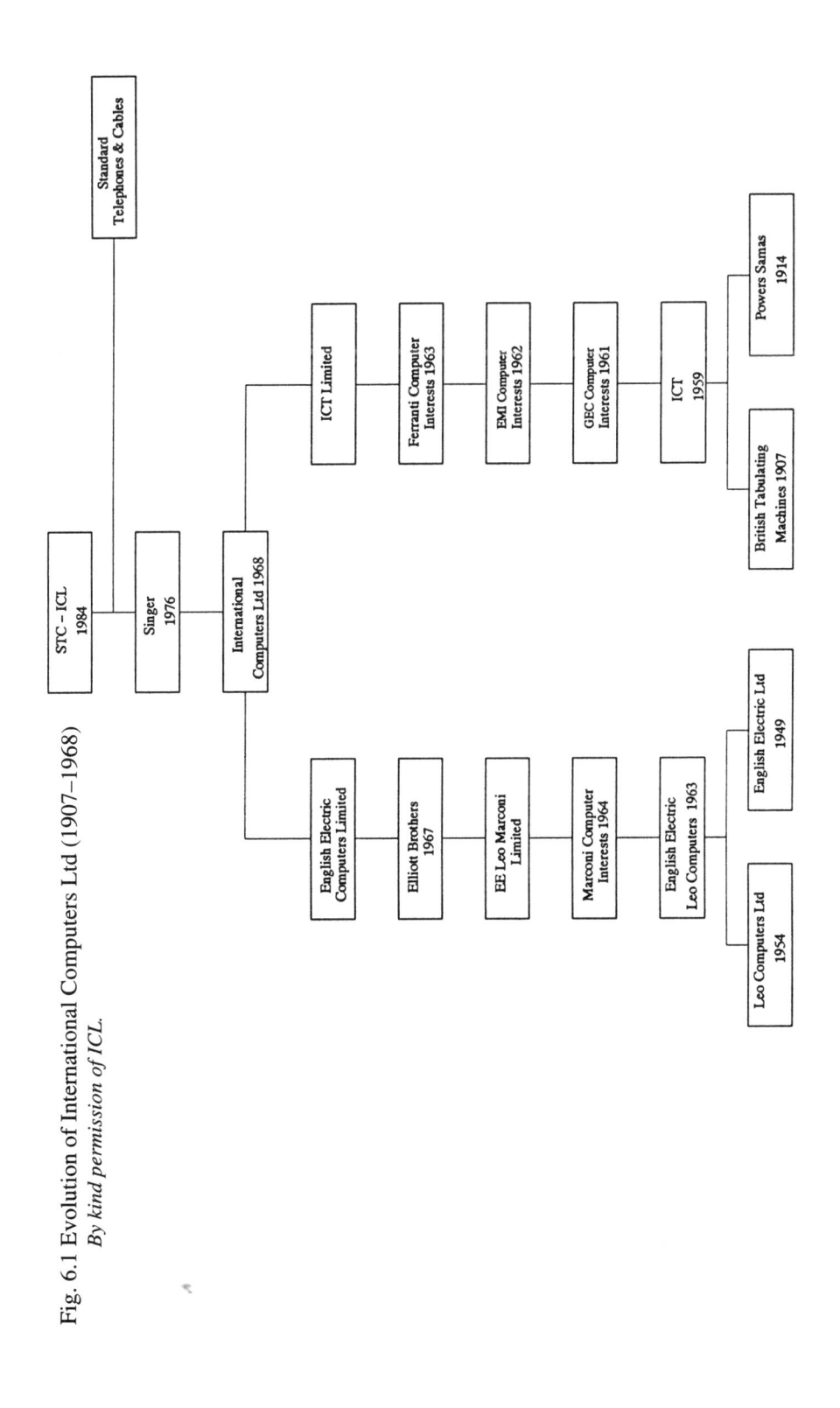

Fig. 6.1 Evolution of International Computers Ltd (1907–1968)
By kind permission of ICL.

Ltd (ICT) led to the formation of International Computer (Investments) Ltd (ICL). ICT had been previously formed from the British Tabulating & Machine Company Ltd and Powers-Samas Accounting Machines Ltd in January 1959, and had subsequently absorbed the computing interests of Ferranti, EMI (Electric and Musical Industries) and GEC. Thus, ICL contained all the original elements (Figure 6.1) of British computing, and subsequently developed the ICL 2900 computer to replace the System 4 and ICT's 1900 series.

Centralised Computer Policy is Challenged

The loss of the computer manufacturing business in November 1964 was a psychological blow to many senior staff at Lyons. Cracks also started to appear in the Lyons' Master Plan; the development was not proceeding as fast as some would have wished and some programs that had been developed were not fulfilling line management expectations. Other methods of processing using smaller mini computers were becoming fashionable and were attracting wide user interest. Mini computers were more compact, required less office space and consumed considerably less power. Fewer technical staff were required to operate and maintain them, which led to other obvious economies. The most appealing feature was their use of generalised packaged programs that could be installed and used by most clerical departments without any particular knowledge of computers. The large technical departments of systems analysts and programmers were becoming rarer although they never completely disappeared. The term "user friendly" was frequently used to describe this new generation of equipment.

In December 1969 a subsidiary, Lyons Computer Services Ltd, was formed in an attempt to bring the increasingly complex computer operations of Lyons under better control. This internal computer services company had three senior executives of the major user divisions on its Board: Desmond Brazier representing the Bakery division, Hugh Brown (1931–1983) representing the Tea division, and John Garner representing the Ice Cream division as well as Frederick Collins representing Central Accounting Functions. There were two other Board members, Leonard Badham (1923–1992), Chairman and a Lyons main board director, and, last but not least, George Stevens, Head of Computers, who was also responsible for finance. The new services company had separate divisions comprising operations, programming, systems analysis accounting and forward planning. The aim of this structure was to centralise the Lyons computer work and to produce uniform standards and procedures. This structure was not a success since the new service company was unable to influence users in the definition of their computer requirements, and those users who failed to define their requirements did not participate. A cause of extreme difficulty was that the user directors, who were on the Lyons Computer Services Board, had dual responsibilities; on the one hand to their divisional directors, who paid their salary, and on the other to their co-directors of Lyons Computer Services Ltd for which they received no payment. They, therefore, lacked commitment to the Lyons Computer Services company, and disagreements on policy standards and other major issues became a fundamental problem. Frequently, the operating divisions, who funded Lyons Computer Services Ltd, wanted the cheapest computer systems for their management; but the cheapest for them was not always the cheapest from a corporate viewpoint. Another irksome difficulty was the allotment of resources and, on this, agreement was almost impossible. Finally, there were personality and political problems that helped to fuel the disagreements. For five years Lyons struggled with this structure but clearly such conflicts were not conducive to the long-term planning of the group's computer capability and the disagreements were having a demoralising effect on staff.

During this period a complete reassessment of the company's hardware needs was undertaken by five of their computer experts, culminating in a report issued on 3 March 1969. For a year the team had carried out a comprehensive study of ten computer manufacturers, later reduced to five, which included Burroughs Control Data Corporation (CDC), International Business Machines (IBM), International Computers Limited (ICL) and UNIVAC. Each manufacturer was evaluated against a pre-selected list of criteria that included hardware, software, languages, utilities software packages, compatibility, support and maintenance. Some 80 separate measuring parameters were used, each having previously been allocated a weighting index. Test runs were carried out on the manufacturers' machines to validate claims. Other performance evidence was examined and many visits and discussions with users and suppliers were conducted. Computer Analysts and Programmers Ltd and the National Data Processing Service were used to advise on and check the validity of the approach, methods and scoring indicators. Eventually, after considerable lobbying by ICL to get the decision reversed, Lyons decided to standardise on a single supplier, and to adopt IBM data processing equipment for the foreseeable future.[11] From the very detailed study, IBM had obtained a clear leading score of 65.7% with the runners-up being UNIVAC (52.8%), followed by Burroughs (52.5%), International Computers Limited (51.6%) and finally Control Data Corporation (37.5%). Acting on the study team's recommendations, an IBM model 360/50 computer, costing £892,852, was installed at Cadby Hall on 9 March 1970, and was fully installed and commissioned by 26 March in a new computer suite occupying 7,500 square feet (twice the area initially required to allow for expansion of equipment), which had been built on the ground floor of Elms House over a period of eight months at a cost of £50,000.

In April 1972 Lyons disposed of their LEO III/46 to the National Data Processing Service (GPO) for £50,000 and in August their LEO III/7 ran its last job. 1972 therefore, for Lyons, saw the end of the LEO saga that had started twenty-five years earlier.

The Service Bureau at Hartree House continued in operation as Baric, and by December 1972 had replaced its LEO III computer with an ICL 1904A valued at over £400,000. The LEO III had been installed in Hartree House in 1962 to enlarge the computer bureau service, to provide program testing facilities for companies buying similar machines and to assist with software development. It was the first commercial time-sharing computer to be brought into service. Richard Shops Limited, one of the first companies to use the bureau and who had earlier threatened litigation in respect of program delays, were still using the service when LEO III/5 was decommissioned. Most of their LEO III programs were rewritten to run on the replacement ICL 1904A computer and those which were not were subcontracted to the National Data Processing Service machine. One of the largest bureau contracts that Hartree House handled was for Mark & Spencer, generating income of over £300,000 a year.

A late flowering of LEO occurred on 15 December 1980, when the Post Office, as it had become known, started the live running of its telephone billing application on an ICL 2960 computer. This work was already being undertaken on the LEO machines, but their age, the cost and difficulty of obtaining spares and the reluctance of engineers to work on older machines gave real cause for concern over their continued reliability. Because of two lengthy industrial disputes preparations for the transfer of the systems to the ICL 2960 had been seriously held up and the Post Office faced the prospect of a major delay in the transfer of work and a heavy resulting loss. Fortunately ICL had provided for the 2900 series a Direct Machine Environment (DME) system whereby a 2900 computer could be set up to run under the control of programs written for other types of machine. This had already effected emulation of both the 1900 and System 4 machines on the 2900. After a feasibility study ICL now undertook a £1-million contract over 18 months to develop a similar facility (DME/LEO 326) to enable the existing LEO programs for the billing application to be run on the Post Office ICL 2960 computer. Because LEO was microprogrammed and the original flow charts and logic diagrams were still available, the LEO programs were able to run on the ICL 2960 and were tested in good time. The project became operational six weeks ahead of the planned date, and the faltering LEO III/44 in use at Cardiff was replaced just in time.

The decision by Lyons in 1970 to adopt IBM equipment marks the end of their commitment to LEO, the project that had led them and the whole commercial world into the field of data processing. The adoption of new equipment did nothing to alleviate the organisational problems that confronted them, and it was decided that, after three years in operation, Lyons Computer Services Ltd needed to be given a new structure. The new organisation encompassed two divisions: an operating unit responsible for the day to day processing activities and a new unit to be known as the Data Processing Function. The operating unit continued to provide computer services to Lyons' divisions and charged commercial rates for the services supplied; in addition it marketed its services to customers outside the Lyons Group, as had been done when Lyons had set up their initial LEO service bureau fourteen years earlier. The sale of spare computer resources, through a marketing agency, proved moderately successful, but by this time other bureaux were active and competition was intense.

The Data Processing Function was staffed by four experienced senior members of Lyons Computer Services, whose brief was to co-ordinate computer activities in the Group, to encourage the exchange of ideas and to provide guidelines and advice on computer policy and practice. A user group was established to work with them in the full discussion of plans and proposals; to ease this work the Data Processing Function was given a research and development budget to allow studies to be carried out for user departments without the need to charge their costs to users.

This structure survived for little more than two years: the demand by Lyons' operating divisions to assume complete control of their data processing and to install non-standard equipment became overwhelming. Those tasks such as payroll and some database applications that were seen to be better handled centrally were continued as before, but users progressively began to install a variety of equipment; in the main this was supplied by IBM, but some equipment from other makers was also adopted. These developments, collectively, were expensive, not only because of the duplication of effort that inevitably resulted, but also because they prevented the group from taking full advantage of the exchange of information that would have been possible had there been full compatibility.

Almost half a century has passed since Lyons took the first imaginative and courageous steps that led to the development and acceptance of commercial computing in this country. Once LEO had passed into other hands and Lyons was left free to decide its own computing policy untrammelled by commitments to the development and manufacture of computers, it was found that the price of those early achievements was an accumulation of intractable problems that had grown steadily over the years. There was too little recognition of the need for close consultation and understanding between computing staff and line management, which resulted in a lack of agreement about the applications to be addressed and their relative priorities. Many computer experts had failed to realise that their proper objective had changed, and that they should now be considering, with operating management, how computers could best be used to improve the running of the business rather than their further use on clerical processing These experts had come to regard their technical expertise as of more value than that of line managers, and no longer sought to explain and simplify their craft. Consequently, many managers increasingly resented this arrogance, and developed a hostility towards automation that would take much effort and time to overcome. Anyway, the Master Plan, which had been developed so carefully by Simmons, and which, he thought, would eventually encompass the whole business, was abandoned, partly because of political opposition but also because of changes in the structure of the company towards decentralisation.

Many of the problems that Lyons faced were shared by other large concerns in their progress from the use of computers in limited and routine applications towards a corporate strategy for comprehensive data processing. There were some that were a particular heritage from the LEO project; the very factors that contributed to the earlier successes may now be seen to have sown the seeds of later troubles. The early programming team was recruited from people who were already working in Lyons, and who therefore had an understanding of how Lyons thought and functioned. This was of inestimable value in reconciling user needs with computer constraints, and the natural rapport overcame much of the potential conflict. But it also masked the need to recognise the inevitability of conflicts in the future and to find ways to resolve them satisfactorily.

The emphasis, by Simmons in particular, on pure requirements was in one sense another factor that aided progress by providing a firm basis for early applications, although it was soon realised in practice that the requirements for any job had to be formulated in the light of the practical means that were available. This emphasis obscured the perhaps much greater importance of the "perceived" requirements of user management because users sometimes suspected that systems were designed to meet the dictates of doctrine rather than to help them in carrying out their function.

Again, the achievements of Lyons between the wars in the field of clerical innovation undoubtedly helped in the rapid development of LEO and its early acceptance. On the other hand they persuaded management that the effects of innovation in this new field could be handled as easily and as smoothly. The computer was soon to become more than a mere clerical tool, and would call for innovation on a far wider basis, throughout the concern, than was realised at the time; had the true impact to operating management been appreciated earlier much of the opposition and mistrust that was generated might well have been avoided.

A further advantage of the LEO team as it struggled with the early technical problems of development was that the management responsible for its progress was also the management to whom many of its users answered. This, too, enabled differences between LEO and its users to be resolved rapidly and easily; but this very ease obscured the necessity of setting up a organisational framework which would, where possible, avoid such conflicts or, where not, allow their satisfactory resolution. The first signs of conflict appeared when an application serving several operational departments (teashops orders) had been installed, but the pressures for progress then were such that the problem was not adequately addressed. With hindsight, it might now be suggested that a complete separation of Lyons systems activities from those of LEO Computers could have avoided many later problems; still, the total resource available then would clearly have been insufficient for such a structure to have been established.

Those years had seen the birth and establishment of commercial data processing when computers were considered the concern of mathematicians only, and the few who had considered their relevance to industry had dismissed the thought. For a brief few years, Lyons alone had the vision to realise their potential and the courage to pursue it. Where other companies with the technical and marketing resources waited on events, Lyons, with a small but passionately dedicated team, demonstrated what could be achieved and helped to lay the foundations of a world-wide industry that has caused a revolution in information processing.

> It is unworthy for men of excellence to labour like slaves over tasks that could be safely relegated to machines.

Gottfried Wilhelm Leibnitz (1646–1716). German philosopher and one of the world's supreme intellects.

SOURCES AND CHAPTER NOTES

Few early historical records associated with the LEO project have survived. Official record keeping did not seem to exist, until the formation of Leo Computers Limited, in 1954, when the discipline of the company Secretariat at least, kept copies of some correspondence. The principal sources used in the writing of this book, therefore, are as follows:

The *Reports of the Directors* and *Annual Reports and Statement of Accounts,* of J. Lyons & Co. Ltd, between 1895–1978. These have been a valuable source of information associated with major company development and have provided a cross reference for dates. Leo Computers Limited—*Minutes of Meetings* between 1958 and 1963 and associated documents and memoranda which passed through the Company Secretary's office. These papers include correspondence in connection with LEO patents and some financial information, although the nature of the latter is limited. Leo Computers' records were destroyed in 1988 and are therefore no longer available to scholars. However, the author has had duplicates of the surviving Minutes bound; these will eventually be placed in a library or museum. They include: *Minutes of the Management Meeting; Marketing Progress Report; LEO Progress Report—Production; LEO Progress Report—Research; LEO Progress Report—Sales; Consultancy and Marketing Report; LEO Programming Progress Report; London Area Progress Report.*

A range of sales and publicity literature, brochures, technical manuals and other documents have provided a rich source of information. They include: LEO technical manuals, *The Layman's Guide to LEO* (written, by Derek Hemy, Ernest Lenaerts and others, to help general management to understand the workings of LEO), *The LEO Chronicle* (a diary of events compiled by Thomas Thompson —research has shown some of this to be inaccurate), technical drawings of LEO, program specifications, the papers of Ernest Lenaerts and user manuals and publications of the companies that installed LEO computers. Some sources have been obtained from trade journals and newspapers, in particular *Electronic Engineering.*

Libraries and museums have provided a range of sources and information and I am particularly appreciative of the friendly helpfulness accorded me during my research. These establishments include: Birkbeck College, University of London; the British Architectural Library, London; the British Library, London; British Telecom Research Laboratories, Ipswich; Bristol

Record Office, Bristol; Cambridge University Library; Hammersmith and Fulham Archives Library, London; Hammersmith Reference Library, London; National Archives for the History of Computing, Manchester University; the University of Melbourne; National Meteorological Archive, Bracknell; National Museum of American History (Smithsonian Institution), Washington D.C.; Newcastle-upon-Tyne Central Library; Newspaper Library, London; The Office of Population Censuses and Surveys, London; The Principal Registry of the Family Division (Probate Registry), London; Public Record Office, Kew; Science Museum, London; Supreme Court Library, London; Tower Hamlets Planning Department, London; the University of Pennsylvania, Philadelphia with special thanks to Gail Pietrzyk.

In most cases the help of those directly involved with the early development of the LEO computer(s) and peripheral devices was sought and information obtained either by interview or correspondence.

J. Lyons & Co. historical archives, which includes a complete run of the *Lyons Mail* and a miscellany of documents connected with the company's history. This source is not generally available to the public. The files of the Lujeri Tea Estate were researched before their destruction in 1988.

Notes to Chapter 1

1. Public Record Office, Kew. Ref. BT31/4383. Sale of Contracts.

2. J. Lyons & Co. acquired the Cadby Hall site, including the original Cadby Hall Pianoforte Manufactory, from Francis Drake Leslie, receiver and manager for Woodhouse & Rawson United Limited. The previous history of the site itself makes interesting reading. Charles Cadby (1811–1884), had acquired 8½ acres of land in the Hammersmith Road when it was known as Crofton Lodge Estate. He had been required to vacate his factory at 38/39 Liquorpond Street, London (now part of Clerkenwell Road) by the Metropolitan Board of Works for street improvements and the new estate seemed ideal for his new premises. He built his new factory and showrooms in 1874, to the design of Lewis Henry Isaacs (1830–1908), on 1½ acres, the remainder of the estate being set aside for ordinary building plots. On the ground floor, fronting Hammersmith Road, Charles Cadby built his new showroom with the works above. A clock with a weather vane in the form of a piano surmounted the building. At the rear of the imposing frontage were a collection of other less attractive buildings, which he used as workshops for piano fabrication, timber storage, packing case shop, stables and a coach house. The stables were still in use by Dobbin & Son when Lyons acquired the site

and they continued to provide stabling for Lyons when they took occupation of the premises. The building work, completed in eight months, had cost £26,024, an increase of £824 from the original quotation since he decided to have a fifth floor added. The keystones of the windows contained carved portraits of celebrated composers of the Italian, German and English schools.

After Charles Cadby's death, on 22 October 1884, the factory stock, comprising some 170 pianofortes and the valuable high grade warehouse timber, was auctioned and the estate sold. The pianofortes fetched £20, each with the exception of the grands. Cadby left his estate to his second wife and eight children. The oldest male heir, Charles Henry, inherited £1,000. He was in poor health and was advised by his doctor to move to a warmer climate. It is thought that he bought a plot of land in South Africa from a map supplied by agents in London, and that when he got there he was astounded to find that he had bought an area of land which took pretty well an entire day to ride round on horseback.

Shortly afterwards, he was approached by people who wished to have the mining concession on his farm, but he turned them away, thinking he was going to die at any time. Besides, he liked the wide open spaces the way they were. Finally, as his nephew recalled many years later, he was made an offer by somebody who came clean with him and told him that he was "probably" sitting on a diamond mine. He then sold his property, partly for cash and partly for shares.

It is not known what became of his family, although in 1931 one of his granddaughters, Muriel Cadby, visited Cadby Hall on her first trip to England from South Africa to see the former family business premises.

Between 1892 and 1894 Cadby Hall had been sold by the original owner to many different trades that operated on the site. The property along the Hammersmith Road, comprising the showrooms and space above, was occupied by the Kensington Stores Company and the buildings to the rear were used by several occupiers including the Maskelyne Typewriter Company, the electrical works of Messrs Woodhouse & Rawson United Limited and the engineering works of Messrs Epstein.

3. During World War II many city teashops suffered damage from bombing, and fewer were in existence in 1945 compared to 1939. Indeed, the teashop located at 54 Fore Street was damaged by the first bomb to fall on the City of London in World War II, at 00.15 a.m. on 25 August 1940. Later, as more establishments became unserviceable, the company introduced emergency teashops which were towed behind vans to areas of distress and devastation to provide basic catering facilities. Food and drink were sometimes provided

free of charge, especially to those made homeless and the emergency services.

Notes to Chapter 2

1. "How Lyons Gained Computer Lead", Oliver Standingford, OBE., The *Lyons Mail*, June 1979. Standingford's assessment of ENIAC's reliability appears wrong. According to Nancy Stern in her *From ENIAC to UNIVAC* (Digital Press, Bedford, MA, 1981), ENIAC's average error free running period was 5.6 hours (1955) during attempted running of 164 hours/week. The operating ratio was: 0:69. Good time: 113 hours.

2. Discussions with Anthony Salmon, 14 May 1992.

3. Originally from Shakespeare's *Henry V*. "We few, we happy few, we band of brothers".

Notes to Chapter 3

1. Forty years on from the first computer calculations, mathematicians are still using computers to calculate prime numbers. In March 1992 Harwell Research Laboratories issued the following press release:

Prime discovery at AEA Technology's Harwell Laboratory, England, "Scientists at AEA Technology's Harwell Laboratory, England, discovered the largest known Prime Number and the 32nd Perfect Number using the Laboratory's Cray-2 Supercomputer and software written by scientists at Cray Research, Inc., USA. This important mathematical discovery was published today in *Nature* magazine (26 March 1992). The new Prime Number was discovered during a routine test of Harwell's Cray-2 Supercomputer. It has 227,832 digits and is equivalent to the numeral 2 being multiplied by itself 756,839 times, minus 1.... the test took nearly 19 hours on one central processing unit (cpu) of Harwell's four cpu Cray-2 system. The number was checked on Cray's new 16 processor Cray Y-MP C90 system at the Company's Chippewa Falls, Wisconsin, USA facility. With a completely different programme on another Cray Research computer, the discovery was independently verified by Richard Crandall, Chief Scientist at NEXT Computer." The Cray-2 Supercomputer was installed at Harwell in March 1987. It is equipped with 4 processing units and has 256 million words (8 bytes) of memory, i.e. 2 gigabytes. In addition there are 25 gigabytes of very high speed disc storage. It is a vector processor and with all 4 processors working simultaneously is capable of 1,700 million floating point operations per second. The machine is a part cylinder which stands 4½ feet high and has a diameter of 4½ feet. It consumes 195 kilowatts of electrical power and is cooled by immersing the 250,000 integrated circuits in a flowing fluorocarbon

Sources and chapter notes 193

liquid. The clock speed of 4.1 nanoseconds is the fastest of any computer currently available. Michael Schomberg, AEA Technology, Harwell Laboratory, Oxfordshire.

See also John Maddox, "The endless search for primality", *Nature*, vol. 356 (26 March 1992) and Nigel Hawkes, "Harwell tots up an almost useless record", *The Times*, (26 March 1992).

2. Thomas Thompson, "The Converter" (16 January 1951). This was a rewrite of an earlier document prepared by STC. The functions of the converter were described as follows:

> (a) to control the reading of teleprinter characters at a speed of 333 elements per second from data tapes attached to two machines alternately connected to the converter.
> (b) to interrupt the teleprinter characters read from the data tapes;
> (c) when the character is a numeral 0–11, to set it up in its binary form;
> (d) to accumulate a running total of the successive digits of a decimal or sterling number, correctly combined in the binary form;
> (e) to multiply this running total by 2, 4 and 8 and add together the appropriate partial products, thus effectively multiplying the running total to date by either 10 (2 and 8), 2, or 12 (4 and 8), in preparation for the addition of the succeeding digit;
> (f) to provide a means of controlling the combination of the partial products referred to under (e) so that under normal decimal conditions the partial products times 2 and 8 are combined together to give a multiplication by 10; but also to provide that the first and second sterling colons in any sterling number change the combination of partial products so as to give a multiplication by 2 and by 12, respectively;
> (g) to provide adding arrangements so that the running total multiplied by the appropriate factors shall be added to the digits just taken in to give a new running total;
> (h) when a minus sign character, or a series of characters making up a designation number, is received, to provide that the appropriate binary digits are inserted in the running total;
> (i) when a space character indicating a short number break is received, to feed the digits of the running total to the calculator in the form of a pattern of 17 pulses (or no pulses), together with 18 marker pulses, the first preceding the first binary position of the running total, and the others being coincident with the binary positions;

194   Sources and chapter notes

(j) when the long number indication character (L) is received before any number, to ensure that 35 positions are provided in the running total instead of the normal 17, and that the arrangements for the insertion of the sign and designation digits and for feeding out the number to the calculator are appropriate;
(k) when a carriage return character is received, to feed the digits of the running total to the calculator in the form of a pattern of 35 pulses (or no pulses), together with a marker pulse for each position, and one in advance of the first position; also to send a number-end pulse to the calculator at the same time as the last marker pulse;
(l) when a carriage return followed by three line feeds is received, to ensure that number-end pulses are sent out to bring the total of them for this block up to 16; also that a block-end pulse is sent out to the calculator at the same time as the last number-end pulse;
(m) to provide, for certain classes of date, that a warning is given if 16 long numbers, or pairs of short ones, are received without a block-end indication after the last and also to cause the converter to stop reading date;
(n) to provide, alternatively to (m), that for other classes of data a block-pulse is sent out to the calculator after each group of 16 long numbers (or equivalent) since the previous block-end indication;
(o) when the (z) character is received to ensure that the running total is fed, not to the calculator, but to the testing apparatus;
(p) when a signal is received from the inlet annex system to show that the annex tube connected to the calculator is not yet empty, to stop the tape machine from which data is being read at the end of the current block of data and to start up again when a signal is received to show that an empty annex tube has now been connected to the feeder;
(q) when the end cross character (+) is read from the tape, to stop reading from that tape but to start up the tape attached to the other machine and commence reading from that.

3. Standard Telephones applied for a patent (732,341) on 2 December 1949. This was the subject of a discussion at a meeting with them and J. Lyons & Co. Ltd on 6 July 1961. They had made claims which had originally been put to them by J. Lyons & Co. Ltd and to which J. Lyons & Co. Ltd objected. Letter from AA Thornton & Co. Patent Agents to Lyons, 29 July 1955.

Original patents for the various components of LEO were taken out as follows:

Main case: Application number 19928/50, 10 August 1950. Inventors, Thomas Thompson, Oliver Standingford, John Pinkerton and Derek Hemy.

Loader: Application number 17170/51, 10 August 1950. Inventors, John Pinkerton and Thomas Thompson.

Reconverter: Application number 17171/50, 10 August 1950. Inventors, Thomas Thompson, Derek Hemy and Oliver Standingford.

Unloader: Application number 17172/51, 10 August 1950. Inventors, John Pinkerton and Thomas Thompson.

Converter: Application number 17173/51, 10 August 1950. Inventors, John Pinkerton, Thomas Thompson, Oliver Standingford and Derek Hemy.

Division circuit: Application number 30765/50, 18 December 1950. Inventors, Leo Fantl and Ernest Lenaerts.

On 3 August 1956 the Patent Office cited certain Raytheon computer patents against the claims of LEO. Two articles published by Raytheon described, in general terms, a computer in which input data is on tape, and is transferred to one of two mercury delay lines used in turn, before being transferred to the internal memory of the calculator; a converse arrangement was used as output. It was said that the computation and recording can proceed simultaneously. This seemed to be the precise feature in the concept of the LEO loader and unloader and although Thomas Thompson undertook to have the matter considered further, no interpretation of the disclosure of the two articles could be found which avoided that conclusion. Letter AA Thornton 3 August 1956. On 13 September 1956 Lyons abandoned the patent application for LEO. Letter 13 September 1956.

4. In the early days of LEO valves were used, or not, depending on their availability. In the course of usage over several months some types were found to be less reliable than others and were replaced with alternatives. As a result there is no definitive list of the types used. However, the following memorandum issued by Ernest Kaye on 14 January 1959 gives some indication of the types and numbers in use on the LEO II at that time.

Valve type	quantity used	valve type	quantity used
A2293	4	M8123	80
E33CC	60	M8195	105
E88CC	2,500	M8206	4
E180F	760	VR105	26
EF80	600	6F33	6
EL34	170	6057	20
EL83	85	6058	1
EL822	1,230	6060L	640
M8083	500	6067L	430
M8098	11		
Total	7,232		

5. *Valve Failure Analysis*, Ernest Kaye, 6 February 1953

6. The Runge–Kutta method is a one step method for numerically solving the Cauchy problem for a system of ordinary differential equations in the form: $u = f(t, u)$. The principal idea was proposed by Carl Runge (1856–1927) and developed later by Wilhelm Kutta (1867–1944) and others. *Encyclopaedia of Mathematics*, vol. 8, p.194.

7. This figure was provided by Anthony Salmon in my discussions with him on 14 May 1993. He recalls going to the Board himself, raising the issue, and in double quick time got their approval. In Thompson's *The LEO Chronicle*, he records a figure of £10,000. Since Anthony Salmon's recollection of other events and figures were remarkably accurate—I was able to check these with written evidence—I am inclined to believe that £20,000 was the true amount, particularly as other figures in Thompson's *Chronicle* were found, after research, to be wrong. He lists a £2,500 donation to Cambridge, for example, when in fact it was £3,000.

8. The figure of £150,000, spent over five years, seems unrealistically low but at that time it was a great deal of money. Today's equivalent would be nearly £2 million. For comparison Lyons profit for 1954 was £686,914.

Notes to Chapter 4

1. Conversation with Ernest Lenaerts, 19 October 1988.

2. *Report on US Visit*, Thomas Thompson and Anthony Barnes, October–November 1955.

3. Discussion with Anthony Salmon, 14 May 1993. Salmon & Gluckstein Ltd was sold to the Imperial Tobacco Company (ITC) in 1902. The ITC had been incorporated from a consortium of companies, including W. D. & H. O. Wills, John Player & Sons Ltd and 11 other independent tobacco companies, in 1901 to fight off the challenge of the ruthless American tobacco baron James Buchanan Duke (1857–1925).

4. *Leo General Management Meeting*, 10 May 1962 and 30 May 1962. *London Area Progress Report*, 7 September 1962. "Average this period 85.1 hrs., average last period 76.5 hrs." (expressed as a percentage of switched on time).

5. *Minutes of the Leo General Management Meeting*, 10 August 1962. "Mr Collier, Chairman of the United Drapery Stores, was also attempting to claim for loss of business sustained because of the delay..."

6. *Lyons/LEO III Project*, John Simmons, April 1961

7. *Lyons/LEO III Project*, from Arthur Robey to John Simmons, 14 December 1961.

8. *Lyons/LEO III Project*, memorandum from Arthur Robey to John Simmons, 14 December 1961. "with a resulting reduction in clerical costs that is sufficient to recover, within 4 years of operation, the capital sum, interests on capital at 6 per cent per annum and the preliminary and operating costs involved which amount to just over £500,000 in the period of the project..."

Notes to Chapter 5

1. *Minutes of the Management Meeting*, 19 June 1959. "There was a general discussion on whether it was worthwhile pursuing this project."

2. Conversation with Ian Brotherton, 18 June 1990.

Notes to Chapter 6

1. "UK Computers—many makes and few sales," *Financial Times*, 1 September 1961.

2. Balance Sheets. Leo Computers Ltd (7 January 1963) and Control Systems Division of English Electric Ltd (11 January 1963)

3. Appointment of John Garner as Accountant of Leo Computers Ltd from 20 June 1960. Anthony Salmon's memorandum to John Simmons and Michael Holmyard (Secretary) June 1960.

4. *Minutes of the Leo Management Meeting*, 14 October 1960.

5. *Minutes of the Leo Management Meeting*, 12 May 1961.

6. *Minutes of the General Management Meeting*, 12 October 1962.

7. *Minutes of the LEO General Management Meeting—Computer Time Commitments* 19 October 1962. "Mr Anthony referred to the report produced by Mr Smith showing how over committed we seem to be on computers."

8. *Leo Progress Report—Research. Item 9 Code Design for Leo IV*, 20 April 1962: "work has begun on this project with coding studies of the Westminster Bank model job."

9. English Electric–Leo Meeting at Lazard's, 8 September 1964: "Mr Anthony told him that we were looking for £2,000,000 to enable us to answer any stockholders' questions on the lines—had we lost money on our investment?"

10. John Hendry writing in *Business History*, January 1987, p. 91 says: "Any sale of Leo Computers Ltd to English Electric must be dressed up as an equal merger so that LEO customers would not be frightened away. English Electric agreed to this as a transitional measure, and a series of merger plans was developed accordingly." This implies that Lyons' intention at this time was to divest themselves completely of computer manufacture. The author's discussions with Anthony Salmon, 14 May 1993, dispute this view. Anthony Salmon made it clear that Lyons had no intention, originally, of disassociating themselves from the merged company, on the contrary, they [Lyons] were determined to stay with computer manufacture. The decision to

eventually sell their interests only came about later when the Marconi difficulties arose and it was clear that lesser shareholders of a new consortium would be unwelcome.

11. The ICL team was led by David Caminer. When the decision to install IBM equipment was made he was naturally very disappointed, particularly as IBM had previously used "unorthodox methods" to obtain orders against LEO machines. He sought meetings with the highest executives in Lyons to try to get the decision reversed but the directors stood by their computer staff.

BIOGRAPHIES

BARNES, Antony Bernard was born on 7 October 1926 of Herbert Bernard Barnes and Sylvia Mary (née Potter) in Liverpool and was educated at Bedford School. Between 1946–1947 he obtained a second class Mechanical Sciences Tripos (part one) and a second class Electrical-Mechanical Sciences Tripos (part two). He served as an Instructor Lieutenant in the Royal Navy and joined Lyons as a Management Trainee, where he worked in the Statistical Office. He transferred to the LEO programming team in November 1950 where his talents were quickly recognised. In 1955 he accompanied Thomas Thompson to the USA on a six-week tour, visiting several computer manufacturers and users. In January 1956 he became the Administration Manager of the Design and Development Section of Leo Computers Limited and in June 1959 the Production Director, reporting directly to Anthony Salmon, the main Lyons Board Director responsible for the whole LEO project. He left Leo Computers Limited shortly after the merger with English Electric.

BROIDO, Daniel (1903–1990). Born in Kirensk, Siberia on 17 May 1903 while his parents were in exile for their political beliefs. His mother Eva (née, Gordon) was born in Lithuania and qualified and practised as a pharmacist. His father, Mark Broido, was a chemical engineer but because of police harassment and imprisonment was a student for 17 years. His mother was a prominent member of the Russian Social Democratic Party and in 1902 was living clandestinely in Russia. During that year both his parents, as yet unmarried, were arrested and sent to Siberia for belonging to the Social Democratic Workers Party. During the long train journey into exile they decided to marry, on the train, and with the help of other prisoners travelling with them formed a quorum of ten Jews and were married in the absence of a Rabbi, borrowing a ring from one of the passengers on the train. Shortly after Daniel Broido's birth his parents escaped to England and Daniel Broido was brought up by his grandmother. At a conference in London in 1903 the Russian Social Democratic Labour Party split into two factions—the Mensheviks ("minority") and the more extreme Bolsheviks ("majority") dominated by Lenin. Broido's parents were associated with the Menshevik faction. His parents returned to Russia in 1905 and again lived illegally, in St Petersburg, working for the Menshevik movement, which itself became deeply divided in 1912. After the revolution of October 1917 his parents found themselves at odds with the ruling Communist Party and from 1920 they lived in exile in Berlin, where Daniel's father worked for the Russian Trade delegation. Daniel was separated from his parents for the entire revolutionary period (1917–1921) and was only able to join them in Berlin as a result of some extraordinary adventures.

Daniel Broido studied at Berlin's Technical University, obtaining his degree in Mechanical Engineering, and started working for the General Electric Company (AEG) and then for Rotaprint. In 1934 Herr Fischer, Director of Rotaprint at that time, made arrangements for Broido to travel to the United Kingdom to work at the Rotaprint agency in London at a time when the German authorities were vetting all workers. Broido believed that this transfer was carefully planned by Herr Fischer and that he owed his life to him. Fischer committed suicide soon after Broido left Germany. During World War II Daniel Broido worked for Caterpillar Tractors on tank design; he volunteered for the Army but was turned down because his work with Caterpillar was considered more important. Because of his having volunteered for the Army and his work on tractor design he was given British citizenship without delay in 1946. Broido returned to Rotaprint but soon left them to join Olding Developments Limited, where he became Managing Director and Chief Engineer. In 1950 Olding Developments Limited was sold to the British Tabulating Machine Company Limited (BTM) and his inventions and patents were transferred to them. He became senior Development Engineer on optical reading machines, becoming a pioneer in this field with over 100 patents to his credit. Among his inventions was the first sterling calculator, single cycle decimal calculator, computing scale, graph reader, and the printing calculator. He invented the first bar code system, which he called mini marks, and patented this on 6 February 1954.

In 1956 Raymond Thompson of Lyons recruited Broido as Chief Mechanical Engineer for all aspects of the LEO computer and he worked closely with Dr Pinkerton, designing optical mark reading machines such as the Lector. When Lyons started to export their computers to Eastern Europe Broido acted as interpreter and Sales Director. He spoke fluent German and Russian and had a very good working knowledge of Serbian. He was transferred to ICL at the time of the mergers and was mainly responsible for East European sales. Between 1966 and 1970 he made 34 trips to Eastern Europe for ICL, of which 21 were to the Soviet Union. He spent a lot of time receiving delegations of engineers and other important guests from the eastern block in promoting sales for ICL computers. Daniel Broido married Nordi Osten in 1940 and they had two sons, Michael and Stephen. Daniel Broido died on 10 October 1990, sadly before he was able to see this story in print.

CAMINER, David Treisman, OBE. Born 26 June 1915 in South Hackney, London of Henry Jack Treisman and Rachel (née Simmons). Joined Lyons in 1936 as a Management Trainee and after a statutory period of learning Lyons' methods was put to work on improving Management Accounts. During World War II he served with the Green Howards as part of the British 8th Army in North Africa, where he was badly wounded, losing a leg during the attack on the Mareth line in Tunisia in March 1943. After recovering from his wounds he returned to Lyons as Manager of the Systems Research Office in 1944. With his meticulous attention to detail he was responsible for the programming team and system specifications for the LEO computer and, undoubtedly, it was his groundwork in office procedures which helped to make the early computer programs so successful. Appointed Director Leo Computers Limited on 9 June 1959.

He transferred to English Electric Leo Computers Limited as General Sales Manager when English Electric and Leo Computers merged. English Electric Leo Computers Limited eventually merged with ICT to form ICL and David Caminer transferred to them as a Senior Executive. In 1981 he was awarded the OBE for his work and direction in the installation of a large ICL computer system in the European Commission Offices in Luxembourg.

COOMBS, Mary Clare, BA (Hons). Born 4 February 1929, daughter of William Blood OBE, MRCS, LRCP, DIH (Senior Medical Officer, J. Lyons & Co. Ltd 1936–1963) and Ruth Gwendolene Susanne, (née Petri). Educated at Putney High School and St Paul's Girl's School and Queen Mary College, University of London. Joined J. Lyons & Co. Ltd. in 1952 as a Management Trainee, starting work in the Statistical Office. After a few months she was invited to join the LEO team as the first woman programmer. Mary worked on many of the early programs including the Lyons and Ford Motor Company payrolls, was transferred to English Electric Leo Computers and subsequently to ICL as a result of the mergers. In 1955 Mary married John Coombs who, for a brief period, had also worked as a LEO programmer. From 1964 Mary ceased full-time work because of family commitments but continued to work part-time in the training department of ICL, editing manuals and for a few months running a computer programming course for severely handicapped residents at Princess Marina Centre at Seer Green, which was also attended by a young offender from Finnamore Wood Camp. This work was jointly sponsored by ICL and Buckinghamshire County Council. At the end of 1969, Mary severed her connections with the LEO team, because she was then unable to return to full-time working. An attempt to join Freelance Programmers Ltd as a Systems Analyst came to nothing because of cut backs on their part. Mary returned to full-time employment again in September 1973 as a primary school teacher, completing a postgraduate certificate in 1973–1976. She retired from teaching in 1985 and is currently working as a buyer in the water treatment industry and participating in the computerisation of her employer's clerical procedures.

FANTL, Leopold. Born 8 August 1924 in Teplitz Schoenau, Czechoslovakia. Came to England in June 1939 on a children's transport. Worked as a farm labourer in Kent and Devon. In 1942 when he was 18 years of age he joined the RAF. After the war he returned to Czechoslovakia to find his parents, and was imprisoned, having been accused of being a spy. While in the RAF he was given technical training and after leaving continued his education through correspondence courses. Joined J. Lyons & Co. Ltd. on 28 March 1949 as a Trainee in the Cadby Hall Labour Planning Department. In 1950 he joined the LEO programming team as a Trainee Programmer. In March 1954 he was promoted to a supervisory grade. In June 1960 Fantl left for Johannesburg, South Africa, to set up a computer bureau that Lyons jointly owned with Rand Mines. He was the Bureau Manager until March 1965 when he returned to London. In February 1970 he returned to Johannesburg and joined Rand Mines, which by now had obtained full ownership, as Chairman of the bureau company. He also joined various Boards within the Rand Mines Group.

Leo Fantl is a keen photographer and he recorded much of the development phases of the LEO computer to film.

GLUCKSTEIN, Isidore (1851–1920). One of ten children born to Samuel Gluckstein (1821–1873) and his wife Ann, sometimes Hannah, (née Joseph) (1819–1885) on 13 August 1851. He was educated at Hartog's and later at the Daventry Foundation School in Whitechapel. He entered his father's tobacco business in 1864 and developed a remarkable financial ability. He married Rose Cohen on 21 June 1876 and they had seven children. With his brother Montague and their brother-in-law they developed the Salmon & Gluckstein tobacco business and founded, with others, the catering and food manufacturing company of J. Lyons & Company Limited. He was a Director of J. Lyons & Company Limited and Strand Hotels Limited from their incorporation until his death at the Grand Hotel, Eastbourne on Friday 10 December 1920. He was buried at Willesden Cemetery on Sunday 12 December 1920.

GLUCKSTEIN, Montague (1854–1922). Brother of Isidore, he was born at 35 Crown Street (now Charing Cross Road) on 18 July 1854. His Father, Samuel Gluckstein, had started the family's first tobacco business from this address. Although younger than Isidore, he was far more at ease with people and had a persuasive and confident manner. Like his brother he was educated at Hartog's Academy and the Daventry Foundation School in Whitechapel, and joined the family's tobacco business. On 6 February 1884 he married Matilda Franks and they had three children, all of whom married consanguineously. In 1893 Montague Gluckstein and others were involved in a legal challenge by the official liquidator in connection with the acquisition of Olympia Limited and contract securements. He eventually lost the case in the High Court and this was deeply wounding to his pride; he held other directorships at the time in the Westminster Electric Supply Corporation, the Guardian Assurance Company and the Pall Mall Electric Light Company. Montague Gluckstein was a Director of J. Lyons & Company Limited (he became Chairman in 1917 after Joseph Lyons died) and Strand Hotels Limited from their incorporation until his death on 7 October 1922.

GLUCKSTEIN, Samuel (1821–1873). One of eight children of Lehman Meyer Gluckstein (1794–1859) and Helena Horn (1797–1854), Samuel Gluckstein was born in Reinberg, Prussia on 4 January 1821 and came to Britain in 1841. His father was a language teacher. On his arrival in Britain Samuel lodged with his aunt, Julia Joseph, in Spitalfields, London and married her daughter Ann (Hannah) on 25 May 1845 at the Great Synagogue in Dukes Place. Samuel and Ann had 12 children, two of whom died in infancy. He was naturalised a British citizen on 10 August 1861. With his brother Henry he started a cigar making business from 35 Crown Street (now Charing Cross Road) and later moved to Leman Street, Aldgate. After partnership disagreements the business was dissolved in the Chancery Court on 25 March 1870 and the assets divided. He started another cigar manufacturing business with two sons (Isidore and Montague) and his son-in-law Barnett Salmon (1829–1897), husband of his daughter Helena. Samuel was not a healthy man; he had been nursed by his wife before their marriage, and he died of diabetes on 23 January 1873 at 34 Whitechapel Road aged 52 years. He left a will and remembered many of his grandchildren, one Hannah Solomon (Salmon) living at 251 Edgware Road. This became the first retail tobacco outlet of Salmon & Gluckstein, the business he did not see prosper. One of his executors was named as Harry Lyons but it is not known whether he was connected with the Lyons family who gave their name to J. Lyons & Company Limited, a business formed later by two of his sons, Isidore and Montague Gluckstein.

GOSDEN, John A., MA. Born on 9 March 1930 in Folkstone, Kent to Arthur Gosden and Sarah (née Curry). He was educated at Monmouth School and Cambridge

University, where he obtained a MA in mathematics in 1953. He worked for J. Lyons & Co. Ltd. between 1953 and 1961 as a programmer and later as Senior Applications Manager and designer of micro code and system software for the LEO III computer. He married Margaret Mary Davis on 21 December 1957. Between 1961 and 1965 John Gosden worked for the Auerbach Corporation as the first editor of Standard EDP Reports. He developed and installed a multi-computer operating system for the US Navy Command and Control Centres. Between 1966 and 1970 he was Department Head responsible for technical advice and planning for The National Military Command Support Centre of the Joint Chiefs of Staff at the Mitre Corporation. The Equitable, New York (a Financial Services Company) employed him from 1970 to 1986 in a number of roles; Second Vice President, Technical Support Department; Vice President, Project Manager; Vice President, Corporate Computer Services; Vice President, Telecommunications; Vice President and Technology Officer and in 1977 he was Chairman of the Federal Advisory Group to review the information systems of the White House for President Carter. He is a Fellow of the British Computer Society and has been Chairman of a National Academy of Sciences Review Committee for the Computer Institute at the National Bureau of Standards, a Trustee of EDUCOM, Chairman of the American Federation of Information Processing Societies Governmental Activities Committee, Chairman of the ACM Publications Board, and a National Science Foundation Visiting Scientist. John Gosden enjoys music, opera, ballet, and the visual arts and in the 1970s raced single-handed catamarans and enjoyed playing tennis and racquetball. He now does voluntary work for the Museum of Modern Art (MoMA) in Manhattan, where he has made his home. He has two children, Harry and Sarah.

GROVER, John. Born 7 December 1924 in Eltham, SE London, of Arthur Grover and Amy (née Hall). Educated at Eltham Selective Central School. Won a 5-year Engineering Apprenticeship with the Royal Ordnance Factory, Woolwich and studied at Woolwich Polytechnic. In 1943 volunteered for RAF air crew training and won pilots wings in 1945. Was course Student of Honour. Decided against long-term commission and left RAF in 1947. Joined J. Lyons & Co. Ltd. as a Management Trainee in Sales Accounts Office on Bakery Sales Ledger Section. In 1950 was invited to join LEO programming team as Trainee Programmer. John married Doreen Turner on 24 May 1952 and they had one daughter. John Grover left J. Lyons & Co. Ltd in 1956 to join Derek Hemy at EMI working on Austin Motor Company payroll and specification of the EMIDEC computer. Became Sales Manager, and, when EMI was absorbed by ICT in 1962, was appointed Chief Computer Executive for half of UK sales force. Appointed Divisional Sales Manager for Northern and Western England and Scotland at the time of the merger of English Electric with Leo Computers Limited. Fellow of the British Computer Society. Retired early and bought a derelict coach house in Arundel, Sussex, which he restored. Hobbies include woodworking.

HEMY, Derek Charles. Born in Wembley, Middlesex, 17 May 1920 to Wilfred Charles Hemy and Bessie Louise (née Short). Educated at St Olave's and St Saviour's Grammar School, Tower Bridge, London. He joined J. Lyons & Co. Ltd in July 1939 as a Management Trainee. In 1940 he joined the Royal Engineers

(Chemical Warfare), and transferred in 1942 to the Royal Corps of Signals to take a commission. A year later, after advanced technical training, he was posted to signals intelligence at Harrogate to form and command the AR13 Department, whose main work was Radio Fingerprinting (RFP)—the identification of individual German transmitters by analysis of wave form characteristics—and TINA—the identification of individual morse operators through the statistical analysis of their transmitting styles. On 1 March 1946 he married Margaret Mary Gordon Kirkwood, who had served in the AR13 Department and, as Chief Classifier, had been responsible for the successful development of the RFP technique. On release from the Army in July 1946 he returned to J. Lyons to work in their Systems Research (later O & M) Office under David Caminer. In September 1947 he became the first member of the LEO team to work on the design and development of the LEO computer; shortly after he wrote the first payroll program and, leading a small team of highly motivated programmers, developed the operating systems, standards and programming techniques for the first commercial computer programs in the world. In the following years, under David Caminer's guidance, the operational use of LEO was established and developed. In December 1954 Electric and Musical Industries (EMI) advertised that they were starting work on computing and Hemy decided to accept the job of running the applications and operations of EMI's new Computer Division and, after handing over his work, left Lyons in 1955. At EMI, Hemy's responsibilities included user specification and overall design of their first computer, which was supplied to the British Motor Corporation. During 1956 he worked in partnership with Godfrey Hounsfield on the EMIDEC (later called EMIDEC 1100) solid state computer, the United Kingdom's first. It was Hemy who first coined the expression "second generation computer" to describe the new computer technology. He transferred to International Calculators & Tabulators (ICT) when they absorbed the computer interests of EMI in 1962 and left them to join the Unilever Organisation Division as a computer consultant in 1963. He advised and assisted many Unilever companies, in the UK and overseas, in the installation and use of computing equipment and techniques. He is now retired and works voluntarily for the Girvan Guild of the Royal National Lifeboat Institution.

KAYE, Ernest Joseph, Bsc (Eng) A.C.G.I. Born in London on 20 June 1922 of Simon and Dinah Kaye (née Hoffman). He was educated at Kilburn Grammar School and Imperial College, London, where he studied engineering between 1940 and 1942. He joined General Electric Research Laboratories in 1942, working in the communications section, on underwater homing torpedoes and later on pulse modulation and electro-mechanical relay systems. He remained there until 1949. He married Marianne Zeisl on 19 May 1947 and has three children. He joined J. Lyons & Co. Ltd. in 1949 as Assistant to Dr John Pinkerton and was jointly responsible for much of the early circuit design of the LEO computer. With Ernest Lenaerts and John Pinkerton he published a series of articles in *Electronic Engineering* during 1954 that won them the Radio Industry Council's award for the best technical writing of the year. Ernest Kaye stayed with Leo Computers Limited through many mergers and finally left to join Control Data, first as Marketing Manager and then United Kingdom Service Manager for the Control Data Corporation. In 1968 he retired from computer activities to run Lewis & Kaye (Hire) Limited, a company specialising in hiring and renting silver, glass and china for film and television productions.

LAND, Frank. Born in Germany in 1928, he came to Britain in 1939 when he was 10 years old. He obtained an Economics Degree at the London School of Economics (LSE) and after a year of research joined J. Lyons & Co. Ltd. as a clerk in the Statistical Office, where he kept the accounts for the Provincial Bakeries and Laboratories. In 1952 he was recruited as a Trainee Programmer on the LEO computer team. Frank Land worked on a large number of Lyons and external customer programs, and when English Electric and Leo Computers Limited merged he was appointed Chief Consultant responsible for Domestic Marketing and the Regional Sales Offices. He returned to the LSE to teach and research in Systems Analysis. He became Professor of Systems Analysis at the LSE and now holds the post of Professor of Information Management.

LENAERTS, Ernest Henry. Born on 4 August 1910 and educated at West Kensington Central School, where he finished with Cambridge School Certificate in 1926. His father Emil and mother Emily (née Warner) could see no future for a boy whose main object in life was to take things to pieces in order to mend them, and decided that he should have a respectable office job. Thus Ernest Lenaerts started working for J. Lyons & Co. Ltd. in a clerical capacity in the Stock Department, a job that he did not much like. After a few years of clean office work under Thomas Thompson he developed enough courage to ask John Simmons how he could qualify himself for a proper job, possibly in the Company's Laboratories. He studied hard at evening classes, which culminated in his London Matriculation Certificate, but was disappointed that he was not selected to join the Laboratory staff. While in the Stock Department he met Gladys Buckledee, whom he married in 1936, and they had two sons, David and Paul. In 1941, tired of office work, he volunteered as a trainee Wireless Mechanic in the RAF. After basic training he was moved into Radio Countermeasures and two years later found himself as Sergeant in charge of three London RAF sites, including Alexandra Palace where the BBC transmitters were being used for jamming purposes. He was invited to return to Lyons after the war and successfully negotiated a post as Radio Mechanic. He spent over a year on various projects, including a 100 Megacycle (microwave) oven which he used to cook sausages in demonstrations to Lyons' Directors. He was approached by his former chief Thompson with a view to being seconded to Dr Wilkes at Cambridge University to assist in the building of the EDSAC computer. He spent the whole of 1948 at Cambridge and during this period greatly improved his knowledge of electronics and of the principles of computers. He returned to Cadby Hall to work with Dr Pinkerton on plans for building LEO, and they, with Kaye and Shaw, were responsible for most of the circuit development for the LEO computer, with Lenaerts contributing much innovation and practical know-how to the LEO computer project. He jointly published with John Pinkerton and Ernest Kaye a series of articles in *Electronic Engineering* during 1954 which won them the Radio Industry Council's award for the best technical writing of the year.

As the LEO II computers were installed in various locations around the country Lenaerts' position as Field Research Manager developed into a more general role of solving a wide range of problems, not always arising from computers themselves but as a consequence of them. As the hardware became more reliable the importance of the man–machine interface became more obvious, giving rise to research projects in their own right. Among these were noise in the computer room, static charge created by fast moving paper and speech recognition as computer input. With the merger of Leo Computers and ICT in 1963, these projects were gradually discontinued and Lenaerts accepted early retirement in the autumn of 1969. He continued working as a consultant for ICL for two more years on the subject of human factors related to ICL's new range of computers, and now lives in Ruislip, West London. Lenaerts was responsible for filing two patents, Ink Ribbon for High Speed Printers (20972/66) and Display Storage Apparatus (19807/69). Among his articles and papers are: "Visual Presentation of Binary Numbers" *(Electronic Engineering,* April 1954), "Leo Operating and Maintenance" *(Electronic Engineering,* August 1954), "Automatic Square-Rooting on a Computer" *(Electronic Engineering,* July 1955), "Study of Static Charge on Paper Tape" *(Journal of Science Institute,* June 1966), "Talking to the Computer" *(New Scientist,* December 1969) "Acoustic Noise in the Computer Room" (for GPO, November 1967).

LYONS, Joseph Nathaniel (Sir) (1847–1917). Born on 29 December 1847, of Nathaniel Joseph Lyons and Hannah (née Cohen), at 50 Lant Street, Southwark, London. Educated at the Jewish Borough School (Kennington), he came from a humble background but had a great love for the arts. He began his career as apprentice to an optician and invented a device called a chromatic stereoscope which he hawked around exhibitions and fair grounds. He turned his hand to water-colour painting, exhibiting at the Royal Institute where he sold several of his works. He also wrote detective stories and co-authored, *Master Crime and Treasures of the Temple* with Cecil Raleigh (1856–1914). As a youth he composed music hall sketches and songs, which he sold in the vestibule of the Pavilion Theatre, Whitechapel (this is where he was to meet his future wife). During World War I he wrote a recruiting song entitled "*Shoulder to Shoulder"* but one of his earliest patriotic efforts in verse was "A Tragedy of the War" which he wrote during the South African campaign. He married Sarah Pysche Cohen (1860–1948) on 24 August 1881.

Joseph Lyons was a self-made businessman of huge energy, able to seize commercial and catering opportunities that frequently required mammoth logistics to organise. Outside his business interests he was also very active in the Territorial Army and played an active part in introducing athletics into its training curriculum. It has been said that he was largely responsible for organising the first Territorial Athletic meeting held at Stamford Bridge in June 1909, which attracted 1,700 entries. He received a knighthood in 1911 for his organisation of the messing arrangements for the Territorial Army.

Joseph Lyons became the company's first Chairman in 1894 and remained a Director until 1917. Under his Chairmanship net profits of the Company were consistently high during the formative years, rising from £11,404 in 1895 to £268,474 in 1917 when he retired. During this time dividends to shareholders were frequently £30 per cent and in 1907–1909 as high as £42 per cent, the highest in the company's history. Sir Joseph Lyons died, after a short illness, at the Hyde Park Hotel on Friday 22 June 1917, aged 69 years.

PINKERTON, John Maurice McLean, PhD, C.Eng, FIEE. John Pinkerton was born at St Pancras, London on 2 August 1919. His father (John McLean Pinkerton), a surgeon, also a medical practitioner, and mother Norah Dorothy (née O'Flyn) encouraged his interest in radio. He listened to his first crystal set, built by his father, when he was only three years old and by the time he was twelve had built his first one valve radio set. He entered Cambridge University to study Natural Sciences in 1937 and was allowed to continue his course after war broke out in 1939. Between 1940 and 1945 he worked on radar research at the Telecommunications Research Establishment, Swanage, and later at Malvern. He returned to Cambridge after the war to read for his PhD. He started work at J. Lyons & Co. Ltd. on 17 January 1949 as an Electronic Engineer and led a small dedicated team, resulting in the design and construction of the LEO computer, which performed its first programmed task in 1951. On 9 June 1959 he was appointed a Director of Leo Computers Limited and was responsible for research. John Pinkerton resigned his Directorship on 24 March 1963 after the merger of The English Electric Company and Leo Computers Limited. He joined ICL on the merger of Leo Computers Limited and ICT and took charge of research projects inherited from English Electric as Research Director. He was a member of the team developing the 2900 series computer. In 1982 he served on an ESPRIT committee on Advanced Information Processing. In 1983 he became Chairman of the Telecommunications Policy Group of BETA, the Business Equipment Trade Association, and represented them in discussions with the Department of Trade and Industry, leading to the 1984 Telecommunications Act. He represented ICL in the European Computer Manufacturers Association. After his retirement in 1984 he started his own consultancy in information technology.

SALMON, Anthony Montague Lawson. Anthony Salmon was the eldest of four boys born to Julius Salmon and Emma (née Gluckstein), first cousins, on 5 May 1916. He was educated at Malvern School and left when he was 17 years old, travelling to Zurich to study German. His father allowed him to start smoking when he was only 7 years old and all the boys were encouraged to take claret with their meals from the age of five. As part of his education his father took him on a luxury cruise visiting Rio de Janeiro and Cape Town. When 18 he studied Italian in Rome and later French in Tours. In 1934 his father opened a shop (Hall Crown), near the Cumberland Hotel in London's Oxford Street, in competition with Marks & Spencer, where Anthony worked for a time. This was not successful and the business was sold to a Canadian company. He was put to work in the Trocadero Restaurant kitchens until the outbreak of World War II when he joined an infantry regiment as a private but, because of illness (duodenal ulcer) was discharged. He returned to Lyons as a tea taster on the understanding of his doctor that he would not taste tea!. He married Valerie née Isaacs in May 1940 and in 1942 took charge of Lyons' laundry subsidiary, James Hayes & Sons. In 1943 he became Managing Director of Henry Telfer Limited, a Lyons meat subsidiary. In 1944 he was also given responsibility for the Tea Estate in Nyasaland, a responsibility he kept until its sale to Brooke Bond in 1977. He became Managing Director of Leo Computers Limited on its formation in 1954 and a main Lyons Board director in 1955. Mr Salmon played an important and crucial role in the marketing of the LEO II and LEO III computers, using his considerable business contacts to generate sales. He played a key part in the first computer sale to W.D. & H.O. Wills through his family's business connections with John Player and others in the tobacco trade. Between 1958–1976 he was responsible for the Estates Division at Head Office. Mr Salmon has two children and among his hobbies lists fly fishing in Scotland and bridge—"and I haven't gone broke yet". He has been an honorary treasurer for the Protection of Children and at one time was involved in the Hammersmith Teenage Project, a unit run by the London Borough of Hammersmith for delinquent children referred to it by the courts.

SHAW, Raymond Tempest. Born in Ilford on 17 April 1924 of Frederick Alfred Shaw and Eliza (née Pember) he received his early education at Sidcup Central School, which he left in 1938. He joined Jacob White & Co., a privately owned Electrical and Mechanical Engineering Workshop where he gained experience in the use of machine tools. In 1940 he joined Standard Telephone & Cable Co. and was employed as assistant to the Chief Chemist to test new materials in the manufacture of thermionic valves. In 1943 Ray Shaw volunteered to serve in the RAF and was trained as a Radar Mechanic associated with airborne systems such as LORAN, GEE, IFF and AYF for navigational aids. He served in Bomber Command and South East Asia Transport (Australia, North Borneo, Singapore), and was demobilised as a sergeant in 1947 and returned to his former employer, Vacuum Science Products. In 1949 he joined J. Lyons & Co. Ltd. as a Senior Design Engineer working on the LEO computer. In 1956 he emigrated to Australia and after a short spell with Amalgamated Wireless of Australia joined the University of Sydney Physics Department at the Adolph Basser's Computing Laboratory as Engineer Computing assisting the Chief Engineer in the development of a magnetic tape backing store for attachment to the University's SILLIAC computer, a derivative of ILLIAC built at the University of Illinois. In 1960 he returned to Britain and joined English Electric Computing Division at Kidsgrove, Staffordshire, assisting in the design of the KDF9 computer. When English Electric merged with Leo Computers Limited he found himself working again with his old chief, Dr John Pinkerton. Ray Shaw was involved in a varied career after the merger, first as a Research Manager in data communications then in a variety of project management roles until 1981, when he became self employed as a Computing Systems Consultant. Ray Shaw married Muriel Margaret Chadwick in 1982. He is a member of the British Computer Society, British Institute of Management, The Society of Ornamental Turners and British Robotic Association.

SIMMONS, John Richardson Mainwaring, MA (1902–1985). Born on 19 March 1902 in Colombo, Ceylon where his father, Sidney Mainwaring Simmons, was a missionary for the Church Missionary Society, himself having been born in Palamcottah, South India of missionary parents. (*The Church Missionary Intelligence* 1902 lists John Simmons' date of birth as 18 March). His mother, Beatrice (née Reynolds), had married his father in Thetford on 8 September 1897 and died at a young age in Colombo on 22 December 1907. His father remarried in December 1909, to Helena Elsie Marion Walker, who was also a Church Missionary Society missionary from 1907. She died at Stifford, Essex on 2 February 1941. After graduating from Cambridge University in 1923 with a first class degree in mathematics he joined J. Lyons & Company Limited as a statistician and management trainee. He was put to work to improve clerical and accounting procedures and reported to the Company Secretary, George Booth. In 1926 he married Muriel Hare at the parish church of Wilton in Somerset, the service being performed his father. An expert on management systems, John Simmons was totally dedicated to improving management information and revolutionised clerical procedures at Lyons during the 1930–1940s which won him wide acclaim both inside and outside the Company. He became Chief Comptroller in 1946 (a title used in Lyons then to identify the one responsible for management accounts and other economic information) and in 1950 was appointed an Employee Director. In 1965 he was given ordinary Director status. John Simmons is remembered for initiating and driving the LEO computer project in 1949 against all odds but with the active support of his peers. This project was brought to a satisfactory conclusion at the end of 1953. In 1962 he was persuaded to write a book, *LEO and the Managers*, Macdonald, which was subsequently adopted as part of the Lyons' management training programme. John Simmons also played a dominant role in the Institute of Administrative Management (founded in 1915 as the Office Machinery Users Association). He joined the organisation in 1933 and was a member of its Governing Council from 1934 until 1968, Chairman from 1938 to 1950, President from 1944 to 1950 and honorary Vice President until his death. The Institute honours his 52-year membership record with an annual lecture in his name. John Simmons applied high standards to his work and demanded the best from those working for him. He retired in September 1968 and died on 14 January 1985 in St Mary's Hospital, after a series of strokes, aged 82 years. There were no children of the marriage and his wife survives him. John had a half sister, Margaret Theodora Mainwaring Simmons, to whom he made a bequest in his Will.

STANDINGFORD, Oliver William, OBE (1912–1980). Born at Brentford, Middlesex of John Standingford and Miyuie Jane (née Francis) on 9 October 1912. He first worked as a Management Trainee in the Stock Department of Lyons in 1930. He served in the Army during World War II and returned to Lyons after war service as Training Manager and later as assistant comptroller. He accompanied Raymond Thompson on a study tour of the United States in 1947 and on their return home submitted to the Lyons Board a report and schematic diagram for a computer system which had been drafted, with Simmons, on the *Queen Elizabeth*. Their report suggested that Lyons should build a computer for clerical purposes. Oliver Standingford left Lyons and became Assistant Comptroller and later a Director of Walkers Dairies Limited in Liverpool, which became part of Lyons Maid Limited.

THOMPSON, Raymond Thomas (1907–1976) MA, Bsc, FCIS, FIOM. The son of a grocer, he came from a poor background. He was born on 10 November 1907 of Walter William Thompson and Lillie Frances (née Huntington) in Doncaster and died on 4 March 1976 after an unsuccessful heart by-pass operation in Harefield Hospital aged 68 years. He was educated at Ilkeston Secondary School in 1919 and won a major scholarship to Pembroke College, Cambridge in 1925. He distinguished himself with a first class Mathematical Tripos Part 1 and a BSc first class honours at London; on leaving university he studied for the Chartered Secretaries' examinations. He started his working career with Owen & Owen Ltd, Liverpool, where he was an assistant secretary. He joined Lyons on 1 June 1931 and in April 1945 was appointed Assistant Secretary; in December 1946 he was appointed Chief Assistant Comptroller and joined the Board of Leo Computers Limited on its formation. Although he had frequent flashes of brilliance and undoubtedly had a quick, agile mind, his management style was thought by many to be arrogant. He did not treat his subordinates with courtesy and was said to be intolerant, but nevertheless he was a very active promoter of the LEO project and his enthusiasm undoubtedly persuaded the Lyons Board to continue to fund the department. He contributed many ideas, supported others and took a very active part in promoting the machine to other parts of industry. Without his involvement it is doubtful whether the project would have succeeded. He was always known as TRT. He was a member of the Institute of Office Management for over 35 years. From March 1946 to February 1949 he was a member of Council, and part of that time acted as Treasurer. He was for many years a member of the Institute's research committee, and was elected a fellow in 1951 to mark his services to the Institute, particularly in connection with the Clerical Job Grading Scheme and preparation of the biennial *Clerical Salaries Analysis*. He was previously Vice-Chairman of Council for two years and Chairman of the Electronic Data Processing Division. In 1966 he joined Shell-Mex and BP Ltd as advisor on computer applications and techniques.

WHEELER, Prof. David John, FRS. Born 9 February 1927 of Arthur William Wheeler and Agnes Marjorie (née Gudgeon). Educated at Camp Hill Grammar School, Birmingham; Hanley High School, Stoke-on-Trent; Trinity College, Cambridge. In 1948, while a research student at Cambridge University, he was seconded to J. Lyons & Co. Ltd for a few weeks to work on business computer programming. Between 1951 and 1957 he was a Research Fellow at Trinity College, Cambridge, and was Visiting Assistant Professor, University of Illinois between 1951 and 1953; Assistant Director of Research, Cambridge University, 1956 to 1966; Reader in Computer Science, Cambridge University, 1966 to 1978. Married Joyce Margaret Blackler in 1957. Published *Preparation of Programs for an Electronic Digital Computer*, 1951 (jointly with Wilkes).

WILKES, Vincent Maurice MA, PhD FRS. Maurice Wilkes was born on 26 June 1913 of Vincent Joseph Wilkes and Ellen (née Malone) at Dudley, Worcestershire. He was educated at King Edward's School, Stourbridge and St John's College, Cambridge where he obtained a Mathematical Tripos (Wrangler). He joined the Cavendish radio group in July 1934 and in 1938 studied for his MA degree; his PhD was obtained in October 1939. During the War he was involved with radar research. In 1946 Maurice Wilkes was appointed Director of the Mathematical Laboratory at Cambridge, a post he held until 1970. It was while he was working at the mathematical laboratory, and inspired by American research, that he built the EDSAC computer, which ran its first successful task on 6 May 1949. He married Nina Twyman in 1947. In 1956 he was made a Fellow of the Royal Society and between 1957 and 1960 was the first President of the British Computer Society. He was made a member of numerous committees, including Adjunct Professor of Computer Science and Electrical Engineering at MIT; Member of Measurement and Control Section Committee, IEE; Member of Council, IFIP; Chairman of IEE East Anglia Sub-Committee; Foreign Honorary Member of the American Academy of Arts and

Sciences. He received many awards including the Eckert–Mauchly Award, the McDowell Award, the Faraday Medal and the Pender Award (University of Pennsylvania). Among his publications are *Oscillations of the Earth's Atmosphere*, (1949); *Preparation of Programs for an Electronic Digital Computer*, (1951) (jointly with Wheeler); *A Short Introduction to Numerical Analysis*, (1966); *Time-Sharing Computer System*, (1968); *Memoirs of a Computer Pioneer*, (1985). Since 1986 he has been a Member for Research Strategy at the Olivetti Research Board and between 1980 and 1986 worked for the Digital Equipment Corporation, USA.

WOOD, Ashley Peter. Born 31 January 1918 of Walter Wood and Florence Ann (née Ames). Educated at Whitgift Middle School, Croydon (now Trinity School of John Whitgift) and left in 1936. Married Joan Dorothy Blundell Moss on 18 November 1939. One son, Michael Peter (7.5.47) and daughter Carolyn Anne (8.4.41). After a short career with Barclay's Bank Peter Wood joined the Lyons' Chocolate Sales Accounts in 1939 and during that year attended a Territorial Camp, from which he was sent to join the Armed Forces in France. He was rescued from Dunkirk and from 1942 was Lieutenant Colonel Commanding Special Services Battalion with the 14th Army in India and Burma, attached to SOE. Later Assistant Adjutant General, Bombay Area, until demobilisation in 1947. He returned to Lyons and worked in the Wages Office as Supervisor for the Premium Bonus System. In 1950 Thompson recruited him to join the LEO team and he was sent to Cambridge University on a two-week course on EDSAC. He was made Operations Supervisor of LEO and later Bureau Manager. He left Lyons in 1965 to join the Ever-Ready Company when Lyons sold them a LEO III computer. He remained with the company, becoming General Manager Management Services, until his retirement in 1983.

APPENDICES

Appendix 1: Program actions on the LEO I computer

Each instruction of a LEO program consisted of three parts that defined the action to be carried out, the address of the compartment affected and a discriminant denoting the length of the compartment. Initially, following EDSAC practice, these parts were written as: Action Letter, Address Number and Suffix (discriminant) Letter. Thus an instruction to add the contents of compartment 106 into the accumulator was written as:

A 106 F   for a short number
A 106 D   for a long number

This was later changed, and a purely numerical notation was used:

28 106 17   for a short number
28 106 19   for a long number

Of the 32 possible actions (0 to 31), only 17 were provided when LEO I was first used; these 17 are identified in the full list below by the insertion, in brackets, of the original action letter beside the corresponding action number.

Eventually, as developments proceeded, 30 actions were available to programmers. Some of the original actions became redundant, but new actions were added; in the end values 0, 9 and 15 were not used, but 29 performed two different functions according to the value of the discriminant. The actions fell into three broad categories:

Sequence control action numbers were: 2, 3, 13, 27 and 29.

Arithmetic and data manipulation action numbers were: 1, 4, 5, 6, 7, 8, 12, 14, 21, 22, 25, 26, 28, 30 and 31.

Input and output action numbers were: 10, 11, 16, 17, 18, 19, 20, 23 and 24.

Action number and name	Description of program action
1 CLEAR	Clear the double compartment specified, and all later compartments in the same tube of the store.
2 CONDITIONAL STOP	If external switch has been set, reset calculator ready to carry out next order when restart button is pressed and light stop lamp, otherwise proceed to next order.

3(E)	TEST POSITIVE	Test sign position of accumulator; if it contains "0", change sequence to the order contained in compartment specified by the address.
4(R)	SHIFT RIGHT	Shift right contents of accumulator by number of positions indicated by position of first "1" in the address.
5(T)	TRANSFER (FROM ACCUMULATOR)	Transfer the most significant 17 or 35 digits of the contents of accumulator into compartment specified by address, and clear the accumulator.
6(Y)	ROUND OFF	Round off contents of accumulator to 34 significant places by adding a 1 into the most significant position of the second half of the accumulator register.
7(U)	COPY FROM ACCUMULATOR)	Copy contents of accumulator into compartment specified by the address without clearing the accumulator.
8	NEGATIVE AGGREGATE	Clear the accumulator and subtract from it the contents of the double compartment specified and all later double compartments in the same tube of the store. This was introduced to facilitate the compiling and checking of check totals on punched cards used to carry forward data. Originally this action called for the input of one character from paper tape.
9(O)	NOT USED	Originally this (letter O) was the code to output one character to the teleprinter.
10	CARD PUNCH OUTPUT	Send out results for punching on a card from first twelve double compartments of the tube specified.
11	TABULATOR OUTPUT	Send out results for printing by tabulator. from the tube specified.
12(S)	SUBTRACT	Subtract from accumulator contents of the compartment specified by address.
13(Z)	STOP	Reset calculator ready to carry out next order when restart button is pressed, and light stop lamp.
14	SELECT	Replace contents of accumulator by contents of compartment specified by the address. Originally this required two actions—5 (transfer) to clear the accumulator followed by 28 (add).

Appendices

16	CONVERT (HOLLERITH)	Convert a number held in Hollerith notation in the specified tube of the store to full binary, and add the binary form into the accumulator; the address specifies decimal or sterling and the number of digits to be converted. Originally this operation was performed by a very laborious program sequence.
17	CONVERT (DECIMAL)	Select long number from address specified, convert from binary-decimal or binary/sterling to full binary, and add result into more significant half of the accumulator.
18	CONVERT (STERLING)	As above.
19	RECONVERT (DECIMAL OR STERLING)	Reconvert long number in full binary form in accumulator and stack resulting digits in punched card notation in special output tube; according to what is specified in the order, express in decimal or sterling, use number of digit positions specified and start new line of results.
20	TAPE INPUT 1	Clear tube of store specified and put into it next block of information in binary-decimal form from No. 1 perforated paper tape.
21(H)	SET UP (IN MULTIPLIER)	Set up in multiplier register contents of compartment specified by address. At Cambridge this was called mnemonically "hold in multiplier".
22(N)	MULTIPLY (NEGATIVELY)	Multiply contents of compartment specified by address by contents of multiplier register, and subtract from contents of accumulator.
23	TAPE OR CARD INPUT 2	Similar to actions 20 and 24 except it applies to No. 2 perforated paper tape or No. 2 card feed.
24	CARD INPUT 1	Clear tube of store specified and put into first twelve double compartments of the tube next block of information from No. 1 card feed.
25(L)	SHIFT LEFT	Shift left contents of accumulator by number of positions indicated by positions of first "1" in order.
26(X)	AUGMENT	Augment contents of accumulator to the contents of compartment specified by address, and clear accumulator. This complements 14 and is equivalent to an Add followed by a Transfer. Originally action X had no effect, did not stop machine.

27(G)	TEST NEGATIVE	Test sign position of accumulator; if it contains negative "1", change sequence to order contained in compartment specified by address.
28(A)	ADD	Add into accumulator contents of compartment specified by address.
29	WITH SHORT DISCRIMINANT (NON ZERO)	Test the contents of the accumulator; if there is a "1" in any position, change sequence to NON-ZERO order contained in the compartment specified by address.
29	WITH LONG DISCRIMINANT (NON ZERO)	Test the contents of the accumulator, if there is not a "1" in any position, change sequence to order contained in compartment specified by address
30(C)	COLLATE	Compare contents of compartment multiplier register and add a "1" into accumulator in all positions where there is a "1" in both numbers.
31(V)	MULTIPLY	Multiply contents of compartment specified by address by contents of multiplier register, and add result to contents of accumulator.

Appendix 2: LEO II features at February 1958

PRINCIPAL PURPOSE:		Commercial data processing and statistical work.
WORD LENGTHS:		19 or 39 bits including sign, and duplicate actions for each length.
TYPE OF INSTRUCTION:		Single address (could be modified by one of three registers) including divide, square root, scale, collate, augment and special data sum check actions.
IMMEDIATE ACCESS REGISTERS:	Capacity:	14 words of 39 bits.
	Type:	mercury delay line.
	Access:	zero effective access.
MAIN QUICK ACCESS STORE:	Type:	mercury delay line.
	Capacity:	2048 of 19 bits each. These may be taken in pairs to form words of 39 bits. 0.16 ms average.
BUFFER STORE:	Type:	mercury delay line.
	Capacity:	32 words of 19 bits each.
AUXILIARY STORE:	Type:	drums of 16,384 words each.
	Capacity:	up to a total of 65,536 words of 19 bits.
	Access:	minimised by use of buffers, revolution time 18 ms.
MODE OF OPERATION:		Serial fixed point.
SPEED OF ARITHMETICAL OPERATIONS:	Additions:	0.34 ms from immediate access register. 0.66 ms from main store.
	Multiply:	0.66 to 3.5 ms from main store.
	Divide:	3.5 ms from main store.
INPUT:		Up to four channels operating simultaneously: Paper tape at 200 rows per second. Punched cards, either punched in binary or any 2-hole code, 200 cards per minute. Magnetic tape, see next page.
OUTPUT:		Up to four channels operating simultaneously: Punched cards, either punched in decimal, binary or any 2-hole alpha code: 100 cards per minute. Line printer, 140 printing positions, 50

Appendices

MAGNETIC TAPE:
different characters, 4 plugboard layouts: 300 lines per minute. Magnetic tape, see below.
Up to eight decks with each pair of input/output magnetic tape channel's peak rate 10,000 digits per second sustaining simultaneous reading and writing, including check at separate head, 4,000 digits per second on each pair of channels.

AUXILIARY PRINTING:
Electric typewriter controlled by conventional punched cards and plugboard, approximately 10 characters per second.

CHECKING FACILITIES:
Magnetic tape was completely re-read at a separate head after writing, and compared with contents of buffer. Punched cards were checked at a separate read station after output. Special orders were provided to make programmed input checks fast and easy. All information in the drum store was parity checked.

OTHER FACILITIES:
Provision was made for automatic conversion and reconversion between binary, decimal and sterling notations, arranging, in addition, for suppression of all non-significant zeros, the insertion of signs, and printing or punching of numbers in true decimal form.
Optimum programming techniques are not required as the access to the store is so rapid. A special assembly program is provided to enable programs to be written in a simple form, all addresses and cross references being then computed automatically. Buffer stores are provided on each of the four input and three output channels and also between the auxiliary and main stores, enabling all work in parallel with the computer. Thus, reading, punching, calculating, printing, reference to the auxiliary store and the operation of any two of the eight magnetic tape decks can all be carried out concurrently.
Input and output channels are each provided with switching facilities to enable immediate changes to be made in the ancillary equipment linked to the computer.

CONFIGURATION COST:
The cost varied according to the equipment required. A complete installation, including

ancillary and data preparation equipment and
spares and maintenance equipment, would be
between £120,000 and £200,000. (See Appendix 4.)

Appendix 3: LEO I and II summary of machine test programs

During the development of the LEO I and II computers a series of test programs were developed to aid maintenance engineers in fault diagnosis. These were in addition to the marginal test programs, designed to identify weaknesses in the machine circuitry before failure occurred, and were run daily prior to operational work. The following is a summary of both the marginal test procedures and test programs as they were in 1957. These procedures were constantly modified and improved to aid the task of fault diagnosis.

Marginal testing

Principles of marginal testing

It was possible to detect gradual deterioration of performance of individual circuits before they had reached the point of failure by means of what was termed marginal checking. An alternating voltage derived from the mains was injected into a large number of circuits throughout the machine, at each of which it may induce a malfunction if large enough. In setting the marginal test program the various voltages were so proportioned that under the standard test conditions each circuit was driven to approximately the same fraction of the breakdown point. Thus it was possible to bring up the marginal test voltage gradually at all points at once. If the standard value could not be reached without inducing breakdown as indicated by the performance of the machine during a test program, then it follows that one or more circuits must be nearer the failure point than on the last occasion a test was carried out.

Application of marginal testing

A particular feature of the marginal testing arrangements was the categorisation into sections and sub-sections so that individual marginal circuits could be rapidly located by analytical procedure. Thus, although there were some 500 marginal testing points (March 1958) it was possible to find the one circuit whose performance had deteriorated in a matter of two or three minutes. The testing was carried out from the control console which incorporated (amongst other facilities) a large Variac transformer for varying the voltage, switches for applying it throughout the machine and an accurate a.c. voltmeter to measure value.

Effects of marginal testing

There were two types of marginal testing faults:

1. Failure of a pulse to operate a circuit because it was either too small or too narrow.
2. Unwanted pulses (breakthrough) or interference which may cause a spurious operation of a circuit.

Pulse amplifiers

These faults could be simulated if the gain of the various pulse amplifiers in the machine were alternatively increased and decreased. This was possible as the amplifiers were of the cathode coupled type. The test was carried out by raising and lowering of grid bias on one or more of the two amplifier valves, by injecting a small a.c. voltage across a fixed small value resistor in series with the variable resistor used for amplifier control. The amplifier gain was thus raised above and below the normal value at a rate of 50 cycles, to an extent determined by the amplitude of the injected voltage. The optimum setting of the gain potentiometer could then be determined as that for which both forms of circuit failure begin at the same injected voltage.

Flip-flops

In this case the arrangement adopted varied the sensitivity to setting and re-setting pulses by varying the gain of the trigger amplifying valve within the package. When flip-flop components drift they usually cause the performance to become asymmetrical, i.e. as setting becomes easier, re-setting becomes more difficult and it is this which is revealed by the test.

Other circuits besides flip-flops and amplifiers were also subjected to marginal testing using the principle of alternating current variations in bias. A slightly different method of marginal testing was adopted with the photoelectric readers where the voltage supplied to the lamp was varied above and below the nominal value. This provided a comprehensive test of the reading efficiency.

Distribution of marginal testing voltages

The circuits subjected to marginal testing were divided into ten *major* groups, each consisting of a logical section of the machine, e.g. store, co-ordinator, input, output, etc. The *major* groups were sub-divided into ten *minor* groups, each consisting of circuit types within the group, e.g. flip-flops, counter, etc. Since these circuits did not have the same sensitivity to marginal voltage, it was necessary to proportion the voltage applied to each circuit by a series of weighting resistors so that when the test voltage was applied to all the circuits all fail at about the same voltage. For the majority of circuits the marginal test point was connected to a socket on the test board. This board had 610 sockets divided into 10 rows having alphabetical designations and 61 columns, numbered 1 to 60.

The maintenance engineer could remove the marginal test voltage from any *major* group by pressing one of the ten *minor* group buttons. He could also remove the test voltage from an individual circuit by earthing the relative socket on the test board.

Some circuits, namely output flip-flop packages and store transmitters and receivers, were not connected to the socket board. Two lines, one associated with 16 transmitters and one with 16 receivers, were taken from the store *major* group switch to the storage rack, where each line was connected to the 16 individual weighting resistors. The test points of output flip-flop valves were connected to form one or more *minor* groups, in the appropriate *major* grouping. Relay valves in the packages were similarly (but separately) treated.

Circuit description

The Variac transformer supplied up to 20 volts at 50 cycles per second to test points by means of the *major* and *minor* group switches. The *major* group switches were ten pole and the *minor* group single pole, each pole of the *major* being connected to a separate switch in the *minor* bank, thus making a 10 × 10 matrix.

Operation of marginal test switches

Normally with all buttons in the reset position, the test voltage was applied to all marginal test points within the machine. If the machine failed when carrying out a test program before the standard 20 volts was achieved, then the engineer could remove margins from the suspected *major* group. If the machine then worked correctly then the faulty circuit was within the *major* group concerned. The search could then be narrowed to the faulty *minor* group by resetting the *major* group button and pressing the *minor* buttons in turn until the machine worked correctly with only one *minor* group button pressed. The *major* and *minor* group in which the faulty circuit was situated was then known. The circuits within this group and their associated sockets could be found by reference to the Marginal Test Index. The engineer could then earth each socket in turn until the machine operated correctly with the test voltage applied to all the circuits except the faulty one, which is released from margins.

Routine method of using marginal tests

If test programs operated correctly when all circuits were subjected to the standard marginal conditions of 20 volts, experience indicated that the small amount of gradual circuit change to be expected during the day was unlikely to cause a fault. If the machine failed a test at 20 volts but passed it at 18 volts it was found safe to postpone the correction of the weakness until it was conveniently opportune. This illustrated the convenience and flexibility of a test which allowed operating margins to be measured.

Flip-flop monitoring

A row of 20 neon indicators was provided on the control console to monitor the state of most of the flip-flops in the machine. It was possible to inspect the state of up to 20 flip-flops at any one time. A switching arrangement using a row of 20 push buttons switches facilitated selection from some 200 flip-flops. The buttons were arranged in two groups of 10, each group controlling one half of the neon indicators. A connecting line was taken from the reset side of each flip-flop and routed through the above switch connections to the grid of one of 20 triode valves. A neon indicator connected between earth and the anode of each valve strikes when the valve is cut off, i.e. when the flip-flop is set.

Appendices

Connecting lines from the *annex full* flip-flops in the three outlet channels were fed to neon indicators located on the outlet switching panel. A button was provided to reset all flip-flops in the machine.

Loudspeaker monitoring

A loudspeaker, situated on the control console, was used to monitor the frequency of operation of any one of the 20 flip-flops which had been selected by the method above. This was extremely useful at detecting any intermittent or sporadic operation of a flip-flop while the machine was in continuous operation. Such conditions were indicated by a change in the tone emitted from the speaker.

Test programs

The programs were so designed that each tested a part of the machine. The magnitude of the part tested varied according to the specific program used and they were divided into two categories:

1. The general or routine test programs.
2. The specific action or special purpose test programs.

The general test programs were designed to give an assurance of the general serviceability of the machine. They were used regularly every day during the maintenance period and the test procedure took about 50 minutes, provided that no lengthy investigation of stoppage was necessary. The programs could also be used when the computer was faulty and no definite indication was known of the whereabouts of a fault. Each program was designed to test a large section of the machine, i.e. store, arithmetic unit, input and output.

The special purpose tests were used for individually testing the more complicated actions of the machine, e.g. conversion, reconversion, multiplication, and for testing smaller parts of the machine, e.g. one tube of the store.

All the test programs were designed to resemble normal programs as much as possible although the patterns of pulses was carefully chosen in order to present the most difficult conditions for the circuits involved and were modified periodically during the tests.

General test programs

Experience showed that the best plan for carrying out a routine test on the computer was to use five separate tests on:

1. The store (known as S4).
2. Arithmetic circuits (known as M1, M2, and M3).
3. Input, conversion and reconversion circuits (known as M4).
4. Output circuits (known as PC punch card, PH for Hollerith printer or PP for Powers–Samas printer).
5. Auxiliary store (designation not known—possibly PD).

The store test

The types of fault checked in this test were:

1. Picking up extra digits in a particular mercury delay tube.
2. Dropping of digits from a particular mercury delay tube.
3. Failure to extract information from one or more mercury delay tubes.
4. Failure to insert information in one or more mercury delay tubes.
5. Corruption of patterns in one mercury delay tube of the store by those going to another.

Each compartment of the store was checked in such a way that not only was it confirmed that the correct pulses had been stacked, but also that they had not been stacked anywhere else. Because a part of the store had to be used to hold the program for checking the remainder, the store test was in two parts.

Arithmetic test

This comprised three individual programs:

1. M1 for testing the arithmetical actions associated with the main accumulator: these comprised shifting, multiplication, add/transfer, hold, round off, suppression, collation and division.

2. M2 for testing the arithmetical actions associated with the subsidiary accumulator: these comprised sequence change, negative, aggregation and suppression.

3. M3 for testing the inter-register actions and access arithmetic.

Each of these programs comprised several individual tests, associated with a particular action, or modification of an action or other variant of an action. If an error occurred within any test the test was stopped. Each of the programs was formed into a loop and the test designed to go round the loop as many times as was necessary to give a comprehensive test. When an error was indicated, the number specified in the tube and compartment positions of the stop order specified the particular test being carried out. Thus if a 17 was indicated as the tube number, this may have indicated that an error had occurred when shifting a negative number to the right, in the main accumulator.

Further facilities were made available by using the conditional sequence change switch where the program could be made to continually repeat the faulty test or to continue with the next part of the test.

Input, conversion and reconversion test

These programs were designed for testing paper tape input to both channels, binary/decimal card to channel 3, conversion and reconversion, fill and clear.

Appendices 225

The program was designed to read a series of pattern blocks of information into the paper tape reader and checked this against the same data which had been read in by the card reader. Where there was a discrepancy the machine stopped. It was impossible to loop on a fault condition during a reading check. The test program was, therefore, arranged so, that, initially, the contents of all three annexes were inspected, and the results of this inspection must be correct before the information was actually read into the store. In this way, if a comparison test failed, it was possible to repeat the test continually to enable a fault to be detected under dynamic conditions.

Output circuit test

Programs designated PH and PP were designed to test the Hollerith (PH) and Powers–Samas (PP) printers. A series of patterns were formed in the output tube and these patterns were printed, a line at a time, to one of the connected printers. The patterns were designed to form an easily recognisable combination so that a wrong character(s) could be quickly identified The program was repeated for each printer connected.

Program number PC was designed for testing punch card devices. A series of patterns was formed in the output tube and punched, one card at a time, by one of the card punches. Approximately 16 different patterns (cards) were produced and the test was repeated several times. The cards thus produced were checked by reading them back into the machine, on a card reader, and comparing with the check pattern held in the various mercury tubes of the store. When a discrepancy occurred the computer stopped and the necessary investigation was made.

Auxiliary test

This program attempted to provide a comprehensive test of the magnetic drum storage and its associated actions. It was divided into three parts:

1. Alternating pairs. Each of a pair of contrasting whole tube patterns was written in turn on to sector "0". after writing, the sector was read and checked. There were five pairs of patterns, each pair being used twenty times before the next pair was tried.

2. Shunting in and shunting out (collating). This module tested the actions 2n. 30 0 0 and 2n. 30 1 0 for values of n from 0 to 15.

3. Whole drum test. In each sector of the drum an individual pattern was stacked, working from sector 0 to sector 255. Within the sector, each double compartment contained the same pattern. All sectors were checked by summation. All sectors were cleared, then each sector was read, summed and checked empty. The test was repeated, but working from sector 255 to sector 0.

Special and individual test programs

The individual test programs could be used when a fault was suspected and where more comprehensive or easier manipulation was required than was provided by the general test programs.

1. Individual storage tube test (S5). This was designed so that any specified storage unit and delay tube could be given a comprehensive test. There were two versions of the program, S5A and S5B. S5B was used for a tube in the top ¾ of the store while S5A was used for a tube in the bottom ¼ of the store. When the program had been fed in, the computer stopped and the tube number had to be inserted on the manual digit selector buttons, and provided that the conditional stop switch was down, the machine would stop if an error occurred. With the conditional stop not operative a fault could be examined under dynamic conditions. The test was concerned with the insertion of a series of readily identifiable patterns into the specified tube.

2. Store holding test. This was designed to check the digit pulse holding properties of each tube of the store and was used when the frequency control unit was to be checked. A standard echelon type pattern was inserted once in each tube and was then inspected in a cyclic sequence. During each cycle a check was made with the standard pattern held in one tube. If a pattern became incorrect, the correct pattern was then restacked. This test also was in two parts, S6A and S6B, each to cover the whole store, minus the three tubes holding the programs.

3. Random number test. This was designed to reproduce the conditions which arise in many of the mathematical jobs and formed a comprehensive test of multiplication, for various combination of numbers.

4. Conversion (T27) and reconversion (T20). Individual test programs were provided for these actions and the tests were used where a fault had been narrowed down to one of these actions. These individual tests were easier to manipulate than the general input/output test in that the tape readers need not be utilised and the test of the particular action was more concentrated. Various test patterns were dealt with during these tests and facilities for looping on to a fault condition were provided.

5. Register holding and sensitivity test (R1). This was used whenever it was necessary to test or install a register unit. A holding and pattern sensitivity test was applied to any special selected register 0–7, 10–13. Two types of test were provided: a simple shifting pattern and a pattern which is set up and then repeated twenty times.

6. Manual test programs. In order to narrow down a fault condition using an individual test program, it was very useful to insert a simple program comprising a few relevant orders by means of the manual digit selector buttons. This program was made as short and simple as possible, in order to simulate the fault condition. Thus a fault was often traced to a particular action, or variant of the action, or to a certain type of data, e.g. conversion of a negative decimal quantity.

Source: Engineer lecture notes (LEO II), 1958

Appendix 4: LEO II prices quoted to NRDC in January 1959

Basic computer:	£ 73,763
Installation:	£ 1,991
1 Input channel punched card/paper tape	£ 2,047
1 Powers output channel	£ 12,628
1 Magnetic tape link	£ 16,896
1 Magnetic drum link	£ 4,646

Total £111,971

Ancillary equipment to be linked:

1 Powers printer		£ 6,479
2 Magnetic drums @	£11,424	£ 22,848
2 Magnetic tape cabinets @	£12,012	£ 24,024
1 LEO paper tape reader desk and control panel with 2 Ferranti readers		£ 1,378

Total £ 54,729

Installation spares and test equipment:

Test rack instruments and computer tool kit	£ 5,679
Category A spares	£ 2,978
Category B spares	£ 3,122
Spare packages and sub-assemblies	£ 1,810
Spare drum control package	£ 789
Standby power supply	£ 517

Total £ 14,895

Grand total: £(111,971 + 54,729 + 14,895)   £181,595

Additional optional equipment:

1 Input channel card/paper tape	£ 2,047
1 Output channel card	£ 3,052
1 Hollerith card reader	£ 1,430
1 Hollerith card punch including LEO card punch check device	£ 2,819
1 Hollerith tool kit	£ 68

Appendix 5: The first clerical jobs: LEO I and LEO II

Internal Work

The earliest operational programs run on LEO were labelled P1, P2 and so on; Bakeries Valuations was originally P1 and Payroll P4. Later the programs were renumbered L1, L2, and so on in order to distinguish them from bureau work carried out for external companies. These programs were labelled E1, E2, and so on. When a job like payroll involved several programs to carry out all its business tasks (the very small size of the store, just 2,048 memory locations in which to hold orders, constant data and intermediate results, greatly restricted the logic which could be incorporated in one program), with intermediate punched card files passing between them, the programs making up a suite had a letter suffixed, for example, L1A, L1B, L1C (originally P4A, P4B, P4C.)

Lyons identified 27 tasks suitable for LEO I and II during the period up to 1961–1962 when the Systems Research Team began to work on the LEO III Master Plan, though not all of them became operational programs. On several occasions, unforeseen problems emerged during feasibility and development phases that caused some projects to be abandoned. One sadness arising from the paucity of archive material is that no record of many of the programs has survived, not even the brief name given to the "L" number.

Some projects involved scientific work rather than conventional clerical tasks, for example, market research for Shepherd & Manning (a subsidiary company) or crystallography analysis for the Lyons Laboratory: the core of LEO's workload, however, were the commercial jobs briefly described in the following paragraphs.

(L1) Bakeries Valuations (later numbered L8)

Originally called P1 and P2, this was the first job programmed and run on LEO 1; it is believed to have been the first regular commercial job run on any programmed computer. The application had been selected, specified and flow-charted by David Caminer. It was initially written by Tony Barnes and later modified and enhanced by John Grover under the supervision of Derek Hemy. It ran for the first time on 5 September 1951 but because of the unreliability of the magnetic tape units in use it was reprogrammed to use paper tape input and output and slow teleprinter for hard copy output. It did not run regularly until 30 November 1951 and was considered "live" on 7 December 1951. A weekly run job, it calculated the value of bakery goods produced and distributed by the several bakery departments, for example, Kup Kake, Danish, Swiss Roll and Individual Fruit Pie, through various channels of sale, comparing despatch totals with stock, and reported any variances.

(L2) Teashops Replenishment

Orders were telephoned daily from some 200 teashop manageresses into Cadby Hall, giving requirements for the next day's business against a standing order. These orders were converted to punched cards while the teashop manageress was making her call; what was heard is what was punched. The staff receiving the calls wore special headphones so that their hands were free to operate the card punch keyboard. Over 40,000 different items of food were supplied. Other management data, such as weather forecast, was fed in by prepared paper tape and by 4.30 p.m. the same day detailed cooking, packing and loading summaries for the despatch of the goods had been completed. These summaries would be used overnight to prepare items in the Cadby Hall kitchens and load the vehicles which would make the deliveries, the last deliveries being loaded first so that they would be in the correct position in the delivery vehicle. Management statistics were produced, printing only those results which required some intervention. A further feature of the job was to reconcile the value of goods delivered against the money banked for each teashop, taking account of returned or damaged goods. Providing the two amounts were within acceptable tolerances a monthly bonus was paid. This operation was carried out to a very tight schedule and an emergency manual system was devised in case the computer broke down at a critical stage.

(L3) Reserve Stores Stock Control

The need for maintaining reserve food stores away from Cadby Hall had started during World War II when Lyons used several of their premises and approximately 100 public wharves to store reserve food stocks. The computerised job ran for only a short period of time for in 1953–1954 with the cessation of rationing, the time had come to reorganise the food depots, making the programs that had been particularly tailored no longer valid. The computer program selected raw materials, or their substitutes, and other goods ordered by Lyons' departments so as to minimise the number of separate calls and took account of the different stock situations by location. It calculated the charges to be made for the consignments and also the rent due to the public wharves and calculated forward stocks, maintained stock balances and valued them, and so on.

(L4) Payroll (Later numbered L1)

This was originally given the number of P4 by Derek Hemy and was the most successful clerical task that was transferred to the LEO computer. It ran uninterrupted on LEO I from 24 December 1953 until 4 January 1965, when LEO I was discontinued. During this period a number of changes were made to the program, it continued to be run on LEO II until the LEO III machines came on stream. Over 40,000 people were employed by Lyons at one time, including some 10,000 in the teashops and their support staff and 3,200 in the Corner Houses. The rest were employed in various other activities of the business, such as clerical and works department. The computerisation of payroll, which was implemented progressively, had a dramatic effect on productivity. Modified versions of L1 were developed for the special wage structures of the Teashops (L14), Corner Houses (L17), Normand Payroll (L23) and Works Department (L27). So successful was computerised payroll that Lyons undertook the payroll for Ford Motor Company (22,000 staff), Tate & Lyle Limited (2,000 staff), Kodak Limited (7,600 staff) and a pay accounting job for Army and Air Force Officers. The Pay Accounting job was run for 9,000 officers every month and special casualty runs were carried out three times a week to give immediate effect to changes of rank, allowances and the like. It was complicated by the variety of allowances and deductions affecting pay and by the retrospective nature of many of them. Special jobs (L11) were run at the end of each income tax year, referred to as Tax Year-End, to provide annual information in respect of National Insurance to the Department of Health and Social Security and Income Tax to the Inland Revenue.

(L4) Tea Blending Control (renumbered after payroll was introduced). A weekly run job which maintained a detailed control over the company's unblended tea stocks comprising many grades and classifications, this job was first run under an old P number (unknown) in 1953 under the title Original Tea Stocks. It controlled the issues of tea from the warehouse into the factory and compared the actual average cost of producing a blend like Orange Label with the standard budget cost. The job was extensively modified and renumbered L4, and the new programs completed their first operational run on 27 July 1956. The new suite of programs were concerned with the analysis, valuation and control of stocks, usage and purchase of tea. The scope of the job extended from the entry into a contract for purchases up to the issue of tea to the factory for blending, though in some instances the tea did not reach the mixing stage but was sold to customers in the original state. Some teas, after blending, returned into stock and were themselves used as basic constituents of the marketed blends. These were known as ullage blends. A blend of tea could be derived from up to 24 different teas which together provided the required characteristics of flavour and body. All teas when bought were earmarked for use in a particular blend and held as part of the blend stock until eventually used for blending. The packet blends were known as colours, for example Red Label and Green Label. In addition there were caterers' blends, fancy blends, china blends, export blends and Black & Green blends. In all, approximately 70 blends were handled.

(L5) Bakery Rail Orders (also called Wholesale Bakery Invoicing)

The system handled the paperwork involved in the distribution of bakery goods by rail from Olympia Station to customers in all the remoter areas of the United Kingdom, for example, those not located within economic delivery van reach of a bakery depot. In the main, dealers enjoyed weekly credit. The orders formed the basic data for the job from which invoices and packing instructions were produced, together with the amount owing for the orders. Additionally the job provided each representative with a list of the amounts he should collect from his dealer, it maintained a control over the cash collected by each representative and produced sales statistics. Orders were taken by travelling salesmen, posted to Cadby Hall, converted into punched paper tape and valued by LEO. The amount to be collected when the salesman next called was printed and written on the order: the orders were then microfilmed and sent back with the goods as an invoice/despatch note. LEO produced summaries showing the total quantity needed of each product, and picking lists so designed that despatch staff could go round the warehouse in the fastest sequence making up each customer's order. LEO also worked out the right number of each size of box needed, for each order. Other programs in the L5 suite calculated totals for orders placed, goods sold and so on, worked out salemen's commission, and kept track of amounts paid and still owed by each customer.

Appendices   231

(L6) Lyons Maid (Ice Cream) Dealer Statistics

Lyons sold ice cream products to 44,000 dealers (shops) from their 50 distribution depots. The statistics produced from this operation assisted Sales Management to control the activities of their representatives. Reports were produced quarterly for each of the 44,000 dealers, for each representative and for each depot. Some figures were consolidated to District and Division levels. Dealers were telephoned from the depots sufficiently often to keep them well stocked with ice cream. Those who did not have telephones were supplied with order cards that they posted to the depots when requiring more product. In addition, each dealer was called on regularly by a representative from the depot to stimulate sales. Sales van journeys were then planned the day prior to delivery. This job also recorded dealer performance statistics, which were analysed at the end of the year so that special discounts could be calculated. It also recorded information so that representatives' commission could be calculated but the actual calculation was outside the scope of this job. The names of some of the products were: Pola Maid, Gaiety Bricks, Zippy, Wonder Cakes, Kups, Mivvi, Koola Fruta, Koola Kreema and Orange Maid.

(L7) *See note below.
(L8) See L1.
(L9) Operations Research.
(L10) *See note below .
(L11) Payroll Tax Year-End.
(L12) Works Department Stock Control and Job Costing.
(L13) * See note below.
(L14) Teashops Payroll.
(L15) * See note below.
(L16) * See note below.
(L17) Corner Houses Payroll.
(L18) * See note below.
(L19) * See note below.
(L20) * See note below.
(L21) Lyons Maid (Ice Cream) Depot Replenishment and Production Programming.

(L22) Caterers Tea Sales Invoicing and Ledgers.

This was a straightforward invoicing job, involving valuing orders for a wide range of food and other products for use in catering establishments, keeping a customer ledger and printing sales statistics.

(L23) Normand Limited Payroll.
(L24) Frood Invoicing and Ledgers.
(L25) Lyons Maid (Ice Cream) Depot Clerical Work.
It was planned to use magnetic recording tape and data transmission equipment for this application but this was abandoned for unknown reasons, probably because of

the unreliability of the Decca magnetic tape units then in use and the emergence of the LEO III machines.

(L26) Bakery Depot Replenishment.
(L27) Works Department Payroll.
(L28) Lyons Maid (Ice Cream) Sales Plan.
(L29) * See note below.
(L30) * See note below.
(L31) Rolls Confectionery Payroll.

No records have survived for those jobs not described. Some are obvious, such as the various department payrolls but others, like Lyons Maid Sales Plan, were probably never specified and disappeared with the introduction of the LEO III computer.

* No records survive for these job numbers. It is possible that numbers were allocated but the projects abandoned before any conclusions were reached. On the other hand numbers may not have been allocated at all; they are included here for completeness so that the reader is not misled into thinking that any numbers have been missed.

External Work

Some early bureau work has been mentioned in the text, e.g. Weather Forecasting, Ford Motor Company Payroll, British Transport Rail Freight Charge Tables, Tax Tables, Weapons Design, etc. The following represents a selection of other jobs run on LEO I and LEO II, some of which were transferred to customers' own machines:

AEI Hotpoint	Invoicing
Atlas Assurance Ltd	NAAFI Pension Fund
	Group Pensions
Bermondsey Borough Council	Payroll
British Hydro-Chemicals	Payroll and Cost Re-allocations
British Oxygen Company	Production Control
	Payroll
CAV Ltd	Payroll
	Cylinder Pressure and Temperature Calculations
	Heat Transfer Calculations
	Cold Starting Calculations
	Pressure and flow characteristics in fuel injection systems
De Havilland Aircraft Company	Aircraft/missile design

Eagle Star Insurance Company	Group Pensions
	Payroll
Ever-Ready Company	Van Sales
Ford Motor Company	Payroll
	Purchases
F. Perkins	Casting Requirements
Gallup Poll	Readership analysis
Glaxo Laboratories	Rebate Valuation
Glyn Mills Limited	Army Bulk Pay
Greenwich Borough Council	Payroll
Guardian & Eagle Star	Group Endowments
Hudson's Bay Company	Mink and Fur Sales Accounting
ICI Metals Ltd	Lightning Fasteners
Ilford Ltd	Sales Accounts
	Payroll
Kodak Ltd	Payroll
National Coal Board	Pneumoconiosis statistics
Nigerian Government	Tax Tables
Nivisons	Stock Yields
Rotax	DC Motor Performance
Sandersons Fabrics	Stock Control
Smiths Clocks & Watches	Stock Control
	Machine Loading
South Eastern Gas Board	Prepayment Meter Checking
	Insurance fund annual renewals, and prepayment billing
Southwark Borough Council	Payroll
Standard Motor Company	Materials Scheduling
Stewart & Lloyds Limited	Multiple Regression
Tate & Lyle Ltd	Payroll
Taylor Woodrow Ltd	Monthly Invoicing (abandoned)
Wedd Durlacher Mordaunt	Jobbers Accounting Procedures
Westminster Bank Ltd	Payroll
	Customer Accounts
Woolwich Borough Council	Payroll

Appendix 6: Sales of LEO II computers

Machine No.	Company	Location	Date	Cost
LEO II/1	J. Lyons & Co. Ltd	London	May 1957	£142,800
LEO II/2	W.D. & H.O. Wills Ltd	Bristol	Sep 1958	£160,000
LEO II/3	Stewarts & Lloyds Ltd	Corby	Jun 1958	£125,000
LEO II/4	Ford Motor Co.(parts)	Aveley	Dec 1958	£125,000
LEO II/5	Leo Computers Ltd	London	Jul 1959	£183,000
LEO II/6	Ministry of Pensions	Newcastle	Nov 1959	£121,000
LEO II/7	British Oxygen Co.	Edmonton	Feb 1960	£161,000
LEO IIc/8	Standard Motor Co.	Coventry	Jul 1960	£125,000
LEO IIc/9	Ilford Limited	Ilford	Nov 1960	£180,000
LEO IIc/10	W.D. & H.O. Wills Ltd	Bristol	Apr 1961	£158,000
LEO IIc/11	Ford Motor Co. (payroll)	Dagenham	Jan 1961	£194,000

Notes

The LEO IIc machines were assembled with core memory and a mixture of transistors and valves

LEO II/2 was the first order taken for a LEO computer and first with Ferranti high speed magnetic drums and Powers-Samas alphanumeric printers.

LEO II/3 was the first delivery of a commercial computer in the United Kingdom.

LEO II/5 was the first LEO computer to have magnetic tape drives.

LEO II/6 was the first LEO computer to have a Bull alphanumeric printer.

LEO II/7 was transferred to Leo Computers Ltd, Hartree House, to become the second bureau machine.

Appendix 7: Program actions on the LEO III computer

The LEO III instruction set showed a marked contrast to those of LEO I and LEO II. Although familiar, basic actions were included, i.e. add, subtract, shift, change sequence or halt, the extra bits in the half-word (19 instead of 17) and the power of the micro code concept allowed for:

Actions which were omitted on LEO I, for example, divide, set-up and step-on loop controls, enter and leave sub-routine or double word arithmetic.

New categories of action required by LEO III's more advanced facilities, for example, storage allocation/protection, setting radix for arithmetic or magnetic tape deck control.

Complex logic to be carried out by a single action, for example, merge, table look-up or floating point arithmetic.

ACTION 0:   HALT AND REGISTER FACILITIES

0	0	0	HALT.
0	0	1	SPARE (same as 0.0.3).
0	d	2	SET (N) for collation in B.
0	0	3	SET RADIX at (N).
0	1	0	COPY (A), (B), (C), to N^1, $N + 2^1$, $N + 4$.
0	1	1	REPLACE (A), (B), (C), by (N^1), $(N + 2^1)$,$(N + 4)$.
0	1	3	SPARE (same as 0.1.1).

ACTION 1:   ARITHMETIC ON LITERALS, TABLE LOOK-UP, ROUND-OFF AND SPECIAL FACILITIES

1	d	0	TABLE LOOK UP using key (A) and table N onwards.
1	0	1	SET QUARTETS for collation in B. Those quartets of B whose corresponding bits in N are 1 are filled with 1s, those whose corresponding bits are 0 are filled with 0s.
1	0	2	ROUND OFF.
1	0	3	INTERCHANGE AREA ADDRESS. Interchange (64 + N1) and (64 + N2).
1	1	1	ADD N to (A).
1	1	2	SUBTRACT N from (A).
1	1	3	SELECT N into A.

ACTIONS 2–15: ARITHMETIC ON VARIABLES, MERGE, CONVERSION AND PATTERN MANIPULATION

2	d	m	TRANSFER (A) to N and clear A.
3	d	m	COPY (A) to N.
4	d	m	ADD (N) to (A).
5	d	m	SUBTRACT (N) from (A).
6	d	m	SELECT (N) into A.

236   *Appendices*

7	d	m	AUGMENT (N) by (A).
8	0	m	MERGE blocks of constant length specified by modification registers 1 and 2 into a block specified by modification register 3, until either of the two input blocks becomes exhausted or the output block becomes full. Item length is (N) binary.
8	1	m	MERGE CONDENSED DATA as above. Item length is specified in binary by a single word entry preceding each item.
9	d	m	MULTIPLY (A) by (N) and place in AB. (A) and (N) must be in common uniform radix.
10	d	m	MULTIPLY (B) by (N) and ADD to (A).
11	d	m	MULTIPLY (B) by (N) and SUBTRACT from (A).
12	d	m	CONVERT (N) and place in A using table held in locations (A) onwards.
13	d	m	DIVIDE (AB) by (N) leaving quotient in A and remainder in B (AB) and (N) must be in common uniform radix.
14	d	m	REPLACE those bits of (N) specified by (B) by the collation of (B) and the sign and modulus form of (A).
15	d	m	COLLATE (N) with (B) and ADD to (A).

ACTION 18:   SHIFT

18	0	0	SHIFT (A) logically.
18	0	1	SHIFT (A) arithmetically.
18	1	0	SHIFT (AB) logically.
18	1	1	SHIFT (AB) arithmetically.

ACTION 19:   FILE CONTROL
           TEST ROUTE N1 engaged, if so repeat the action; if not, take action as follows.

19	0	0	OUTPUT one block to route N1.
19	0	1	INPUT one block from route N1.
19	0	2	RUN BACK to last mark on route N1 (Magnetic tape only).
19	0	3	RUN ON to next mark on route N1 (Magnetic tape only).
19	1	0	BACKSPACE one block on route N1 (Magnetic tape only).
19	1	1	REWIND route N1 (Magnetic tape only).
19	1	2	UNLOAD route N1 (Magnetic tape only).
19	1	3	INPUT the first word of the block, and run forward to the next block end without further transfer of information (Magnetic tape only).

ACTIONS 20–22: FLOATING POINT ARITHMETIC.

20	0	m	ADD (N) to (A*).
20	1	m	SUBTRACT (N) from (A*).
21	0	m	TRANSFER (A*) to N and clear A*.
21	1	m	COPY (A*) to N.

Appendices

22	0	m	MULTIPLY (A*) by (N) and place in A*.
22	1	m	SELECT (N) into A*. Place the number of non-significant zeros in (N) in compartment 0 and (N), scaled until Q10 is non-zero, in sign and complement form in A.

ACTION 23: **INDIRECT MODIFICATION AND LOCKOUT FACILITIES**

23	0	0	STEP ON AND TEST indirect modifier by N.
23	0	2	SET TAG for MASTER ROUTINE and ENTER MASTER ROUTINE.
23	0	3	SELECT TAG of N into A.
23	1	m	COPY (A) into TAG of N.

ACTION 24: **MODIFY NEXT INSTRUCTION ADDRESS AND OTHER FACILITIES**

24	0	0	MODIFY DIVISION NUMBER AND ADDRESS WITHIN DIVISION OF NEXT INSTRUCTION. Locations N, (N), ((N)), etc. are searched until a positive modifier is found.
24	0	1	MODIFY DIVISION NUMBER AND ADDRESS within division of next instruction by (N).
24	0	2	SELECT N into A.
24	0	3	SUPPRESS DIVISION NUMBER of address of next instruction; THEN MODIFY ADDRESS of next instruction by (N).
24	1	0	UNCONDITIONAL SEQUENCE CHANGE to N.
24	1	1	SELECT MODIFICATION GROUP.
24	1	2	SUPPRESS DIVISION NUMBER of address of next instruction; THEN MODIFY ADDRESS of next instruction. Locations N, (N), ((N)), etc., are searched until a positive modifier is found.
24	1	3	COPY INDICATORS to N.

ACTION 25: **MODIFICATION AND INDICATOR FACILITIES**

25	0	m	STEP ON AND TEST modifier M by N.
25	1	0	SET INDICATORS N.
25	1	1	CLEAR INDICATORS N.
25	1	2	COLLATE INDICATORS against N and select results into A.
25	1	3	CONDITIONAL HALT if any of the INDICATORS specified by N are set.

ACTION 26: **MODIFICATION AND SUB-ROUTINE FACILITIES AND TESTS FOR ROUTES.**

26	0	0	ENTER SUB-ROUTINE N.
26	0	1	LEAVE SUB-ROUTINE N.

238   *Appendices*

26 0 2   ENTER PRIORITY CONTROL.
26 0 3   EXIT FROM MASTER ROUTINE.
26 1 0   TEST ROUTE N1.
26 1 m   SET MODIFICATION REGISTER M at (N^1).

ACTION 27:   TEST ACCUMULATOR

27 0 0   CHANGE SEQUENCE to N if (A) is zero.
27 0 1   CHANGE SEQUENCE TO N if (A) is non-zero.
27 0 2   CHANGE SEQUENCE to N if (A) is positive or zero.
27 0 3   CHANGE SEQUENCE to N if (A) is negative.
27 1 0   CHANGE SEQUENCE to N if (AB) is zero.
27 1 1   CHANGE SEQUENCE to N if (AB) is non-zero.
27 1 2   As 27.0.2.
27 1 3   As 27.0.3.

ACTIONS 28/29: DATA REARRANGEMENTS

28 0 0   {BULK COPY words from locations starting at the
28 0 1   {location specified in A to locations starting at
28 1 0   {N, or CLEAR locations starting at N, as specified
28 1 1   {by d, m and the table entry (A).
28 0 2   UNPACK FIXED FIELD DATA from N onwards according to table specified in A.
28 0 3   UNPACK VARIABLE FIELD DATA from N onwards according to table specified in A.
28 1 2   EDIT into N onwards according to table specified in A.
28 1 3   CONDENSE into N onwards according to table specified in A Delete non-significant zeros and insert number ends.
29 0 0   EDIT FOR HOLLERITH OUTPUT.
29 0 1   EDIT FOR ANelex OUTPUT.

ACTIONS 30/31: DOUBLE LENGTH ARITHMETIC

30 0 m   DOUBLE LENGTH TRANSFER Transfer (AB) to $N + 2^1$, N^1.
30 1 m   DOUBLE LENGTH COPY. Copy (AB) to $N + 2^1$, N^1.
31 0 m   DOUBLE LENGTH ADD. Add $(N+2^1)$ (N^1) to (AB).
31 1 m   DOUBLE LENGTH SUBTRACT. Subtract $(N + 2^1)$ (N^1) from (AB).

Appendix 8: Components required to manufacture a LEO III

The following table represents the component quantities in the mainframe and other units of a LEO III computer, excluding the peripheral devices such as magnetic tape units and printer. They were calculated for the manufacture of the LEO III/6 machine that was delivered to Shell Mex at Manchester. Component quantities varied depending on the configuration and machine type, and should be viewed as approximate only.

Resistors, fixed	101,626
Resistors, variable	1,183
Capacitors fixed	37,880
Transformers power	161
Diodes semiconductor	76,800
Transistors	35,830
Relays	826
Switches	446
Fuses	474
Lamps, neon	2,049
Lamps, filament	459
TOTAL	257,734

Source J. J. Woolsey.

Appendix 9: Sales of LEO III computers

Machine number	Type	Operational dates	Purchasing company
LEO III/1	s	1962–1972	Leo Computers Ltd, London (Bureau)
LEO III/2	s	1962–1972	Leo Computers Pty. Johannesburg, SA
LEO III/3	s	1962–1966	Dunlop Rubber Co. Ltd, Birmingham (transferred to BOC)
LEO III/4	s	1963–1975	London Boroughs Joint Computer Committee (Metropolitan Boroughs of Greenwich, Bermondsey, Southwark, Woolwich, Deptford, Camberwell)
LEO III/5	s	1963–1971	CAV Ltd, London
LEO III/6	s	1963–1972	Shell-Mex & BP Ltd, Manchester (moved from Hemel Hempstead in 1965)
LEO III/7	s	1963–1972	J. Lyons & Co. Ltd, London
LEO III/8	s	1963–1976	Tubemakers Pty. Ltd, Sydney, Australia
LEO III/9	s	1963–1974	HM Customs & Excise, Southend
LEO III/10	s	1963–1971	Board of Trade, Eastcote
LEO III/11	s	1963–1970	Smith & Nephew Ltd, Birmingham
LEO III/12	326	1963–1967	Leo Computers Ltd, Minerva Road (experimental 326 machine)
LEO III/13	s	1964–1975	BOC Ltd, Manchester
LEO III/14	s	1964–1972	Shell-Mex & BP Ltd, Manchester (moved from Hemel Hempstead in 1965)
LEO III/15	s	1964–1969	Shell Australia, Melbourne
LEO III/16	s	1964–1971	Kayser Bondor Ltd, Baldock
LEO III/17	s	1963–1975	Manchester Corporation

Appendices *241*

LEO III/18	s	1964–1978	Cerebos Ltd, London
LEO III/90	s	1964–1965	NDPS (GPO), London (became 111/39)
LEO III/19	s	1964–1966	DNS (GPO), Lytham St Annes (became 111/94)
LEO III/20	s	1964–1973	Colonial Mutual Life, Melbourne, Australia
LEO III/21	s	1964–1973	Tote Investors Ltd, London
LEO III/22	s	1964–1971	H. J. Heinz Co. Ltd, London (sold to Renold Chains 1971–1975)
LEO III/23	360	1965–1971	Dunlop Rubber Co. Ltd, Birmingham (transferred to Freemans 1971–1973)
LEO III/24	s	1965–1970	Allied Suppliers Ltd, London (transferred to Phoenix Insurance Co. 1970–1973)
LEO III/25	s	1965–1974	Inland Revenue, Worthing
LEO III/26	326	1965–1980	NDPS (GPO), London
LEO III/27	326	1965–1975	Freemans Ltd, London
LEO III/28	s	1965–1972	Coventry Corporation
LEO III/29	360	1965–1975	Shell Mex & BP Ltd, installed at Manchester for system testing then moved to Hemel Hempstead to replace LEO III/6
LEO III/30	s	1965–1975	Royal Bank of Scotland, Edinburgh
LEO III/31	360	1965–1975	Shell Mex & BP Ltd, Hemel Hempstead (replaced LEO III/14)
LEO III/32	s	1965–1974	Colvilles Ltd, Motherwell
LEO III/33	s	1965–1973	Phoenix Assurance Co., Croydon
LEO III/34	326	1965–1977	NDPS (GPO), London
LEO III/35	s	1965–1973	South Western Gas Board, Bath
LEO III/36	326	1966–1975	DNS (GPO), Lytham St Annes

LEO III/37	s	1965–1972	British Insulated Callenders Cables, Prescott
LEO III/93	360	1965–1979	Vypocetni Laborator Dopravy (VLD),* Prague, Czechoslovakia
LEO III/38	s	1965–1977	HM Dockyard, Rosyth (originally at Portsmouth)
LEO III/39	s	1965–1973	Ever Ready Co., London (was 111/90)
LEO III/40	s	1966–1973	Consolidated Glass, Germiston, SA
LEO III/41	360	1966–1977	NHKG,* Ostrava-Kunice, Czechoslovakia
LEO III/42	s	1965–1974	Renold Chains Ltd, Manchester
LEO III/43	360	1966–1977	HM Dockyard, Portsmouth (replaced LEO III/38)
LEO III/44	326	1966–1981	NDPS (GPO), Cardiff (was at Docos House, London)
LEO III/45	s	1966–	Wedd Durlacher Mordaunt, London
LEO III/46	326	1966–1972	J. Lyons & Co. Ltd, London (sold to NDPS London)
LEO III/47	326	1966–1980	Ustredi Duchodoveho Zabezpeceni (UDZ),* Prague, Czechoslovakia
LEO III/48	s	1966–1977	HM Dockyards, Devonport
LEO III/94	s	1967–1974	London Boroughs Management Service Unit (London Boroughs of Tower Hamlets, Hackney and later, Haringey; was III/19)
LEO III/49	326	1966–1972	Shell Australia, Melbourne
LEO III/51	326	1966–1981	NDPS (GPO), Edinburgh (moved to Kensington in place of III/46)
LEO III/55	326	1966–1981	NDPS (GPO), Portsmouth
LEO III/56	360	1967–1977	HM Dockyard, Chatham
LEO III/58	326	1966–1981	NDPS (GPO), Derby

Appendices

LEO III/66	326	1969–1977	DNS (GPO), Glasgow (moved to Bristol)
LEO III/67	326	1969–1981	NDPS (GPO), Derby
LEO III/68	326	1969–1981	DNS (GPO), Glasgow (moved to Edinburgh in 1974)
LEO III/69	326	1969–1981	NDPS (GPO), Kensington, London
LEO III/70	326	1969–1981	NDPS (GPO), Bristol

* VLD = Transportation Computing Laboratory (Railways).
NHKG = New Metallurgical Plant of Klementa Gottwald (Steel).
UDZ = Social Security Centre (Social Security).

Notes:
There were three basic machine types available. The model "s" was the standard machine. The model "360" was a faster configuration and the model "326" was the fastest in the LEO III range. The table below gives the store and arithmetic cycle times as measured in microseconds. (one microsecond is equal to one millionth of a second). The exception was LEO III/2, this was a slower pre-production machine derived from the LEO III/1 prototype.

Machine type	Store speed	Arithmetic unit speed
(s)	13.5μsec	34.0μsec
360	6.0μsec	12.0μsec
326	2.5μsec	5.0μsec

Source: English Electric–Leo Computers Ltd data sheet

LEO III/2 was the first LEO III computer delivered outside Lyons.
LEO III/23 was the first delivered model 360 machine.
LEO III/26 was the first delivered model 326 machine.
LEO III/34 was the only known machine using data transmission facilities.
LEO III/43 was shown at the Prague Exhibition of 1966.
LEO III/56 was shown at the Moscow Exhibition of 1967.

Machines with serial numbers in the nineties were insertions in the production schedule; 91 and 92 were not built, nor were III/50, III/52, III/53, III/54, III/57, III/59, III/60, III/61, III/62, III/63, III/64 and III/65.

Machine numbers III/66 to III/70 were scheduled when the production line was re-opened at Winsford for the repeat order placed by the Post Office with the new English Electric-Leo company.

244 *Appendices*

Appendix 10: Standard utility software supplied with LEO III

Program number	Utility program description
06001	Magnetic tape post mortem
06050	CLEO file production and post mortem
06060	General purpose print
06091	Magnetic tape copy
06096	Magnetic tape comparison
07002	3-tape omnisort
07003	4-tape omnisort
07004	Restartable 4-tape omnisort
07005	General merge program
08000	Intercode translator
08001	Sort generator program
08002	Store post mortem print out
08003	Program collection utility
08004	Master routine generator
08005	Intercode trial data amender
08050	Autolector reception program
08051	Xeronic printer edit routines
08060	CLEO compiler
08067	CLEO store print
09004	Sentinel production (magnetic tape heading record)
09005	Independent store post mortem (master area)
09006	Independent store post mortem (program area)

Appendix 11: Sales of Autolector (Document Reader)

Autolector was conceived by Leo Computers Limited and was a development of Lector, a machine that was designed to read and translate marks made on documents such as salesmen's order forms, payroll attendance time sheets, meter reading cards and so on. The development of Autolector was a joint venture by Leo Computers Limited and Parnall & Sons of Bristol, who were responsible for the paper transport and optical scanning systems. Parnall had previously been successful in manufacturing and selling mark reading machines to Littlewoods Pools Limited, Vernons Pools Limited and the Gateway and Sainsbury supermarket businesses. Autolector was designed for high volume document processing. The forms were stacked into portable cassettes that were loaded on a conveyor; the conveyor could be loaded continuously without interrupting the free running of the machine. One machine was successfully used to mark a physics Advanced level GCE paper in the summer of 1969. The Oxford and Cambridge Joint Examining Board, who borrowed the machine, used it in the same year to mark one of the three "A" physics papers. The examination forms were read at 1200 per hour, both faster and more accurate than the previous manual process. Only those papers with objective questions could be handled. Autolector forms were selected individually from the cassettes by a vacuum pick-up and then carried by alignment rollers to the revolving vacuum drum, on which they were held smooth and flat for reading. Forms could be read at between 270 and 400 per minute depending on size. Forms of a similar size were read at a constant speed irrespective of data content.

Autolector could handle form sizes of widths between 7.5 and 8.5 inches and lengths of between of 9 and 16 inches. The machine was fitted with a form jam detector and a double feed sensing device. A micro switch was fitted to the output tray to stop the machine if this became full. The output tray was also fitted with a vibrating device so that documents could be progressively moved down the output tray for easy unloading.

Machine dimensions were: length 3.38 m (11' 1"), height 0.94 m (6' 3") width 0.94 m (3' 1"). The whole weighed 2,032 kg (4,480 lb).

Autolectors were used by the following:

J. Lyons & Company Limited, London. (Two machines).
Allied Suppliers Limited, London.
HM Dockyard, Chatham, Kent.
HM Dockyard, Portsmouth, Hampshire.
HM Dockyard, Devonport, Devon.
HM Dockyard, Rosyth, Scotland.
Dunlop Limited, Birmingham.
South-East Regional Examinations Board.

Total 9 machines

Appendix 12: Sales of Xeronic printers

In 1956 the Central Research Laboratories of Rank Precision Industries Limited became interested in exploiting the photoelectric technique of printing known as xerography. Then, they were already studying means of solving the difficult problem of making a high speed printer without fast-moving mechanical parts and with great reliability, and the formation of their associated company within the Rank Organisation Limited, Rank XeroX Limited, in conjunction with Haloid-XeroX Inc. of Rochester, New York, provided the answer to much of their problem. By the formation of this new Anglo-American company the Copyflo patent rights and knowledge in the use of xerography held by Haloid-Xerox Inc. became available to Rank-XeroX Limited. Copyflo was originally developed to reproduce American Navy charts from 35 mm film during World War II, which were in great demand and tedious to produce photographically. The technology was developed further for Xeronic.

The Xeronic printer was developed in the Rank Research Laboratories under the original Directorship of Dr Nyman Levin and later Dr Arthur Starr and Keith Huntley, who was head of the Electronics Laboratory. Following its development it was manufactured and marketed initially by the Data Systems Division of Rank Precision Industries Limited, a company within the Rank Organisation supplying cinematographic apparatus, and later by Rank Data Systems Limited, a subsidiary of the Rank Organisation set up to manufacture and market the Xeronic. The speed of the Copyflo printer was doubled for Xeronic.

A prototype machine was exhibited at Britain's first Electronic Computer Exhibition in 1958. It could only print one sentence but this was sufficient to demonstrate the principle. The words chosen, "now is the time for all good men to come to the aid of the party", were produced repetitively at 1,500 lines per minute.

Rank Data Systems Limited exhibited on the Rank-XeroX Limited stand at the British Trade Fair in Moscow in 1961, although they were unable to show their printer. Instead, Ian Brotherton gave, on 23 May 1961 at the House of Engineering, a lecture which stimulated much interest with the Russians. Following this, the Russians placed an order for a machine but agreement could not be reached on how to supply and service it, the Russians wanted to undertake the servicing themselves, and the order was ultimately cancelled.

The first Xeronic printer was supplied to Ferranti Limited for use on their Orion computer. AEI Limited also took delivery of one for use on their 1010 computer (RAF Hendon) and a third was delivered to EMI Limited for their EMIDEC 2400 computer that was in use at the Ministry of Pensions, Newcastle.

First machines used a 4-form formhead, which was later modified to take 32 forms.

The printers were not a commercial success. Cheaper, more reliable mechanical line printers introduced from America were more attractive to users, and these predominated until the mid-1970s, when laser technology made a significant impact.

The following companies installed Xeronic printers:

Ferranti Ltd (never used).
Commercial Union Assurance Co., Exeter (two machines).
Compagnie d'Assurances Générale, Paris.
Ministry of Pensions and National Insurance, Newcastle (two machines).
Royal Air Force, Hendon.
J. Lyons & Co. Ltd, London.(a second machine was installed to replace one destroyed in a fire).
Government Communications Headquarters (GCHQ) Cheltenham, Gloucestershire (two machines).
NDPS (GPO) Charles House, Kensington, London (bought by Lyons but never used).
Mutuelle Générale Française Accident, Le Mans, France.
Zusatzversorgungskasse, Weisbaden, Germany.
I/S Data Centrallen, Copenhagen, Denmark.

Total 15 machines.

Appendix 13: How LEO I worked—a semi-technical description

Two documents were produced in the early years of LEO to explain the way computers worked to those concerned with the project and to management and staff in departments where computer applications were planned and implemented. The first of these, *A Non-technical Description of EDSAC*, was compiled in 1948–1949 and issued in June 1949, mainly for use internally; the second, which was developed from it, was intended for wider use. It was issued in August 1951 as *A Layman's Guide to LEO*, and in its original form comprised about 75 pages; it was subsequently revised and supplemented to deal with the buffering and input–output facilities that were added to LEO as it was developed, and later versions were over 150 pages in length.

The following notes are based on the original versions of these documents. Because at the time they were written there was no general awareness of the binary notation, over half of the texts were devoted to an explanation of binary arithmetic. This material is omitted here. The explanations of the nature and operation of the computer are set down in the following paragraphs in a very much abbreviated form, which nevertheless follows the structure of the originals. It is hoped that this will enable the reader not only to appreciate the nature of LEO, but to see it through the eyes of those who brought it to fruition. The term "computor" [sic] is spelt in the original form.

1. Electronic Calculators

An electronic calculator is so called because it works mainly by electronic, as opposed to electrical or mechanical, means. Whereas electrical engineering is concerned with the behaviour of electricity in conductors, electronic engineering essentially employs circuits incorporating electronic (or radio) valves. Such a valve, as the word implies, is a kind of highly sensitive tap for controlling variations in electrical pressure. The effects of changes in electrical pressure when transmitted through a valve are conveyed not along a wire but across space, usually a vacuum, inside the glass envelope of the valve.

By the use of valves in the calculator it was possible to control very brief variations or surges of electrical pressure, called pulses. It was by means of these pulses that the calculator was able to do its work.

2. Information in the Calculator

The information needed by the calculator for its operations was of two kinds:

> 2.1 The numbers to be worked on, any intermediate results and the final results to be printed.

> 2.2 A specification, in numerical form, of all the operations necessary to produce the final results; these were termed Orders, and the complete series of orders the program.

Both orders and numbers are held in the form of short pulses of electrical pressure, each lasting just under one millionth of a second (.97) and separated from the next pulse position by the same amount. Each pulse position denotes a binary digit whose value is "1" if the pulse is present, or "0" if the pulse does not occur. In this way a binary number may be represented by a train of pulse positions travelling along a conductor; thus the sequence:

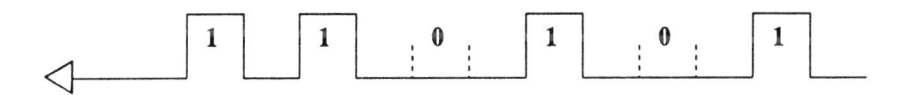

would correspond to the binary number, 110101 (or decimal 53)

3. Storage of Information

Clearly, some form of storage is required, so that the orders determining the operations can be available in sequence and the numbers can be selected as required. This is achieved by circulating the information round closed loops, to be available recurrently. However, since the speed at which electrical impulses travel along a conductor is that of light (186,000 miles per second) and the time occupied by one pulse, with its interval, is almost two microseconds, a loop of wire two fifths of a mile long would be needed to hold only a single pulse (one binary digit). The storage of information travelling at this speed is clearly not practicable, and the transmission speed needs to be reduced radically. In LEO this is accomplished by introducing into the storage loop a "delay line". A delay line consists of a steel tube 1" in diameter filled with mercury, terminated at each end by a piezo-electric crystal. It is a natural property of such a crystal that, when an electric pulse is applied to it, it vibrates and transmits a compression pulse to the mercury; conversely, when a crystal is vibrated mechanically (by a compression pulse) it emits an electrical vibration—an electrical pulse to the circuit with which it is connected. Thus when a train of pulses is fed to the crystal at one end of the delay line corresponding mechanical pulses are transferred to the mercury to travel along the tube to the crystal at the other end where they are converted back to the original pattern of electrical pulses. However, since in the mercury there are mechanical, their speed of transmission is reduced to 4,760 feet per second compared with the electrical speed of nearly 200,000 miles per second. In LEO each delay line is 5' 4" long and this enables a train of 576 mechanical pulses to be circulated in the line serially, as shown in the diagram overleaf:

```
←——————— 5' 4" delay tube ———————→
┌─────────────────────────────────────────┐
│ Mechanical vibrations travel along tube at 4,760 feet per second │
│ • • • • • • • • • • • • • • • • • • • • │
│                                         │
│  crystal                       crystal  │
└─────◁───────────┬───────────────◁───────┘
              Electronic circuits
```

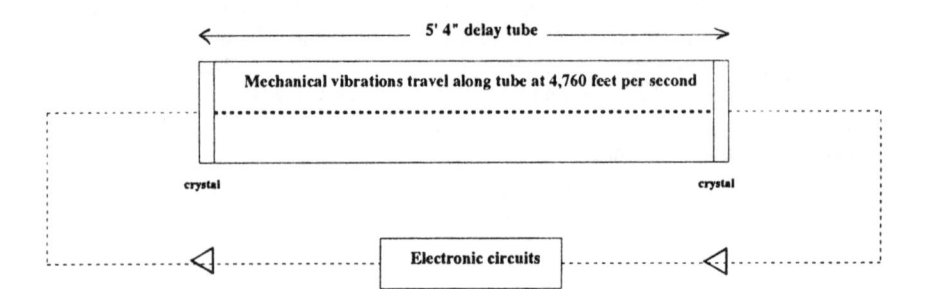

Electronic pulses available to machine travelling at 186,000 miles per second

Thus each pulse in turn is passed through the electronic circuit associated with the tube, and each pulse (or digit of information) is available there for use every 1.12 milliseconds (576 pulse intervals of 1.95 microseconds). The information so stored is organised in 32 "compartments" of 18 digits, each compartment holding one number or order. To select a specific compartment, therefore, it is necessary to specify the time within the cycle at which the compartment will emerge into the electronic circuit, and therefore for an electronic "clock" to be maintained in LEO which counts the passage of compartments.

In all, LEO has 64 of these delay lines, so that to designate a compartment it is required to specify the number of the line, followed by the number of the compartment (its "time") within that line. These two numbers together constitute the address of the compartment; for the tube number six binary digits are used, and for the "time", five. The eleven digits of the address thus corresponds to the decimal compartment addresses 0 to 2047.

4. General Organisation of the Calculator

The main parts of the calculator are:

    4.1 Co-ordinator
    4.2 Store
    4.3 Starter
    4.4 Reader
    4.5 Computor
    4.6 Recorder

The general relationship of these parts is represented in the diagram below:

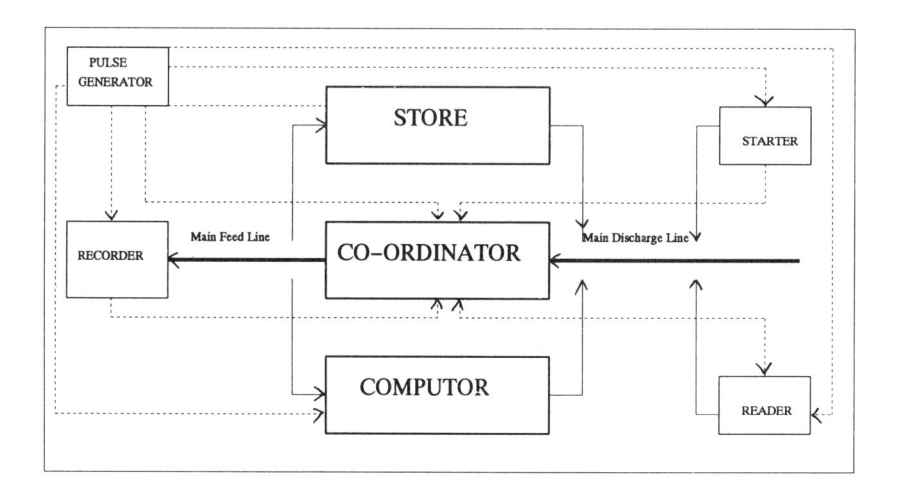

```
┌─────────────────────────────────────────────────────────────────┐
│   ┌──────────┐                                                  │
│   │ PULSE    │··············································     │
│   │ GENERATOR│                                            :     │
│   └──────────┘         ┌─────────────┐                     :     │
│        :        ┌─────>│    STORE    │                     v     │
│        :        │      └─────────────┘              ┌──────────┐ │
│        :        │             │                     │ STARTER  │ │
│        v        │             v  v                  └──────────┘ │
│   ┌──────────┐  │ Main Feed Line  ┌─────────────┐ Main Discharge Line     │
│   │ RECORDER │<─┼─────────────────│CO-ORDINATOR │<──────────────  │
│   └──────────┘  │                 └─────────────┘       ^        │
│        :        │                    ^  ^               :        │
│        :        │                    │  │               :        │
│        :        │      ┌─────────────┐                  v        │
│        :········└─────>│  COMPUTOR   │             ┌──────────┐  │
│                        └─────────────┘             │  READER  │<·│
│                                                    └──────────┘  │
└─────────────────────────────────────────────────────────────────┘
```

4.1 The Co-ordinator

This is the "nerve centre" of the machine because its primary purpose is to select in the appropriate sequence the orders to be executed, to interpret them and to send signals to the other parts to ensure that the required operations are performed and that information is correctly routed. It receives back signals when operations have been completed, so that it can initiate the next step and select the following order for execution. The full lines in the diagram show the paths by which information flows, and the broken lines indicate the links through which control is executed.

Information from any of the other parts of the machine always flows into the "Main Discharge Line" which leads into the co-ordinator; information which is to pass to the "Store", the "Computor" and the "Recorder" flows from the co-ordinator through the "Main Feed Line".

The course of action of the co-ordinator itself is governed by the programme of orders held in the store; the co-ordinator has a "Sequence Register" whose contents specify the address of the storage compartment holding the next instruction to be carried out, and, except where a change of sequence is called for, the last step that the co-ordinator takes in executing an order is to add one to the contents of this register.

The co-ordinator makes constant use of the "Clock Pulse Generator". This unit produces a constant supply of pulses of standard duration and frequency (pulses of 0.97 microseconds at intervals of 1.94 microseconds), which are used to synchronise all parts of the machine and enable the co-ordinator to count the passage of compartments through the store and to control the opening and closing of switches that define the flow of information throughout the calculator.

4.2 The Store.

The store as has been explained, takes the form of 64 delay lines. The store operates only in response to signals transmitted from the co-ordinator. Each delay line is connected to the Main Discharge and Feed Lines through electronic switches or "gates"; when the contents of a specified compartment are required from the store the co-ordinator selects the discharge gate of the tube stated in the address and applies a signal to open that gate for the time that the compartment is available, by reference to the address and the "clock". When information is to be transferred into the store, a similar operation is performed to open the appropriate Feed Gate of the store for the time of the transfer.

4.3 The Starter

Since the co-ordinator can operate only by carrying out orders taken from the store, it cannot start working unless there is already a program in the store. On the other hand, information can only be transferred into the store under the control of the co-ordinator.

At the start of operations therefore it is necessary to provide a means of setting into the store an initiating series of orders which enable the co-ordinator to proceed with any job presented to it. It is the task of the Starter to insert these Initial Orders into the store, and, when they have been inserted, to pass a signal to the co-ordinator to select the first of the Initial Orders to be executed. These orders are permanently wired into a rotary switch, and when the starter is pressed they are converted into electronic pulses and stored in fixed compartments in the store.

4.4 The Reader

The reader is the means whereby the program of orders and data for a job are taken into the machine. It is a device which can "read" information presented to it in the form of rows of holes punched into a paper tape and convert the holes into groups of pulses to be used in the calculator. Each row of information on the tape represents one decimal digit or character, and its conversion into the required binary form is carried out by the calculator under program control.

4.5 The Computor

The computor is that part of the machine which performs the arithmetic calculations by means of electronic circuits. When the co-ordinator interprets an order that calls for a calculation, by the appropriate switching pulses it first causes the required number to be fed from the store and sent to the Computor; the co-ordinator then transmits switching pulses to the Computor to set it up to carry out the specified calculation.

Appendices

In addition to the various circuits which perform the arithmetic manipulations, the computor contains a number of "Registers"; these are delay line circuits similar to those used for the Store, but of shorter length since they are used to hold only a single number at a time. These registers are used to provide temporary storage, in rapidly accessible form, for numbers on which arithmetic is being carried out. The most important of these registers is the Accumulator, from which any result to be transferred from the Computor to the Store is derived.

4.6 The Recorder

The recorder is the means by which the results of a program are issued by the Calculator for external use. It can be arranged to have these results either printed on a teleprinter or punched into a paper tape; in either case the results are translated from binary form into the five-element code (for decimal digits or characters) by the Calculator under program control.

5. Physical Characteristics

The physical layout does not correspond closely to the main parts described previously. The physical components of the Calculator can be classified under four headings:

   5.1 The mercury delay lines
   5.2 The main electronic circuits
   5.3 The input and output devices (Reader and Recorder)
   5.4 The power supply and switchboard

5.1 The Mercury Delay Lines

These are arranged in five batteries of 16 lines each. Four are used for the store; the fifth is used to provide spare tubes in the event of breakdown. The five batteries are kept together in a "vault" at a constant temperature, since temperature changes would affect the transmission speed of pulses through mercury. Each line is a tube of mild steel 5'4" long with a bore of 1".

5.2 The Main Electronic Circuits

The largest space is occupied by eighteen racks of electronic equipment, comprising valves of different types and their associated components. The eighteen racks are related to the main parts of the machine that have already been described as follows:

   8 are associated with the store.
   3 with the co-ordinator.
   3 with the computor.
   3 with the input and output devices.
   1 with the clock pulse generator.

254   Appendices

Each rack is seven feet high, three feet wide and about one foot deep and accommodates ten to twelve panels, in which are set the valves and other components. There is also a control desk containing electronic and electrical equipment used to monitor the working of LEO; it also accommodates the Starter.

5.3 Input and Output Devices

The original input and output equipment was accommodated on an office table beside the control desk.

5.4 Power Supply and Switchboard

In all there are about 4,000 valves [sic] which consume a total of about 25 kilowatts of power. Partly because of this relatively high consumption, but more particularly because the normal supply needs to be both transformed and refined, LEO has its own special power supply and switchboard. The switchboard itself is adjacent to the rest of LEO but part of the power supply is in the basement of the building.

Because of the power consumed during operation the main electronic racks are provided with special ventilation plant to draw off the surplus heat. The total area required to accommodate LEO and its equipment is about 2,500 square feet.

Note 1. As high speed input–output facilities were added to LEO, the fifth battery of delay lines was used in part to provide buffer storage for input and output; until that stage only one of the electronics racks was used. For the high speed facilities designed by STC several smaller but similar racks were added.

Note 2. The number of valves increased as LEO was developed.

6. Arithmetic in LEO

The original documents deal at length with addition, subtraction, multiplication and division of both positive and negative numbers; in this abridged appendix only the addition of two positive numbers is dealt with, to illustrate the approach to logical design.

As mentioned earlier, thermionic valves may be used as taps to enable or prevent the flow of pulses in electronic circuits in such a way as to carry out arithmetic operations.

For this purpose valves are incorporated in a number of standard circuits to constitute "logical elements" which perform basic manipulations on trains of pulses representing binary numbers.

The Junction. "J" has two inputs, "a" and "b" and one output "t". A pulse will appear in "t" if there is a pulse in either of the inputs.

The Gate. "G" provides an output pulse in "t" only if there are pulses in both inputs, "a" and "b".

The Suppressor. "S" reproduces in output "t" a pulse in input provided that there is no pulse in "b". If there is a pulse in "b", then no pulse can occur in "t".

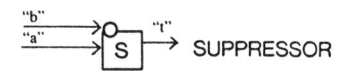

"b" → "t"
"a" → S → SUPPRESSOR

The Pulse Delay. "D" has only one input; a pulse arriving in "a" will occur in "t" one pulse interval later (shifted left by one binary position).

"a" → D → "t" DELAY

To illustrate how these logical elements are used to effect arithmetic operations it is proposed to consider the addition of two binary numbers, "a" and "b":

"a" 01101100 (decimal 108)
"b" 00101010 (decimal 42)

These numbers are assumed to flow to the adding mechanism through two lines, "a" and "b", with pairs of digits, starting with the least significant, arriving in successive pulse intervals. It will be seen that for the first three digit positions a Junction will suffice to give the correct result (100 plus 010 = 110), since only one pulse occurs in any pulse interval:

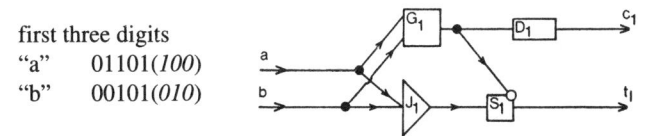

first three digits
"a"   01101(*100*)
"b"   00101(*010*)

However in the next binary position there is a pulse in both inputs and this must give no pulse in output "t"; instead, it must be arranged to carry over a pulse into the next (fifth) pulse interval. For this, provision must be made to detect two simultaneous pulses, and as a result to suppress the pulse on "t" that would otherwise be output from "J", and to produce a carry pulse in the following interval. This is accomplished by adding the elements shown below.

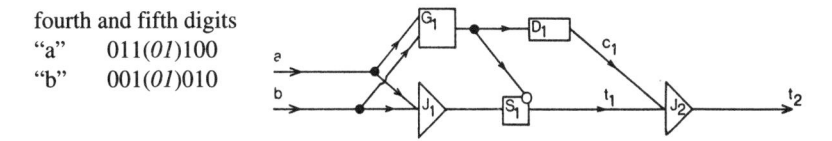

fourth and fifth digits
"a"   011(*01*)100
"b"   001(*01*)010

At this stage the outputs "t" and "c" can be fed to a second Junction "J_2" to bring the numbers together in lines "t_1" and "c_1" to provide the correct answer in line "t_2".

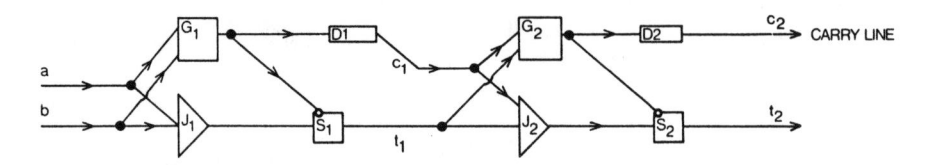

In the sixth, seventh and eighth positions:

(*011*)01100
(*001*)01010

The circuits already built up are sufficient to produce the correct numbers in the lines "t_1" and "c_1" but in the seventh position there is a pulse in both "t_1" and "c_1" therefore in the total line "t_2" the pulse from "j_2" must be suppressed and a new carry pulse must be created in the eighth position. This is done by providing leads from "c_1" and "t_1" to a gate "g_2" which detects the coincident pulses in them. A lead from "g_2" to a suppressor "s_2" in "t_2" suppresses the pulse from "j_2"; and a lead from "g_2" to another one-pulse delay "d_2" forms the new carry pulse in the eighth position in "c_2", which must be added to "t_1". This is done by feeding it back into "c_1" at the junction "j_3". The pulse arriving at "j_3" from "c_2" passes to "j_2" and "g_2" where it is added to "t_1" by the same process as a carry from "c_1", thereby giving the pulse in the total line "t_2" which now has the final total 10010110 (decimal 150).

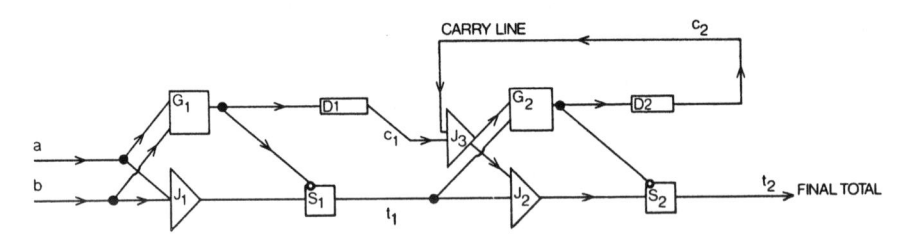

Other arrangements of these logical elements are used in LEO for multiplication and for dealing with negative numbers; subtraction is effected by taking the complement of the number to be subtracted and then using addition.

Appendix 14: Summary of LEO characteristics

LEO 1	Logic circuitry:	Thermionic and Ge diodes. Hard valve amplifiers. Wholly serial.
	Storage type:	Mercury delay tubes.
	Storage size:	2,048, 17-bit words.
	Store access time:	500μsecs
	Backing store:	None
	Word size:	17 or 35, 4-bit character.
	Add time:	1,300μsecs.
	Channels:	Four input and output.
	Peripherals:	Paper tape read, card read/punch, line printers.
	Innovative features:	Automatic clock pulse frequency control. Convert and reconvert instructions. Analytical marginal testing. Data preparation and checking equipment.
LEO II	Logic circuitry:	Thermionic and Ge diodes. Hard valve amplifiers. Wholly serial.
	Storage type:	Mercury delay tubes.
	Storage size:	8,192, 19-bit words.
	Store access time:	125μsecs.
	Backing store:	Magnetic drum.
	Word size:	19 or 39, 6-bit character.
	Add time:	520μsecs.
	Channels:	Four input and output.
	Peripherals:	Paper tape read, card read/punch, line printers and magnetic tape.
	Innovative features:	Interleaved pulses in store. Additional arithmetic registers. Alphanumeric output to printers. New instruction sets.
LEO IIc	Logic circuitry:	Thermionic and Ge diodes. Hard valve amplifiers. Transistor core store. Serial arithmetic, parallel storage.
	Storage type:	Core storage. Memory tube registers and I/O buffers.
	Storage size:	8,192, 19-bit words.
	Store access time:	80μsecs.
	Backing store:	Magnetic drum.
	Word size:	19 or 39, 6-bit character.
	Add time:	360μsecs.
	Channels:	Four input and output.
	Peripherals:	Paper tape read, card read/punch, line printers and magnetic tape.
	Innovative features:	Transistorised core storage accelerating many instructions especially moves within store.

Appendices

LEO III	Logic circuitry:	Diode/transistor. Wholly parallel.
	Storage type:	Core storage. Transistor registers.
	Storage size:	65,536, 21-bit words.
	Store cycle time:	13.5μsecs.
	Backing store:	Magnetic disc.
	Add time:	34μsecs.
	Channels:	Up to 8 in all.
	Peripherals:	Paper tape read/punch, card read/punch, line printers, magnetic tape and document reader.
	Innovative features:	Microprogrammed instructions, floating point instructions, mixed radix arithmetic, tagged store reservation scheme. Multiprogramming. Input and output buffers in main store. Standardised input and output interfaces. Operating system. CLEO programming language.
LEO 360	Logic circuitry:	Diode/transistor. Wholly parallel.
	Storage type:	Core storage. Transistor registers.
	Storage size:	65,536, 21-bit words.
	Store cycle time:	6μsecs.
	Backing store:	Magnetic disc.
	Add time:	12μsecs.
	Channels:	Up to 8 in all.
	Peripherals:	Paper tape read/punch, card read/punch, line printers, magnetic tape and document reader.
	Innovative features:	As for LEO III but with faster micro programme logic and store with 6μsecs cycle.
LEO 326	Logic circuitry:	Diode/transistor. Wholly parallel.
	Storage type:	Core storage. transistor register.
	Storage size:	65,536, 21-bit words.
	Store cycle time:	25μsecs.
	Backing store:	Magnetic disc.
	Add time:	5μsecs.
	Channels:	Up to 8 in all.
	Peripherals:	Paper tape read/punch, card read/punch, line printers, magnetic tape and document reader.
	Innovative features:	As for LEO 360 but with all or part of core store having 2.5μsecs cycle time.

Appendices

The LEO III word consisted of 48 bits: 40 information bits, 2 sign bits, 2 parity bits and 4 tag bits. Separate tag bits were used to identify each program and its associated storage areas to ensure that in no circumstances could one program corrupt that of another.

Each word could represent: 1×10 digit number with sign and parity; 2×5 digit numbers (separately addressable) each with sign and parity; 1×40-bit number with sign and parity; 2×20-bit binary numbers (separately addressable) each with sign and parity; sterling amount up to £9,999,999 19s 11d with sign and parity, 5× alphanumeric characters; 1 floating point number with 39-bit mantissa and 21-bit exponent occupying 1½ words or two program instructions.

Peripheral equipment and associated devices.

Paper tape input	1,000 char/sec for 5-, 7-, 8- channel tape
Punched card input	600 c.p.m. for 80 column cards
	800 c.p.m. for 51 or 80 column cards
	2,000 c.p.m. for 40 column cards
Paper tape output	110 char/sec
Punched card output	100 c.p.m.
High speed line printer	1,000 lines per minute
	64 different characters and 160 print positions
Monitor typewriter	10 characters per second
Magnetic tape	Ampex TM2 and TM4 tape drives. Six information tracks, 1 parity track and 1 clock track
Transfer rates	28,125, 60,000 and 96,000 char/sec
Discfile	16- or 32-disc units, giving storage for 29.5 or 59 million characters, with access time of 230 m.sec. and peak transfer rate of 120,000 char/sec
Model 3488 random access equip.	Magnetic card storage allowing 340 million characters per retrieval unit, with facilities for linking a large number of units together. Transfer rate of 80,000 char/sec and random access time of 285 to 365 m.sec

Source: John Pinkerton for LEO 1 and LEO II and English Electric–Leo Computers Ltd data card for LEO III.

INDEX

AA Thornton & Company, 194
Abrahams, Lawrence, 16
Accounting & Tabulating Co (GB), 14
Accounts department, 29, 49
ACE project, 70
Advanced Study Computer, 70
AEI computer, 155, 172
Aiken, Howard, 37
Alliance Assurance Company, 107
American threat, 172
American visit report, 37
Ampex magnetic tape, 125
Analytical engine, 13
ANelex Corporation, 125
ANelex printer, 126, 146, 156
Anglo-Vaal Group, 130
Aris, John, 109
    Xeronic printer, 156
Ashby, Charles, 177
Associated Automation Ltd, 180
Atlas computer, 71
Atomic weapons Research Est., 154
Autolector, 149
    capital cost, 152
    characteristics, 149, 151
    complete list, 245
    HM Dockyards, 151
Automatic Relay Calculator, 99
Avery Weighing Machines Ltd, 148

Babbage, Charles, 12
Badham, Leonard, 182
Baird, Barry, 137
Bakeries valuations, first job, 86
Bank of America, 102, 104
Bardeen, John, 97
Baric Bureau Services, 184

Barnes, Tony, 48, 49
    biography, 200
    directorship, 102
    EE merger, 176
    first LEO job, 60, 86
    LEO III derivative, 173
Bartlett & Gluckstein, 100
Baudot, Maurice, 14
BBC, 75
Beharrel, Edward Sir, 130
Belcher, Wing Commander, 103
Bell Laboratories, 97
Bennett, Harold, 38
Bentz, Jim, 87
Birkbeck College, 99
Black & Green Tea Company, 22
Bletchley Park, 14
Blood, Mary, 49, 180
    biography, 202
Board of Trade, 107
Booth, Andrew, 99
Booth, George, 28, 38, 40
    ENIAC, 35
Boots Pure Drug Company, 115
Boulton, Dr, 87
Böwe guillotine, 159
Brattain, Walter, 97
Brazier, Desmond, 182
Breummer, Bruce, 36
British Empire Exhibition 1924/5, 21
British Oxygen Company, 115
British Railways (Western), 115
British Road Services, 107
British Rubber Users Research Ass, 99
British Tabulating Machines, 14, 68, 91, 98, 142, 172, 182
British Trade Fair Moscow 1961, 144

British Transport Commission, 107
Broido, Dan, 140, 143, 144
   biography, 200
   BTM, 142
   East Europe, 144
   joins Lyons, 143
   Moscow, 145
   naturalised, 140
   Tabulator 7, 140
   Tabulator 7 patents, 142
   Xeronic printer, 156
Brotherton, Ian, 154
Brown, Hugh, 182
Buffering storage, 84
Bureau charges, 113
Bureau of Census (US), 102
Bureau operations, 88
Bureau service, 112
Burroughs Machines Ltd, 172, 183
   B6700 computer, 136
   evaluation, 184
Burroughs, William, 13
Bushby, Frederick, 89
Butler, RA Chancellor, 107

C-T-R, 13
Cadby Hall, 20, 22, 23, 24
Calculating machines, 13
   first used by Lyons, 27
   in use by Lyons, 30
Cambridge, 42, 63, 70
   Bushby course, 89
   design approach, 56
   Lyons donation, 38
   Lyons visit, 38
   parts procurement, 72
   Reporter, 38
Caminer, David, 42, 43, 49, 51, 52, 84, 111, 125, 149
   backing store, 99
   biography, 201
   consultancy, 107
   directorship, 102
   document reader, 146
   EE merger, 176
   full marketing, 130
   leadership, 52
   lecturing, 110
   LEO III prices, 171
   programming, 43, 52
   salesman, 105
   sends Fantl to SA, 129
   software, 43
   South Africa order, 129
   specifies first job, 86
   start at Lyons, 43
   Systems Research Office, 43
   visits RCA, 97
Camper & Nicholsons Ltd, 77, 92
Cape Asbestos, 130
Carlson, Chester, 153
Cavendish Laboratory, 37, 211
Central Mining Finance Ltd, 129
Ceylon Tea Company, 23
Chartered Institute of Secretaries (SA), 129
Checking department, 29
Chelius, Barbara, 130
Clements, Arthur, 130
CLEO programming language, 126
Clerical economics (LEO III), 132, 133
COBOL programming language, 105
Coffins, 73
Coles, Marjorie, 49
Collins, Frederick, 182
Colonial Mutual Life Assurance, 136
Colossus, 14
Commercial Bank of Scotland, 107
Comptometer, 13
Computer Analysts & Programmers Ltd, 183
Computer Society of South Africa, 129

Computer test programs, 223
Control Data Corporation evaluation, 184
Coombs, John, 49
Coombs, Mary, see also Blood, 110
Corbett, Alan, 137
Core memory, LEO II, 97
Cottage Laboratory Ltd, 154
Courtaulds bureau work, 128
Coventry Gauge & Tool Company, 78
Cox, Jean, 47
Creed, 112
Creed punch paper tape equip., 81
Customs and Excise, 107

Data Processing Function (Lyons), 185
Data transmission, 126
Davis, John, 155
Day, Bob, 130
De Havilland Propellers Ltd, 107
    bureau work, 88
De La Rue Bull Machines Ltd, 172
Decca magnetic tape, 97, 171
Decimal Association, 30
Defense Department Pentagon, 102
Delay line storage, 73
DEUCE computer, 176
Difference engine, 12
Disposal computer interests, 174
Document reader, 145
    characteristics, 148
Documentation, 50, 52, 60, 86, 115
    Bakery job, 60
    engineering, 59
    operating, 59, 60
    program, 56
    test programs, 60
    user, 60
Dortmund Society for Technology, 144

Duke, James Buchanan, 197
Dunlop Rubber Company, 130
Dutton, Wally, 47, 85, 86

Eckert—Mauchly Award, 212
Eckert, J. Presper, 34, 35
EDSAC, 38, 40, 41, 44, 45, 51, 52, 63, 64
    addressing, 55
    branch instructions, 53
    function E, 53
    Lyons hear of, 36
    machine orders, 55
    Manchester comparisons, 71
    marginal testing, 79
    memory, 71
    modular testing, 56
    payroll program, 56
    procedures, 54
    sequence register, 53
    stages, 54
    storage addressing, 54
    subroutines, 54
    succeeds, 66
    terminology, 54
    valves, 72
    Wheeler's program, 66
Edwards, W.J., 33, 42
Electronic Computer Exhibition, 114, 155
Electronic Control Company, 35
Elliott Automation Ltd, 115, 171, 180
EMI, 115, 172, 182
EMIDEC 2400, 144, 149, 156
English & American Insurance Co, 107
English Electric Company, 115
    LEO partnership, 175
English Electric Computers Ltd, 180
    ICT merger, 180
    System 4, 180

English Electric Leo Computers Ltd
    merge with Marconi, 177
English Electric Leo Ltd, 175
English Electric Leo Marconi
Computers Ltd, 178
ENIAC
    acceptance by Army, 34
    closed down, 35
    construction detail, 34
    Honeywell v. Sperry trial, 36
    Lyons interest, 36
    operational, 34
    patents dispute, 35
    purpose, 34
    reliability, 36
    use of, 35
Enigma, 14
ERNA, 104
Ever Ready Company, 107
Expenditure, LEO development, 94

Fantl, Leo, 49, 50, 82
    biography, 202
    De Havilland, 88
    initial orders, 70
    joins team, 47
    Met. Office work, 89
    patents, 195
    South Africa, 129
    test programs, 59
Fault categorisation on LEO I, 81
Felt, Dorr, 13
Ferranti Ltd, 115, 171, 182
    Atlas computer, 171
    magnetic drum, 99, 112, 171
    Mark I computer, 71
    Mercury computer, 171
    Orion computer, 171
    paper tape, 68, 112
    Pegasus computer, 171
    Sirus computer, 171
    Xeronic printer, 155

Financial Times, 115
First job run on LEO P1, 87
First LEO computer order, 113
Flint, Charles, 13
Flow charting, 51
Flowers, Thomas, 14
Ford Motor Company, 107
FORTRAN programming language, 105
Franco-British Exhibition 1908, 21

Gamages Department Store, 78
Garner, John, 182
GCHQ (Xeronic), 168
General Electric Company, 72, 182
General Electric Company (AEG), 140
General Post Office, 107, 138
    Colossus, 14
    Dollis Hill, 14
    LEO III/46, 184
    National Data Processing
    Service, 184
German market (LEO III), 144
Gibbs, Gordon, 47
Gibson, Robert, 47, 127
Gill, Stan, 70, 89
Glaxo Laboratories Ltd, 115
Gluckstein tobacconist shop, 17
Gluckstein, Henry, 16
Gluckstein, Isidore, 16, 17
    biography, 202
Gluckstein, Montague, 16, 17, 18, 20, 21, 92, 95
    biography, 203
Gluckstein, Samuel, 16, 17
    biography, 203
Goldstine, Herman, 36
Gosden, John, 50
    biography, 203
    CLEO, 127
    LEO III, 50

Greenwich Borough Council, 111
Grover, John, 48, 49, 50, 60, 86
    biography, 204
    first LEO job, 87
Gyngell, Peter, 136

Haley, Colin, 176
Haloid Company of Rochester, 153
Handley Page Aircraft, 50
Hansard, 107
Hartree House, 112, 116, 127, 184, 234
    EE merger, 177
    ICL 1904A, 184
    Marks & Spencer, 184
    Richard Shops Ltd, 184
Hartree, Douglas, 36, 37, 112
Harvard Computational Laboratory, 102
Harvard Mark I computer, 37, 103
Harvard Mark II computer, 50, 103
Heath & Company (Calcutta), 24
Hemy, Derek, 43, 47, 48, 49, 51, 52, 58, 61, 62, 69, 70, 75, 76, 83, 88, 89
    biography, 204
    Cambridge, 50, 51
    coding, 52
    coding sheets, 57
    De Havilland, 88
    demonstration, 77
    diagnosing faults, 58
    documentation, 59
    early programming, 54
    EMI, 88
    first LEO job, 86
    first payroll program., 55
    first program., 43
    initial orders, 55, 70, 89
    joined LEO, 42
    machine speed study, 81
    Met Office, 89
    O&M office, 43
    Ordnance Board, 87, 88
    patents, 195
    payroll speeds, 92
    publication, 189
    Runge–Kutta, 88
    start at Lyons, 42
    System Research Office, 43
    test programs, 79
Herman, Peter, 130
Herschel, John, 12
Hinds, Mavis, 89
Hirst, Frank, 136
HM Treasury, 115
Hogarth Press, 143
Hollerith Company (UK), 173
Hollerith, Herman, 13, 14, 34
Hollingdale, Stuart, 39
Honeywell Bull, 97, 171
Honeywell Controls Ltd, 172
Honeywell v. Sperry Trial (ENIAC), 36
Horniman W.H. & F.J., 22
Hunt, William, 34
Huntley, Keith, 153, 154, 155

IBM, 171, 173, 175, 186
    1401, 173
    1401 announced, 173
    701 to 705, 104
    announce first system, 94
    evaluation, 184
    Germany, 144
    Greenock, 173
    Lyons choose, 184
    Lyons talks, 40
    System 360, 180, 184
    Thompson visit, 102
    Williams tube, 70
ICT, 14, 171
    merger English Electric Computers, 180
ICT Pegasus 2 computer, 128

Imperial Chemical Industries, 115
Imperial Tobacco Company, 107
Initial orders, 55, 69
Inland Revenue, 90, 107
Institute of Administrative Mgt, 32
International Computers & Tabulators, 172
International Computers Ltd, 182, 183
    DME, 185
    ICL 2960, 184
    Lyons evaluation, 184
International Systems Control Ltd, 172

Jack Olding & Company, 140
Jenkinson, Sid, 50
Joseph, Ann, 16
Joseph, Norman Sir, 130
Journal of Office Management, 172

Kaye, Ernest, 46, 63, 69
    biography, 205
    Camper & Nicholsons, 78
    Lenaerts, 46
    procurement, 46
    valve types, 195
KDF computer, 176
    KDF 9, 180
Keypunching, 82, 140, 151
Kilby, Donald, 176
Klementa Gottwalda Steelworks, 137
Kodak Ltd, 107

Laboratories, 50
Labour Planning Department, 48
Land, Frank, 49, 143
    biography, 206
Law, Thomas, 154
Lazard Brothers, 175
Lector, 146
    capital cost, 152
    characteristics, 146, 148
    first business application, 146
Legal & General Insurance, 50, 107
Lenaerts, Ernest, 42, 46, 49, 59, 63, 69
    after WW II, 41
    ANelex printer visit, 126
    biography, 206
    buffering, 84
    Cambridge, 40, 41
    demonstration, 77
    EDSAC, 41
    EDSAC intro, 41
    job offer, 41
    LEO area, 45
    LEO provisioning, 45
    paper shortages, 42
    patents, 195
    returns Lyons, 45
    start at Lyons, 40
LEO
    R&D, 173
LEO Computer Users Association, 180
Leo Computers Ltd, 102
    English Electric partnership, 175
    funds dry up, 174
LEO English Electric merger, 175
LEO family, 125
LEO funding difficulties, 174
LEO I
    acronym, 67
    actions, 213
    Anthony Salmon influence, 84
    audible speaker, 73
    Board confirms start of, 66
    budget, 38
    buffering storage, 84
    Camper & Nicholsons Ltd, 77
    card punch/read decision, 68
    categorisation of faults, 81
    characteristics, 257

closed down, 179
converting binary, 64
cost analysis, 38
Creed paper tape, 82
De Havilland work, 88
delay line coffins, 73
delay line storage, 73
design features, 71
directors visit, 84
disposal, 180
engineering control, 63
engineers console, 78
error free input, 82
examining store contents, 73
first bureau job, 88
first job, 86
first payroll, 91
how it worked, 248
initial objectives, 63
initial orders, 69
input/output reassessed, 68
instruction set, 213
interactive programming, 73
invoicing job failure, 120
learning process, 69
machine time use, 84
marginal testing, 79
Mean time between faults, 92
Meteorological Office work, 89
monitoring oscilloscopes, 73
operating documentation, 60
operational control, 73
other jobs, 228
paper tape verification, 82
patents, 94
payroll processing speed, 92
peripheral speeds, 81
Pinkerton's approach, 63
Pinkerton redesign, 69
Pinkerton STL concerns, 68
power supplies, 75
proceed alone, 40

project complete, 92
project expenditure, 94
Queen Elizabeth visit, 84
reliability, in search of, 79
space allocated, 45
STC contract, 64
STC replacement cost, 91
STL cancelled, 91
STL doubts, 67
STL patents, 68
STL proposal, 67
tabulators, 68
tax tables, 93
tea stocks job, 120
team spirit, 62
teashops job, 117
test equipment, 64
training, 108
types of input, 83
US visit report, 38
valve testing, 80
valves, 72
Wayne Kerr, 63

LEO II
  bureau charges, 111
  characteristics, 257
  close down, 180
  construction starts, 96
  Decca tapes, 112
  design, 96
  Duke of Edinburgh visit, 112
  features, 217
  Ferranti magnetic drum, 99, 112
  Ferranti paper tape, 112
  first jobs, 228
  first order, 113
  first salesman, 105
  improvements on LEO I, 96
  instruction set, 213
  job with most calculations, 112
  Lenaerts' character, 98
  longest job, 111

Index

marketing, 106
microprogramming, 97
Mills' new role, 105
physical security, 110
pre sales work, 106
prices, 113, 227
recruitment, 108
sales, 234
training, 109
valve types used, 196
LEO II complete list, 234
LEO II/1 delivered to Lyons, 110
LEO II/2 computer, 113
LEO II/3 computer, 113
LEO II/5 computer, 112
LEO III
    actions, 235
    Australian order, 137
    bureau work, 128
    characteristics, 123, 258
    clerical economies, 133
    commissioning, 138
    complete list, 240
    Czech. order, 137
    first sale, 129
    GPO, 138
    instruction set, 235
    largest export order, 144
    LEO Minerva, 174
    Lyons takes delivery, 133
    maintenance, 165
    Master Plan falters, 135
    model 326 for Lyons, 165
    more exports, 136
    part quantities, 239
    Pegasus 2, 128
    prices, 133
    programming language, 126
    reliability problems, 127
    service costs, 171
    utilities, 244
LEO III complete list, 240

LEO III derivative, 173
LEO III sales, 240
LEO III/1 computer, 127
LEO III/46
    service cost, 165
LEO III/46 (Lyons), 164
LEO III/7, 133, 164
LEO IV, 174
LEO losses, 169
LEO maintenance cost, 171
LEO Minerva, 174
LEO Raytheon patents, 195
LEO trading data, 170
Levin, Nyman, 153, 154
Levy, Edwin, 21
Levy, Henry, 105
London Boro's Joint Computer Cmttee, 139
Lyons
    Accounts department, 29
    Articles of Association, 19
    banquets, 22
    business diversification, 23
    Cambridge visit, 38
    Checking department, 29
    company origins, 16
    Corner House, 23
    decimal notation use, 31
    disposal computer interests, 174
    during WW I, 25
    earliest records, 19
    first exhibition, 19
    first formation, 18
    first teashop, 20
    Glasgow exhibition, 19
    Greenford, 24
    IBM talks, 40
    incorporation, 20
    laboratories, 24
    Lujiri estate, 24
    meal/sales statistics, 25
    microfilm, 32

office innovation, 31
Paris exhibition 1889, 19
preparation LEO I, 45
second formation, 19
shareholders (2nd Co), 19
Stock department, 29
subvention payments, 169
tea sales, 24
tea sales growth, 22
Trocadero restaurant, 20
White Books, 30
Lyons Computer Services Ltd, 182
Lyons Electronic Office, 67
Lyons, Joseph, 18
biography, 207

Machines Bull, 175
Mackie, Alex, 137
Magnetic tape
Ampex models, 127
Ampex/Pegasus, 128
Decca 3000, 97
Harvard Mark II, 103
IBM, 94
LEO II, 112
LEO II drive cost, 227
LEO III, 125
LEO III post design, 128
LEO III problems, 127
librarian, 134
Orion computer, 171
see also appendices, 259
STL, 64
Xeronic printer, 155
Maintenance, LEO III, 165
Maitland, Commander MP, 107
Manchester University, 44
computer, 70
magnetic drum, 99
Williams tube, 70
Marconi Company Ltd, 178

Marconi Wireless Telegraph
Company, 176, 177
merge with EE Leo, 177
Marconidata H6000, 126
Marginal testing, 79, 220
Marketing computers, 106
Master Plan, 132, 186
clerical economies, 133
cost of, 132
falters, 135, 182
Master Routine, 50, 57
Masters, J.C., 105
Matheson, Louis, 136
Mauchly, John, 34, 36
Meteorological Office, 89
Metropolitan Life Insurance Co, 103
Microfilm use, 32
Microprogramming, LEO II, 97
Mills, Geoffrey, 31, 43, 105
personnel job, 105
training courses, 109
Minerva Road, 47, 112, 138, 174
Ministry of Pensions, 156
Minsk University, 144
Monroe Calculating Company, 172
Moor School, 36
Moor School, Pennsylvania, 34
Morgan, Tony, 130
Moscow Exhibition 1967, 138
Mullard Ltd, 72
Murton, Peter, 136

Napier, John, 11
National Cash Register, 13, 115, 172
National Coal Board, 107
National Computing Centre, 109
National Data Processing Service, 167, 183, 184
National Development Foundation (SA), 129
National Physical Laboratory, 50, 70, 115

National Research Dev. Corp., 70
Noble, Ben, 51
Normand Limited, 50

O&M, 31, 43, 105, 132
Office Machinery Users Association, 32
Olding Developments Ltd, 140
Olivetti, 175
Ordnance Board, 87

P1 the first LEO job, 87
Packard Bell Computer Corp, 172
Parnall–Lyons partnership, 149
Parnall & Sons Ltd, 148
Parnall, Henry, 148
Parnall, William, 148
Pascal, Blaise, 12
Patents, 94
Paton, George Sir, 136
Payroll, 55
Penney, William Sir, 154
Pennsylvania, University of, 34, 36, 190
Petru, Jiri, 138
Philco Corporation of America, 168
Phillips, 175
Pidgin, Charles, 34
Pietrzyk, Gail, 36
Pinkerton, John, 44, 45, 46, 47, 61, 64, 72, 73, 77, 82, 143, 145, 148, 149, 154, 156
    ANelex printer visit, 126
    BBC, 110
    biography, 208
    Broido, 143
    Cambridge, 44
    change of plan, 68
    Computer Bulletin, 76
    directorship, 102
    document reader, 146
    EE merger, 176
    Esmond Wright, 64
    interview, 44
    job application, 44
    joins Lyons, 45
    learning process, 69
    Lector, 143
    lecturing, 110
    LEO II proposal, 96
    LEO job offer, 45
    Leo redesign, 69
    Parnall, 149
    Parnall patents, 152
    patents, 195
    RCA visit, 97
    STC concerns, 68
    STC replacement cost, 91
    Xeronic, 156
Plant, Miss, 47
Pollock, Neil, 115
Potter magnetic tape, 125
Powers Accounting Machines Ltd, 14
Powers Samas Company, 14, 33, 97, 182
Powers, James, 14
Powers-Samas, 136
Prague Exhibition 1966, 138
Princeton University, 35, 36, 70
Programming
    absolute address, 54
    addressing, 56
    batch totalling, 61
    Cambridge, 51
    check totals, 60
    diagnosing faults, 58
    documentation, 59
    dumps, 59
    engineer tests, 60
    exception reports, 60
    first steps, 53
    flow charts, 60
    instruction limits, 57

instruction set, 213, 235
interactive changes, 59
limitations, 57
log-book, 59
machine speed, 58
modular testing, 56
payroll, 62
stages, 56
storage, 57
subroutines, 54
trials/tests, 56
user expectations, 61
Provincial Bakeries, 50

Radio Corporation of America, 97, 180
Radley, Gordon Sir, 175, 178
Rand Mines Ltd, 129
Rank Data Systems Ltd, 155
Rank Organisation Ltd, 153
Rank Precision Industries, 153
Rank Xerox Ltd, 153
Raytheon LEO patents, 195
Recognition Equipment Inc, 168
Recordak, 32
Remington Rand Ltd, 172
Restrictive Practices Act, EE Leo merger, 176
Richard Shops Limited, 184
Richardson, Jack, 177
Robinson, Clifford, 177
Rotaprint, 140
Royle, Derek, 177

Sales Accounts Office, 48
Salmon & Gluckstein, 17
Salmon, Anthony, 84, 113, 130, 171
    biography, 208
    EE merger, 175, 178
    Marconi, 177
Salmon, Barnett, 16, 17
Salmon, Geoffrey, 85

Salmon, Harry, 66
Salmon, Isidore Sir, 30
Salmon, Samuel Sir, 136
Samastronic, 98, 112, 113
Samuel Gluckstein & Company, 16
Science Museum, 12, 180
Servicing LEO III, 165
Shaw, Raymond, 46
    Australia, 47
    biography, 209
Shell Australia, 136
Shockley, William, 97
Siemens, 82, 99, 175
Siemens Edison Swan Ltd, 115
Simmons, John, 38, 39, 40, 41, 42, 43, 66, 68, 87, 96, 132, 186, 187
    accounting, 29
    biography, 209
    career commence, 28
    consolidates a/cs, 30
    decimal notation, 30
    directorship, 102
    IAM, 32
    invents LEO name, 67
    Lenaerts' letters, 41
    Master Plan, 132
    office changes, 32
    office consultant, 32
    promotion, 32
    research centre, 31
Simple Electronic Computer, 99
Smith, Graham, 137
South African Bureau, 129
South Eastern Gas Board, 107
Spicer, Charles, 14
Spowers, Allan, 137
Standard Telephone & Cables, 172
Standard Telephone Company, 64
Standard Telephones & Cables, 115
Standingford, Oliver, 33, 35
    biography, 210
    Cambridge, 37

ENIAC, 35
Harvard, 37
patents, 195
US visit, 37
Stanford Research Institute, 104
Starr, Arthur, 154
Statistical Office, 48, 86
Stern, Nancy, 36
Stevens, George, 143, 182
Stewarts & Lloyds Ltd, 107, 115
STL
    equipment concern, 68
    Esmond Wright, 64
    patents, 68
    project cancelled, 91
    proposal, 67
    reliability, 68
Stock department, 29, 40
Strand Palace Hotel, 175
Subvention payments, 169
Sutcliffe, Reginald, 89
Swade, Doran, 12
Synthesis instructions, 55
System 4 computer, 180
System Research Office, 31, 42

Tabulating Machine Company, 13
Tate & Lyle Ltd, 111
Tea stocks, 120
Teashops, 50, 117, 188
Teitelbaum, Ruth, 36
Telegraph Condenser Company, 72
Test programs, 220
Thompson (RD) & Company Ltd, 159
Thompson, Derek, 32
Thompson, Stanley, 149
Thompson, Thomas, 29, 32, 35, 40, 41, 42, 43, 48, 50, 59, 85, 86, 143, 144
    at Harvard, 103
    backing store, 99

biography, 210
Broido, 144
Cambridge, 37
demonstration, 59, 77, 85, 86
directorship, 102
document reader, 145
East Europe, 145
EE merger, 176
ENIAC, 35, 36
Goldstine, 36
Harvard, 37
Hemy, 48
IBM, 104
inspiration, 76
lecturing, 110
Lenaerts, 41
LEO I close, 179
LEO II, 96
Moscow Trade Fair, 144
patent infringement, 94
patents, 195
payroll, 92
Pentagon, 103
promotion, 32
recruits Broido, 143
shortcomings, 76
South Africa, 129
starts at Lyons, 28
TRT, 28
US comments, 102
US report, 40
US visit, 37, 48, 102
Xeronic, 156
Tootill, Geoffrey, 39
Training, LEO I, 108
Transvaal Consolidated Land & Exploration Co Ltd, 129
Transvaal Society of Accountants, 129
Tubemakers Australia Pty, 136

Union Corporation, 130

UNIVAC, 94, 103
    evaluation, 184
US Army Ordnance Corps, 34
US Bureau of Census, 34
Ustredi Duchodoveho Zabezpeceni, 137

Valve testing, 80
Valve types, LEO II, 196
Valves, 14, 34, 72, 73, 78, 79, 80, 97, 99, 195
van Rooyen, Faith, 130
Verification, 82
Vickers, 14
Victorian Computer Society, 137
von Neumann, John, 35, 36
Vypocetni Laborator Dopravy, 137

Watson, John, 40
Watson, Thomas, 13
Wayne Kerr Laboratories, 63, 77, 92
Westinghouse Company, 102
Wheeler, David, 47, 72, 73
Wheeler, David Prof.
    biography, 211
    EDSAC program, 66
    initial orders, 55, 69
    payroll, 56
    publication, 56
    vacation work, 52, 54
White Books, 30
Wilkes, Maurice, 36, 40, 41, 44, 50
    biography, 211
    EDSAC, 37
    initial orders, 70
    Lyons, 37
    Moor School, Pennsylvania, 36
    publication, 56
Williams, Frederick, 70
Wilmott, Joe, 134
Wood, Peter, 50, 212
Wright, Esmond, 64

Xeronic printer, 153
    capital cost, 159, 165
    complete list, 246
    fire, 165
    mark VI, 168
    marketing budget, 154
    Ministry of Pensions, 156
    principals, 153
    Rank abandons, 168
    replacement, 167
    workings, 156
Xerox 914, 154
Xerox Corporation, 168

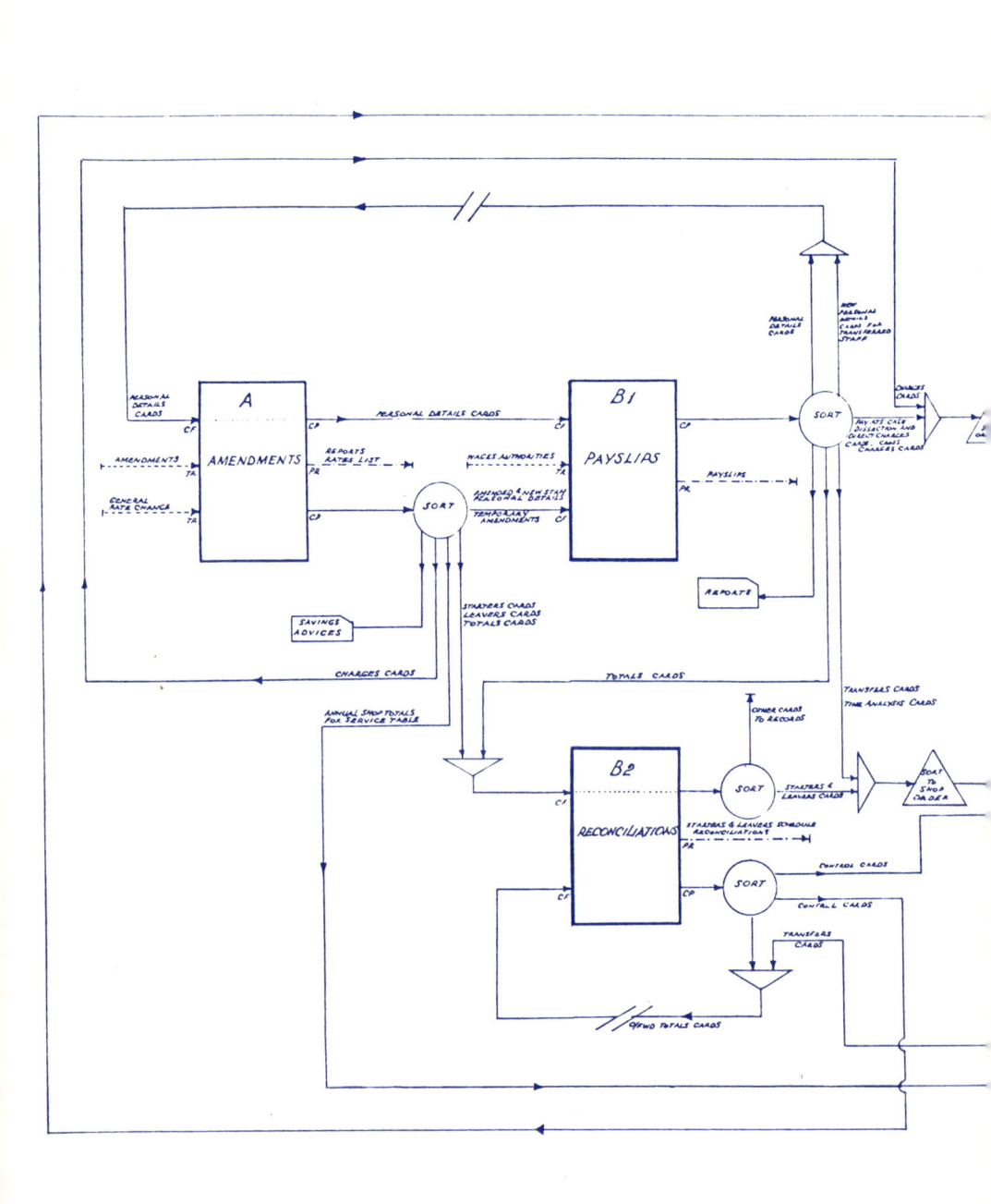